Demystifying the Dark Side of AI in Business

Sumesh Dadwal
Northumbria University, UK

Shikha Goyal
Lovely Professional University, India

Pawan Kumar
Lovely Professional University, India

Rajesh Verma
Lovely Professional University, India

A volume in the Advances in Human Resources Management and Organizational Development (AHRMOD) Book Series

IGI Global
PUBLISHER of TIMELY KNOWLEDGE

Published in the United States of America by
IGI Global
Business Science Reference (an imprint of IGI Global)
701 E. Chocolate Avenue
Hershey PA, USA 17033
Tel: 717-533-8845
Fax: 717-533-8661
E-mail: cust@igi-global.com
Web site: http://www.igi-global.com

Library of Congress Cataloging-in-Publication Data

Names: Dadwal, Sumesh, 1973- editor.
Title: Demystifying the dark side of AI in business / edited by Sumesh Dadwal, Shikha Goyal, Pawan Kumar, Rajesh Verma.
Description: Hershey, PA : Business Science Reference, [2024] | Includes bibliographical references and index. | Summary: "The book intends to provide comprehensive knowledge to the researchers, academicians, professionals, and students from cross disciplinary interests to gain insights on the theoretical and practical implications of Artificial Intelligence for better understanding and decision making"-- Provided by publisher.
Identifiers: LCCN 2023052955 (print) | LCCN 2023052956 (ebook) | ISBN 9798369307243 (hardcover) | ISBN 9798369307250 (ebook)
Subjects: LCSH: Information technology--Economic aspects. | Technological innovations--Economic aspects. | Artificial intelligence--Moral and ethical aspects.
Classification: LCC HC79.I55 D465 2024 (print) | LCC HC79.I55 (ebook) | DDC 658/.0563--dc23/eng/20231207
LC record available at https://lccn.loc.gov/2023052955
LC ebook record available at https://lccn.loc.gov/2023052956

This book is published in the IGI Global book series Advances in Human Resources Management and Organizational Development (AHRMOD) (ISSN: 2327-3372; eISSN: 2327-3380)

British Cataloguing in Publication Data
A Cataloguing in Publication record for this book is available from the British Library.

Advances in Human Resources Management and Organizational Development (AHRMOD) Book Series

ISSN:2327-3372
EISSN:2327-3380

Editor-in-Chief: Patricia Ordóñez de Pablos, Universidad de Oviedo, Spain

MISSION

A solid foundation is essential to the development and success of any organization and can be accomplished through the effective and careful management of an organization's human capital. Research in human resources management and organizational development is necessary in providing business leaders with the tools and methodologies which will assist in the development and maintenance of their organizational structure.

The **Advances in Human Resources Management and Organizational Development (AHRMOD) Book Series** aims to publish the latest research on all aspects of human resources as well as the latest methodologies, tools, and theories regarding organizational development and sustainability. The **AHRMOD Book Series** intends to provide business professionals, managers, researchers, and students with the necessary resources to effectively develop and implement organizational strategies.

COVERAGE

- Entrepreneurialism
- Executive Compensation
- Corporate Governance
- Organizational Development
- Training and Development
- Succession Planning
- Process Improvement
- Worker Behavior and Engagement
- Organizational Learning
- Performance Improvement

IGI Global is currently accepting manuscripts for publication within this series. To submit a proposal for a volume in this series, please contact our Acquisition Editors at Acquisitions@igi-global.com or visit: http://www.igi-global.com/publish/.

The Advances in Human Resources Management and Organizational Development (AHRMOD) Book Series (ISSN 2327-3372) is published by IGI Global, 701 E. Chocolate Avenue, Hershey, PA 17033-1240, USA, www.igi-global.com. This series is composed of titles available for purchase individually; each title is edited to be contextually exclusive from any other title within the series. For pricing and ordering information please visit http://www.igi-global.com/book-series/advances-human-resources-management-organizational/73670. Postmaster: Send all address changes to above address.

Titles in this Series

For a list of additional titles in this series, please visit:
http://www.igi-global.com/book-series/advances-human-resources-management-organizational/73670

Fostering Organizational Sustainability With Positive Psychology
Elif Baykal (Istanbul Medipol University, Turkey)
Business Science Reference • © 2024 • 338pp • H/C (ISBN: 9798369315248) • US $275.00

Overcoming Cognitive Biases in Strategic Management and Decision Making
Enis Siniksaran (Istanbul University, Turkey)
Business Science Reference • © 2024 • 295pp • H/C (ISBN: 9798369317662) • US $285.00

Human Relations Management in Tourism
Marco Valeri (Niccolò Cusano University, Italy) and Bruno Sousa (Polytechnic Institute of Cavado and Ave, Portugal)
Business Science Reference • © 2024 • 316pp • H/C (ISBN: 9798369313220) • US $275.00

Innovative Human Resource Management for SMEs
Shuja Iqbal (School of Management, Jiangsu University, China) Komal Khalid (King Abdulaziz University, Saudi Arabia) and Andi Cudai Nur (Universitas Negeri Makassar, Indonesia)
Business Science Reference • © 2024 • 449pp • H/C (ISBN: 9798369309728) • US $250.00

Workplace Cyberbullying and Behavior in Health Professions
Muhammad Shahzad Aslam (School of Traditional Chinese Medicine, Xiamen University Malaysia, Malaysia) Yun Jin Kim (School of Traditional Chinese Medicine,,Xiamen University Malyasia, Malaysia) and Qian Linchao (School of Traditional Chinese Medicine, Xiamen University Malaysia, Malaysia)
Business Science Reference • © 2024 • 282pp • H/C (ISBN: 9798369311394) • US $275.00

Promoting Value Creation Through Organizational Effectiveness and Development
Thais González-Torres (Rey Juan Carlos University, Spain) and José-Luis Rodríguez-Sánchez (Rey Juan Carlos University, Spain)
Business Science Reference • © 2024 • 255pp • H/C (ISBN: 9781668484791) • US $250.00

IGI Global
PUBLISHER of TIMELY KNOWLEDGE

701 East Chocolate Avenue, Hershey, PA 17033, USA
Tel: 717-533-8845 x100 • Fax: 717-533-8661
E-Mail: cust@igi-global.com • www.igi-global.com

Editorial Advisory Board

Table of Contents

Detailed Table of Contents

is utilized to assess AIDA (attention, interest, desire, and action) effectiveness. By counting the number of users that watched, liked, visited the profile, or engaged in a certain action after seeing the advertisement, Instagram's marketing effectiveness was determined. This chapter examines how ChatGPT, an NLG model powered by OpenAI's GPT-3 technology, might enhance chat-based e-commerce and other sectors including news, education, entertainment, finance, and health. The authors evaluate ChatGPT's present use cases in various fields and consider potential new uses. They also talk about how this technology may be used to provide people with more individualized content. They examine ChatGPT's potential to improve customer service for businesses in our final section.

The blending of AI with every aspect of the stream, whether it is medicines, natural disaster predictions, disease epidemiology, future prediction, etc., has been crucial and impactful in today's world. On the flip side, there are several problems that humans face with the incorporation of AI into their day-to-day lives. The first and foremost aspect is implementing AI-based technologies, which require high capital as these are costlier in addition to their infrastructure establishment and talent acquisition. The second problem is security concerns, as AI often works and provides future predictions based on past data that might be sensitive to an individual or a firm that it stores in its server, which raises concerns concerning privacy and security breaches. The third point includes the interaction of company personnel with their client physically. Some other cons of incorporating AI include the loss of massive jobs known as unemployment and bias and ethical issues that might arise.

The detection and prevention of financial statement fraud is a critical concern in maintaining the credibility and reliability of financial reporting. In response to this ongoing challenge, researchers are exploring innovative solutions that leverage artificial intelligence (AI) technology. This study investigates the potential application of AI techniques, such as machine learning algorithms, natural language processing, and data mining, in enhancing forensic accounting practices for detecting and preventing financial statement fraud. Furthermore, the

will be achieved. In this chapter, the authors discuss the fundamentals of contemporary AI as well as a number of illustrative applications. Artificial intelligence (AI) is the ability of computers, computer programmes, and other systems to mimic human intelligence and creativity, autonomously come up with solutions to issues, be able to reach judgements, and make choices. Additionally, there are ways in which existing artificial intelligence outsmarts humans. Additionally, it will examine the forecasts for artificial intelligence and provide viable solutions to address them in the next decades.

The growing adoption of artificial intelligence (AI) in the retail industry has triggered a significant evolution in the shopping experience. However, concerns have surfaced regarding their potential psychological effects on consumers, which can sometimes lead to stress and confusion. As retailers continue to harness AI technology to enhance customer engagement and optimize their operations, it becomes increasingly important to confront and manage the potential risks and uncertainties that come with its swift deployment. The study considered 237 online retail customers to know the factors that determine the negative aspects of artificial intelligence and their impact on the purchase intention of online retail customers towards AI-enabled e-retail platforms. Financial information and security, consumer trust and AI autonomy, reliability issues due to novelty of the concept, and malfunctioning of systems are the factors that negatively impact the purchase intention of online retail customers towards AI-enabled e-retail platforms.

This chapter delves into the fusion of artificial intelligence (AI) and Sustainable Development Goals (SDGs), emphasizing the need to navigate safety risks and ethical concerns. AI offers substantial potential in addressing sustainability challenges across various domains, such as energy conservation, workplace management, and advertising. However, its integration may influence employee well-being and data privacy. To effectively achieve SDGs, organizations must adopt proactive

Preface

The book *Demystifying the Dark Side of AI in Business* explores the area of unaddressed drawbacks of artificial intelligence (AI) and its effect on contemporary business practices. AI is radically altering industries and workplaces, thus it's important to understand the potential risks and challenges associated with integrating AI into corporate processes. This book compiles works by eminent researchers, academicians, and professionals from several fields to shed light on the dark side of artificial intelligence, drawing from a wide spectrum of worldwide views. The book covers various critical subjects like unethical AI implementation, safety issues, negative social implications, unforeseen consequences, and legal concerns surrounding AI adoption with academic rigour and careful analysis.

This book explores the need for strong governance to address the challenges posed by artificial intelligence. It draws attention towards the unrestrained utilization of AI and stresses the risks posed by improper use of the technology by people, organizations, and society as a whole. The book gives readers the skills they need to successfully traverse the challenges of using AI by providing real-world case studies and useful insights.

The book addresses important subjects such as safety dangers, governance, ethical problems, social repercussions, and future perspectives. By highlighting the negative implications of AI, this work ensures a balance between the potential benefits and the inherent potential risks connected with this revolutionary technology. This comprehensive book provides a deep grasp of the theoretical and practical consequences of artificial intelligence, catering to a broad audience of academicians, scholars, researchers, professionals, and students with varying interests. The studies compiled in this book highlight the understanding of artificial intelligence in multidisciplinary organizational contexts such as marketing, finance, operations, law, hotel management and human resource management.

TARGET AUDIENCES

The intended publication's main target audience consists of academics and professionals who need specific reference material on the theme *Demystifying the Dark Side of AI in Business*. Teachers, legislators, managers, consultants, organization development specialists, and undergraduate and graduate business students are among the secondary target audience members who utilize the same reference materials. While the book will primarily focus on academic topics, readers outside of academic and professional circles will also find the writing style to be accessible and engaging.

The readers will gain varied research perspectives on the often-overlooked negative aspects of Artificial Intelligence (AI) and its implications for organizations. The book carefully examines the darker aspects of artificial intelligence (AI), addressing concerns like unethical implementation, safety risks, negative social impacts, unintended consequences, and the legal complexities surrounding AI adoption. Through real-world case studies and practical insights, the book equips readers with the knowledge to navigate the complex terrain of AI deployment, enabling them to make intelligent and responsible decisions. This compilation brings together a variety of perspectives from leading researchers, academicians, and professionals across the globe.

KEY FEATURES OF THE BOOK

The book offers a thorough examination of the frequently disregarded drawbacks of AI. Furthermore, it addresses a variety of subjects including unethical application, safety hazards, adverse social effects, unforeseen repercussions, and legal issues. The book provides a variety of insights into the dark side of artificial intelligence by bringing together essays from eminent academics, academicians, and professionals from several disciplines, drawing on global viewpoints. The primary focus is on the necessity of strong governance to handle the issues raised by AI, stressing the possibility of human exploitation and addressing the pitfalls for individuals, organizations, and society as a whole from AI misuse.

This book is a useful tool that provides a fair assessment of the theoretical and practical ramifications of artificial intelligence. The book goes beyond theoretical investigation, it intends to give its readers the tools they need to make sense of the complicated world of artificial intelligence by covering important subjects like financial risks, information technology dangers, legal issues, marketing ramifications, and more. By doing this, it promotes the cautious adoption of AI, finding a careful balance between the disruptive technology's inherent hazards and possible rewards.

ORGANISATION OF THIS BOOK

This book is organised into 12 chapters. A brief description of the chapter is given in the next sections.

Chapter 1: A Comparative Study on Artificial Intelligence and Courtroom Practices With India, UK, and USA

The chapter is related to the applicability of AI in business and court room related practices. it includes mechanism of AI, ethical principles that have been formulated by organizations, a comparative analysis of AI used in countries and its position in India.

Firstly, In the modern business world, the fast-growing AI is considered to be the OpenAI's CHATGPT, so the mechanism of this particular AI will be discussed.

Secondly, the concept is based on AI and business. the gains of business through AI and the method in which AI has been used in different companies. just a glimpse of it.

Thirdly, the court room practice, it includes what is meant to be a court and the usual procedure that starts there and the major issue that calls for AI in courts, the method of usage of different AI used in different countries and the new AI that has been launched in India for courts

Fourthly, the concept related to information technology, and AI in research, and the gains that court and other legal offices earns via the AI. Fifthly, covering the principles on efficiency of justice the EU principles that governs AI implementation and process. Sixthly, the position in India, the LAWBOTPRO AI, its comparison with SUPACE and SUVAS, the dark side of AI in court practice which can also be considered in a business which includes its reliability and limitation periods as well.

Chapter 2: A Conceptual Study on Instagram Marketing: Examining the Effect of AI on Several Business Sectors Using AI Chat GPT on Marketing Effectiveness

This chapter explores how employing AI Chat GPT affects marketing efficiency, notably on the Instagram platform—especially marketing on the Instagram platform. To make wise judgments about content strategy, it is important to gather organized information and practical content ideas, increase desired, improve consumer emotions and experiences, and assess the performance of their postings. By watching the success of Instagram marketing, a descriptive qualitative method using virtual ethnography is utilized to assess AIDA (Attention, Interest, Desire, and Action) effectiveness. Instagram marketing effectiveness was determined by counting the number of users that watched, liked, visited the profile, or engaged in a certain action after seeing the advertisement. According to the study's findings, users can pay close attention to and actively participate in marketing content developed using AI Chat GPT, which increases their interest in the company's goods and services. By utilizing AI Chat GPT on the Instagram platform, these results can assist businesses in increasing the efficiency of their marketing efforts. Almost every few decades, a new invention drastically alters the course of human history. Anything that significantly increases the level of living qualifies as an innovation, like the internet. What significant historical event will follow this one? It is located here and is known as Chat GPT. It was created by the robotics research organization Open AI. The ChatGPT natural language analysis (NLP) model enhances OpenAI's GPT-2 transformer-based model for language with the GPT-3 collection of massive language patterns combining unsupervised and reinforced learning techniques. The technique facilitates informal text communication between users and AI systems. It could be used in the creation of virtual assistants for voice and text discussions as well as customer support software.

Chapter 3: AI's Double-Edged Sword: Examining the Dark Side of AI in Human Lives

The AI is s a double edged sword, in recent years, blending AI with every aspect of the stream, whether it is medicines, natural disaster predictions, disease epidemiology future prediction, etc. has been crucial and impactful in today's world. On the flip side, there are several problems that humans face with the incorporation of AI into their day-to-day lives. The first and foremost aspect is implementing AI-based technologies, which require high capital as these are costlier in addition to their infrastructure establishment and talent acquisition. The second problem is security concerns, as AI often works and provides future predictions based on past data that might be sensitive to an individual or a firm that it stores in its server, which raises concerns concerning privacy and security breaches. The third point includes the interaction of company personnel with their client physically. As everyone is aware, AI plays the best role in automation, but lack of contact might reduce customer satisfaction in the long run from a business point of view. Some other cons of incorporating AI include the loss of massive jobs known as unemployment and bias and ethical issues that might arise. So, we should be aware of these problems while implementing them into the business.

Chapter 4: Artificial Intelligence Challenges and Its Impact on Detection and Prevention of Financial Statement Fraud: A Theoretical Study

The chapters discuss the detection and prevention of financial statement fraud and its significance in maintaining the credibility and reliability of financial reporting. In response to this ongoing challenge, researchers are exploring innovative solutions that leverage artificial intelligence (AI) technology. This proposed chapter will serve as a valuable resource for researchers, practitioners, and policymakers interested in the intersection of AI and forensic accounting. It will provide a comprehensive overview of the potential challenges and impact associated with leveraging AI to enhance fraud detection and prevention efforts in the realm of financial statement fraud.

Chapter 5: Artificial Intelligence in Business: Negative Social Impacts

People who work on Artificial Intelligence (AI) technologies that directly affect people's social or ethical lives face different types of problems. These include philosophical questions about how possible it is to build ethics into algorithms and technical issues with AI development. One of the challenges is dealing with the ethical and social effects of putting people and technology together. This chapter aims to make a map of the leading social impact of AI and suggestions for how to deal with these effects. AI offers many opportunities for fundamental changes and significant industry improvements. This disruptive technology allows impressive things, like self-driving cars, serving food in restaurants, guiding robots, etc. Many people disagree about how artificial intelligence will affect society. However, people believe that AI improves everyday life because it can do simple things, making life easier, safer, and more efficient. Others say that AI is dangerous for privacy, makes racism worse by making people look the same, and puts people out of work by taking their jobs. The main things that were done to fix this social effect were to get more people talking about it and to make laws, principles, and methods for controlling how AI is used. This chapter mainly discusses the negative social impacts of AI in business.

Chapter 6: Beyond the Hype: Unveiling the Harms Caused by AI in Society

The chapters discuss that AI offers numerous, and previously unheard-of, prospects for significant enhancements and fundamental changes in a variety of industries albeit with some negative sides this . Amazing things like driverless vehicles, face recognition payment, guide robots, etc. are now possible because of disruptive technology.

More specifically, AI energizes digital business, supports the creation of smart services, and encourages digital transformation. Currently, when businesses seek to apply the digital first approach, AI is regarded as one of the top five developing technologies. Despite the fact that information technology has many advantages for businesses, authors have cautioned against its negative aspects. This is also true with AI technologies. It is acknowledged that AI has the potential to create risks for individuals, organizations, and society. Stephen Hawking, a renowned physicist, issued this scary caution: "Success in creating effective AI could be the biggest event in the history of our civilisation. Or the worst. So we cannot know if we will be infinitely helped by AI or ignored by it and side-lined, or conceivably destroyed by it." AI significantly impacts the loss of human decision-making and makes humans lazy

Chapter 7: Cyber Security Challenges and Dark Side of AI: Review and Current Status

Experts believe that cyber security is a field in which trust is a very unstable phenomenon because of its agnostic nature and in this era of advanced technology, where AI is behaving like a human being, when both meet, everything is not bright, but things are scarier in the next upcoming wave of AI. In a time when offensive AI is inevitable, can we trust AI completely?

When hackers are using AI to harness their skills to attack. In this chapter, the negative impact of AI has been reviewed while meeting with cyber security at the intersection of technology, Business disruption, forcefully wrong decision making, generation of fake news, deep fake videos, and creation of unethical content in the name of liberty with help of smart AI, etc. are some major issues which has been quoted as an example while analyzing these issues, the dark side of AI has been analyzed while mapping it with the ethical vectors of technology in the light of cyber security. The use of AI for launching security attacks, exploiting vulnerabilities, and creating malicious actors for weaponizing machines either using them as a tool or as a target, etc. and similar activities have been reviewed thoroughly up to date, along with it, the challenges and gray areas which need to be addressed urgently has been also discussed along with it its existing solution from a literature review point of view.

Chapter 8: Dark Gamification: A Tale of Consumers' Exploitation and Unfair Competition

This chapter discusses that use of Gamification has captivated the interest of consumers from all spheres of life and marketing holds a dominant position. It enhances customer engagement and loyalty through non-gaming contexts like social media marketing, e-mail marketing and customer relationship management. Gamification's growing use in the service environment has caught the attention of practitioners and marketers alike. However, everything has a positive and negative aspect, and gamification is no exception. Although there are many studies on gamification in the marketing arena, there are very few primary and secondary studies that focus on the negative side of gamification. In this chapter, we explore this lesser attended side of gamification with focus on addiction, exploitation, manipulation, and unfair competition. To address these issues, gamification designers must employ game design aspects that limit overuse and remove focus solely on extrinsic incentives. We feel that this study can help gamification specialists and marketers prevent harmful consequences by minimizing certain game design aspects.

Chapter 9: Future Perspectives of Artificial Intelligence in Various Applications

AI technology has a lengthy history and is continually evolving and expanding. It focuses on intelligent agents, which are composed of gadgets that observe their surroundings and then take appropriate action to increase the likelihood that a goal will be achieved. In this essay, we will discuss the fundamentals of contemporary AI as well as a number of illustrative applications. Artificial intelligence (AI) is the ability of computers, computer programmes, and other systems to mimic human intelligence and creativity, autonomously come up with solutions to issues, be able to reach judgements, and make choices. The majority of artificial intelligence systems have the capacity to learn, which enables individuals to gradually increase their performance. Recent studies on artificial intelligence (AI) techniques, such as machine learning, deep learning, and predictive analysis, aimed to improve planning, learning, reasoning, thinking, and action-taking skills. Accordingly, the suggested study aimed to investigate how human intelligence differed from artificial intelligence. Additionally, there are ways in which existing artificial intelligence outsmarts humans. Additionally, we critically examine what the most advanced AI now available is capable of, why it still falls short of human intellect, and what obstacles still stand in the way of AI's ability to match and surpass human intelligence. Additionally, it will examine the forecasts for artificial intelligence and provide viable solutions to address them in the next decades.

Chapter 10: Impact of Negative Aspects of Artificial Intelligence on Customer Purchase Intention: An Empirical Study of Online Retail Customers Towards AI-Enabled E-Retail Platforms

The chapters presents empirical research and discusses its darker side from the point of view of online retail customers. There are many kinds of risks associated with AI-human interaction. These may be privacy issues, sharing of personal information, deep exploration of information by AI tools for provide best services to the customers, etc. The data were collected from 286 customers which fulfils the minimum requirements of EFA (Exploratory Factor Analysis). Only those respondents were considered for filling the complete and final questionnaire who experienced AI based online retail shopping. Multiple regression was applied to determine the effect of various benefits of AI in online retailing on Customer Satisfaction. The independent variables in the form of factors were represented by the "Factor Scores" obtained from the EFA process.

Findings: Highest impact is shown by Financial Information & Security, followed by Personal Information and Movement Pattern and Malfunctioning of Systems and Reliability Issues due to the Novelty of the Concept, the variable 'Monotonous and Stereotypical" was not found contributing to significantly to the purchase intention.

Chapter 11: Sustainable Development and AI: Navigating Safety and Ethical Challenges

This Chapter delves into the fusion of Artificial Intelligence (AI) and Sustainable Development Goals (SDGs), emphasizing the need to navigate safety risks and ethical concerns. AI offers substantial potential in addressing sustainability challenges across various domains, such as energy conservation, workplace management, and advertising. However, its integration may influence employee well-being and data privacy. To effectively achieve SDGs, organizations must adopt proactive strategies to manage these inherent risks, ensuring a harmonious integration of AI and sustainability for a promising and equitable future.

Chapter 12: Unmasking the Shadows: Exploring Unethical AI Implementation

The last chapter explores unethical issues in AI implementations. Unethical AI implementation is a real issue and finding examples is easy. Many are concerned by companies using facial recognition technology for security or advertising purposes - this practice not only violates ethics but is damaging to privacy as well as leading to social injustice. Furthermore, concerns have been voiced regarding government use of AI for monitoring citizens; many fears this use violates human rights or leads to oppressive regimes; these issues have long since arisen since AI's mainstream adoption. In this paper, we share various examples, research conducted on AI ethics has uncovered many challenges related to designing ethical systems that are widely accepted, with multiple limiting factors identified as potential impediments. One difficulty lies in defining ethical principles and their interpretation by different cultures, professions and social groups. Also, we bring out another challenge that lies in the fact that many of those developing and using AI work within industries, firms or government organizations with profit maximization at heart and are less concerned with other issues besides profit maximization - this can especially be seen among for-profit tech firms and governments using AI to monitor populations.

Sumesh Dadwal
Northumbria University, UK

Shikha Goyal
Lovely Professional University, India

Pawan Kumar
Lovely Professional University, India

Rajesh Verma
Lovely Professional University, India

Chapter 1
A Comparative Study on Artificial Intelligence and Courtroom Practices With India, UK, and USA

S. Sivasankar
https://orcid.org/0009-0003-1363-925X
SASTRA University, India

ABSTRACT

This chapter explores the applicability of AI in courtrooms and the related practices. Inspired by the works of AI developers in India and globally including LAW BOT PRO, CHATGPT, COMPAS, and HART, this chapter addresses the evolution of machine learning and artificial intelligence, its mechanism, applicability in business matters, courtroom practice, how AI is involved in the general practice of court, and its position globally and in Indian perspective. It addresses concepts regarding AI that are used in countries like the United States and the United Kingdom and its legal implications, the comparative study on the working mechanism of these AI in different countries, the ways it will aid within the legal or court system, the ethical principles as per the European Union (EU), the distinction between AI for court and AI in court, the challenges it faces entering the justice system, whether it will replace lawyers, and is it trustworthy.

INTRODUCTION

Our generation should be considered as the beginning era of man-made, non-human intelligence. The concept of life is unknown to the time. Several approaches have been made on existence of life yet the source of life is still a mystery. An intelligence

DOI: 10.4018/979-8-3693-0724-3.ch001

is evolved by a natural human to assist himself was started way before several decades in the form of machines and at present it gained its splashing momentum by enhancing its activities as if done by a human being. It assists mankind in several streams. To be cautious it was at the first instance created only for assisting human kind activities. Just like the nervous system it has neural networks and a determined decision-making skill just like human. The major question is whether all human's decision wise? No, that's the difference between them. It runs on a pre-determined rules to make decision rather what a natural human do. The major difference is that it is a programmed one and not in physical presence rather it is travelling through the signals of consisted networks.

These machine learning systems by way of utilizing algorithms and learn from data by using artificial neural networks to stimulate the way human brain works is termed as Artificial Intelligence, AI. It was started as an image and speech recognition and now it has been developed into autonomous vehicles and entered into at least with a specific aspect in every profession. Let me put the problem straightforward here. Do the advent of AI in every profession leads to the problem of techno-human unemployment? Will it be regarded as the new world order? In simple terms, if not accepted now, there always lies a future where technology grows and will there be a position of AI based labour or employment system being adopted where no man has a choice of getting employed? It again leads to the debate, whether technology be considered superior than the human resource?

The first artificial intelligence system was developed in 1956 and it was a computer programme designed to play checkers, a game. It was created by Arthur Samuel (McCarthy & Feigenbaum, 1990) one of the participants in the Dartmouth conference and it was there the term Artificial Intelligence coined. We can analyse how an AI developed from a game of checkers to play the profession of employed persons almost in every aspect. Further it is not the one which always got programmed. Samuel's checkers programme was the first example of a machine learning algorithm, which he trained to play checkers by having it play games against itself and learn from its mistakes (McCarthy et al., 2006). So, we cannot go into the assumption that how a programmed AI functions the job of an employee. But the real question here is how can an AI take over a profession? There is an ultimate difference between an employment and a profession. Let us take the example of software developer, he works with an AI and the takeover by AI is a simple job that an AI develops a system. But it is not the case with a profession especially considering a legal profession. To be particular, the courtroom profession.

CHATGPT AND ITS MECHANISM

Situation seeks a perfect answer. So, the one who is the protagonist here, on whom there are certain doubtful beliefs among people to be questioned on its usability, have given a clarity on what way it is working. "It is received as CHATGPT is a large language model that uses deep learning techniques to generate human-like texts. It is based on the generative pre-trained transformer (GPT) architecture, which uses a transformer neural network to process and generate texts. The model is pre-trained on a massive dataset of texts, like books, articles, and websites, so it can understand the patterns and structure of natural language. When given a prompt starting point, the model uses this pre-trained knowledge to generate text that continues the given input in a coherent and natural way."

What is meant by "large learning language model?". It digests huge quantities of text data and infer relationships between words within the texts. The basic training given to the GPT is to predict the word in a sequence of words also known as next-token-prediction (Binz & Schulz, 2023), which helps to predict the next word in a sequence and masked-language-modelling, which helps to predict the middle word in a sequence. Basically, what happens is the input data is processed individually and sequentially rather than as a whole corpus. This means that during training, the context window is fixed and only extends beyond a single input for a number of the phases in the process. This limits the complexity of the relationships between words and the meanings that can be derived.

In response to this issue, in 2017 a team at Google Brain introduced transformers. Unlike LSTMs, transformers can process all input data simultaneously. The model can assign variable weights to various input data components in connection to any point of the language sequence by use of a self-attention mechanism. This feature enabled massive improvements in infusing meaning into large language models and enables processing of significantly larger datasets.

The first GPT was introduced in 2018 by an open AI named it as GPT1. And the model continued to evolve into a GPT-2 in 2019 and by 2020 with GPT model-3 and by 2022 it was evolved as InstructGPT and CHATGPT.

Every single GPT model has a transformer architecture that is made up of an encoder to handle the input sequence and a decoder to construct the output sequence. The encoder and decoder both provide a mechanism for multi-head self-attention that enables the model to differentially weight various parts of the sequence in order to infer meaning and context (Ghojogh & Ghodsi, 2020). The encoder additionally uses masked-language modelling to comprehend the links between words and produce more intelligible replies. It is the self-attention mechanism that drives CHATGPT.

The following are the step-by-step process on how the AI generates the answers and suggestions,

1) It creates a query, key and a value vector for each token from the input it has received.
2) It calculates the similarities between the query from step one and the key of every other token by taking the product of two vectors together
3) Then it generates normalized weights by feeding the output from step 2.
4) It generates the final vector representing the importance of the token within the sequence by multiplying the weights (how much stressed the word was…) and finally give its suggestions.

AI AND BUSINESS

So far, we have seen how the CHATGPT functions. Now the question arises why we need an AI. The answer is simple. "Ease of doing business and other works." So next popup that comes to our mind is "Does the invent of AI leads to make another approach of doubting the service of we humans?"

We can take the answer in a two-fold approach as a coin. The CHATGPT and other similar AI's have been developed primarily for the purpose of business benefit. The free service of these AI that common people can afford is basically a research engine. But the true nature of work that these AI does is behind the subscriptions of premium and many businessmen were buying it now. The answer lies there.

1) Firstly, purchasing it leads to ease of doing the business. Its cost efficient than that the business pays the employees routinely. They can rely on one thing on many matters rather than approaching different departments for various works.
2) On the second hand, many businesses think employee as a burden of costs, they have to pay many employees if the span of the business is vast. They have an approach of underestimating the capability of the employees and often creates a sense of doubtfulness that the decision or the creative ideas given by employees many not worthy or accurate enough. Example of these is the forecasting department and investing departments of the company.

Analysing both the sides we can presume that employees are getting wasted. But we cannot say that they are sceptical on employees rather they are relying more on AI. But the end result is the same on all positions of employees.

Let's take an illustration, Alibaba, a Chinese corporation, operates the biggest e-commerce site in the world, selling more items than both Amazon and eBay put together. Artificial intelligence (AI) plays a crucial role in Alibaba's daily operations and is employed to foretell potential client purchases. The business creates product descriptions for the website automatically using natural language processing. Alibaba's City Brain project to develop smart cities is another way the company employs artificial intelligence. By tracking every vehicle in the city, the project employs AI algorithms to assist alleviate traffic congestion (Marr, 2019).

Robotic Process Automation (RPA) is used by many businesses like IBM, Deloitte, Microsoft. They use RPA to automate rote tasks which is the fundamental of any AI to learn by repetition. Enhanced customer experiences is the one which personalises customer's like over a product or service based on his search history and past transactions. Amazon, the best example of utilising AI solutions to improve customer service. The forecasting department gets affected by certain business which use AI in predicting market. According to Forbes repot Nissan is planning to use AI in an attempt to design new models in real time to shorten the time to market for new models. But the concern here is a clean data should be produced to AI. The prediction is good only if the data given is clean and clear. But certain company requires AI to enhance its user relationship such as Google and social media platforms such as Instagram. These are industry specific needs. They use Artificial Intelligence to perform tasks based on the analysis of information. It can recommend new products based on our search engine history, recommend trips based on analysis on vacation by flight history.

As per Forbes, business owner's concerns of using Artificial Intelligence falls on technology dependence, technical skills to use AI, human workforce reduction, privacy concerns, provide business or customers with misinformation, bias errors a negatively impact customer relationships.

Here's a situation where two companies let's say A and B are purchasing a special AI named X. Both companies are IT. If A company requests X to suggest few marketing techniques and it gives its best solutions so that A company can predict the future market. Now B company asks X to predict the market and the situation of A in future. Will X provide what it suggested A company? It is troublesome even if it provides the exact suggestion or a suggestion that too nearly resembles the strategy of company A. AI provides information with a pre collected data. If that data is being shared the system will turn itself as a best answer to the question and it will prioritize it and share its best answer. Even though it is said the company should have made certain agreements or contracts regarding its privacy and sensible questions or suggestions yet chance are still high on technical faults, and there may arise a situation where the AI finds certain loopholes in the contract and may provide information to others which with due intelligence can be interpreted.

The generative Artificial Intelligence has legal conundrum on Intellectual property rights. To be precise in the domain of IPR, the Artificial Intelligence does not consider the copyright of original authors in account of providing information. Since it is the basic ideology behind the working of AI that whatever the queries that is given, it should give suggestion in its own way rather mentioning what the original source data.

This copyright issue should be considered in the same manner if a company is misusing the intellectual right of other company. Since a company is an Artificial person, it should consider the position of the original authors if AI is interpreting in the process of business. At the least business should consider mentioning this in their disclosure agreement with other parties. The person who is to be made liable is the way forward. Is it whether the business or the contracting parties or the AI. To avoid this there can be a development in the system where the AI should list the original authors in the end. But it is rare that AI developers mention the original source data as it ultimately affects the purpose of AI and thereby cutting the profits the developers and creators earn.

According to the McKinsey global survey report (*The State of AI in 2021*, 2021) the percentage of workforce or labour displacement from 2020 to 2021 is higher. It cannot be said that arrival of AI in companies' department functions and thereby leading downsizing as illegal but we can safely land on quoting that they are morally wrong. Now, we are clear in saying that reports of AI risks are more in developed economies than in developing economies with a unitary difference. It was also reported that it will create 2.9 trillion US Dollar of business value and 6.2 billion hours of workers productivity. It is based on business centric, customer centric rather on workers or employee centric. "Human resources are essential for operating a business" is only temporary, because at the historical time there was no other option than to utilize the human. But now AI replacing human resource significantly to technological resource.

As far as these AI's occupying the business units and companies there is no major problem but the real situation arises when these AI try to occupy the professions. We are aware about how the business, profession and occupation differ.

COURTROOM PRACTICE

A court is a gathering of professionals who aid, administers and renders justice. A court stands on a specific place or location where the affected party and the party whom they are fighting against, appears and argue before the court of professionals and receive justice.

There are two division system inside the court. It is bar and bench. The bar, represents the advocates who appear on behalf of the either affected party or the respondent and argues before the bench, the judges by aiding them in all matters related to the law in which the case is subjected to and the interpretations of various provisions and statutes will be done and then the judge hears both parties and comes with the judgement that is beneficial for either party.

How the Day Starts in a Court

The day starts with filing of cases. In every court there is a registry headed by a registrar or a joint registrar. There every plaint, petitions, application, memorandum of appeal etc., have to be filed by advocate or a person duly appointed by him. It can also be the advocates office clerk who is to be duly appointed. Then the officer in charge of filing the counter shall endorse the date of receipt of the document presented. Once the pleadings, applications, documents are presented appropriately in a required manner, they are ready for filing; the Registrar makes the registration of the same and prepares a list of cases for the hearing.

Then a writ of summon is issued on the opposite side to call them that a case has been filed against them and they should file a response application or pleading. Then the court make admissions of hearings and dispose the case off.

The real drag is the pendency of cases. The recent National Judicial Data Grid (NJDG) shows that 3,89,41,148 cases are pending at the district and taluka levels and 58,43,113 are still unresolved at the high courts (Sagar, 2021). The reason for this happening is low staffs, slow process of registration, adjournments, inadequate benches, the number of appeals in a case, profession of service turned to money making among various advocates, abuse of public interest litigation PIL, lack of adequate arrangement to monitor. These were also said by the union law minister, Shri Kiren Rijiju (Press Trust of India & Business Standard, 2023). To overcome these problems many countries employed Artificial Intelligence to assist the court practices. Further the law minister said for implementing phase two of the e-Courts project there is a need to adopt new, cutting-edge technologies of machine learning (ML) and artificial intelligence (AI) to increase the efficiency of justice delivery system. It was conceptualized with a vision to transform the Indian Judiciary by ICT (Information and Communication Technology) enablement of Courts. It is a pan-India Project, monitored and funded by the Department of Justice, Ministry of Law and Justice, for the District Courts across the country.

The first level of e-court project was conducted during the COVID19 pandemic, where e-filings and virtual hearings were conducted.

Supreme court Portal for Assistance in Court Efficiency (SUPACE) was recently launched by the supreme court of India. It was created to first comprehend the judicial operations that call for automation, after which it helps the court increase efficiency and decrease pending cases by encapsulating those that can be automated. Similarly, there are steps taken in other countries like,

- US: COMPAS (Correctional Offender Management Profiling for Alternative Sanctions).
- UK: HART (Harm Assessment Risk Tool).
- China/Mexico/Russia: Giving legal advice, approving pensions.
- Estonia: Robot judge for adjudicating small claims.
- Malaysia: Supporting sentencing decisions.
- Austria: Sophisticated document management.
- Argentina/Colombia: Prometea (Identifying urgent cases within minutes).
- Singapore: Transcribing court hearings in real-time.

Information Technology

The fact that the artificial intelligence only needs a specific and crystal-clear facts otherwise information as input is undeniable. This also made it unquestionable that the courts also should have a clear information about the case. Most of the cases that are put to hearing are not complex to deal. It is to be noted that everything is information from the facts that have been received in the court, the process or the procedure that's taking place and the outcome. Many cases only need a simple assessment and can be disposed off early, the only specimen required is the information and all other process are inbuilt in the AI for specific purposes. This has great advantage on the civil cases than the criminal proceedings.

Considering the civil cases in every court the complexity of the information and predictability of the outcome need to be identified. Nearly large proportion of the civil cases have high predictability on outcome. So, the court rulings will be produced by automatic process based on the data supplied. On the first hand the court need the digital submissions of filing the suit or information and there is no need to re-enter it manually. Case processing can be done partially or fully automated if the outcome is highly predictable. To accomplish this a smart e-portal is also necessary which was done by the supreme court during phase one trial of its e-court project during pandemic.

How AI Aids in Research

A CoCounsel, an AI legal assistant (*Case Text's Open AI. GPT-4 Version.*, n.d.). Can you conduct research on what courts in this jurisdiction have done in cases presenting similar fact patterns to the case we are working on? and other similar questions can be asked of by a junior associate using CoCounsel, which is powered by technology from Open AI, the company that created ChatGPT. Case text is a part of what is certain to develop into a rapidly expanding ecosystem of legal technology businesses providing AI products built on extensive language models.

There are other chances to employ AI to deliver legal services in a more fully automated manner. In order to encourage innovation in this field, legal and legislative frameworks will need to be changed. This will also allow for the identification and mitigation of related risks.

One of the most time-consuming duties in a lawsuit is figuring out how to make sense of the vast number of papers that are produced during discovery and extract their structure, significance, and key details. AI will significantly speed up this process, doing tasks that would typically take weeks without it in a matter of seconds. Or take into account creating motions that you will submit to a judge. AI can be used to quickly create first drafts that cite pertinent case law, present arguments, and refute (as well as anticipate) points put forth by opposing lawyers. The final draft will still require human input, but AI will make the process go much more quickly.

Examples include contracts, the many forms of paperwork that are filed with a court during a legal proceeding, answers to interrogatories, summaries for clients of recent events in a legal situation, visual exhibits to be used during trial, and pitches intended to attract new clients. During a trial, AI might potentially be employed to analyse the trial record in real-time and give attorneys advice on which witnesses to cross-examine. This is what the US and UK court systems are doing in real time.

What AI Can Do for Court

In a first the supreme court of India used AI for live transcription of its proceedings to the public at large. Now there is a separate e-portal for the various courts in India. There is still a need to develop a mechanism to file the case electronically through the website which would make the job of the registrar easier by also fixing the chronological date and time of hearing and the adjournments if any. Recently the supreme court of India have also started using AI for translating the orders, decree and the judgements both in English and the regional languages which helps the locals to understand the day-to-day proceedings of court. AI have also been used by advocates and other competent persons to compile draft, contracts and responding in legal advice to clients, drafting land documents such as patta, sale deed, mortgages, gift, general attorney and many by providing specific information.

1) Grouping facts and key information:

When large paper works are used it will psychologically cause distress among the court officers say registrars, clerks. But when the information being collected without any manual work by way of AI, the amount of work can be done at present is greater than it was before. AI collects key information and groups chronologically and then the judge assesses and confirms the information gathered. This system is being followed in US and UK by eDiscovery and digital case system respectively. It is only to be on the safe side, the document investigation is conducted by the jury. Comparing the manual research works, this method is more accurate and results in speedy disposal of cases according to the jury of US and UK.

2) Counselling:

AI is also being used in an advisory position. Once the government in any country allow public to use advisory AI free of cost, the clients no longer be charged for hefty fee due of advocates. This type of advisory AI is trending this year 2023, due to the launch of DONOTPAY in US. It is an AI robot which replaces the lawyer where the client can directly move the court once the application is done and the clients can connect their EarPods with the AI robot and it actually does hear the case and arguments put forth, analyse and then suggest the way the client can give counter argument or opinion. But this robot AI currently allowed on parking ticket related cases in US which was appreciated by the public.

3) Predictive justice:

It was the prediction and accuracy of AI that brings some chance of hope in court system according to many scholars and specifically the developers of these AI. We are not aware of the working process of those AI in detail due to their secrecy in development and there are chances of copyright issue if misused. A team of programmers in the US has created a model that is intended to forecast the actions of the Supreme Court of the United States (SCOTUS). By only using the data available prior to the decision, this model will outperform the baseline model at both justice and case level as well as at parametric and non-parametric levels. It achieved 70.2% accuracy at case outcome level and 71.9% at justice vote level (Katz et al., 2014). It said that this AI can be applied out of sample to the entire past or future of the court and not for a single term purpose only. This is the exact view said by those developers. It is in similar to COMPAS used in US for reducing the risk of its outcome and predictions which also have similar capacity of tests as mentioned above. In US view COMPAS is more reliable.

There is a software and a company named "RAVEL" (Artificiallawyer, 2017). Artificial lawyer first caught up by the CEO and co-founder Daniel Levis. He caught the inspiration by attending Stanford school of law and wanted to create a machine learning AI and he achieved it. For the time being, RAVEL treats US law from three angles: case law, judge behaviour, and court type. The RAVEL is not for public operation rather it is being acquired by law firms by subscriptions and the insights of process making mechanism not exactly revealed.

PRINCIPLES ON EFFICIENCY OF JUSTICE

The European commission for efficiency of justice (ECPEJ) (Dymitruk, 2019) carved out certain ethical principles that to be followed by the AI in the justice making process.

1) Principle of respect of fundamental rights: ensuring that the design and implementation of artificial intelligence tools and services are compatible with fundamental rights. For example, it should neither be biased over religion nor assume an aesthetical idea as to a country which is a harbour of religion, India. It should be par with the IT rules;
2) Principle of non-discrimination: specifically preventing the development or intensification of any discrimination between individuals or groups of individuals; there should be equal treatment and fair trial;
3) Principle of quality and security: with regard to the processing of judicial decisions and data, using certified sources and intangible data with models conceived in a multi-disciplinary manner, in a secure technological environment;
4) Principle of transparency, impartiality and fairness: making data processing methods accessible and understandable, authorising external audits; the user of the AI must show the process, idea and understanding, the choices and assumptions made to the public or to the concerned authority and it should be further examined.
5) Principle "under user control": avoiding a prescriptive approach and making certain that users are active, educated, and in control of their decisions. Users must be in charge of their decisions, be aware of what the AI is doing, and comprehend what it is doing. This implies that users must have no trouble departing from the algorithm's result (*Ethical Principles on AI in Courts by European Union:*, n.d.).

Beyond State v. Loomis (Liu et al., 2019), a recent case in the United States, the accused Loomis was charged with attempting to flee a traffic officer and operating a motor vehicle without owner's consent. The trial court with the aid of COMPAS predicted the verdict based on the accused's criminal history, level of education and so on, and sentenced to imprisonment for six years including probation. Then an appeal was made stating that AI tools have violated his process rights and the reasoning given was not to reveal the trade secret concerns and hence the method in which Loomis risk deducted cannot be revealed thereby violating right to information or reasoning behind justice. This case Demonstrates how unrestrained and unchecked outsourcing of public power to machines may undermine human rights and the rule of law. This case showcases the issues of the 'legal black box' and the 'technical black box' to identify the risks posed by rampant 'algorithmizing' of government functions to due process, equal protection, and transparency.

COMPARATIVE RESULT: HOW FAR US AND UK ACHIEVED

As described earlier, pre-COVID period welcomed the AI implementation in legal system. We have also seen how AI got effected in US and UK by RAVEL, DONOTPAY and HART. By now the pandemic got reduced and declining and we have to understand the stand that has been taken by these countries which dominantly developing artificial intelligence these days, specifically the post-COVID period.

The US supreme court have published "2023 year - end report on federal judiciary" (*2023 SC US Endreport AI and Law*, n.d.) where the US supreme court while recognizing the potential of AI warns on "dehumanizing the law". The US Chief Justice John G Roberts. Jr, notably pointed that it carries hazards, especially when used incorrectly. He emphasised that much of the legal system's decision-making involves human assessment, discretion, and nuanced knowledge. Simply entrusting such power to an algorithm is likely to produce unsatisfying and unjust results, especially given that AI models can incorporate unintentional bias. He also particularly mentioned that "In criminal cases, the use of AI in assessing flight risk, recidivism, and other largely discretionary decisions that involve predictions has generated concerns about due process, reliability, and potential bias," wrote Roberts. "At least at present, studies show a persistent public perception of a 'human-AI fairness gap,' reflecting the view that human adjudications, for all of their flaws, are fairer than whatever the machine spits out."

The impact of AI already taking place in the US where two lawyers were fined of 5000 USD for filing cases with the use of CHATGPT which generated non-existent and fabricated cases. Their defence was good faith and innocence. It is evident that it is the lawyers got fined and not the AI or the related developing company. Though legally speaking it is the lawyers who believed the contents were true and AI being newly developed, its personality needs to be identified to make it criminally liable. The report also stated that "But any use of AI requires caution and humility. One of AI's prominent applications 2023 Year-End Report on the Federal Judiciary made headlines this year for a shortcoming known as "hallucination," which caused the lawyers using the application to submit briefs with citations to non-existent cases. (Always a bad idea.) Some legal scholars have raised concerns about whether entering confidential information into an AI tool might compromise later attempts to invoke legal privileges."

UK- a committee was formed with the union of the House of lord's justice and home affairs which made a report on 28th November 2022 on "technology rules? The advent of new technologies in the justice system". (*AI Technology and Justice System*, n.d.) This investigated the application of artificial intelligence (AI) technologies in the criminal justice system. The report focused on tools that use algorithms or machine learning technologies to assist in the application of the law in England and Wales. This includes algorithmically modified technologies used to discover crimes, discourage criminal activity, and to rehabilitate or punish offenders. The technologies referred were predictive policing, visa streaming and facial recognition tools. The committee highlighted AI's potential to improve efficiency, productivity, and problem resolution in the justice system. However, it stated a lack of minimum standards, openness, evaluation and training in AI technology meant that the public's human rights and civil freedoms could be endangered. The committee stated that tackling these concerns would "consolidate the UK's position as a frontrunner in the global race for AI, while respecting human rights and the rule of law". The committee believed that precise documentation, evaluation by subject experts and transparency when evidence is subject to algorithmic manipulation. It also took into consideration that the government has no cross-departmental strategy on the use of new technologies in justice system as well as no clear line of accountability for technological misuse.

The UK government disagreed on certain important recommendations set out by this committee and here are few of that, it was not convinced that a new independent national body and certification system should be established. It stated that while certification was effective in some situations, it might also foster false confidence and be costly and it disagreed with the notion of making transparency a statutory principle. It stated that several police departments were already being transparent about the technologies they utilise by posting tools, information, and impact evaluations on their websites. While agreeing to certain recommendations still it is peculiar to take into consideration the said idea such that transparency, misuse, data falsifications and accountability be maintained and identified.

POSITION IN INDIA

Usage of AI upon the works of the judicial system was welcomed only to the extent of live transcription of supreme court cases, e-filing of petitions and plaint and translation of judgements to regional languages but not to the extent of delivering justice. SUPACE, supreme court portal for assistance in courts efficiency which leverages machine learning to deal with huge chunks of case data. A language translation AI tool named, SUVAS, Supreme Court Vidhik Anuvaad Software was launched to translate judicial documents.

A law student has developed an AI called LAW BOT PRO, addressing the issue of gathering information on the legal issues they are facing (Bar & Bench & Bar & Bench, 2023). Law Bot Pro is a revolutionary app that offers a comprehensive and user-friendly platform for finding legal information, Law Bot Pro is a ground-breaking tool. The intelligent chatbot is one of the main characteristics of Law Bot Pro. Since the chatbot is designed to respond to questions in simple terms, more people may easily obtain legal knowledge. Users only need to enter their legal query into the chatbot, and it will respond with a precise and succinct response. Instead of depending on CHATGPT which can handle multiple purposes other than legal search, the developer preferred to develop a new chat box which handle only searches relating to legal issues. It will provide higher accuracy for direct questions.

"It is not made for legal professionals, yet", says Giri, the developer, whose main aim was to launch the first version specifically for narrative queries. The app in the future will offer a variety of resources, including case laws, statutes, regulations, and legal articles, among others for professionals as well.

Everything is fine if it helps the court to give justice. But not the justice delivery system itself. There are lot of reasons why the justice delivery system is not suitable in Indian scenario according to the study.

1) Trustworthy: People tend to believe what others say as true rather than what the AI says when their personal life is involved. People choose the system to which they have been adopted, which can be analysed when India adopted the parliamentary system similar to UK because we were adopted to the system, the British's practiced. This applies both to the case of legal advice and rendering justice. People in India trust the professionals and they believe their words because of their skills, experience and knowledge. There is absolutely a chance of appeal or a re-examination if the justice delivered by AI which will become a double work. It can be said that the personality of each judge differs but AI have a similar personality over any cases. But when a justice is delivered, multiple analysis should be made to give a just and fair justice. That's why there are different benches in courts.
2) Predictive justice - justice assumed? AI tools such as COMPAS and HART used in US and UK respectively is said to have achieved 70.2% accuracy at the outcome level and 71.9% at justice vote level (Katz et al., 2014b). Does the representatives of the deceased are satisfied with the chance of justice at 71% against the murderer? Or a company files a case to recover the damages and losses incurred due to the bribe done by competitors on manager, for the actual loss incurred or just a portion of the loss? If justice is given by AI, it is based on the prediction on how the real judges would react and its accuracy depends on that assumption. Rather than justice administering AI bots, those

AI which provides legal information are considered accurate because their input is already saved over the historic laws and cases. Something which comes out of prediction is not a justice. The judgement should be a 100% accurate which is difficult to be achieved by AI than the manual method.

3) Role of advocate: advocates and lawyers are the one that aid the bench in administering justice. Advocates are professionals who completed bachelors in law and passed the bar examination and practice in the courts. There are over 1.3 million advocates and lawyers registered in India. If AI replace the role of advocate, it not only ceases the job but also the hard work and passion put into the profession. Justice won't see emotions but the lawyers do. What a client need is to make sure the lawyer understands his emotion and that's how the lawyer devolve into the case and help his client. There are many people who do not know the operation of internet and other devices in rural and semi-urban areas. They rely on natural lawyers and seek their advice. AI can be used in helping the lawyers in search of precedents and case related researches helping them to address cases instantly. AI cannot be made complementary to lawyers. The legal system places great importance on a lawyer having a thorough understanding of the facts of a case and their potential consequences. This may be difficult to replicate with AI, as it may be unable to grasp the nuances of a case and therefore provide an incorrect solution. Furthermore, the risk of relying too heavily on technology is that it could result in a legal system that is only as good as its technology is. This could lead to a negative impact on the quality of justice, as AI systems are likely to be less experienced than human lawyers.
4) How far reliable? Unlike other countries India give importance to all religion and treats them equally. It is the harbour of religion. There are many schools of thoughts apart from the main source and even people from tribal areas have their own customs and traditions. If a case is involved with a religious issue how far the AI can give verdict without bias and how far it is reliable? In reality case concerning religious issue can be addressed on the way it is being practised apart from the codified law. We can see this in Sabarimala case where we have to consider the tradition and practice. Also, in Ayodhya Ram mandir land dispute over place of worship, the essentiality whether a particular religion need a place to practice their worship is necessary or not need to be considered along with the codified law i.e., constitution of India. Certain cases won't have preceding judgements like the above-mentioned cases. So, it is difficult for AI to predict and render proper justice without any bias.
5) Limitation as to information: there are more AI to fulfil a specific task which cannot be ignored. But every AI collects information only as to the past records. There is a specific period the time of collecting information stops. But it can

be continued again if user permits. The current version of CHATGPT January 2023 is only trained on data through September 2021. This means that the chatbot cannot intercept more recent data. We can consider certain AI are lacking current state of affairs. If there is a sudden change in law, approaching AI is troublesome. The duty of those in legal profession is to accumulate knowledge regarding all affairs especially in real time. It is to be noted that the above mentioned applies to those AI which was authorised in justice making process.

6) Independence of judiciary: there are three organs of the government or democracy namely judiciary, legislative and executive. Independence of judiciary not only means the independent appointing process of judges but also remind us that the three organs should not encroach upon the functions of other organs. Is independent of judiciary gets affected by the invocation of AI in justice rendering system? What the constitution makers thought of judicial independence is there shall be a free and fair justice rendered without the interference of the other organs but all should work together to promote democracy. In that case can technology interfere the process of judiciary? Justice making is an art with systematic process. Systematic process says there shall be regulations in governing justice. The constitutional makers were aware of the fact that technology will improve faster in upcoming decades. Inspite of that they gave regulations on appointing the judges. We also cannot ignore that in the way of societal change anything can be regulated with the society's need and preferences including advancements in certain areas. The area in which art and technology differs is the individual skills, experience and especially the emotions. The ultimate objective of judiciary is to render justice which can be done perfectly unbiased way by the human judges. Technology has no way in entering the justice giving process rather it has all scope in aiding the way the work to be done.

In light of the likelihood that judicial reforms will have an impact on the external aspect of independence, judges should be shielded from any pressure or intervention that might encourage them to cave. This protection should be extended to any procedural regulations that might directly or indirectly influence a judge's decision. Therefore, the implementation of AI in courts through judicial reform should not promote the exercise of control over national courts.

the implicit establishment of liability administrations for judges operating in the environment of courts bedding AI rudiments which may exercise pressure over judicial opinions; the reduction of judges' hires, which would put them at risk of bribery; or decrease the support of the bar, which would lead to an increase in the workload for individual judges.

In order to effectively manage these systems in courts, expert knowledge is required to monitor their functioning and identify potential issues. There are three potential outcomes: training of judges; training of AI technicians to assist work in the courtroom; or a combination of both. In the case of judges, what knowledge and skills are required to effectively manage AI issues? At this stage, the answer is unclear. In the second case, involving AI technology, the possible expansion of independence safeguards for them is essential. Any technical professional working in this area should not be subject to any external pressure or interference. A related issue is how the technician interacts with the judge, as well as how liability (in the event of damage or AI-related issues) is allocated. A shared regime of liability may be appropriate in the light of the joint responsibility of the expert and the judge. At this stage, it is important to note that, regardless of the liability regime, any AI-assisted court judges should not have any form of influence over judicial functions.

CONCLUSION

If AI is able to give accurate results, then it will cause lawyers to lose their job. Everyday technology is getting advanced. The custom of law as an art will become one with science and technology. Lawyers are an integral part of the legal system. If AI replaces lawyers, then it means that lawyer is not necessary and it will contradict the above said limitations of using AI in a country like India.

There is a difference between AI as the court and AI in the court. Lawyers play a vital role in legal system and the same way the legal system regards lawyers essential for justice as they have a thorough understanding of facts of a case and through their experience, they can analyse the consequences. This particular setup is difficult for AI to be on par with the experience and analysing skills of a lawyer over the years. There is a chance that AI may not grasp the nuances of the case and may render incorrect solutions. As already said, if AI takes over the justice system, then it will lead to a negative impact on society that justice is only good as its technology is. There is a good opportunity of utilising AI for research purposes by lawyers so they can handle multiple cases and render speedy disposal. But using AI for rendering justice and replacing lawyers all at once is not possible.

REFERENCES

2023 *SC US endreport AI and law*. (n.d.). www.supremecourt.gov. https://www.supremecourt.gov/publicinfo/year-end/2023year-endreport.pdf

AI technology and justice system. (n.d.). https://lordslibrary.parliament.uk/ai-technology-and-the-justice-system-lords-committee-report/

Artificiallawyer. (2017, February 12). *AL Interview: Ravel and the AI revolution in legal research.* ArtificialLawyer. https://www.artificiallawyer.com/2017/01/23/al-interview-ravel-and-the-ai-revolution-in-legal-research/

Bar & Bench. (2023). Law student develops Law Bot Pro, a free legal AI app. *Bar And Bench - Indian Legal News.* https://www.barandbench.com/apprentice-lawyer/law-student-develops-indias-first-free-legal-ai-app

Binz, M., & Schulz, E. (2023). Using cognitive psychology to understand GPT-3. *Proceedings of the National Academy of Sciences of the United States of America, 120*(6). Advance online publication. doi:10.1073/pnas.2218523120 PMID:36730192

Case text's open AI. GPT-4 version. (n.d.). Case Text.

Dymitruk, M. (2019). Ethical artificial intelligence in judiciary. *ResearchGate.* https://www.researchgate.net/publication/333995919_Ethical_artificial_intelligence_in_judiciary

Ethical principles on AI in courts by European union. (n.d.). https://www.coe.int/en/web/cepej/cepej-european-ethical-charter-on-the-use-of-artificial-intelligence-ai-in-judicial-systems-and-their-environment

GhojoghB.GhodsiA. (2020). Attention Mechanism, Transformers, BERT, and GPT: Tutorial and Survey. *Research Gate.* https://doi.org/ doi:10.31219/osf.io/m6gcn

KatzD.BommaritoM. J.BlackmanJ. (2014). Predicting the behavior of the Supreme Court of the United States: A General approach. *Social Science Research Network.* doi:10.2139/ssrn.2463244

Liu, H., Lin, C., & Chen, Y. (2019). Beyond State v Loomis: Artificial intelligence, government algorithmization and accountability. *International Journal of Law and Information Technology, 27*(2), 122–141. doi:10.1093/ijlit/eaz001

Marr, B. (2019). *Artificial intelligence in practice: How 50 Successful Companies Used AI and Machine Learning to Solve Problems.* John Wiley & Sons.

McCarthy, J., & Feigenbaum, E. A. (1990). In memoriam: Arthur Samuel: Pioneer in Machine learning. *AI Magazine, 11*(3), 10–11. doi:10.1609/aimag.v11i3.840

McCarthy, J., Minsky, M., Rochester, N., & Shannon, C. E. (2006). A proposal for the Dartmouth Summer Research Project on Artificial Intelligence, August 31, 1955. *AI Magazine, 27*(4), 12. doi:10.1609/aimag.v27i4.1904

Press Trust of India & Business Standard. (2023, February 22). *Union law minister Rijiju lauds use of AI to transcribe SC proceedings*. https://www.business-standard.com/article/current-affairs/union-law-minister-rijiju-lauds-use-of-ai-to-transcribe-sc-proceedings-123022201258_1.html

SagarA. (2021). The Role of Judiciary in India and Pendency of Cases: an overall view. *Social Science Research Network*. doi:10.2139/ssrn.3798261

The state of AI in 2021. (2021, December 8). McKinsey & Company. https://www.mckinsey.com/capabilities/quantumblack/our-insights/global-survey-the-state-of-ai-in-2021

Chapter 2
A Conceptual Study on Instagram Marketing:
Examining the Effect of AI on Several Business Sectors Using AI ChatGPT on Marketing Effectiveness

Pramod Ranjan Panda
GIET University, India

Swapna mayee Sahoo
GIET University, India

Saumendra Das
https://orcid.org/0000-0003-4956-4352
GIET University, India

Rohit Bansal
https://orcid.org/0000-0001-7072-5005
Vaish College of Engineering, Rohtak, India

Sabyasachi Dey
Trident Academy of Creative Technology, India

Nayan Deep S. Kanwal
University Putra Malaysia, Malaysia

Hassan Badawy
Luxor University, Egypt

ABSTRACT

The purpose of this study is to look into the applications of AI Chat GPT that affect marketing efficiency, notably on the Instagram platform. In the success of Instagram marketing, a descriptive qualitative method using virtual ethnography is utilized to assess AIDA (attention, interest, desire, and action) effectiveness. By counting the number of users that watched, liked, visited the profile, or engaged in a certain action after seeing the advertisement, Instagram's marketing effectiveness was determined. This chapter examines how ChatGPT, an NLG model powered by OpenAI's GPT-3 technology, might enhance chat-based e-commerce and other sectors including news, education, entertainment, finance, and health. The authors evaluate ChatGPT's present use cases in various fields and consider potential new uses. They also talk about how this technology may be used to provide people with more individualized content. They examine ChatGPT's potential to improve customer service for businesses in our final section.

DOI: 10.4018/979-8-3693-0724-3.ch002

1. INTRODUCTION

OpenAI's ChatGPT chatbot platform, powered by artificial intelligence, has the potential to revolutionize human interaction with technology. It uses machine learning and natural language processing to enable conversational conversations between people and machines, enabling applications in various sectors such as customer service, entertainment, education, finances, and healthcare. ChatGPT's sophisticated features understand discourse context, making it better suited for most systems. Its widespread use will have a profound impact on society, with virtual assistants enabling interactive recreational activities, AI-powered tutoring solutions in schools, and digital financial guidance for insurance companies. In healthcare, ChatGPT can improve patient care by utilizing predictive analytics applications to spot patterns in medical data faster than humans. Its ability to interpret complex questions enables successful data finding, especially in industries like hospitals. The development of ChatGPT has numerous opportunities to improve society and people's lives in education, entertainment, money, health news, and productivity. The explored that AI Chat GPT helped companies create better content and enhance platform user experiences, particularly on the Instagram platform. Further research is needed to determine the impact of AI Chat GPT on marketing efficiency. The present study has investigated the conceptual developments on Chat GPT usage in social media and search engine optimization through AI where the marketing effectiveness tool like AIDA explored the mood, sentiments and emotion of customer before an attempt of purchase. The study has been classified into seven sections. The section two provided the objectives of the study, section three is on the literature review, section four articulated on the ChatGPT, section five investigated on social media marketing using AI and AIDA, section six provided the discussion and section seven articulated on conclusion.

2. AIMS OF THE CHAPTER

- Employs a descriptive qualitative approach using virtual ethnography.
- Users are able to actively engage in marketing content created with AI Chat GPT.
- Chat GPT improves upon OpenAI's GPT-2 model by using the extensive linguistic patterns from the GPT-3 dataset.
- Encompasses features such as mood, emotion, and subject analysis.
- Enables the creation of several chat threads to facilitate authentic interactions between people and bots.

- This text examines the challenges that hinder the progress of artificial intelligence (AI) and explores the potential applications of ChatGPT in different industries.
- Examines the potential of ChatGPT in delivering customized content and enhancing customer support.

3. LITERATURE REVIEW

Effectiveness is a measure of a company's success or failure in achieving its objectives. Success depends on achieving goals, and if an organization achieves its objectives, it has succeeded. Effectiveness indicators describe the diverse outcomes of program outputs in accomplishing program objectives. A successful work process contributes more to the accomplishment of stated goals, indicating the efficiency of a process within an organizational unit (Mardiasmo, 2017).

According to Beni (2016) effectiveness as the link between production and objectives, assessing an organization's procedures, methods, and production levels. An action is considered effective if it significantly impacts service delivery capacity. In the public sector, effectiveness and success are related, with the capacity to deliver community services significantly impacted by societal goals and their stated purpose.

The goal of artificial intelligence (AI), a multidisciplinary approach combining linguistics and computer science, is to develop machines that are capable of carrying out tasks that traditionally call for human intellect (Sarker, 2022). These comprise, according to Korteling (2002), the capacity for comprehending, analyzing, and interpreting abstract concepts as well as the capacity for responding to intricate human qualities like attention, emotion, and creativity, among others.

The Dartmouth Summer Research Project on AI, which was conducted in the middle of the 20th century (McCarthy et al., 2006), provides an overview of the development of AI as a scientific topic. The outcome was the creation of machine learning (ML) algorithms, which allow prediction or decision-making based on patterns in sizable data sets (Jordan & Mitchell, 2015).

ChatGPT is an AI-based large language model (LLM) developed by OpenAI that can produce text input responses similar to human responses. It interprets and responds to questions using a text-based interface using the generative pre-trained transformer (GPT) architecture (Brown et al., 2020).

However, concerns have been raised about possible biases based on data sets used in ChatGPT training, which could limit its functionality and produce factual mistakes. Additionally, security issues, cyberattacks, and the spread of incorrect information via LLM must be considered (Deng & Lin, 2022).

A company's social media marketing might be enhanced by using ChatGPT into marketing strategies, especially on Instagram. marketing on social media, especially on Instagram. In the era of industry 4.0 and quick technical advancement, using the internet and social media for communication, information sharing, and search is becoming more and more commonplace in daily life (Hazizah & Padli Nasution, 2022). Businesses may utilize social media, which includes Instagram, to interact with consumers and sell their products and services (Sulianta, 2014).

The internet has great potential for serving as a marketing channel for businesses and individuals in the business world. These advantages have led an increasing number of companies to begin operating online. The level of rivalry for customers or clients in the context of internet marketing is intensifying as more companies venture into the world of online commerce. The struggle for customers or clients is becoming more and more intense in the context of internet marketing (Dharma, 2023).

Social media's quick development made it possible for people all around the world to use it. Due to the growth of websites like Facebook, Twitter, Instagram, TikTok, and others, social media is no longer a novelty to people all over the world. a result of the growth of websites like Facebook, Twitter, Instagram, TikTok, and others, the entire world. This is supported by information from the Ministry of Communication and Information (Budi Dharma et al., 2022).

In comparison to earlier forms of communication, social media has a number of benefits, including the ability to share knowledge, expand networks and communities, and disseminate information (Sulianta, 2014). Online activities can be carried out by using message attraction to grab the audience's attention, sending messages, and getting feedback through social media. Social media may transmit information quickly and has a far wider audience than any other method of communication (Sulianta, 2014).

According to (Kotler, 2009), social media is a channel for customers to interact with businesses and one another while also exchanging text, photographs, audio, and video information. Twitter, Facebook, and Instagram are the social media platforms used, according to past research's findings.

Each social media platform has unique qualities that it can use to promote things to users. According to Puspitarini and Nuraeni (2019), Instagram is a photo-sharing program that enables users to capture images, add digital filters, and share them with other social networking sites as well as the Instagram owner directly. Instagram contains supporting components such profiles, followers, hashtags, push alerts, the ability to link to other social networks, location tags, and others, according to Diamond (2015). According to study (Jayanti, 2014), businesspeople use Instagram to market their brands by offering information through explanations in the form of photographs information presented through images with explanations in the subtitles.

Businesses can communicate with their customers through Instagram's commenting feature to build consumer trust. a belief in customers. study (Andini N.P. et al., 2014).

4. ABOUT CHATGPT

OpenAI has developed a ChatGPT NLP model for natural language processing, using the Transformer architecture for real-time interactions. The model, developed through millions of social media conversations, understands user input and responds naturally. It learns conversational themes from these conversations, making communication with AI systems easier for individuals. ChatGPT is useful in various professions, such as automated customer care and assistance. It uses reinforcement learning techniques, allowing it to improve even after exposure to new data sets or circumstances. This tool allows for the development of interactive programs that understand user inputs and deliver human-like outcomes without requiring manual work from engineers or developers.

4.1 The Purpose of ChatGPT as a Component of Open AI

ChatGPT is a new NLP chatbot platform developed by OpenAI to enable robots and computers to communicate more organically and understand human speech. It uses machine learning techniques to learn from human-to-human conversations without training data, aiming to reduce misunderstandings and inaccurate inferences. The goal is to create powerful conversational AI bots that can handle challenging tasks and make interactions simple through text, voice, or in-person. Transfer learning, contextual understanding, and multi-turn discourse modeling are some of the sophisticated NLP approaches used. ChatGPT has significant enhanced machine and human interactions, with applications in customer service, healthcare systems, and virtual assistants. These advancements aim to facilitate communication between people on opposing sides.

4.2 ChatGPT: E-Commerce Tool for New Healthcare

ChatGPT, a technology that combines machine learning and natural language processing, is increasingly being adopted by various economic sectors. It offers automated customer assistance options, enhancing productivity and cost-effectiveness. E-commerce businesses can benefit from ChatGPT's chatbot capabilities, which can quickly address customer issues without incurring additional costs for human staff. This reduces costs and enhances the overall user experience.

The healthcare industry, particularly telemedicine services, can also benefit from ChatGPT. Due to medical privacy laws, patient connections must be handled with care. AI-powered capabilities can speed up patient registration forms while ensuring compliance standards are observed.

In conclusion, ChatGPT's technology will have a significant positive impact on both commercial and consumer sectors. It can lower labor expenses for customer support staff, streamline processes in healthcare institutions, and foster more engaging interactions between businesses and customers. Organizations may gain from incorporating ChatGPT into their operations, resulting in improved customer service and reduced costs.

4.3 ChatGPT: A New Tool to Marketing Digitally Revolutionize

ChatGPT, a new technology combining natural language processing and machine learning, is revolutionizing digital marketing by creating conversational AI chatbots that understand customer needs, address issues, and assist in purchasing. This automation saves businesses time on administrative tasks while still providing a personalized experience. ChatGPT can be used in conjunction with other technologies like analytics software or AI programs to enhance the effectiveness of digital marketing initiatives. Benefits include better customer relations, enhanced efficiency, cost savings, and greater adaptability. By combining natural language processing methods with AI models trained on large datasets from various industries, businesses can gain perspectives not typically available through technological advancement. This approach provides a competitive edge and saves money, as better campaign outcomes and ROI levels are closely related to investing time and money in labor-intensive manual tasks. Overall, ChatGPT offers numerous benefits for businesses in digital marketing, providing a competitive edge and cost savings.

4.4 ChatGPT: The Upcoming Major E-Commerce Event

ChatGPT is a revolutionary technology that uses machine learning and natural language processing to create chatbots that assist customers. This technology can significantly reduce customer support costs and improve response times, benefiting e-commerce businesses by reducing labor expenses and customer support time. ChatGPT also allows businesses greater control over their messages and delivery, a task that would be difficult to achieve manually. It also offers businesses a better understanding of international customer demands in various languages, enabling them to access new markets and increase earnings. It can also be used during heavy internet traffic to prevent lead loss. ChatGPT also provides businesses with critical understanding of their clients' behavior, enabling them to tailor their offers based on user interactions.

4.5 ChatGPT: A New Healthcare Trend

ChatGPT, a revolutionary invention, has the potential to revolutionize various sectors, particularly healthcare. Its quick and precise natural language processing capabilities can expedite and improve jobs in the healthcare sector, such as monitoring medical data and providing patient care. ChatGPT can also be used to enter information into electronic health records (EHRs) for data tracking, saving time and reducing errors. This not only saves time for healthcare professionals but also increases the accuracy of the data. Furthermore, ChatGPT's improved efficacy reduces the likelihood of errors, thereby enhancing the accuracy of the data. In essence, ChatGPT's rapid and precise natural language processing capabilities could significantly impact the healthcare sector, enhancing efficiency and accuracy in various tasks.

4.6 Use of ChatGPT and Healthcare

ChatGPT, a natural language processing system, has the potential to revolutionize the healthcare sector by providing personalized patient care, streamlining administrative processes, and enhancing nurse-physician communication. It can provide virtual support and emotional support during challenging times, reducing the need for in-person visits and costs. ChatGPT can also streamline administrative tasks like appointment scheduling and document filing, allowing medical staff to focus on critical tasks. It can also enable physicians to communicate more closely online than face-to-face. However, more research is needed to address ethical implications. Overall, ChatGPT has significantly improved patient care outcomes.

4.7 AI in the Medical and Pharmaceutical Field

The medical industry is rapidly evolving due to new technologies, with AI potentially significantly impacting this growth. AI can analyze medical images, identify anomalies, and design personalized patient care. It can also perform time-consuming tasks like appointment scheduling and data entry. Scientists are exploring AI's potential for more precise disease diagnosis and treatment.

4.8 ChatGPT Could Drastically Affect Healthcare

ChatGPT, an artificial intelligence chatbot, has the potential to significantly impact the healthcare sector by providing personalized, natural-language interactions. By responding authentically and naturally, chatbots can improve communication with patients and become more successful. AI-enabled chatbots can prioritize symptoms for specific illnesses and provide general guidance on healthcare needs. They can also act as the first point of contact for mental health therapy by offering consultations and expert advice.

4.9 ChatGPT: A Chatbot That Is Modernizing How People Consider Healthcare

ChatGPT is changing how people perceive healthcare by providing individualized health advice and solutions without physically visiting a doctor or hospital. It can assist users in getting medical advice, understanding their health risks, and making informed decisions about their overall health and wellness. With its cutting-edge technology, ChatGPT can also anticipate medical emergencies, allowing users to handle them before they worsen.

4.10 The ChatGPT Technology's Potential in Education

In education, ChatGPT's capabilities could revolutionize interpersonal communication by automating virtual assistants, online tutoring, and customer support. The educational industry can now provide customized learning experiences tailored to students' unique needs. Teachers can create lesson plans based on students' interests and aptitudes, providing timely feedback and allowing professors and teachers to submit their work. ChatGPT can also be used as a virtual assistant at educational institutions, responding to campus services and course details without constant human help. To improve teacher-student interactions and classroom performance, it is a wise choice to use this new technology immediately into any teaching and learning process.

4.11 Finance Industry's ChatGPT

ChatGPT is a digital transformation software that can significantly benefit financial institutions, particularly in the banking sector. It offers numerous applications that automate tasks such as account verification and response to simple customer inquiries, allowing banks to focus on more complex queries that require interaction with real people or support from other divisions within the bank. ChatGPT uses natural language processing (NLP) to modify its responses for each user based on their previous interactions and data accumulated over time. Many banks are already online, making them quicker and more convenient.

The implementation of machine learning algorithms ensures high accuracy levels even when responding to unusual or unusual inquiries, ensuring that clients always receive rapid, correct solutions. With the competitive nature of existing banking services, investing in ChatGPT makes sense.

4.12 Advantages of ChatGPT for Finance and Banking

ChatGPT offers numerous benefits, including improved customer service in banking and finance industries, automated processes for account balance monitoring, and enhanced customer loyalty. It also reduces risk by analyzing customer contact patterns and identifying fraudulent activities. ChatGPT allows customers to set budgets, track spending, and make financial decisions, offering personalized advice based on their risk tolerance, objectives, and investment skills. It also helps detect fraudulent activities by analyzing customer interactions and abnormal behavior. Overall, ChatGPT enhances customer experience and trust in the banking and finance sectors.

4.13 ChatGPT: A Platform for Digital Transformation

Businesses can enhance their operational, social, and business processes with ChatGPT online transformation software. It allows for the automation of sales funnel operations and customer service processes, providing a wide range of tools for developing new products and services in line with changing consumer needs. ChatGPT's AI-driven features enable businesses to develop fresh strategies based on current information gathered from various sources, including social media websites. In addition to analytics, ChatGPT provides users with valuable insights into potential future growth opportunities and methods to improve operations, potentially boosting ROI.

4.14 A Key Tool for Developers Is ChatGPT

GPT (Generative Pre-Trained Transformer) is a powerful tool for developers, used to create text production models, language translation models, and code completion systems. It can be used as a beginner's tool for bug fixing and can provide examples of code structures depending on the programming language. GPT can also examine source codes more thoroughly than most human readers, detecting differences between software components before they are examined. It can also create new lines of source code from previously produced examples, allowing developers to quickly build a range of different versions of their application until they find the perfect one. This reduces the time needed to find software issues and provides illustrations of how to develop useful solutions in various programming languages. GPT is an essential tool for developers managing difficult debugging tasks and is a valuable resource for those dealing with complex debugging tasks.

4.15 ChatGPT's Role in Supporting Customer Support

Customer service is aided by ChatGPT, an AI-powered virtual assistant. ChatGPT might offer pre-written answers to commonly asked queries, lessen the load on customer support agents, and speed up response times. It may also provide proactive advice and assist clients in finding answers more rapidly. Customers will also find it straightforward to contact with customer service representatives using ChatGPT's chatbot interactions, which allow natural discussions. Customers may now obtain the assistance they require without having to wait on hold or have lengthy chats with customer support representatives.

4.16 An Effective Alternative for Call Center Professionals

The cloud-based platform ChatGPT offers call center workers a productive substitute. It enables customer support representatives to address client enquiries in real time with speed and ease. Artificial intelligence (AI) technology used by ChatGPT enables it to comprehend customer inquiries, find pertinent data, make suggestions for potential solutions, and provide the most suitable response. In order to give consumers a more thorough response to their requests, it can also access multiple data sources. This shortens processing times and lessens the need for expensive human intervention.

4.17 ChatGPT Will Rule the Human Race in the Future

The future of chatbots, such as ChatGPT, is uncertain due to the rapid development of AI and technology innovations. While some experts worry about the potential loss of human employment due to long-term effects of AI-powered automation, it is not a significant concern. ChatGPT has shown remarkable ability in producing natural language responses from data sets, but it is still far from becoming as intelligent as a real human. AI systems lack emotional intelligence, making them difficult to understand complex social situations or interact with humans outside of controlled situations. Furthermore, additional technological advancements are required before robots can completely replace people in all jobs. Despite these concerns, it is unlikely that robots will rule supreme over humans within our lifetimes, given the trends, advances, and spending on research and development in these sectors.

4.18 ChatGPT AI and Business in the Future

ChatGPT AI is a powerful tool that can significantly change how companies communicate with their customers. It offers a natural and effective conversational platform, allowing businesses to save costs, improve customer service, and gain insights into consumer behavior. With its rapid language processing capabilities, it is essential for expanding businesses. ChatGPT AI's machine learning capabilities enable it to respond more accurately than traditional chatbots and stay updated with industry trends. This work contributes valuable knowledge on conversation generation using generative pre-training models like ChatGPT to academics and industry specialists. Understanding its inner workings and potential applications can help develop the next generation of artificial intelligences that behave spontaneously, similar to humans.

4.19 Google Chrome Is a Leading Browser in the World

Google dominates the browser market with Google Chrome, which has a 66% global usage share as of April 2020. The closest competitor is Microsoft Edge/ Internet Explorer, which has a 16% market share. Mozilla Firefox and Apple Safari account for 12% and 8%, respectively. Google Chrome's success is attributed to its usability and rich feature set, making it a desirable option for both SEO experts and casual internet users. It also offers strong connectivity with other Google services and regular updates, ensuring users receive the latest security patches. Google dominates the search algorithm market, being used for 90% of all desktop and mobile searches. Microsoft Bing is its main rival, accounting for 7% of global searches. Google holds a 98%+ market share in the mobile industry, with 70% of users using Chrome, 15% using Safari, 7% using Edge/Internet Explorer, 5% using Firefox, and 2% using Opera. This gives Google an edge over competitors like Microsoft Bing and Yahoo! and allows it to continue providing innovative solutions that meet consumer requirements.

4.20 Open AI ChatGPT Could Be the Search Engine's Future Dominator

Microsoft Open AI's ChatGPT technology is a cutting-edge artificial intelligence system that can enhance online information searches. It uses machine learning algorithms and natural language processing to interpret customer inquiries, providing precise responses. Unlike traditional search engines that rely on keywords, ChatGPT can understand conversational queries in natural language, enabling faster navigation through large amounts of data with higher accuracy. It also provides personalized search results, impacting various spheres of life, including commercial operations and education.

4.21 A Future Vision of ChatGPT in 2040

2040's GPT Chat Importance

- Enables efficient communication with AI bots.
- Allows natural, real-time conversations on various subjects.
- Automates operations requiring manual labor, lowering customer care costs.
- Adaptable, providing personalized interactions.
- Significantly lowers customer care costs.

4.22 Social Media and Intelligence Analytics

AI has revolutionized information processing and technology understanding, significantly impacting social media growth and business marketing. The integration of AI has led to improved statistics in social media marketing and shifted the marketing paradigm from traditional strategies to digitalization. With the rise of emojis and hashtags, it's challenging to gather quantifiable proof of favoritism and resistance. Advanced analytics are essential for understanding both structured and unstructured data, and the use of AI in social media indirectly helps in analyzing the latest marketing trends. The integration of AI in social media has transformed marketing strategies and made data collection more meaningful.

4.23 Social Media and Transformation of Business

Social media has significantly impacted various sectors, including the corporate sector, marketing, and technology. The adoption of AI has led to a shift from manual to digital processes, with marketing being the most affected. Social media has also improved marketing strategies, with the emergence of virtual and augmented reality advancing AI. This has enabled corporate transformation, allowing companies to expand their presence, reach a wider audience, and improve brand image. Social media has also brought businesses and customers closer, increasing consumer satisfaction. For commercial organizations, social media is a cost-effective method.

4.24 AI's Effect on Successful Business

We'll talk about how AI may help social media marketers by facilitating content development, ensuring a consistent online presence, automating bidding, and enhancing audience targeting in this part. The most common uses of AI in modern life are Alexa, Siri, and Bixby. Artificial intelligence is more complex by definition. Businesses pay social media experts to curate content and present more user- and revenue-friendly statistics on the website. On the page, this boosts incoming traffic and leads.

5. SOCIAL MEDIA MARKETING WITH AI'S SUPPORT AND POTENTIAL

AI can significantly enhance social media marketing by speeding up content development, ensuring a consistent online presence, automating bidding, and improving audience targeting. AI is expected to outperform traditional marketing techniques and is expected to win in competition. AI-assisted social media marketing strengthens companies and provides additional leverage, especially in increasing sales. Unlike traditional methods, AI offers a modern solution, allowing customers to have a unique experience through interactive customization. When paired with AI, social media marketing is unstoppable in its pursuit of success, as both are based on rapidly developing technology. The best possible convergence between social media and AI will result from their ongoing, complex growth and development.

5.1 Artificial Intelligence: Social Media's Present and Future

Artificial intelligence has become the most in-demand technology in recent decades, controlling the world and potentially reliant on humanity in the future. It has significantly impacted various sectors, including retail, aviation, hospitality, and in-service sectors. Social media has also been significantly impacted by AI, allowing businesses to grow and connect globally. The goal of social media is to build new relationships, transfer knowledge, and maintain social presence, all of which can have positive or negative consequences on each other.

5.2 AIDA MODEL

- **Attention**

Advertisements must capture the interest of their target audience, whether readers, listeners, or viewers, in order to effectively promote goods or services.

- **Interest**

After grabbing the target's attention, the service or product supplier must consider how to keep the target's interest and pique their curiosity about upcoming attention-grabbing promotions. Because of this, the target must be encouraged to become more interested and pay attention to the communications by employing terms that pique curiosity.

- **Desire**

The promotion is successful in luring the target to utilize these goods and services if the target already has an interest in wanting the marketed product or service. Certain sentences must pique the target's interest in what they want to possess, utilize, enjoy, or do.

- **Action**

It is now up to the service or product provider to convince customers to act as quickly as feasible and use the promoted good or service. In this situation, it's important to pick the appropriate command words to ensure that the target hears and sees the promotion. As a result, the target will not think twice about choosing to employ the supplied good or service.

5.3 Social Media on Instagram

The marketing sector is essential to implementing business plans since marketing strategy is essential to obtaining corporate success. The company's position in the market can be improved or maintained by implementing a detailed marketing strategy and seizing sales-boosting opportunities. Business people communicate, distribute, and provide their goods and services using promotional media to pique the interest of potential clients. Meanwhile, promotion may be seen as a type of marketing communication, which refers to any actions taken to spread information that can persuade or influence consumers to purchase the supplied products in order to enhance sales Creating brand loyalty among consumers is a goal of marketing (Nabilah et al., 2021).

Social media serves as a platform for user-to-user engagement. In (Reinhart Abedneju Sondakh et al., 2019), stated that social media is a platform that focuses on the existence of its users and encourages user interaction. Social media is utilized as online content that can improve user connections in a web-based social network.

As per research (Hidayat & Suhairi, 2022) digital marketing has a significant impact on buying interest, Instagram is one of the social media and digital marketing tools that business people can use to support their marketing performance. The Instagram application is currently used widely by the global community, including in Indonesia. Instagram is one of the social media platforms that may be used for direct marketing. As a result, Instagram can be used as a marketing tool by the food and beverage sector. It is simpler for someone to promote goods or services because the Instagram application has supportive features.

5.4 Use of AI ChatGPT by Business Actors

Figure 1 shows how businesses use AI Chat GPT to gather structured data for Instagram content, aiming to gain positive customer responses and understand the effects of using bots in marketing strategies. Bots can influence consumer purchasing decisions

Figure 1. Example of AI ChatGPT usage
Source: Author's own contribution

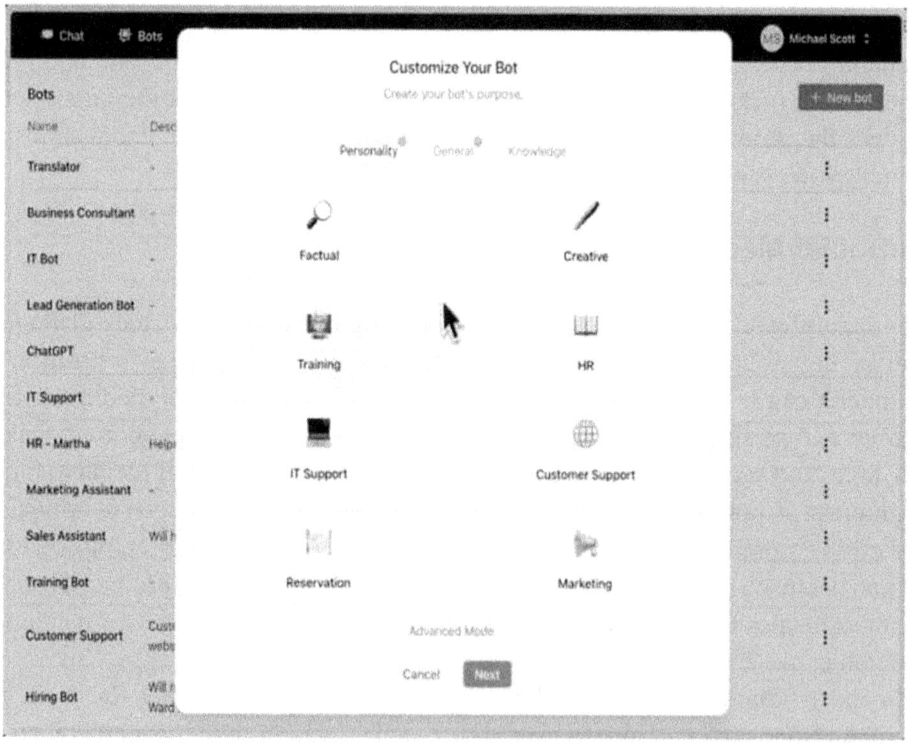

and market behavior through their conversational style, behavioural style, and use of universal phrases and speech. This enhances the customer experience and emotions desired by the company/brand, ultimately influencing their purchasing decisions.

5.5 Instagram Post Impressions Feature

Instagram provides data on post impressions, which can be categorized into user profiles, hashtags, home feeds, and explore sites (see Fig. 2). These insights can help assess user submission effectiveness and inform content strategy decisions. Researchers and practitioners can modify content to increase reach and engagement. Instagram post impressions can be used to evaluate content effectiveness, including reach, likes, shares, and saves, as well as the number of people visiting a product. The AIDA concept on Instagram post impressions can be used to gauge the success of marketing campaigns, allowing for more targeted and effective content creation.

Figure 2. Posts made without AI ChatGPT
Source: Author's own contribution

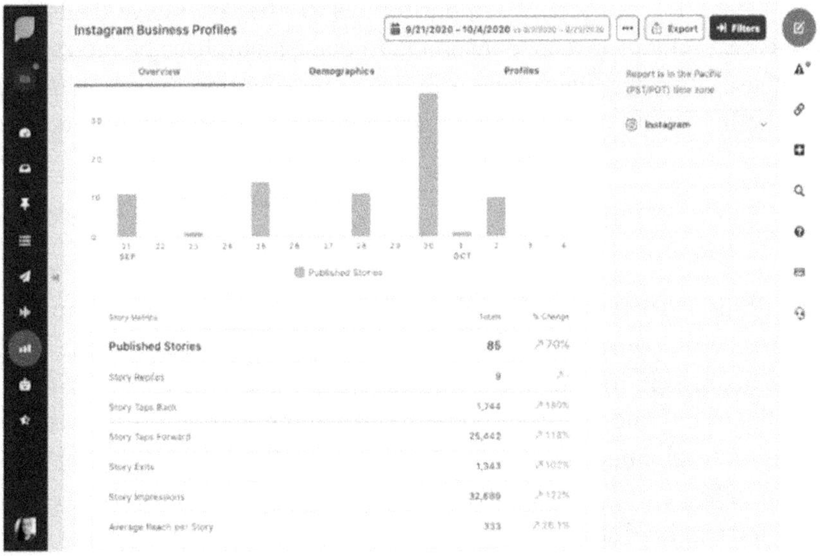

- **Attention**

Chat GPT is a tool that can help companies create captivating advertising messages that captivate their audience. Its wide language capabilities enable it to create sentences and paragraphs that pique their interest. For example, it can provide advice on creating headlines for advertisements that pique reader interest. This study examines content created using Chat GPT and content on Instagram. By counting the number of individuals who see the advertisement or the number of ad impressions, users can gauge their interest in the company's advertisement.

- **Interest**

Chat GPT can enhance user interest by making product recommendations based on their interests and likes. By utilizing the attention mechanism, Chat GPT can understand user requests and make suitable recommendations, potentially driving interest and influencing buying behavior. The number of people who like, save, or share an advertisement is a reliable indicator of user interest.

- **Desire**

At this point, the user ought to feel as though they are the true owners of the product or service. GPT Chat can assist with offering customer's special discounts and perks. Chat GPT can identify opportunities to offer exclusive deals, rewards, or discounts that will encourage consumers to make a purchase by interacting with users. purchase. You may determine user desire by counting the number of people who visit the Instagram profile or look at the descriptions of the offered goods or services.

- **Action**

At this point, the user is required to take a certain action, such purchasing a good or service or going to a café. GPT Chat can make suggestions for goods or services according on the user's requirements and interests. Chat GPT can compile a list of pertinent items and help the user choose the best option for the client using data gleaned from prior interactions. Count the number of people who visit a café or make a purchase after seeing a product advertisement to determine user behavior.

5.6 Instagram Posts Viewed With the AIDA Concept

Figure 3 and Table 1, Table 2, Table 3 and Figure 4 show the number of Posts made by businesses in the last 3 months with AI Chat GPT and distributed as per AIDA model

Figure 3. Posts made by businesses in the last 3 months with AI Chat GPT
Source: Author's own contribution

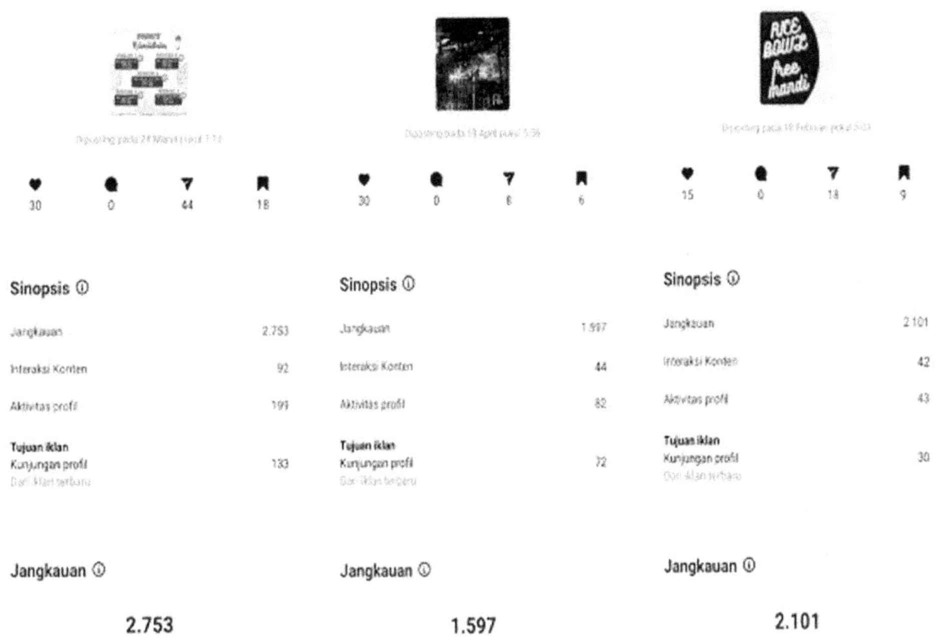

Table 1. Number of users who viewed marketing posts

Figure	Reach	Reach	Reach
Figure 2	275 Account	284 Account	230 Account
Figure 3	2.753 Account	1.597 Account	2.101 Account

Table 2. Number of Instagram user activities based on interest

Figure	Content Interaction	Content Interaction	Content Interaction
Figure 2	10 Account	6 Account	11 Account
Figure 3	92 Account	44 Account	42 Account

Table 3. Number of users who visited the instagram profiles of business owners

Figure	Visit Profile	Visit Profile	Visit Profile
Figure 2	8 Account	11 Account	15 Account
Figure 3	133 Account	72 Account	30 Account

- **Attention**

In order to attract a customer's attention, a message must be compelling regardless of the format or media in which it is presented. Potential customers or buyers who have been targeted receive broad or focused attention. This can be expressed using strong, unambiguous language, vivid images, and sentences with their own characteristics that are intriguing or memorable. We can measure user attention by calculating the number of people who saw the advertisement or the number of ad impressions (Kotler, 2009).

Table 2.1 demonstrates that, as compared to image 2, the Instagram post in image 3 yields highly good outcomes. When compared to the image 2 post, this is quite satisfying because it demonstrates that the marketing content produced by AI Chat Gpt may be viewed by Instagram users up to thousands of accounts. With these outcomes, chat GPT might comprehend the merchants' desire to produce content for the proper audiences, particularly coffee fanatics. According to what the business want, a high level of focus can help the audience recognize the business actor's brand. Business actors' brands are recognizable by the broader audience, who sees the corporate actor's marketing messages.

- **Interest**

Someone's curiosity, desire to watch, and attention to what they hear and see increase when a message piques their interest. Due to the curiosity generated by the advertisement, buyers pay attention to the message. User interest can be gauged by how many people save, like, or share an advertisement. The number of Content exchanges in figures 2 and 3—two representations of this activity—can be seen.

According to Table 2, users who are very interested in marketing content are depicted in figure 3 by users who save, like, and share marketing content with other Instagram users. This demonstrates how AI Chat GPT can boost the effectiveness of interest in the information it produces, generating curiosity among Instagram users about the content produced.

- **Desire**

This desire leads to the consideration of the drives and explanations for why people buy items. There are two different types of buying motivations: intellectual and emotional. Here, rational motives take into account the benefits and downsides for buyers, whereas emotional incentives come from sentiments associated with product purchasing. You may determine user demand by counting the number of people who visit Instagram accounts or look at the details of the products or services being offered.

The users only need to complete one more step to take action at this point, according to the results in Table 3's row three. Users can view other content on the business actor's Instagram profile after clicking through from one marketing piece, which is incredibly advantageous for business actors. With these outcomes, it can be seen that AI Chat GPT's marketing materials are quite successful in encouraging users to visit the profiles of business actors.

- **Action**

Customers take action because they are fervently eager to buy the offered good, counting the number of individuals who visit the cafe or make purchases as a result of seeing product promotions. The results of capturing chatlogs of consumers who respond upon marketing content produced by AI Chat GPT demonstrate this.

5.7 Information Using GPT AI Chat

According to Darling-Hammond in (Newton & Williams, 2022) the Direct Message feature on Instagram allows for contact between two people or a group of people and the exchange of information. When consumers wish to talk with us, we can access the contents of the current chat using the direct messaging feature, and we can also respond to customers to uphold and establish the relationship between sellers and buyers.

Every post that uses AI Chat GPT in its marketing material includes multiple users who take action to directly buy products made in the marketing content, as shown in chatlogs captured in Aunty Ann Cafe's direct message, which can be seen in Figure 4. This demonstrates that the marketing materials offered by AI Chat GPT actively contribute to marketing effectiveness, as is evident from the AIDA principle discussed above.

6. DISCUSSIONS

There is little question that the introduction of artificial intelligence-driven solutions across a variety of industrial sectors, like as those provided by Chat GPT, has altered how organizations operate in the present. These breakthroughs provide substantial competitive benefits over traditional approaches, which, if they haven't already, could do so soon given how poorly they perform in relation to current AI capabilities. They provide them access to effective automation solutions that enable quicker processing

Figure 4. Capturing chatlogs of users who took action on marketing
Source: Author's own contribution

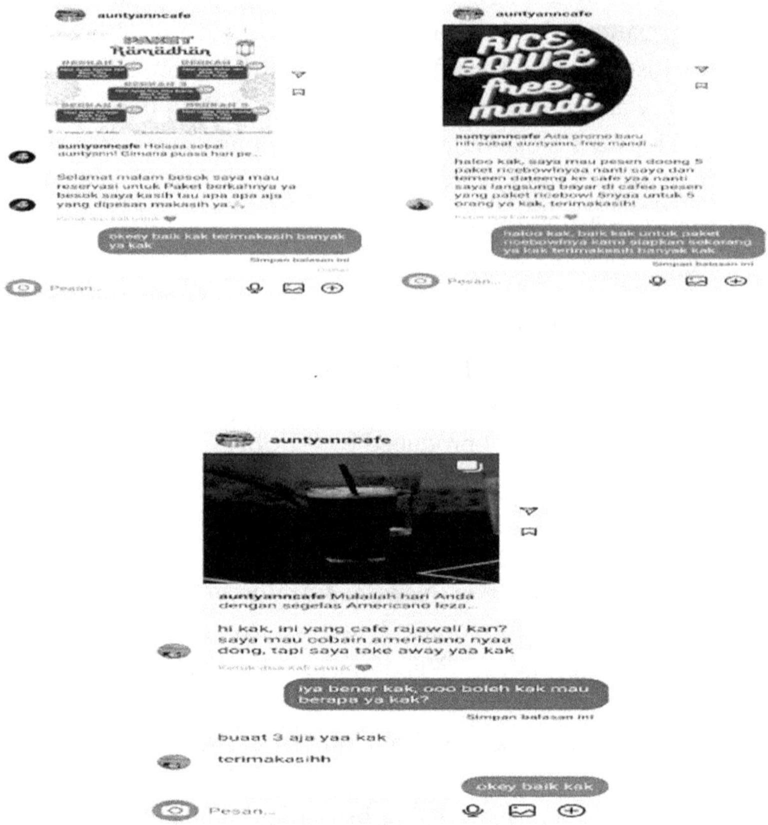

times and increased production levels across all departments in order to achieve this. It is simple to understand why so many businesses use this sort of technology in routine operations given the potential financial and operational benefits it offers.

7. CONCLUSION

The effectiveness of marketing using the ChatGPT and AI applications are the burgeoning area of research where the application of AIDA concept explored the emergence of mood, emotion and sentiment analysis. According to the AIDA concept the results of the table above exhibit that Chat GPT has a significant impact on the attention section. In this study, the conceptual analysis on ChatGPT using AI and Instagram is having a positive impact of customer decision-making as well as purchase intention. Though the analysis has highlighted the applications of AI in social media is very impressive the marketing effectiveness undermine with respect to the applications of attention, interest, desire and action. It observed that the AIDA concept have a significant impact on marketing effectiveness in modern business domain where a huge usage of social media is imperative.

REFERENCES

Andini, N. P. (2014). Pengaruh viral marketing terhadap kepercayaan pelanggan dan keputusan pembelian (Studi pada Mahasiswa Fakultas Ilmu Administrasi Universitas Brawijaya angkatan 2013 yang melakukan pembelian online melalui media sosial instagram). *Jurnal Administrasi Bisnis, 11*(1).

Brown, R., Rocha, A., & Cowling, M. (2020). Financing entrepreneurship in times of crisis: Exploring the impact of COVID-19 on the market for entrepreneurial finance in the United Kingdom. *International Small Business Journal, 38*(5), 380–390. doi:10.1177/0266242620937464

de Deus Chaves, R., Chiarion Sassi, F., Davison Mangilli, L., Jayanthi, S. K., Cukier, A., Zilberstein, B., & Furquim de Andrade, C. R. (2014). Swallowing transit times and valleculae residue in stable chronic obstructive pulmonary disease. *BMC Pulmonary Medicine, 14*(1), 1–9. doi:10.1186/1471-2466-14-62 PMID:24739506

Deng, J., & Lin, Y. (2022). The benefits and challenges of ChatGPT: An overview. *Frontiers in Computing and Intelligent Systems, 2*(2), 81–83. doi:10.54097/fcis.v2i2.4465

Dharma, B., Syarbaini, A. M. B., Rahmah, M., & Hasby, M. (2023). Enhancing Literacy and Management of Productive Waqf at BKM Al Mukhlisin Towards a Mosque as a Center for Community Worship and Economics. *ABDIMAS: Jurnal Pengabdian Masyarakat, 6*(1), 3246–3255.

Diamond, A. (2015). Effects of physical exercise on executive functions: going beyond simply moving to moving with thought. *Annals of Sports Medicine and Research, 2*(1), 1011.

Hazizah, S. N., & Nasution, M. I. P. (2022). Peran Media Sosial Instagram Terhadap Minat Berwirausaha Mahasiswa. *Fair Value: Jurnal Ilmiah Akuntansi dan Keuangan, 5*(4).

Hidayat, T., & Suhairi, S. (2022). Pengaruh Persepsi Nilai, Harga dan Promosi Digital Marketing Terhadap Minat Beli Pasca Pandemi di Suzuya Mall Tanjung Morawa. *Cakrawala Repositori IMWI*, *5*(2), 607–615.

Jordan, M. I., & Mitchell, T. M. (2015). Machine learning: Trends, perspectives, and prospects. *Science*, *349*(6245), 255–260. doi:10.1126/science.aaa8415 PMID:26185243

Korteling, J. E. (2016). Determining training effectiveness. Paris: North Atlantic Treaty Organization (NATO) Research & Technology Organisation (RTO).

Kotler, P. (2009). *Marketing management: A south Asian perspective*. Pearson Education India.

McCarthy, H. D. (2006). Body fat measurements in children as predictors for the metabolic syndrome: Focus on waist circumference. *The Proceedings of the Nutrition Society*, *65*(4), 385–392. PMID:17181905

Nabilah'Izzaturrahmah, A., Nhita, F., & Kurniawan, I. (2021, October). Implementation of Support Vector Machine on Text-based GERD Detection by using Drug Review Content. In *2021 International Conference Advancement in Data Science, E-learning and Information Systems (ICADEIS)* (pp. 1-6). IEEE.

Newton, J. R., & Williams, M. C. (2022). Instagram as a special educator professional development tool: A guide to teachergram. *Journal of Special Education Technology*, *37*(3), 447–452. doi:10.1177/01626434211033596

Puspitarini, D. S., & Nuraeni, R. (2019). Pemanfaatan media sosial sebagai media promosi. *Jurnal Common*, *3*(1), 71–80. doi:10.34010/common.v3i1.1950

Sarker, I. H. (2022). Ai-based modeling: Techniques, applications and research issues towards automation, intelligent and smart systems. *SN Computer Science*, *3*(2), 158. doi:10.1007/s42979-022-01043-x PMID:35194580

Sondakh, R. A., Erawan, E., & Wibowo, S. E. (2019). Pemanfaatan Media Sosial Instagram Pada Akun@ Geprekexpress Dalam Mempromosikan Restoran Geprek Express. *Llmu Komunikasi*, *7*(1), 279–292.

SondhiS. (2023). Aspects of Dharma. *Available at* SSRN 4552530.

Sulianta, F. (2021). Distictive Sport Youtube Channel Assesment Through The Methodological Approach Of Netnography. *Turkish Journal of Computer and Mathematics Education*, *12*(8), 381–386.

Susilawati, C., Miller, W., & Mardiasmo, D. (2017, August). Sustainable housing innovation toolkit. *12th World Congress on Engineering Asset Management and 13th International Conference on Vibration Engineering and Technology of Machinery*.

Tadi Beni, Y. (2016). Size-dependent electromechanical bending, buckling, and free vibration analysis of functionally graded piezoelectric nanobeams. *Journal of Intelligent Material Systems and Structures*, *27*(16), 2199–2215. doi:10.1177/1045389X15624798

Chapter 3
AI's Double-Edged Sword: Examining the Dark Side of AI in Human Lives

Love Singla
https://orcid.org/0000-0002-8159-7712
Maharaja Agrasen University, India

Ketan preet Kaur
Bahra College of Law, Patiala, India

Napinder Kaur
https://orcid.org/0000-0002-5009-2631
Lovely Professional University, India

ABSTRACT

The blending of AI with every aspect of the stream, whether it is medicines, natural disaster predictions, disease epidemiology, future prediction, etc., has been crucial and impactful in today's world. On the flip side, there are several problems that humans face with the incorporation of AI into their day-to-day lives. The first and foremost aspect is implementing AI-based technologies, which require high capital as these are costlier in addition to their infrastructure establishment and talent acquisition. The second problem is security concerns, as AI often works and provides future predictions based on past data that might be sensitive to an individual or a firm that it stores in its server, which raises concerns concerning privacy and security breaches. The third point includes the interaction of company personnel with their client physically. Some other cons of incorporating AI include the loss of massive jobs known as unemployment and bias and ethical issues that might arise.

DOI: 10.4018/979-8-3693-0724-3.ch003

Demystifying the Dark Side of AI in Business

INTRODUCTION

The introduction of artificial intelligence into daily life has revolutionized the day-to-day needs of human beings, from the automation of ceiling fans to future predictions of several problems like the Air Quality Index (AQI), groundwater quantity level, etc., with the use of algorithms known as 'Machine Learning.' Thus, the term 'machine learning' coined by Arthur Samuel has been defined as a branch of artificial intelligence that is computer-based automation and continues learning of algorithms based on their prior experiences without the intervention of any programming or humans. This involves the initial information/data requirements of good quality, which are further distributed among training and testing datasets. These datasets (training and testing) are used by the machines (computers/laptops) by using different machine learning algorithms or models with variability in algorithms based on model requirements. Machine learning, also called ML, is a branch of computational intelligence (AI) that deals explicitly with developing computer systems capable of acquiring knowledge and improving performance through data analysis. ML comprises various approaches, allowing software programs to enhance their performance gradually. Machine learning algorithms are specifically designed to identify and analyze correlations and patterns within datasets. Historical data is input for several tasks, including prediction, information classification, data clustering, dimensionality reduction, and content generation. This is exemplified by recent machine learning-powered apps like ChatGPT, Dall-E 2, and GitHub Copilot. Machine learning has broad use in several sectors. Recommendation engines are utilized by many industries, such as e-commerce, social networking, and news organizations, to provide material to customers based on their previous actions. Machine learning systems and vision algorithms are crucial in ensuring the safe navigation of self-driving automobiles on the highways. Machine learning is employed in the healthcare field to detect medical conditions and provide recommendations for treatment strategies accurately. Additional prevalent machine learning applications encompass identifying fraudulent activities, filtering out spam, detecting malware threats, predicting maintenance needs, and automating corporate processes. Machine learning is a potent tool for problem-solving, enhancing corporate operations, and automating processes. However, it is also an intricate and demanding technology requiring the extensive experience and substantial resources. Optimal algorithm selection necessitates a profound understanding of the mathematics and statistics. Adequate training of the machine learning algorithms often requires significant quantities of high-quality data to get precise outcomes. Comprehending the findings can be challenging, especially when dealing with results generated by intricate algorithms, such as neural networks with deep learning that mimic the human brain. Machine learning models can incur significant expenses in the execution and optimization.

Artificial intelligence applications are like a Double-edged sword; they make our lives simpler and more manageable, but on the other end, they might damage our lives physically and biologically. Increased AI usage makes humans dependent, which might harm our race. Different sectors, like healthcare, medicine, and business, face different kinds of problems initiated by using artificial intelligence.

Coming of disadvantages is always complementary to the advantages of AI in every sector. Some of the general drawbacks include –

1. **Exorbitant expenses**: The capacity to develop a machine capable of emulating human intelligence is a significant accomplishment. It necessitates a substantial amount of time and energy and can incur a significant financial burden. Artificial intelligence (AI) also requires up-to-date technology and software to remain current and satisfy the latest demands, resulting in substantial expenses.
2. **Lack of originality or innovative thinking:** One major drawback of AI is its inability to develop unconventional thinking. AI can acquire knowledge and improve performance based on pre-existing data and previous encounters. Still, it needs more capacity for originality in its problem-solving methods. An exemplary instance is the bot Quill, which can generate earning reports for Forbes. These reports solely consist of data and facts already supplied to the bot. While the autonomous ability of a bot to create an article is commendable, it lacks the inherent human element found in other papers published by Forbes.
3. **Joblessness:** An example of the application of artificial intelligence is the use of robots, which are replacing jobs and contributing to an increase in unemployment (in certain instances). Hence, it is argued that substituting humans for chatbots and robots inevitably entails a potential risk of unemployment. Robots are commonly employed to replace human labor in manufacturing industries, particularly in technologically advanced countries such as Japan. However, this is not universally true, as it simultaneously generates new prospects for human employment while also substituting humans to enhance productivity.
4. **Changes in job and training requirements:** The integration of AI in training can drastically alter the skill prerequisites for positions associated with movement, such as instructors, trainers, and personnel managers. In a scenario where retraining adults for these occupations is considered arduous or costly, the current practice of training overseen and conducted by humans may be favored. Employing AI for training entails the capability of AI to execute

particular assignments that humans conventionally carry out. Teachers and trainers can utilize AI-powered XR training or AI-based assessment to evaluate students' skills and create tests. Similarly, AI-powered online career guidance tools can assist career counselors or PES case workers in offering appropriate training recommendations to job seekers. Introducing AI technologies for training may increase the demand for digital skills in occupations associated with training and recruitment. The ability of AI to execute tasks traditionally performed by humans indicates the potential for time liberation to allocate to other duties. While it may be necessary to give part of the newly available time to utilizing or comprehending the AI tools for training purposes, there may still be more time left for other tasks. Shifting jobs necessitates reconfiguring responsibilities for teaching and career counseling occupations, which can be difficult if the workforce lacks the necessary skills. Approximately 16% of Vocational Education and Training (VET) teachers need more computer skills or improve their digital problem-solving abilities. Additionally, about one in four teachers need more confidence in utilizing digital tools for classroom instruction or delivering student feedback. Humans possess a comparative advantage over AI in executing creative or advanced cognitive activities, such as critical thinking or decision-making in intricate scenarios. Furthermore, while AI tools can be imbued with human-like qualities such as humor and empathy, individuals may still prefer the presence and engagement of other humans, particularly in times of hardship or emotional turmoil. Given these apparent advantages, it is recommended that trainers and job counselors utilize the extra time provided by AI technologies to focus more on people facing more intricate issues. Consequently, this would redirect the attention towards developing more advanced cognitive and social abilities required for these vocations. For specific individuals, this may necessitate further schooling and training. Several national AI policies prioritize the retraining of individuals who are displaced by AI, intending to facilitate a just transition during the deployment of AI. For example, Singapore has created a manual on job restructuring in the era of AI, highlighting the importance of engaging in discussions about the reasons behind job transformation, the specific aspects that require modification (including conversations about those that), and the process of implementing the change (Fadel et al., 2019; *Teachers and Leaders in Vocational Education and Training*, 2021).

5. **Induce Human Laziness:** AI solutions streamline most monotonous and recurring jobs. Our reliance on cognitive abilities has diminished as we no longer need to commit information to memory or engage in problem-solving activities to accomplish tasks. Excessive dependence on AI can pose challenges for future generations.

6. **Lack of ethical principles:** Integrating ethics and morals into an AI system might be challenging due to their inherent complexity and subjective nature. The exponential advancement of artificial intelligence has sparked apprehensions regarding the potential scenario where AI could proliferate beyond human control, ultimately leading to the eradication of humanity. This occurrence is commonly known as the AI singularity.
7. **Devoid of emotion:** From a young age, we have been educated that computers and other machines lack emotions. Human beings operate collectively, and effective administration of teams is crucial for attaining objectives. Undoubtedly, robots outperform people when operating at their full potential. Nevertheless, it remains a fact that the interpersonal bonds that underpin teams, which are essential for collaboration, cannot be substituted by computers.
8. **Unchanged:** Humans cannot develop artificial intelligence because it relies on pre-programmed knowledge and prior experiences. Artificial intelligence excels in performing repetitive tasks, but any modifications or enhancements need manual code alteration. AI cannot be accessed and utilized the same way as human intellect, but it can retain unlimited data.

Machines can solely accomplish activities for which they have been specifically designed or programmed. When confronted with duties beyond their designated scope, appliances often encounter failure or produce outcomes that lack utility, hence potentially yielding detrimental consequences. Therefore, we need the ability to create something traditional.

Specific sectors face distinct drawbacks while implementing AI.

1. **Marketing industry:** The main reason is the absence of human interaction and originality. Although AI can automate diverse marketing processes and produce insights based on data, it may need help reproducing the distinctive human aspects of branding, such as emotive bonding, intuition, and creative ideation. By depending exclusively on data and predetermined patterns, AI algorithms may overlook unconventional or creative marketing strategies that necessitate human ingenuity and intuition.
2. **Education industry:** An inherent drawback of AI in education is the possibility of ethical and privacy issues. AI systems gather and evaluate a substantial volume of data about students, encompassing their academic achievements, conduct, and personal details. It is imperative to secure sensitive data handling using suitable privacy measures.
3. **Creativity:** An inherent drawback of AI in creativity is the possible absence of novelty and genuineness in creative works generated by AI. Although AI systems can imitate established styles and trends, there is a continuous discussion

on whether AI can genuinely exhibit creativity in a manner comparable to humans. AI-generated creations may be deficient in profoundness, emotional attachment, and distinctive viewpoints stemming from human encounters and sentiments.

4. **Transportation industry:** An inherent drawback of AI in transportation lies in the ethical and legal dilemmas it poses. Autonomous vehicles, such as self-driving cars, raise concerns over culpability in accidents. Assigning liability in a collision involving an AI-controlled vehicle can be intricate. Furthermore, ethical considerations, such as distributing scarce resources or prioritizing passengers over pedestrians, may need to be considered when AI systems choose traffic management or accident prevention. Addressing these moral quandaries and formulating suitable standards and regulations for AI in transportation is an intricate and continuous endeavor.
5. **Healthcare industry:** The healthcare industry is one of the most emerged and transformed companies, and the hike in healthcare costs might drive this shift. Still, the need for more experts due to integrating IT-based techniques with healthcare is primarily in companies (decrease cost with better solutions (Chan et al., 2019). There are numerous problems/ difficulties faced by healthcare systems around the globe, including difficulty in access, higher prices, more wastage, insufficient equipment, erroneous diagnostic testing kits, overworked physicians, and gaps in information transmission/exchange (Cruciger et al., 2016a). To curb these problems, artificial intelligence has played a critical role in streamlined healthcare, medical research, and care delivery systems. Artificial intelligence can be helpful in many places, like diagnostics, treatment choices, and communication between patients and clinicians using AI-powered methods (Holzinger et al., 2017; Hummel & Braun, 2020; Schmidt-Erfurth et al., 2018a). These techniques can assist medical practitioners in patient care and clinical data management. AI can make remarkable progress in being more personalized, predictive, interactive, and preventive in healthcare (Lee et al., 2018a).

With these benefits, drawbacks also leave doubt on the usage of AI in the minds of practitioners. Some of the significant disadvantages include-

1. **The issue regarding data gathering**: The primary problem is the unavailability of pertinent data. Both machine learning and deep learning models necessitate ample data for optimal performance. Employ a comprehensive algorithm to categorize or forecast a diverse array of occupations. The most notable progress in ML's capacity to produce increasingly sophisticated and precise algorithms has taken place in industries with convenient access to extensive datasets. The

> healthcare industry faces an intricate challenge regarding the availability of information (Ji et al., 2019). Due to the personal nature of patient records, organizations are typically hesitant to share health data. A further challenge arises when the data required for a method is not easily accessible after its initial implementation. Systems based on machine learning (ML) ideally exhibit continuous improvement as additional data is included in their training set. Overcoming internal business resistance may provide a challenge in achieving this goal. A paradigm change is necessary in healthcare to apply information technology and artificial intelligence effectively. This shift involves moving away from personal patient treatment and focusing on enhancing overall healthcare. Specific contemporary algorithms can function on an unimodal or less extended scale instead of multimodal learning. Additionally, the increasing utilization of cloud computing servers can reduce the challenge of storing these continuously growing datasets (Lubarsky, 2010a).

AI systems elicit worries about the security and privacy of data. Due to their significance and susceptibility, hackers frequently target health records during data breaches. Hence, it is imperative to protect the confidentiality of medical documents (Baowaly et al., 2019). Due to the progress of AI, individuals may erroneously see artificial systems as human and grant permission for surreptitious data collection, resulting in significant privacy problems (Ji et al., 2019). Obtaining patient consent is crucial in addressing data privacy concerns, as healthcare professionals may utilize patient information extensively for AI research without explicit patient authorization. In 2018, Google acquired DeepMind, a prominent company specializing in artificial intelligence for healthcare. Upon the revelation that the NHS had sent data on 1.6 million patients to the DeepMind company servers without obtaining the patients' agreement, the Streams program, which utilizes an algorithm to treat patients with severe renal impairment, faced scrutiny. An examination of the privacy of patient data was conducted in the USA regarding Google's Project Nightingale. The issue of data privacy has become more significant since the formal hosting of the app on Google's servers (Baowaly et al., 2019; Hamid, 2016). The General Computational Regulations of Europe and the Health Research Regulations, enacted in 2018, are recent legislation that could address this issue by imposing limitations on gathering, utilizing, and disseminating personal data. Nevertheless, enacting diverse laws in different nations poses collaboration and cooperative research challenges. Consequently, data privacy legislation that addresses this problem may limit the data that can be accessed to train AI systems nationally and globally (*FDA Permits Marketing of Artificial Intelligence-Based Device to Detect Certain Diabetes-Related Eye Problems | FDA*, n.d.). Implementing more rigorous data security standards is imperative to ensure these constraints are not impeding innovation in the sector.

One approach enhances data encryption on the client side, while another utilizes federated learning to train models without dispersing the data (Lubarsky, 2010b).

Evaluating the accuracy of the data utilized in creating algorithms poses an equally difficult task. Since patient data has an estimated half-life of approximately four months, specific predictive algorithms may be less effective in forecasting future outcomes due to their limited ability to replicate prior events. In addition, medical records could be more organized due to frequent errors and uneven storage. Datasets utilized in developing AI systems will inevitably contain unanticipated deficiencies, even with diligent efforts to purify and scrutinize the data. Despite the anticipated benefits of widespread implementation of electronic medical records, the development of practical algorithms could be improved by regulatory and compatibility difficulties across institutions, limiting the amount of data that can be exploited (*Dentons - Regulating Artificial Intelligence in the EU: Top 10 Issues for Businesses to Consider*, n.d.).

2. **Advancements and Worries in Algorithms:** The presence of biases in the data collection techniques used to inform model building can lead to potentially biased outcomes. For example, the lack of adequate representation of minority groups due to racial biases in the creation of datasets could result in inferior prediction outcomes. Various techniques are available to address this bias, including developing training sets that include multiple ethnicities. However, AI models can independently address prejudice, such as the current stereotype neural network that mitigates the impact of uncertain factors. The effectiveness of these measures in eradicating bias in the actual world will be determined over time (*Dentons - Regulating Artificial Intelligence in the EU: Top 10 Issues for Businesses to Consider*, n.d.; *FDA Permits Marketing of Artificial Intelligence-Based Device to Detect Certain Diabetes-Related Eye Problems | FDA*, n.d.).

The advancement of AI technology poses a novel obstacle after data gathering. Overfitting occurs when the algorithm forms irrelevant connections between patient characteristics and results. This happens when excessive variables impact the outcomes, causing the algorithm to produce imprecise predictions. Therefore, the system may perform effectively within the training dataset yet yield ambiguous results when predicting future events. Data leakage is a cause for concern. The method's predictive power for events outside the training dataset is reduced when the algorithm achieves exceptionally high accuracy in its predictions, as there is a possibility that a variable inside the dataset may have inaccurately influenced the outcome. Nevertheless, a new dataset is necessary to validate and resolve this problem, as indicated by previous studies (Fernandes et al., 2020; Gama et al., 2022; Neill, 2013).

A standard critique directed against AI systems is the well-known "black-box" dilemma. Deep learning algorithms often need more capacity to offer compelling justifications for their predictions. If the recommendations are inaccurate, the system cannot legally justify its actions. Furthermore, it complicates the task for scientists to comprehend the correlation between the facts and their forecasts. In addition, the "black box" may lead to a complete loss of trust in the medical system. While this discussion is still in progress, it is essential to highlight how many commonly prescribed medications, like Panadol, work needs to be better understood. Additionally, most doctors only have an elementary grasp of diagnostic imaging methods such as magnetic resonance imaging and computed tomography (CT). Developing AI systems that are comprehensible to humans is an ongoing area of research, and Google has just released a tool to assist in this endeavor (Wolff et al., 2020).

3. **Ethical considerations:** Artificial intelligence has been the subject of ethical issues since its inception. The primary problem is accountability rather than data privacy and security concerns. Given the severity of the repercussions, the existing system must assign responsibility to individuals when they make unfavorable choices, particularly within the medical domain. Artificial intelligence (AI) is sometimes perceived as a "black box" due to concerns among researchers about the difficulty of understanding the process by which an algorithm arrives at a specific result. It has been proposed that the issue of the "black-box" dilemma is of lesser importance for algorithms utilized in less critical applications, such as non-medical ones, and instead prioritize efficiency or improvement of operations. However, responsibility becomes significantly more significant when considering AI applications that aim to improve medical results, especially in cases of errors. Consequently, the responsibility for a system failure is not readily discernible. Attributing blame to the doctor can be challenging, given their lack of involvement in developing or supervising the algorithm. Nevertheless, the developer's responsibility may seem unrelated to the clinical environment. Using machine learning for moral choices in healthcare is forbidden in China and Hong Kong (Lee et al., 2018b; Reed et al., 2018; Schmidt-Erfurth et al., 2018b). The need for established ethical principles for appropriately utilizing artificial intelligence (AI) and machine learning (ML) in the healthcare sector has exacerbated the problem. The ethical utilization of artificial intelligence (AI) in healthcare settings is disputed due to the need for standard criteria for its implementation. Regarding this matter, the United States of America has initiated establishing standards for assessing the security

and effectiveness of AI systems, which has been undertaken by the Food and Drug Administration (FDA). The NHS is developing criteria to demonstrate the efficacy of such innovations to streamline the evaluation process and facilitate the adoption of AI-driven solutions. Both endeavors are ongoing and pose challenges for courts and regulatory authorities in approving activities that rely on artificial intelligence. Engaging in public discourse concerning these ethical quandaries is crucial, intending to establish a universally applicable ethical framework that serves patients' best interests (Alami et al., 2021).

4. **Issues related to societal matters:** Humans have long been concerned that the presence of artificial intelligence (AI) in the healthcare industry could lead to the loss of their employment. Specific individuals harbor skepticism. Many individuals are apprehensive and even antagonistic towards AI-based projects because of the perceived risk of being substituted. However, this viewpoint is primarily rooted in misinterpreting AI throughout its different forms. Refrain from considering the long time AI will take to replace healthcare staff effectively; introducing AI does not mean that jobs will become obsolete. Instead, it implies that these jobs would require restructuring and adaptation. Due to human involvement and the inherent unpredictability of several medical procedures, it is unlikely that they will ever possess the same level of linearity and organization as an algorithm. The presence of skepticism towards AI, while comprehensible, undeniably hinders the broader use of this technology. Regarding the outcomes and effectiveness of AI, being ignorant can result in having false expectations. Overestimating the existing capabilities of AI may lead to disillusionment among the population. It is crucial to have more open discussions among the general public on the use of AI in healthcare to tackle these attitudes among patients and medical professionals (Cruciger et al., 2016b; Díaz et al., 2019).
5. **Issues with the practical application of clinical procedures**: The primary challenge to successful implementation is the need for empirical evidence substantiating the efficacy of AI-based drugs in planned clinical trials. Most AI research has been focused on its performance in the commercial environment, resulting in a need for more knowledge regarding its impact on patient outcomes. Most healthcare AI research has been conducted in non-clinical settings. Consequently, broad generalizations based on research findings can take time and effort. Randomized controlled trials, considered the most reliable method in medical research, need evidence of the advantages of artificial intelligence in healthcare. Businesses exhibit hesitancy and need help implementing AI-based solutions due to the need for more practical data and the inconsistent quality of research (Alami et al., 2021).

Had artificial intelligence gained widespread acceptance, it may have been implemented into medical procedures to enhance efficiency. The usability of information systems is crucial for achieving effective load reduction. AI-based treatments should not impede practitioners' efficiency when analyzing or investigating electronic medical data. The price tag encompasses the time and money necessary to educate medical practitioners in proficiently utilizing the technology. There have been limited examples of effectively integrating AI into clinical therapy, with most cases still in the experimental stage (Denti & Hemlin, 2012). The lack of stakeholder input during the development phase has hindered successful integration in numerous instances of innovation adoption.

Obtaining input from diverse individuals is essential for creating a solution that can be easily incorporated into clinical practice. Following the SARS and Ebola pandemics, numerous improvements in AI were achieved to improve outcomes through methods such as enhanced epidemiological forecasting and expedited diagnosis. Nevertheless, the rapid advancements in this field have certain limitations. The effectiveness of these advancements in healthcare relies on their smooth integration into current procedures to avoid confusion or hindering clinicians who lack AI training. Additionally, clinical research has encountered challenges with the algorithms used (Damschroder et al., 2009; Davenport & Kalakota, 2019).

6. **Prejudiced and discriminatory algorithms:** Bias is not confined to the social and cultural realms; it also exists in the technological sphere. Biased software and technical artifacts can arise due to inadequate design or the use of inaccurate or imbalanced data in algorithms. Hence, artificial intelligence only reproduces the existing racial, gender, and age biases prevalent in our society, thereby exacerbating the socioeconomic disparity between the affluent and the underprivileged. You are likely familiar with Amazon's contentious experiment involving a less conventional recruitment method that took place a few years ago. The candidate search tool utilized artificial intelligence to evaluate individuals on a rating scale ranging from one to five stars, similar to the review system employed by Amazon customers. Amazon's computer models for screening job applications exhibited bias toward male applicants and discrimination against resumes, including the term "women," due to a decade of data collection (Hagendorff, 2020).

The absence of diversity within development teams is a significant issue, as is the prejudiced character of the data employed in constructing the product. Their cultural biases and misunderstandings become deeply ingrained in the essence of technical advancement, primarily due to a limited range of perspectives. Consequently, firms that do not adopt diversity face the risk of developing products or services that exclude significant portions of the population.

A study published four years ago revealed that specific facial recognition algorithms inaccurately categorized fewer than 1% of Caucasian males while misclassifying nearly 33% of African-American females. Despite the show's designers claiming that the program is of high quality, the participants they used to measure its effectiveness consisted of over 77% males and 83% white individuals (Damschroder et al., 2009; Davenport & Kalakota, 2019; Denti & Hemlin, 2012; Schönberger, 2019).

CONCLUSION

The concern of AI is addressed by emphasizing several difficulties in execution associated with AI. The challenges of adopting AI successfully included data privacy concerns, social and ethical dilemmas, hacker vulnerabilities, and developer-related barriers. According to our assessment, the presence of AI in the current era is inevitable. Substantial technological advancements have taken place since the beginning of the modern era. Technologies like AI will rapidly increase and become a necessity worldwide. Despite being developed in the contemporary period, AI is constrained and has limited capabilities. Currently, this technology is utilized to do specific tasks by focusing on identifying objects through sensors, and subsequently, the AI takes suitable action based on predetermined rules. The fundamental goal of today's scientists is to construct a complete worldwide AI based on sophisticated and trustworthy computations. The specialized tasks performed by this advanced AI are more complex than those performed by the current AI. Implementing AI systems in healthcare should be viewed as a continuous learning process, requiring a more advanced systems-thinking approach in the health industry to address these challenges. Artificial intelligence can enhance adult educational systems. This is imperative due to the rapid evolution of our work environment. However, only 40% of individuals in the OECD engage in education and training annually, which is much lower for marginalized groups in the labor market. Furthermore, the problem of training quality persists, and it might be challenging to synchronize training with the demands of the job market and the aspirations of people's career paths. AI has the potential to enhance other technology-based training solutions greatly, and, in certain situations, it can also surpass certain aspects of human services.

AI can intervene at many stages of adult learning when employed for training. Before providing training, it is beneficial to evaluate the need for skills by utilizing digital availability data to analyze emerging skill requirements from the recent past. Additionally, skills profiling techniques can be used to analyze the supply of skills. After evaluating the disparities in skills between individuals and the requirements of accessible professions, artificial intelligence can assist in identifying appropriate training alternatives to address those gaps. AI enables the customization of training content to suit individual needs and can be adjusted in real time based on progress. AI may now facilitate training in novel ways, overcoming physical and psychological obstacles by offering secure platforms for experimenting and learning from mistakes.

This working paper examines the possible benefits and downsides of utilizing artificial intelligence (AI) for training based on a comprehensive study of the pertinent literature and consultations with experts in AI and training. Doing this provides essential insights for policymakers, government and private employment agencies, and companies contemplating the implementation of AI tools in their training programs.

Utilizing AI to teach can enhance training engagement, particularly among presently underrepresented demographics, by reducing the obstacles individuals face during training and boosting their motivation to participate. Additionally, specific AI solutions for training have the potential to enhance the alignment between training programs and the requirements of the labor market. Furthermore, these solutions can also mitigate bias and discrimination in the workplace.

However, despite the potential advantages of using AI tools for training, there are also significant disadvantages. These include the possibility of reducing the inclusivity of adult learning systems due to the requirement of digital skills to operate the tools, as well as the substantial amount of data and advanced technological infrastructure necessary for the development of AI tools. Employing AI for training could significantly alter the skill prerequisites for occupations associated with training and recruitment. Furthermore, artificial intelligence gives rise to substantial ethical concerns.

Further research and policies are necessary to fully harness the promise of AI and ensure that its use for training yields positive results for everyone. These should address the requirements for digital skills, the expenses associated with adoption, and the creation of reliable and user-centered AI solutions that can be easily understood. Several OECD countries have implemented policy measures to enhance training programs for digital skills, including AI skills. They also promote innovation and AI adoption among small and medium-sized enterprises (SMEs). Additionally, these countries offer retraining opportunities for individuals whom AI has displaced. They have also developed guidelines for trustworthy and explainable AI aligning with the OECD AI Principles. Furthermore, they are facilitating experimental models or co-regulatory approaches to formally test and gain a deeper understanding of the impact of AI systems. Given that AI can shape an individual's career trajectory when utilized for training, it is recommended that future policy and research focus on the uses of AI in this field.

REFERENCES

Alami, H., Lehoux, P., Denis, J. L., Motulsky, A., Petitgand, C., Savoldelli, M., Rouquet, R., Gagnon, M. P., Roy, D., & Fortin, J. P. (2021). Organizational readiness for artificial intelligence in health care: Insights for decision-making and practice. *Journal of Health Organization and Management*, *35*(1), 106–114. doi:10.1108/JHOM-03-2020-0074 PMID:33258359

Baowaly, M. K., Lin, C.-C., Liu, C.-L., & Chen, K.-T. (2019). Synthesizing electronic health records using improved generative adversarial networks. *Journal of the American Medical Informatics Association : JAMIA*, *26*(3), 228–241. doi:10.1093/jamia/ocy142 PMID:30535151

Chan, H. C. S., Shan, H., Dahoun, T., Vogel, H., & Yuan, S. (2019). Advancing Drug Discovery via Artificial Intelligence. *Trends in Pharmacological Sciences*, *40*(8), 592–604. doi:10.1016/j.tips.2019.06.004 PMID:31320117

Cruciger, O., Schildhauer, T. A., Meindl, R. C., Tegenthoff, M., Schwenkreis, P., Citak, M., & Aach, M. (2016a). Impact of locomotion training with a neurologic controlled hybrid assistive limb (HAL) exoskeleton on neuropathic pain and health related quality of life (HRQoL) in chronic SCI: A case study. *Disability and Rehabilitation. Assistive Technology*, *11*(6), 529–534. doi:10.3109/17483107.2014.981875 PMID:25382234

Damschroder, L. J., Aron, D. C., Keith, R. E., Kirsh, S. R., Alexander, J. A., & Lowery, J. C. (2009). Fostering implementation of health services research findings into practice: A consolidated framework for advancing implementation science. *Implementation Science : IS*, *4*(1), 1–15. doi:10.1186/1748-5908-4-50 PMID:19664226

Davenport, T., & Kalakota, R. (2019). The potential for artificial intelligence in healthcare. *Future Healthcare Journal*, *6*(2), 94–98. doi:10.7861/futurehosp.6-2-94 PMID:31363513

Denti, L., & Hemlin, S. (2012). *Leadership and innovation in organizations: A systematic review of factors that mediate or moderate the relationship*. doi:10.1142/S1363919612400075

Dentons - Regulating artificial intelligence in the EU: top 10 issues for businesses to consider. (n.d.). Retrieved December 19, 2023, from https://www.dentons.com/en/insights/articles/2021/june/28/regulating-artificial-intelligence-in-the-eu-top-10-issues-for-businesses-to-consider

Díaz, Ó., Dalton, J. A. R., & Giraldo, J. (2019). Artificial Intelligence: A Novel Approach for Drug Discovery. *Trends in Pharmacological Sciences*, *40*(8), 550–551. doi:10.1016/j.tips.2019.06.005 PMID:31279568

Fadel, C., Holmes, W., & Bialik, M. (2019). *Artificial intelligence in education: Promises and implications for teaching and learning*. The Center for Curriculum Redesign.

FDA permits marketing of artificial intelligence-based device to detect certain diabetes-related eye problems. (n.d.). Retrieved December 19, 2023, from https://www.fda.gov/news-events/press-announcements/fda-permits-marketing-artificial-intelligence-based-device-detect-certain-diabetes-related-eye

Fernandes, M., Vieira, S. M., Leite, F., Palos, C., Finkelstein, S., & Sousa, J. M. C. (2020). Clinical Decision Support Systems for Triage in the Emergency Department using Intelligent Systems: A Review. *Artificial Intelligence in Medicine*, *102*, 101762. doi:10.1016/j.artmed.2019.101762 PMID:31980099

Gama, F., Tyskbo, D., Nygren, J., Barlow, J., Reed, J., & Svedberg, P. (2022). Implementation Frameworks for Artificial Intelligence Translation into Health Care Practice: Scoping Review. *Journal of Medical Internet Research*, *24*(1), e32215. doi:10.2196/32215 PMID:35084349

Hagendorff, T. (2020). The Ethics of AI Ethics: An Evaluation of Guidelines. *Minds and Machines*, *30*(1), 99–120. doi:10.1007/s11023-020-09517-8

Hamid, S. (2016). *The opportunities and risks of artificial intelligence in medicine and healthcare*. Academic Press.

HolzingerA.BiemannC.PattichisC. S.KellD. B. (2017). What do we need to build explainable AI systems for the medical domain? https://arxiv.org/abs/1712.09923v1

Hummel, P., & Braun, M. (2020). Just data? Solidarity and justice in data-driven medicine. *Life Sciences, Society and Policy*, *16*(1), 1–18. doi:10.1186/s40504-020-00101-7 PMID:32839878

Ji, S., Gu, Q., Weng, H., Liu, Q., Zhou, P., Chen, J., Li, Z., Beyah, R., & Wang, T. (2019). De-Health: All Your Online Health Information Are Belong to Us. *Proceedings - International Conference on Data Engineering*, 1609–1620. 10.1109/ICDE48307.2020.00143

Lee, S. I., Celik, S., Logsdon, B. A., Lundberg, S. M., Martins, T. J., Oehler, V. G., Estey, E. H., Miller, C. P., Chien, S., Dai, J., Saxena, A., Blau, C. A., & Becker, P. S. (2018). A machine learning approach to integrate big data for precision medicine in acute myeloid leukemia. *Nature Communications, 9*(1), 1–13. doi:10.1038/s41467-017-02465-5

Lubarsky, B. (2010). Re-identification of "anonymized data." *Georgetown Law Technology Review. Available Online:* Https://Www. Georgetownlawtechreview. Org/Re-Identification-of-Anonymized-Data/GLTR-04-2017 *(Accessed on 10 September 2021).*

Neill, D. B. (2013). Using artificial intelligence to improve hospital inpatient care. *IEEE Intelligent Systems, 28*(2), 92–95. doi:10.1109/MIS.2013.51

Reed, J. E., Howe, C., Doyle, C., & Bell, D. (2018). Simple rules for evidence translation in complex systems: A qualitative study. *BMC Medicine, 16*(1), 1–20. doi:10.1186/s12916-018-1076-9 PMID:29921274

Schmidt-Erfurth, U., Bogunovic, H., Sadeghipour, A., Schlegl, T., Langs, G., Gerendas, B. S., Osborne, A., & Waldstein, S. M. (2018). Machine Learning to Analyze the Prognostic Value of Current Imaging Biomarkers in Neovascular Age-Related Macular Degeneration. *Ophthalmology Retina, 2*(1), 24–30. doi:10.1016/j.oret.2017.03.015 PMID:31047298

Schönberger, D. (2019). Artificial intelligence in healthcare: A critical analysis of the legal and ethical implications. *International Journal of Law and Information Technology, 27*(2), 171–203. doi:10.1093/ijlit/eaz004

Teachers and Leaders in Vocational Education and Training. (2021). doi:10.1787/59d4fbb1-en

Wolff, J., Pauling, J., Keck, A., & Baumbach, J. (2020). The economic impact of artificial intelligence in health care: Systematic review. *Journal of Medical Internet Research, 22*(2), e16866. doi:10.2196/16866 PMID:32130134

Chapter 4
Artificial Intelligence Challenges and Its Impact on Detection and Prevention of Financial Statement Fraud:
A Theoretical Study

Archna
Lovely Professional University, India

Nidhi Bhagat
Lovely Professional University, India

ABSTRACT

The detection and prevention of financial statement fraud is a critical concern in maintaining the credibility and reliability of financial reporting. In response to this ongoing challenge, researchers are exploring innovative solutions that leverage artificial intelligence (AI) technology. This study investigates the potential application of AI techniques, such as machine learning algorithms, natural language processing, and data mining, in enhancing forensic accounting practices for detecting and preventing financial statement fraud. Furthermore, the research examines the inherent challenges and limitations involved in implementing AI systems within forensic accounting. The findings of this research contribute valuable insights to organizations, regulatory bodies, and forensic professionals, assisting them in their efforts to combat financial fraud and promote the accuracy of financial reporting systems.

DOI: 10.4018/979-8-3693-0724-3.ch004

1. INTRODUCTION

Artificial Intelligence (AI) stands as a technological advancement bound to have a deep influence on the legal domain and the role of forensic accountants as expert witnesses. A forensic accountant's testimony, like any expert witnesses is pivotal for effectively presenting cases in court. Given the intricacies of many cases, forensic accountants often need to sift through data to discern reliable information, a process that can be both costly and time-intensive (Capraş & Achim, 2023). The integration of AI holds the potential to streamline this task, offering a more efficient approach (Cao, 2022). This inevitably requires courts, legal practitioners, and forensic accounting experts to familiarize themselves with this emerging technology and understand its impact on jury decisions (Mehta et al., 2022). Recent research also highlights the application of AI in fraud detection, which can significantly aid forensic accountants in their investigations (Y. Hilary et al., 2022; Chaquet-Ulldemolins et al., 2022; Zioviris et al., 2022). Moreover, AI's role in improving forensic accounting services has been observed in sectors like healthcare, where it contributes to fraud prevention (Obiora et al., 2022). As we move forward, it is evident that the synergy between forensic accounting and AI will play a crucial role in enhancing the legal landscape and the effectiveness of expert witness testimony. Considering the significant role played by forensic accountants as expert witnesses, the ongoing adaptation to AI within the legal framework becomes a pertinent subject for forensic accounting research (Capraş & Achim, 2023). Moreover, the way in which forensic accountants incorporate AI into a dynamic legal environment will also influence the trajectory of forensic accounting research (Cao, 2022). Forensic auditing encompasses the process of examining historical financial data to gather evidence that can be presented in legal proceedings. The term "forensic" is associated with financial facts and their manipulation, as well as the presence of financial fraud. According to Oberholzer, forensic auditing is a variant of investigative audit or accounting that places emphasis on tracking down instances of financial fraud (Ogunode & Dada, 2022). This field of forensic accounting offers a comprehensive understanding of various types of fraud occurrences while also actively working to prevent such fraudulent activities and institute anti-fraud measures. With the advent of information technology in the contemporary era, there has been a growing interest among academics and professionals to harness the capabilities of Artificial Intelligence (AI) in the realm of forensic accounting (Sharma & Panigrahi, 2020). This interest stems from the intention to enhance efforts against financial fraud. Forensic accounting is a crucial tool in detecting fraud, employing specialized skills to uncover suspicious financial patterns and anomalies (Kaur et al., 2020). These professionals conduct thorough investigations, analyze large volumes of data, and scrutinize relevant documents to identify potential red flags. With their expert testimony and collaboration with law enforcement and other experts, forensic accountants help bring fraudsters to justice and offer recommendations to prevent future fraudulent activities, safeguarding organizations from financial harm (Kurshan & Shen, 2020). Forensic accounting holds a crucial position in uncovering and examining instances of fraud (Fedyk et al., 2022). It involves identifying suspicious patterns and irregularities in financial data that may indicate fraudulent activities. By conducting in-depth investigations, forensic accountants gather evidence and determine the extent of the fraud, quantifying the financial losses incurred. Their expertise also extends to providing expert testimony in legal proceedings related to fraud cases and assisting the court in making well-informed decisions (Mhlanga, 2020). Additionally, forensic accountants help organizations implement fraud prevention measures by identifying weaknesses in internal controls and recommending improvements.

Furthermore, forensic accountants assist in tracing and recovering misappropriated assets, contributing to asset recovery efforts. Their due diligence in financial transactions and risk assessments helps organizations identify potential risks and enhance their fraud prevention strategies (Ghandour, 2021). AI plays a pivotal role in the realm of fraud detection, greatly benefiting the field of forensic accounting (Mehta et al., 2022). By leveraging the capabilities of AI-powered algorithms, forensic accountants are empowered to efficiently and accurately process large volumes of financial data, including transaction records and invoices. This capacity enables them to swiftly identify potential red flags and patterns that may indicate fraudulent activities (Caron, 2019). One of the key advantages of AI in fraud detection is its ability to detect anomalies that might escape traditional methods. Machine learning algorithms can learn from historical data and identify deviations from regular financial patterns, allowing forensic accountants to uncover unusual or suspicious transactions that might go unnoticed (Königstorfer & Thalmann, 2020).Moreover, AI offers the advantage of real-time monitoring, enabling forensic accountants to track financial transactions as they occur continuously. This immediacy allows them to promptly identify and respond to potential fraud, helping organizations mitigate losses and prevent further damage. AI's pattern recognition capabilities are particularly valuable in uncovering complex fraud schemes (Cirqueira et al., 2021). By analyzing multiple cases, AI can identify similarities and connections between seemingly unrelated incidents, helping forensic accountants reveal more extensive fraud networks and understand the broader picture of fraudulent activities. Through natural language processing (NLP), AI systems can interpret unstructured data like emails, chat logs, and social media posts. This functionality provides valuable insights into fraudulent communications and interactions, further supporting the investigative process. Predictive analytics is another powerful feature of AI in fraud detection (Zioviris et al., 2022). By analyzing historical data, AI can predict future fraud risks, enabling organizations to take proactive measures to prevent fraud before it occurs. AI systems can also assist in prioritizing and categorizing fraud cases based on severity and likelihood of success. This functionality helps forensic accountants allocate their resources more efficiently, focusing on cases that require immediate attention or present higher risks (Vijai, 2019). Automating routine tasks is yet another benefit of AI in fraud detection (Chaquet-Ulldemolins et al., 2022).

This chapter will help the readers improve their learning and cognitive skills regarding using AI in financial fraud detection. Also, this chapter aims to explore the diverse challenges that practitioners and forensic accounting experts might encounter while incorporating AI, particularly in light of the historical precedence of expert testimonies in legal proceedings (Victor et al., 2020). The work done in this chapter will further augment the preexisting frameworks developed by other authors to help build up future theories on the said subject. Modern technological interventions like AI, ML, IoT, etc, can help detect financial fraud, which can help corporations bring more sustainable profits.

This chapter has been divided into the following subthemes for deeper insight: the conceptual framework of the research, challenges and impact related to AI in forensic Accounting and the future scope of the study.

To maintain the integrity and dependability of financial reporting, the chapter begins by highlighting how crucial it is to identify and stop financial statement fraud. Scientists have recognized this continuous difficulty and focused on creative fixes, especially with artificial intelligence (AI) technologies. This study's primary goal is to look at how artificial intelligence (AI) methods, such as data mining, machine learning algorithms, and natural language processing, may be used to improve forensic accounting procedures for the identification and defence against financial statement fraud. Despite the intricacies involved, the study adopts a methodical approach to investigate the inherent difficulties and constraints related to the application of AI systems in forensic accounting. The research's conclusions provide insightful information that advances the body of knowledge held by regulatory agencies, forensic specialists, and organizations, supporting their efforts to prevent financial fraud and advance the accuracy of financial reporting systems. A thorough discussion is presented throughout the chapter, including the justification for integrating AI, the study's methodology, important discoveries and insights, and a conclusion that offers suggestions and possible avenues for further research in this developing subject.

2. LITERATURE REVIEW

The primary objective of this research is to assess the efficacy of forensic accounting in fraud prevention. This comprehensive analysis investigated three key dimensions: the competencies and attributes of forensic accountants, the methodologies employed in forensic accounting, and the challenges and opportunities pertaining to the development of the forensic accounting field. The central findings highlighted that the skills, capabilities, and techniques intrinsic to forensic accounting render it a potent tool for detecting and preventing fraud. Furthermore, it advocates for the recognition of forensic accounting as an autonomous profession. It also holds educational value, potentially enriching accounting and audit curricula in academic institutions. (Capraş, I. L., & Achim, M. V. 2023). The advent of expansive datasets and artificial intelligence has ushered in novel prospects for leveraging sophisticated models like machine learning to unearth instances of fraud. This section furnishes a comprehensive outline of the complexities associated with utilizing machine learning for fraud detection. Y., Hilary, G., Ke, B. (2022). AI in finance involves applying AI techniques to various aspects of financial operations, attracting attention for decades. This review takes a distinct approach by providing a comprehensive roadmap of challenges, techniques, and opportunities in AI research within finance over the years. It outlined the landscape of financial operations and data, categorizes AI research, and explores data-driven analytics and learning in finance. (Cao, Longbing 2022). This study investigated the pivotal role of forensic accounting in increasing fraud prevention efforts at both corporate and national levels. To ensure the sustained success of fraud prevention strategies, the study recommends that public and corporate management demonstrate commitment and ethical leadership, invest in ongoing training for anti-fraud personnel, and address the pressing issue of cybercrime through the implementation of legal treaties and frameworks. (Ogunode, O. A., & Dada, S. O. 2022). The empirical study conducted in Nigeria investigated the impact of forensic accounting services on fraud prevention among healthcare firms, whereby the findings revealed that the application of forensic accounting services has significantly reduced fraud incidences and effectively prevented fraud at a 1% significance level. The study recommended the establishment of robust internal control systems to introduce checks and balances among staff, thereby minimizing fraud and restoring confidence for potential investors. (Obiora, F. C., Onuora, J. K. J., & Amodu, O. A.2022). Top of FormThe rise of Artificial Intelligence (AI) in the global economy, driven by its analytical capabilities, is leading to increased automation. This shift presents an opportunity for credit fraud detection (CFD) using advanced techniques like autoencoders. However, the challenge lies in regulatory compliance and interpretability. This study proposes a transparent approach by combining feature selection and a novel auto-encoder-based technique. This enables an understanding of the relationship between inputs and outputs for each analysis, enhancing feature ranking accuracy. The findings highlight influential factors in the model's outcomes, and the proposed method surpasses previous results in accuracy. The paper's contribution lies in its advanced CFD model and a novel methodology for enhancing transparency and interpretability in AI techniques (Chaquet-

Ulldemolins, Jacobo 2022). Artificial intelligence (AI) is instigating substantial changes within the banking sector, especially in domains such as credit scoring, risk evaluation, customer experience, and portfolio management. Among its challenges, fraud detection in transaction streams is critical. Recent advancements have introduced deep learning models to address this, focusing on identifying and forecasting potential fraud by estimating normal/fraudulent transaction distributions and detecting deviations. This paper introduces a novel multistage deep learning model: two autoencoders are employed for latent data and feature selection space learning, followed by a deep convolutional neural network to detect fraud. The approach aims to identify fraud in the latent data representation rather than the original data, improving efficiency and accuracy (Zioviris et al., 2022). There has been a global increase in the prominent use of artificial intelligence, which combines machine capabilities with human intelligence, enhancing the effectiveness of traditional methods in addressing financial data manipulation. This study seeks to explore the intermediary role of artificial intelligence tools in the field of forensic accounting and their contribution to the detection of financial fraud. Using structural equation modelling, the research model aims to assess how forensic accounting impacts the identification of financial fraud. The findings of this study can provide valuable insights for professionals, highlighting the advantages of AI technology in the realm of forensic accounting and its potential to enhance fraud detection efforts (Mehta et al.; J. K., 2022).Top of FormDecision support systems and fraud detection are essential in tackling the growing issue of fraud in digital banking. However, the integration of Artificial Intelligence (AI) for decision support introduces challenges due to the lack of transparency in AI predictions, leading to a need for Explainable AI (XAI). While XAI has been employed to provide transparent AI predictions through various explanation methods, existing research lacks a user-centric perspective and discussions about the practical deployment of principles. In this research, a methodology grounded in design science and informed by Information Systems (IS) theory is employed. The objective is to formulate and assess design principles that synchronize the responsibilities of fraud experts with explanation techniques for user-centric Explainable AI decision support. The efficacy of these principles is substantiated through a combination of expert interviews and simulations. (Cirqueira, Douglas, Markus Helfert, and Marija Bezbradica 2021) The emergence of digital payment methods has led to substantial shifts in the landscape of financial crimes. Consequently, conventional strategies for identifying fraud, such as rule-based systems, have experienced a decline in effectiveness. Artificial intelligence (AI) and machine learning (ML) approaches, founded on principles of graph computing, have garnered notable attention in recent times. Graph-oriented methodologies present distinct opportunities for addressing financial crimes. In this article, we delve into the hurdles encountered during the application of current and upcoming graph-based solutions. Furthermore, the evolving patterns in financial crimes and digital payments point toward emerging complexities that challenge the sustained efficacy of detection techniques. Our analysis examines the landscape of threats, leading us to assert that it offers crucial insights for developing graph-centric solutions (Kurshan et al., H 2020). The research paper examined the challenges faced by forensic accountants in dealing with the implications of blockchain technology for fraud prevention and detection. The decentralization of blockchain and its potential for automating financial processes disrupt traditional accounting and auditing. The study, based on qualitative library research, reveals that blockchain is not entirely immune to malicious activities. It suggests that technology will impact accountants' core functions but leaves open the question of its overall effects on the roles of forensic accountants and auditors. Oladejo, M. T., & Jack, L. (2020). The investigation revealed that AI significantly impacts digital financial inclusion, particularly in domains such as identifying, assessing, and managing risks, mitigating information asymmetry challenges, offering customer support and assistance through chatbots, and enhancing fraud detection and cybersecurity measures. It is advisable for worldwide financial establishments, non-financial corporations, and governmental bodies to adopt and amplify the use of AI tools and systems. (Mhlanga David, 2020) examined the integration of AI techniques in the field of fraud detection and forensic accounting. The paper discusses various AI approaches, including machine learning, data mining, and expert systems, and their applications in identifying patterns of fraudulent activities within financial data. It also highlights the benefits, challenges, and future research directions in leveraging AI for fraud detection (Sharma et al., P. K. (2020). This review paper presents a comprehensive overview of artificial intelligence (AI)--based approaches for fraud detection in financial statements. It explores various AI techniques, such as neural networks, support vector machines, and fuzzy logic, and their applications in identifying fraudulent patterns and anomalies. (Zolbanin, H. M., Nabati, M., & Lee, T. S. (2019) This review paper presented a comprehensive overview of artificial intelligence (AI)-based approaches for fraud detection in financial statements. It also analyses various AI techniques, such as neural networks and support vector machines, and their applications in identifying fraudulent patterns and anomalies. Additionally, the paper examines the limitations and suggests future research directions in this evolving field (Zolbanin et al., T. S 2019). The results of the textbook encompassing manual present a comprehensive primer on fraud examination and forensic accounting, offering an in-depth understanding of the subject matter. Encompassing various areas, such as financial statement fraud, asset misappropriation, and corruption, it provides a vast scope of knowledge. Readers will gain valuable perspectives on the investigative methods and approaches employed in the practical application of forensic accounting (Albrecht et al., M. F 2018). Focused on the integration of artificial intelligence (AI) technologies, this survey paper provides an overview of accounting and auditing approaches in fraud prevention. It examines the potential of AI in detecting and preventing financial fraud, including the utilization of data analytics, intelligent decision support systems, and anomaly detection algorithms. The paper also addresses the challenges and ethical considerations associated with the adoption of AI in fraud prevention (Spathis et al., C 2018). The evolution of AI from research labs to practical implementation, driven by standardized computer vision, speech recognition, and machine translation, along with learning-based technologies like digital advertising and intelligent infrastructures, has been enabled by data abundance, computational advancements, and methodological progress. This shift promises AI systems that interact frequently and autonomously in personalized contexts, but it presents significant challenges. These encompass the need for AI systems to make timely decisions in unpredictable environments, withstand sophisticated adversaries, handle extensive data while maintaining user-friendliness, and navigate the limitations of post-Moore's Law computing. The paper suggests addressing these challenges through research in systems, architectures, and security to fully harness AI's potential for societal improvement and individual well-being (Stoica et al., ... & Abbeel, P. 2017) presented a comprehensive exploration of the rise of artificial intelligence within the domains of accounting and auditing. It delves into the existing capabilities of cognitive technologies and their anticipated effects on human auditors and the auditing process. Additionally, the article offers instances from the industry wherein the Big 4 accounting firms have integrated artificial intelligence. Conclusively, it addresses potential biases linked to the development and utilization of AI and ponders the ramifications for forthcoming research (Julia et al., 2017). explored the utilization of artificial intelligence (AI) methods, such as neural networks, genetic algorithms, and expert systems, for fraud detection in the accounting domain. It discusses the advantages of employing AI techniques in analyzing large datasets, identifying anomalous transactions, and enhancing the effectiveness of fraud detection processes (Jubb et al., C. W 2014).Top of Form.In this handbook, readers gain comprehensive insights into understanding, preventing, and detecting corporate fraud. It covers various forms of fraud, including financial statement fraud, and provides practical strategies and techniques for organizations to bolster their efforts in fraud prevention. The book serves as a valuable resource for professionals seeking to strengthen their anti-fraud measures (Wells et al., 2011). This textbook provides a comprehensive overview of forensic accounting and fraud examination. It covers essential topics such as legal considerations, investigative procedures, evidence collection, and findings presentation. Additionally, the book explores the integration of technology, including data analysis techniques, into the practice of forensic accounting (Kranacher et al.; J. T., 2011). This research article investigates the relationship between audit committee characteristics and auditor litigation, with a specific focus on the role of audit committees in preventing and detecting financial fraud. It highlights the significance of effective corporate governance in mitigating fraudulent activities and enhancing financial oversight (Kaur et al.; L., 2020)

3. CONCEPTUAL FRAMEWORK OF THE RESEARCH

The next section shows conceptual framework (see Fig. 1)

Figure 1.
Source: Prepared by Authors

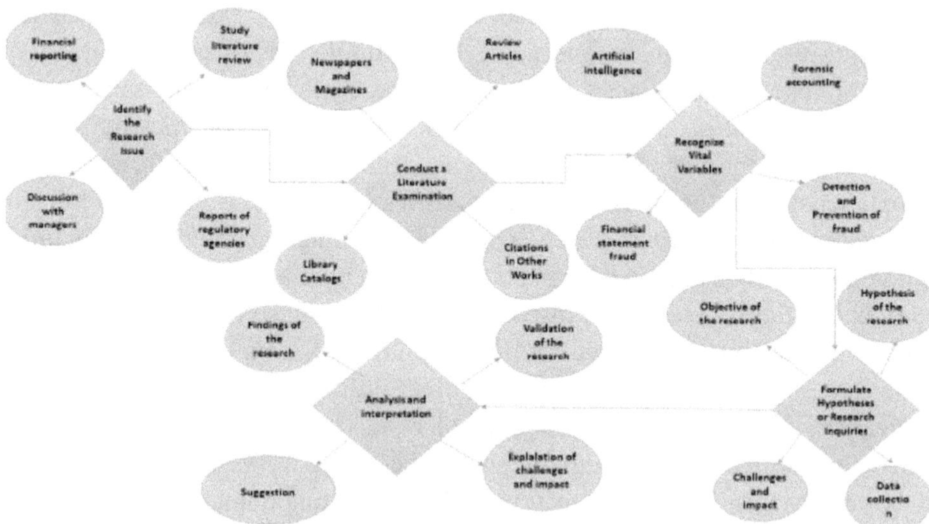

4. DATA

The objective of this research is to examine the challenges and their impact related to artificial intelligence (AI) in fraud detection within the field of forensic accounting, with a focus on analyzing secondary data sources. Data is collected through secondary data sources, including reputable academic journals, books, research reports, and databases that offer valuable insights into the integration of AI techniques in fraud detection within forensic accounting. Collect comprehensive data on various aspects related to AI in fraud detection, such as AI methodologies, applications, benefits, challenges, and limitations, specifically within the context of forensic accounting. Data Analysis performs a systematic literature review, systematically organizing and categorizing the collected secondary data based on key themes, such as AI techniques employed, fraud detection methodologies utilized, and prevailing practices in forensic accounting. Thoroughly analyze and synthesize the information gathered from secondary sources, facilitating a comprehensive understanding of the role of AI in fraud detection and its implications for the field of forensic accounting.

5. ANALYSIS AND INTERPRETATION

5.1 Challenges and Impact Related to AI

The advent of AI technology has sparked significant digital upheaval across the 21st-century banking landscape. This stems from the capability of AI solutions to drive innovation, enhance decision-making, and efficiently address intricate issues within banking institutions. Various AI tools can empower banks to make more precise predictions and adeptly respond to emerging challenges. Thus, AI equips banks with a competitive edge in the market. Nonetheless, capitalizing on AI opportunities requires addressing several potential pitfalls. Concerns encompass privacy breaches, job displacement, data availability and quality, and ensuring alignment between AI strategies and business objectives. While existing literature highlights the potential and challenges of AI in banking, most studies are descriptive and rely on secondary data sources. Subsequent research should employ rigorous empirical methods to offer substantial evidence regarding the scope of AI's opportunities and challenges within the banking sector (see figure 4.2).

- **The proliferation of AI-driven automation could render specific skills outdated:** The potential transformation of traditional roles and the potential obsolescence of certain skills due to AI-powered banking systems raise concerns about job losses. Consequently, ensuring user acceptance of AI within the banking sector could pose a significant challenge.
- **Privacy violation concerns:** The effectiveness of most AI systems in the banking sector is made possible by collecting and analyzing large amounts of customer-related data. This includes factors such as demographic profile information, spending patterns, physical interactions, credit and debit card particulars, social media profiles, and more. Consequently, there is a concern regarding the privacy and security of consumers when utilizing AI technology.
- **Suppression of innovation and flexibility:** Relying excessively on AI for automating decision-making and problem-solving tasks might diminish employees' creative thinking and adaptability.

- **Limited resources for AI implementation and operations:** The expenses associated with setting up and maintaining a large-scale AI system pose significant limitations, particularly for smaller banks that have constrained available resources. Beyond the initial expenditures, maintaining optimal AI technology operations would necessitate skilled data science professionals.
- **The prospect of a digital divide:** Individuals without access to contemporary personal devices like computers, smartphones, and tablets, as well as those lacking internet connectivity and digital skills, might find it challenging to utilize banking AI systems. This could particularly impact individuals with lower socio-economic statuses, limiting their ability to benefit from these technological advancements in banking.
- **Insufficient availability of high-quality datasets for training and testing AI algorithms:** Many AI technologies depend on extensive amounts of unstructured datasets, which may not always be accessible.
- **Incorporating AI into traditional banking operations:** There is limited proof regarding the successful integration of AI with traditional banking procedures. This could result in the inability to fully harness the potential benefits of AI implementation.
- **Erosion of the personal and emotional connection:** AI cannot entirely substitute human bankers and physical branch networks. It is essential to redefine the roles of human bankers to cultivate meaningful interactions between bankers and customers.

After reviewing the research, the result of the study also realizes that these aspects represent challenges associated with AI in the realm of fraud detection.

- **Repetitive task:** The challenge of repetitive tasks in AI fraud detection refers to the potential automation of routine and mundane activities within the fraud detection process. Automated AI might lack the nuanced understanding that human experts possess when interpreting data in a broader context, potentially leading to false positives or negatives.
- **Integration with Human Expertise:** AI should augment human forensic accountants, not replace them. Human insights and expertise are crucial for interpreting results and considering broader investigation contextual factors.
- **Bias in AI:** The learning of AI depends upon the historical data, and if that data has biases, the AI might inadvertently perpetuate them. In forensic accounting, objectivity is vital, but AI systems inheriting human biases may undermine the integrity of investigations.
- **Transparency issue:** Transparency concerns in AI fraud detection pertain to the difficulty in comprehending and validating the decisions made

by AI systems, especially those perceived as opaque. These challenges can undermine accountability, introduce biases, and hinder adherence to regulations.

- **Lack of Training Data for Rare Events:** AI systems rely on historical data for training, and rare or unique fraud events might have limited representation in the dataset. Consequently, the AI may need help to accurately identify infrequent fraudulent activities.
- **"Black box "problem:** The black box challenge in AI fraud detection pertains to the inherent complexity of specific machine learning models, rendering their inner workings challenging to comprehend for humans. This lack of transparency creates issues in explaining the rationale behind fraud detection decisions, giving rise to worries about accountability, biases, and adherence to regulations.
- **The complexity of Financial Fraud:** Fraudsters constantly evolve their tactics, making it challenging for AI systems to keep up with emerging and sophisticated fraudulent schemes. As a result, AI may struggle to detect new types of financial fraud effectively.
- **Regulation and Compliance:** Utilizing AI in forensic accounting must align with relevant laws and regulations, particularly concerning data privacy and security. Adhering to these requirements can be complex and time-consuming for organizations.
- **Lack of Resource Requirements:** Implementing AI systems demands significant computational power and expertise. Smaller firms or those with limited resources might need help in adopting and maintaining advanced AI technologies.
- **Limited Context Understanding:** AI systems might struggle to grasp the broader context of financial transactions, potentially leading to misinterpretations of complex relationships and legitimate business activities.

5.2 Analysis of the Study

Implementing AI systems in forensic accounting presents substantial challenges and limitations that necessitate careful consideration. A primary hurdle is acquiring accurate and relevant financial data from diverse sources, as AI's decision-making heavily relies on such information. The interpretability and explainability of AI models are crucial for transparency and legal compliance in forensic accounting. However, many AI algorithms, intense learning ones, need more transparency, making it easier to comprehend their reasoning. Furthermore, the potential for human biases in the training data can lead to biased outcomes, compromising the objectivity required in forensic investigations. Moreover, financial fraud continually evolves, demanding

Figure 2. Challenges and impact of AI in forensic accounting
Source: Prepared by Authors

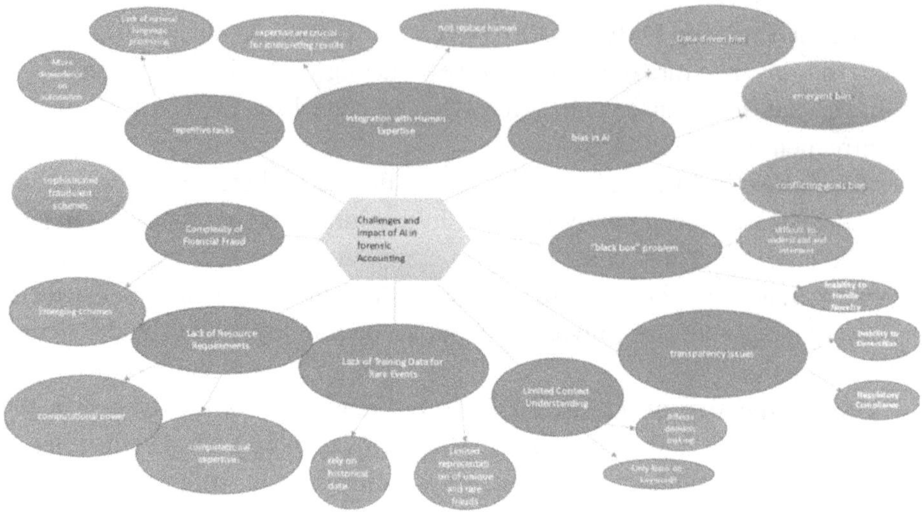

adaptable AI systems that can keep pace with emerging fraudulent techniques. Addressing regulatory compliance, managing resource constraints, and striking the right balance between human collaboration are additional critical challenges that must be addressed to successfully implement AI in forensic accounting. Despite these obstacles, thoughtful integration of AI with human expertise has the potential to enhance fraud detection and improve the efficiency of financial investigations significantly.

This research aims to discuss the challenges and their impact related to using artificial intelligence (AI) by experts in forensic accounting. It highlights the significance of this topic within forensic accounting research, examining existing legal frameworks and proposing potential amendments to the Federal Rules of Evidence to accommodate the integration of AI in courtrooms. Ultimately, the essay concludes by advocating for rule changes that establish standards for AI reliability and argues that the role of forensic accounting experts, as well as other forensic experts, becomes even more crucial in light of these technological advancements to aid the fact-finding process. The authors observe that AI systems are not meant to entirely replace human auditors; instead, they aim to assist in expediently and accurately gathering data, thereby affording auditors more time for tasks necessitating higher-level judgment. AI, mainly through "machine learning," identifies inconsistency in data, such as unanticipated spikes in orders in specific regions, unusually high individual expense items, or favourable terms related to equipment leases from suppliers. Present technology automates repetitive tasks traditionally handled by human auditors, such as analyzing text and images in financial statements. However, accounting firms are progressing towards "natural language processing" to achieve a more advanced level of analysis that comprehends a document's context, utilizing this insight to create financial statements. While some within the accounting field assert that the demand for human accountants remains, others recognize the need for accountants to adapt their skills to this evolving technology. Additionally, opinions vary on whether the demand for entry-level accountants might decline. A positive aspect is that since AI aims to complement specific accounting functions rather than entire jobs, its adoption is expected to progress gradually, causing less immediate disruption.

5.3 Findings of the Study

The research findings on the impact of AI in fraud detection reveal several crucial aspects. Firstly, ethical considerations emerge as a key factor, emphasizing the need for responsible AI implementation to avoid biases and discrimination. Secondly, the transparency and interpretability of AI models play a significant role in building trust and ensuring the system's decision-making process is understandable and reliable. Thirdly, continuous monitoring and updates are essential to keep the AI effective against evolving fraud techniques. Moreover, the study underscores the importance of human oversight in validating AI-generated alerts and handling complex cases that require human judgment. The research also stresses the significance of using high-quality data and robust security protocols to maintain data integrity. Collaboration and knowledge sharing among organizations and authorities emerge as beneficial for improving AI models in fraud detection. Additionally, education and training are shown to enhance decision-making and prevent over-reliance on AI technology. Aligning with legal and regulatory requirements is vital for ethical AI deployment in fraud detection. Furthermore, minimizing false positives is crucial for maintaining the efficiency of fraud detection processes. Lastly, the research highlights the role of accountability and clearly defined responsibilities in ensuring fair and efficient practices when using AI in fraud detection.

Mitigating the negative impact of AI in fraud detection necessitates a responsible and ethical approach. To achieve this, transparency and interpretability of AI models should be prioritized, ensuring that the system's decision-making process is understandable and trustworthy. Continuous monitoring and updates are vital to keep the AI effective against evolving fraud techniques. Human oversight should be integrated into the process to validate AI-generated alerts and handle complex cases. Data quality and security protocols must be robust to protect sensitive information. Collaborative efforts, education, and training can enhance the understanding of

AI's capabilities and limitations. Adhering to legal and regulatory requirements is crucial, and efforts to minimize false positives should be made to optimize the fraud detection process. Clear accountability and defined responsibilities help maintain a fair and efficient system while maximizing the benefits of AI in fraud detection.

5.4 Suggestions

A multifaceted approach is recommended to address and minimize the potential adverse effects of AI in fraud detection. First, adopting explain ability techniques such as Explainable AI (XAI) is crucial. These methods aim to demystify the decision-making processes of AI models, rendering them more comprehensible to human experts and enhancing their trust in the system's outcomes. Second, fostering collaboration between AI systems and human experts is paramount. By capitalizing on AI's efficiency and speed while also leveraging human intuition and contextual understanding, a harmonious synergy that balances automation with accurate detection of fraudulent activities can be achieved. Continuous learning stands as another pivotal strategy. Outfitting AI models with the capacity to adapt and learn from emerging fraud patterns ensures that the technology remains up-to-date and efficacious against evolving tactics employed by fraudsters. Hybrid approaches that combine AI-driven automation with regular human oversight provide an equilibrium between efficiency and precision. While AI expedites processes, human experts critically evaluate complex cases, rectify errors, and infuse situational awareness. Establishing and adhering to ethical guidelines for AI deployment in fraud detection is imperative. These guidelines safeguard against biases, guarantee fairness, and ensure responsible use of technology. Regular audits that evaluate the performance and potential biases of AI models can offer insights into areas of improvement and necessary adjustments. Creating a feedback loop where human experts contribute insights into AI-generated decisions enhances accuracy and performance over time, as their domain expertise complements AI's computational capabilities. Providing education and training to human experts about AI technology enhances their proficiency in working seamlessly alongside AI systems. Benchmarking AI-generated outcomes against human-expert decisions facilitates the identification of disparities, refining AI models and enhancing their alignment with human judgment. Stringent adherence to regulatory compliance ensures that AI systems meet established standards, particularly in transparency and accountability. Employing diverse and representative training data mitigates biases present in AI systems and their outputs, fostering more equitable and accurate fraud detection. Public awareness campaigns are crucial in educating individuals about AI's role in fraud detection, addressing concerns, and building public trust in the technology. By enacting these multifaceted measures, the negative impact of AI in fraud detection can be proactively minimized, allowing the benefits of enhanced automation and accuracy to prevail.

6. CONCLUSION

In conclusion, the results of this investigation illuminate the intricate web of consequences arising from integrating AI into fraud detection. This intricate tapestry comprises a mesh of ethical, technical, and operational factors, each playing a pivotal role in shaping the landscape of fraud prevention. Ethical concerns loom large, accentuating the imperativeness of implementing AI with a strong sense of responsibility. The emphasis here is on mitigating biases and averting discriminatory practices to safeguard fairness within the fraud detection domain. Transparency and interpretability emerge as linchpins in fostering trust and reliability in AI models. It is incumbent upon all stakeholders to be able to comprehend and validate the decision-making mechanisms underpinning these systems. Moreover, this research underscores the ever-evolving nature of fraud and the indispensability of ongoing surveillance and updates to keep AI systems effective against the backdrop of constantly changing fraudulent tactics. Human oversight, we find, remains an irreplaceable component, especially when it comes to verifying AI-generated alerts and addressing intricate cases that necessitate human judgment. The bedrock of this entire endeavour lies in having access to high-quality data and robust security protocols, which are indispensable for maintaining the integrity of data—a fundamental prerequisite for successful fraud detection. A clarion call for collaboration and knowledge-sharing among organizations and regulatory bodies resounds throughout this study, signalling a pathway toward refining AI models in the realm of fraud detection. Education and training, it is revealed, are indispensable tools to empower decision-makers and forestall unwarranted overreliance on AI technology. Conforming to legal and regulatory frameworks is of paramount importance to ensure the ethical deployment of AI in the pursuit of fraud detection. Efficiency emerges as another key consideration, with a pressing need to minimize false positives in order to streamline fraud detection processes. Finally, the study underscores the critical significance of accountability and well-defined roles and responsibilities in upholding equitable and efficient practices when harnessing AI for fraud detection. In summary, the research findings impart invaluable insights to guide organizations and regulatory authorities as they navigate the intricate terrain of AI-driven fraud detection. These insights underscore the necessity of adopting a comprehensive approach that carefully balances technological advancements with ethical considerations and human expertise.

7. FUTURE SCOPE OF THE RESEARCH

The entire financial industry is facing the jolts of generated AI to ensure corporations are able to scale through any eventual arising due to their intervention. Future integration of cutting-edge AI technologies, such as predictive analytics and deep learning, might result in a forensic accounting framework that is more complex and flexible. As these technologies advance, their use in a variety of sectors might transform the identification and avoidance of financial fraud by addressing unique industry-specific issues.

AI's advantages—such as its capacity for greater efficiency and accurate data analysis—make it a potent weapon in the ongoing fight against fraud. However, to guarantee strong data privacy safeguards and mitigate any algorithmic biases, ongoing efforts are necessary.

In order to successfully use AI-driven forensic accounting procedures, ethical concerns and human judgement are essential components, and this collaborative synergy between AI and human knowledge remains crucial. This study provides organizations with more than just insightful information.

REFERENCES

Albrecht, W. S., Albrecht, C. O., Albrecht, C. C., & Zimbelman, M. F. (2018). *Fraud Examination. Cengage Learning.*

Alzahrani, R. A., & Aljabri, M. (2022). AI-Based Techniques for Ad Click Fraud Detection and Prevention: Review and Research Directions. *Journal of Sensor and Actuator Networks*, *12*(1), 4. doi:10.3390/jsan12010004

Aslam, F., Hunjra, A. I., Ftiti, Z., Louhichi, W., & Shams, T. (2022). Insurance fraud detection: Evidence from artificial intelligence and machine learning. *Research in International Business and Finance, 62*, 101744.

Babich, V., Birge, J. R., & Hilary, G. (Eds.), *Innovative Technology at the Interface of Finance and Operations. Springer Series in Supply Chain Management* (Vol. 11). Springer.

Bao, Y., Hilary, G., & Ke, B. (2022). Artificial intelligence and fraud detection. *Innovative Technology at the Interface of Finance and Operations*, *I*, 223–247. doi:10.1007/978-3-030-75729-8_8

Cao, L. (2022). Ai in finance: Challenges, Techniques, and Opportunities. *ACM Computing Surveys*, *55*(3), 1–38. doi:10.1145/3502289

Capraş, I. L., & Achim, M. V. (2023). An Overview of Forensic Accounting and Its Effectiveness in the Detection and Prevention of Fraud. *Economic and Financial Crime, Sustainability and Good Governance*, 319-346.

Caron, M. S. (2019). The transformative effect of AI on the banking industry. *Banking & Finance Law Review*, *34*(2), 169–214.

Chaquet-Ulldemolins, J. (2022). On the black-box challenge for fraud detection using machine learning (ii): nonlinear analysis through interpretable autoencoders. *Applied Sciences, 12*(8), 3856.

Choi, D., & Lee, K. (2018). An artificial intelligence approach to financial fraud detection under IoT environment: A survey and implementation. *Security and Communication Networks*. doi:10.1155/2018/5483472

Cirqueira, D., Helfert, M., & Bezbradica, M. (2021). Towards design principles for user-centric explainable AI in fraud detection. In *International Conference on Human-Computer Interaction*. Cham: Springer International Publishing. 10.1007/978-3-030-77772-2_2

Dhieb, N., Ghazzai, H., Besbes, H., & Massoud, Y. (2020). A secure AI-driven architecture for automated insurance systems: Fraud detection and risk measurement. *IEEE Access : Practical Innovations, Open Solutions*, *8*, 58546–58558. doi:10.1109/ACCESS.2020.2983300

Fawcett, T., Haimowitz, I., Provost, F., & Stolfo, S. (1998). AI approaches to fraud detection and risk management. *AI Magazine*, *19*(2), 107–107.

Ghandour, A. (2021). Opportunities and challenges of artificial intelligence in banking: Systematic literature review. *TEM Journal*, *10*(4), 1581–1587. doi:10.18421/TEM104-12

Jakšič, M., & Marinč, M. (2019). Relationship banking and information technology: The role of artificial intelligence and FinTech. *Risk Management*, *21*(1), 1–18. doi:10.1057/s41283-018-0039-y

Jubb, C. A., Nigrini, M. J., & Mulford, C. W. (2014). Artificial intelligence and the detection of fraud. *Journal of Emerging Technologies in Accounting*, *11*(1), 89–108.

Kaur, D., Sahdev, S. L., Sharma, D., & Siddiqui, L. (2020). Banking 4.0:'The Influence of Artificial Intelligence on the Banking Industry & How AI Is Changing the Face of Modern-Day Banks. *International Journal of Management*, *11*(6). Advance online publication. doi:10.34218/IJM.11.6.2020.049

Kokina & Davenport. (2017). The Emergence of Artificial Intelligence: How Automation is Changing Auditing. *Journal of Emerging Technologies in Accounting, 14*(1), 115–122. doi:10.2308/jeta-51730

Königstorfer, F., & Thalmann, S. (2020). Applications of Artificial Intelligence in commercial banks–A research agenda for behavioural finance. *Journal of Behavioral and Experimental Finance, 27*, 100352. doi:10.1016/j.jbef.2020.100352

Kranacher, M. J., & Riley, R. (2019). *Forensic accounting and fraud examination*. John Wiley & Sons.

Kranacher, M. J., Riley, R. A., & Wells, J. T. (2011). *Forensic Accounting and Fraud Examination*. John Wiley & Sons.

Kumar, S., Aishwarya Lakshmi, S., & Akalya, A. (2020). Impact and Challenges of Artificial Intelligence in Banking. *Journal of Information and Computational Science, 10*(2) 1101–1109.

Lui, A., & Lamb, G. W. (2018). Artificial intelligence and augmented intelligence collaboration: Regaining trust and confidence in the financial sector. *Information & Communications Technology Law, 27*(3), 267–283. doi:10.1080/13600834.2018.1488659

Mehta, K., Mittal, P., Gupta, P. K., & Tandon, J. K. (2022). Analyzing the impact of forensic accounting in the detection of financial fraud: The mediating role of artificial intelligence. In *International Conference on Innovative Computing and Communications: Proceedings of ICICC 2021,* Volume 2 (pp. 585–592). Springer Singapore. 10.1007/978-981-16-2597-8_50

Mhlanga, D. (2020). Industry 4.0 in finance: The impact of artificial intelligence (AI) on digital financial inclusion. *International Journal of Financial Studies, 8*(3), 45. doi:10.3390/ijfs8030045

Mhlanga, D. (2020). Industry 4.0 in finance: the impact of artificial intelligence (AI) on digital financial inclusion. *International Journal of Financial Studies, 8*(3), 45.

Obiora, F. C., Onuora, J. K. J., & Amodu, O. A. (2022). Forensic accounting services and its effect on fraud prevention in Health Care Firms in Nigeria. *World Journal of Finance and Investment Research, 6*(1), 16–28.

Ogunode, O. A., & Dada, S. O. (2022). Fraud Prevention Strategies: An Integrative Approach on the Role of Forensic Accounting. *Archives of Business Research, 10*(7), 34–50. doi:10.14738/abr.107.12613

Okoye, E. I. (2009, November). The role of forensic accounting in fraud investigation and litigation support. In The Nigerian. *The Academy Forum*, *17*(1).

Oladejo, M. T., & Jack, L. (2020). Fraud prevention and detection in a blockchain technology environment: Challenges posed to forensic accountants. *International Journal of Economics and Accounting*, *9*(4), 315–335. doi:10.1504/IJEA.2020.110162

Olaoye, C. O., & Olanipekun, C. T. (2018). Impact of forensic accounting and investigation on corporate governance in Ekiti State. Journal of Accounting. *Business and Finance Research*, *4*(1), 28–36.

OyedokunP.EmmanuelG. (2016). Forensic Accounting Investigation Techniques: Any Rationalization? *Available at* SSRN 2910318.

Pearson, T. A., & Singleton, T. W. (2008). Fraud and forensic accounting in the digital environment. *Issues in Accounting Education*, *23*(4), 545–559. doi:10.2308/iace.2008.23.4.545

Ryman-Tubb, N. F., Krause, P., & Garn, W. (2018). *How Artificial Intelligence and machine learning research impacts payment card fraud detection: A survey and industry benchmark*. Engineering Applications of Artificial Intelligence.

Sharma, D., & Panigrahi, P. K. (2020). Forensic Accounting and Artificial Intelligence: A Review. *Journal of Forensic Accounting Research*, *5*(1), 1–28.

Singleton, T. W., Singleton, A. J., Bologna, J., & Lindquist, R. J. (2019). *Fraud Auditing and Forensic Accounting*. John Wiley & Sons.

Soviany, C. (2018). The benefits of artificial intelligence in payment fraud detection: A case study. *Journal of Payments Strategy & Systems*, *12*(2), 102–110.

Spathis, C., Doumpos, M., & Zopounidis, C. (2018). A survey on accounting and auditing approaches to prevent fraud in the era of artificial intelligence. *Journal of Financial Crime*, *25*(2), 429–448.

Stoica, I., Song, D., Popa, R. A., Patterson, D., Mahoney, M. W., Katz, R., . . . Abbeel, P. (2017). A Berkeley view of systems challenges for AI. *arXiv preprint arXiv:1712.05855*.

Victor Nicholas, A. (2020). The Impact of Artificial Intelligence on Forensic Accounting and Testimony—Congress Should Amend "The Daubert Rule" to Include a New Standard. *Emory Law Journal Online*, *2039*, 1–26. https://scholarlycommons.law.emory.edu/elj-online/3

Vijai, D. C. (2019). Artificial intelligence in Indian banking sector: Challenges and opportunities. *International Journal of Advanced Research*, *7*(5), 1581–1587. doi:10.21474/IJAR01/8987

Vijai, D. C. (2019). Artificial intelligence in Indian banking sector: Challenges and opportunities. *International Journal of Advanced Research*, *7*(5), 1581–1587. doi:10.21474/IJAR01/8987

Wells, J. T. (2011). *Corporate Fraud Handbook: Prevention and Detection*. John Wiley & Sons.

Winston, P. H. (1992). *Artificial intelligence*. Addison-Wesley Longman Publishing Co., Inc.

Zioviris, G., Kolomvatsos, K., & Stamoulis, G. (2022). Credit card fraud detection using a deep learning multistage model. *The Journal of Supercomputing*, *78*(12), 14571–14596. doi:10.1007/s11227-022-04465-9

Zolbanin, H. M., Nabati, M., & Lee, T. S. (2019). Fraud detection in financial statements: A review of artificial intelligence-based approaches. *Computers & Industrial Engineering*, *136*, 621–635.

Chapter 5
Artificial Intelligence in Business:
Negative Social Impacts

Sanjeev Kumar
https://orcid.org/0000-0002-7375-7341
Lovely Professional University, India

Mohammad Badruddoza Talukder
https://orcid.org/0000-0001-7788-2732
Daffodil Institute of IT, Bangladesh

Fahmida Kaiser
https://orcid.org/0009-0002-4113-207X
Daffodil Institute of IT, Bangladesh

ABSTRACT

People who work on artificial intelligence (AI) technologies that directly affect people's social or ethical lives face different types of problems. These include philosophical questions about how possible it is to build ethics into algorithms and technical problems with AI development. One of the challenges is dealing with the ethical and social effects of putting people and technology together. This chapter aims to make a map of the leading social effects of AI and suggestions for how to deal with these effects. AI offers many opportunities for fundamental changes and significant industry improvements. This disruptive technology allows impressive things, like self-driving cars, serving food in restaurants, guiding robots, etc. Many people disagree about how artificial intelligence will affect society, although people believe that AI improves everyday life because it can do simple things, making life easier, safer, and more efficient. Others say that AI is dangerous for privacy, makes racism worse by making people look the same, and puts people out of work by taking their jobs.

DOI: 10.4018/979-8-3693-0724-3.ch005

INTRODUCTION

"Artificial intelligence" (AI) can mean many different things. People use the term to talk about a way to make computers and other machines seem smarter (C. Zhang & Lu, 2021). People think it is a machine made to do men's jobs faster and better. Others see it as "a system" that can take in data from the outside world, figure out what it means, learn from it, and then use that knowledge to do certain things and reach specific goals through flexible goal setting (Misra et al., 2022). There is no doubt that AI will change how people do their jobs. The scary news stories focus on how robots will take away jobs, but the real challenge for people is to find new jobs that value and use their unique skills (Talukder et al., 2023). AI will significantly affect our society, and we need to think about and plan for its many economic, legal, political, and regulatory effects. When a driverless car hurts a pedestrian, it is hard to figure out who is at fault, and it is also hard to stop a global arms race in driverless cars. These are only two things that must be fixed (Gunning & Aha, 2019). Even though it is hard to say how likely this is, it is generally agreed that new technologies always have unintended effects (Briganti & Le Moine, 2020).

The traits and characteristics of each type of artificial intelligence may help in this regard. People will probably all have trouble because of these unexpected effects of AI. The first kind is called constrained AI or weak AI. AI can be made to do things like recognize faces, drive itself, or use Siri to search the internet. AI is used in many systems today, but many are probably just simple AIs that are laser-focused on one clear goal. Some scientists think that weak artificial intelligence could be dangerous if it goes wrong, destroys nuclear power plants, or messes with the electric grid. Artificial general intelligence (AGI), also called artificial intelligence (AI), is the theoretical intelligence of a machine that can understand or learn any intellectual task a human can do, helping humans solve the problem at hand. The long-term goal of many researchers is to make AI, which is essential for everyday life. AGI stands for "artificial general intelligence," which is the same as "artificial intelligence" (AI). Even if humans are better at some things than limited AI, like playing chess or doing math, this is not a big deal (Zhao et al., 2021). Vital artificial intelligence (AI) is different from regular AI in that it can be taught to act like a human mind, to be good at any task that is given to it, and even to have perception, beliefs, and other cognitive abilities that are usually only found in humans. All of these things are used to show what are called "human-like skills." On the other hand, AGI can do better than humans on almost all intelligence tests.

How to stop artificial intelligence from getting so good at what it was made to do that it breaks moral or legal laws is another problem that needs to be solved (Ristiandy, 2020). Even though the primary goal of AI is to help people get better, society would be hurt if AI did this incorrectly, which is possible. People have to think about what motivates them when they make AI systems. The power of artificial intelligence systems comes from the data that goes into them. Our right to privacy is being violated as more and more details about each person's day are collected in seconds, minutes, and hours. If businesses and governments decide what to do with people based on what others know about them, it could lead to social despotism, which is what China's social credit system does.

AI STANDS FOR "ARTIFICIAL INTELLIGENCE"

Artificial intelligence (AI) is the ability of computers to take in information, put it together, and conclude it. This is different from the intelligence shown by humans and other animals (C. Zhang & Lu, 2021). This is done in tasks like speech recognition, computer vision, translating from one language to another, and other input mappings. Artificial intelligence (AI) is when technology, especially computer systems, tries to act like intelligent people. Expert systems, natural language processing, voice recognition, and machine vision are all examples of specific AI applications (Kaul et al., 2020).

Since its establishment as an academic field in 1956, artificial intelligence has undergone several cycles of excitement, disappointment, and funding loss (often called an "AI winter"), new approaches, successes, and renewed financing (Kumar et al., 2024). AI research has explored and rejected numerous methods, including modeling human problem-solving, formal logic, massive knowledge libraries, and brain simulation. Machine learning, which is heavily statistical and mathematical, dominated the discipline in the first two decades of the twenty-first century. This approach has solved many complex problems in industry and academics (Amisha et al., 2019).

HOW DOES AI WORK?

As interest in artificial intelligence (AI) has grown, vendors have been in a hurry to show how AI is used in their products and services. People often think of AI as just technical, like machine learning. AI needs a base of specialized hardware and software to build and train algorithms for machine learning. No one programming language is used mainly for AI, but Julia, Python, R, Java, and C++ all have features that AI developers find helpful (Baidoo-Anu & Owusu Ansah, 2023).

AI systems often take in a lot of labeled training data, which people then use to look for correlations and patterns. These patterns are then used to predict what will happen in the future. In the same way that a chatbot can learn to have honest conversations with people by looking at examples of their text, an image recognition algorithm can learn to recognize and describe things in photos by looking at millions of examples. Making text, photos, music, and other media is possible using generative AI techniques (Baidoo-Anu & Owusu Ansah, 2023).

In AI programming, data is gathered, and rules are made to turn it into knowledge. The rules, sometimes called algorithms, tell computer equipment how to do a particular task in detail. This kind of artificial intelligence programming aims to choose the best way to achieve a particular result (Talukder et al., 2023). The self-correcting function of AI programming tries to improve algorithms over time and ensures the most accurate results. AI creativity uses neural networks, rule-based systems, statistical methods, and other AI technologies to make creative pictures, writings, music, and ideas(Liao et al., 2020).

THE BAD THINGS AI IS DOING TO SOCIETY:

1. AI Could Cause People to Lose Their Privacy

AI is very interested in both data from the past and data from the present. According to Walsh (2023), AI is a warning about "filter bubbles," which are the strange places one could end up in if one does not check an algorithm. Without consumer education to help people decide whether to use AI on edge, where their data can stay private, or in the cloud, where it is always at risk, what people say will become more "on the record." This may have happened accidentally, like when anyone kept getting magician videos after "liking" a particular America's Got Talent clip. The troubling thing is that these algorithms are used without rules in places like healthcare. AI already has problems, such as bias and a lack of technical clarity (Schiliro et al., 2020).

This relationship has existed for ages, with groups not having any influence over one another. Even the most totalitarian governments in the past lacked the technological prowess necessary to effectively spy on and record the private activities of their citizenry(Gupta et al., 2020). This has altered during the last 50 years. Governments and businesses can now gather, store, and process enormous amounts of data about their inhabitants and the citizens of the entire world thanks to the advancement of computers and mass data storage techniques. Even more recently, the creation of data-capable sensors has expanded the possibilities for how, when, where, and what kinds of data can be gathered (Y. Zhang et al., 2021).

Finally, AI businesses, who have long remained impartial in the privacy discussion, have started to see the potential in the data organizations already have.

2. Unemployment

People are starting to worry that automation and AI will change how people work and put people out of work. Because of this, people want to know which jobs robots will do in the future. Some experts say that because of significant changes in the world's jobs, between 75 million and 375 million people (3 to 14 percent of the world's workforce) may change jobs and learn new skills by 2030 (Mutascu, 2021). This shows how different the predictions are, from very optimistic to very pessimistic, and how little agreement there is among business and technology professionals about how the labor market will change. In other words, figuring out how many jobs would be lost might not be easy (Vaishya et al., 2020).

In an industry that is becoming more automated, it will be hard for many governments to ensure that people have the skills and help needed to move to new jobs (Ristiandy, 2020). This is especially important because automation significantly affects low-skilled jobs like office work, construction, and logistics. Since people with less education have fewer job options, the growth of robots and AI threatens low-paying jobs. This flaw in AI could worsen economic inequality and cause many people to lose jobs. As people have seen in the past, economic uncertainty has the potential to pose a significant threat to our democracies by making people less likely to trust democratic institutions and causing widespread dissatisfaction (Ashoori & Weisz, 2019). Considering this, how AI changes the workplace could make people more likely to vote for populist parties and less likely to vote for representative liberal democracies.

3. Insufficient Transparency

Since Al could be wrong in several ways, honesty is essential. The data that has been given may not be complete or may not have been cleaned up well. Another possibility is that the engineers and data scientists mistakenly chose the skewed data sets to train the model (Shen et al., 2023). Because there are so many possible problems, it is hard to find them and figure out why the AI is not working as it should. Even when it is not going well, it does not always matter. Testing and quality assurance tools and processes are used to quickly find bugs during a typical application development process (Larsson & Heintz, 2020).

AI is more than just code, even if some machine learning algorithms are unclear or kept secret because the inventors' business goals depend on it. Mistakes cannot be found by looking at the underlying models. So, people do not know much about any biases or flaws that AI might have. American courts use algorithms to determine if a defendant is "likely" to commit other crimes and decide bail, sentencing, and parole (Alam, 2021). The problem is that the rules and information about how these things work are not very strict. Without enough protections and federal rules that set criteria or require an evaluation, these instruments could weaken the rule of law and limit people's rights.

4. Prejudice and Bias Caused by Algorithms

This brings us to the next topic, "Bia," which is not just a social or cultural problem; it also shows up in technology. When algorithms are given wrong or biased information, people can make the wrong software and other technological things (Mehrabi et al., 2022). AI worsens social and economic inequality and makes race, gender, and age bias in society even worse. People have probably heard about how Amazon uniquely hires people. The algorithm gave applicants one to five stars, like how people review things on Amazon to find prospects using artificial intelligence. Amazon's computer models were trained to evaluate applicants by looking at patterns in resumes sent to the company over ten years (Wan et al., 2021). Because of this, people often preferred male candidates and penalized applications that used the word "women." Bias can lead to accidental or purposeful discrimination (Ferrer et al., 2021). An AI system could be biased in many ways, but it almost always involves private information about protected groups. If the training data set does not have enough examples from the target audience, then some protected groups may be mistreated. For example, suppose people use the whole city, including the poorer neighborhoods, to train an AI system on school performance data from the wealthier neighborhoods. The results may be biased against students from specific ethnic backgrounds (Benlian et al., 2020).

It is commonly known that human decision-making is biased. Some researchers have emphasized how judges' judgments might be unwittingly impacted by their characteristics, and it has been demonstrated that companies offer interviews to applicants with similar resumes but names that are thought to reflect different racial groups at varying rates. Additionally, people are prone to misusing information. Even though a clear connection between credit history and behavior at work has not been proven, businesses may check the credit histories of potential workers in ways that may harm minority groups. Human decisions are also challenging to investigate or analyze because people may exaggerate the elements they take into account or fail to recognize the influences on their decisions, which leaves space for unconscious bias.

5. Profiling by AI Is Not Accurate Enough

AI can describe people in terrifyingly accurate ways. When their ability to gather personal data was tested in a competition, it was found that algorithms to find patterns could predict a user's expected future location by looking at their past location data (Ntoutsi et al., 2020). When the whereabouts of friends and other social acquaintances were considered, the prediction was a lot more accurate. The bad things about AI are sometimes emphasized too much. People might think it does not matter if people find out where one goes because one has nothing to hide. To start, this is probably not entirely right. People could choose to keep their personal information private even if they do nothing wrong or illegal (Tikhamarine et al., 2020). People would not live in a house with glass walls; what about the other places where anyone's teen daughter has lived? Would anyone feel safe if everyone knew where the girl was and what she thought would happen? Without question. Because knowledge is power, when people tell other people something, people lose control over them.

6. Disinformation

Spreading false information is a problem with artificial intelligence. False information comes out of AI (Whyte, 2020). Online bots could make fake texts like news articles that have been changed to support false views or tweets, adding to the worries about misinformation. In the future, targeted disinformation campaigns will use deep fakes more often, putting our democratic processes at risk and dividing society. The Covid-19 outbreak is directly caused by "human exploitation and damage to our natural environment. The AI language tool GPT-3 recently tweeted to dispel doubts about climate change by saying it could not talk about temperature increases because they were no longer happening. The Atlantic, which says that the term "fake news" has become more popular recently, says that online bots and sophisticated fakes could make it hard to tell the difference between fact and fiction (Larsson & Heintz, 2020). This would hurt people's faith in their political systems.

7. The Power of Big IT Companies

Big Tech controls the AI market. Since 2007, Google has bought at least 30 AI companies. These companies work on everything from recognizing faces in photos to giving computers more realistic voices, giving Google a significant market share (Misra et al., 2022). Google is not the only one that controls access. Google, Apple, Facebook, Microsoft, Amazon, and the most prominent Chinese companies spent up to $30 billion on AI research, development, and acquisitions in 2016. This is out of an estimated $39 billion spent worldwide on AI in 2016 (Misra et al., 2022). When companies worldwide take over AI businesses, people risk changing the direction of AI technology in a big way. Because researchers are the best at search, social networks, online shopping, and app stores, these companies almost monopolize user data. So, people are the main places where the rest of the market gets AI. Because of this power imbalance, strong tech businesses could overthrow democratically elected governments.

8. Robots That Cook

Now, robots can cook, which is pretty cool in hospitality (Talukder, 2020a). Even though the technology is expensive in the tourism industry, it may improve over the next few years, just like how automated check-out machines have taken over hospitality (Talukder, 2020b). Even though technology may speed up some things, losing chance meetings with others may make our lives less enjoyable (Tussyadiah, 2020). As technology improves, many tourism and hospitality industry jobs may become obsolete(Talukder& Hossain, 2021). For the few remaining jobs, there may be problems with occupational risks and the problems AI causes. However, did people know that the spouse of the person who created the ATM never uses one? The girlgets her money from the bank instead.

What happens when the automated system's sensors and cameras collect private information about customers and employees? If this kind of customization is allowed, it might be possible to access critical medical information, like records of allergies or illnesses, for which complete anonymity is the only practical solution.

9. Personalized Shopping Might Not Always Be a Good Idea

Amazon knew people were about to buy a pair of white Nikes. Online stores often use AI to give customers personalized recommendations. Keep track of people's browsing habits, preferences, and interests across various companies, apps, and websites (Pillai et al., 2020). AI could help businesses sort through petabytes of data more quickly and smartly to predict how customers will act and give each customer a solution that fits their needs. To give the customer a personalized shopping experience, one must know this much about them. It is more excellent than people expected. Nevertheless, the amount of information digital companies collect about people and their financial interests may be so substantial that people could use that information against us is scary (Liao et al., 2020).

10. Digital Assistants That Can Talk

Most phones have digital voice help, which people use occasionally. Users can find information using voice-activated searches and information returned to them. Many first-world homes now have digital voice assistants that can be used to book train tickets, change the volume on the radio, and send messages to close friends and family (Benlian et al., 2020). However, it is never safe to use them. Digital voice assistants have been accused of secretly recording private conversations, sending them to a random contact in the address book, and sending 1,700 confidential audio files to another user (Benlian et al., 2020).

11. Versatile Housing

Homes are becoming "smart" like smartphones are, with thermostats that remember people's preferences and daily routines so people can welcome us home at the right temperature (Wan et al., 2021). Some refrigerators can suggest wines to accompany someone's dinner and make shopping lists based on what one needs to buy. Smart home devices and appliances work naturally with digital assistants that can be controlled by voice, so people have to turn on more lights, say, "more light."

12. E-Mailing and Sending Messages

Most people send at least one e-mail a day, and often more. Sometimes, people also send many SMS messages and are active on social media (Talukder, 2021). AI's ability to predict text makes it easier to write messages (Hancock et al., 2020). Writing many messages throughout the day might be more accessible(Kaur et al., 2022). This could sometimes lead to exciting talks. Do not think there will be any problems because the words one's computer or phone learns could tell the wrong people much about others.

13. Software That Can Tell Who Is Who

Face recognition features on smartphones and CCTVs in public places have made it easy for people to use facial recognition technology daily. The AI in smartphones is often used to lock and unlock doors (Baidoo-Anu & Owusu Ansah, 2023). The information stays on people's devices, so one must not type in a password or security code. It looks like it is pretty safe. Even if the punishment is worse, there are still people the crime has hurt. Some people could wake themselves up by using their faces to unlock their phones. If the technology is broken, unauthorized people can access the information on phones. Also, it might become common, making it less scary for other people to scan one's face. It is debatable whether or not the device helps stop crime, but "security concerns" are often used to support its use, and it is connected to CCTVs (Pillai et al., 2020). Even a perfect face recognition system that never mistreated some people (like our current systems seem to do) would be wrong. These methods make it harder to keep one's privacy, stay anonymous, and say what anyone wants. When someone is constantly being watched, it is hard to live a whole life, say and debate things that could be controversial or critical of the government, or just be yourself.

14. Software Programs That Stream

After a long day, Netflix and other streaming services help many of us wind down. Based on what one has watched before, the company's recommendation engine, which AI powers, makes suggestions for future shows (including genres, actors, periods, and more) (Kaur et al., 2022). The tool asks about people's viewing habits and the activities people choose. Recommendation algorithms make people less likely to try new things because people are put at risk by letting everyone who looks at someone's computer know what people think about politics or sexuality.

15. AI Could Slow Down the Progress of Society

History shows that risky decisions made by "outliers"—people willing to share new ideas about how the world works—often turn out well for society (Singh et al., 2020). Most AI systems predict the future based on what has happened in the past. AI could make it harder for outliers to change the game's rules and move society forward.

16. AI Could Make It Harder for People to Make Decisions

Even though AI has made people's lives easier, it limits what men can do. AI gives people the tools they need to study and manage people. Because "AI does it better," "AI does not think outside the box," or "AI thinks acting on its own is dangerous," none of these things will make people's lives better. Instead, people will make things worse (Ashoori & Weisz, 2019).

17. If AI Predictions Are Wrong, AI Could Endanger People

The type of data used to teach AI depends on how good the data is. From an industry point of view, this is a problem because training data for real failures of critical systems is often not good enough. A risk exists when wrong predictions lead to things that could be very bad, like industrial accidents or oil spills (Ferrer et al., 2021). This means that "explainable AI" and hybrid AI need to be the top priorities.

18. Hackers Could Use AI to Trick People Into Giving Them Money Through Social Engineering

Hackers have always been better than the rest of us at using technology. Con artists could hurt society if they use deep fakes and deep learning models to trick people into giving them money, personal information, and sensitive intellectual property by pretending to be trustworthy people and businesses. by acting like the people or groups People support (Hacker et al., 2023).

19. AI Threatens the Safety of People

Think about what would happen if AI took over policing, which is in danger of happening now (Ntoutsi et al., 2020). A computer should never do police work. People could be in scary situations if people do not know how to use technology correctly. Some harmful effects could be automatic killing and invasions of privacy. AI can positively impact information technology. Talukder et al. (2022) explained that blue ocean technology improved the hotel industry.

20. High Prices

When a computer can think like a human, the possibilities are mind-blowing. It might take money, time, and other resources (Mutascu, 2021). AI is very expensive because it needs the most up-to-date hardware and software to work and meet its goals.

21. Not Anything Special

One of AI's most significant flaws is its inability to think creatively or outside the box. AI can learn over time with the help of information it has been given and what it has learned in the past, but it cannot use new strategies. A good example is Quill, a robot that writes earnings reports for Forbes (Amisha et al., 2019). Only information that has already been given to the bot is used in these reports. Even though it is impressive that a bot can write an essay independently, the essay does not have the human touch of other Forbes articles.

22. Make People Unresponsive

Artificial intelligence (AI) technology handles most boring and repetitive tasks(Amisha et al., 2019). People use their brains less because people do not have to remember information or solve problems to do their jobs. This addiction to AI could cause problems for people in the future.

23. No Morals

Morality and ethics are essential parts of being human that are hard for AI to copy. Many worry that humans might not be around for much longer if AI develops quickly. The time for AI has come (Vasquez et al., 2014).

24. Emotionless

People learn early on those machines, and robots cannot understand feelings. People need strong team leadership to reach their goals because people are social animals. There is no question that robots are better at their jobs than humans. Human interactions make teams work, and computers cannot replace that (Vasquez et al., 2014).

25. Nothing Has Changed

Artificial intelligence already has built-in knowledge and experience, making it impossible for humans to grow. AI is excellent at doing things repeatedly, but a person must program any upgrades or changes (Whyte, 2020). Even though AI can store infinite information, it is not as accessible or valuable as the human mind. Machines often break down or do strange things when asked to do things not made or designed for. This could have terrible results. Because of this, people cannot give anyone anything typical.

26. Sing Methods of Social Engineering

In a 2018 study on how technology could be abused, social manipulation was found to be one of the most significant risks of artificial intelligence. This worry is getting closer to the truth as politicians depend increasingly on platforms to get their ideas across. For example, Ferdinand Marcos Jr. made a "troll army" on the TikTok app during the last election to get young Filipinos to vote for him (Shen et al., 2023).

The TikTok platform uses AI to fill users' newsfeeds with media-related content people have already seen. Most complaints about the app involve this process and the fact that the algorithm cannot recognize dangerous or misleading content. This makes it hard to believe that TikTok can protect its users from such content(Tussyadiah, 2020).

Deep fakes have spread into the political and social spheres, making it harder to tell what is real and what is not on the internet. Technology makes it easy to change a person's appearance in a picture or video. It has made a nightmare situation where it is hard to distinguish between real and fake news. This allows evil people to spread false information and war propaganda.

CONCLUSION

Uncontrolled AI is to blame for the current AI problems because it does not consider how it will affect society or how resources will be shared. In a free market, it would be silly to think that the pros of data monopolization would be well balanced by the cons of societal problems.

This point of view also says that the issue goes beyond monopolistic power. There is no guarantee that all big tech companies will use different ways to organize and use AI. Antitrust is a helpful tool, but it is not the best or only way to deal with the bad things that could happen because of AI. The focus should be on re-directing technological innovations away from those that increase corporate control through automation and data collection and toward those that give people and employees more options and abilities. Priorities should also be given to the organized collection and management of data and the use of cutting-edge AI techniques to change user behavior, online engagement, and information sharing. How Al acts in the future with their friends and coworkers will affect how he lives in the long run. It will be harder to tell the difference between AI's destructive effects on society in the future than today. The necessary plans and decisions should be made as soon as possible to make things less scary.

REFERENCES

Alam, A. (2021). Possibilities and Apprehensions in the Landscape of Artificial Intelligence in Education. *2021 International Conference on Computational Intelligence and Computing Applications (ICCICA)*, 1–8. 10.1109/ICCICA52458.2021.9697272

Amisha, N., Malik, P., Pathania, M., & Rathaur, V. K. (2019). Overview of artificial intelligence in medicine. *Journal of Family Medicine and Primary Care, 8*(7), 2328–2331. doi:10.4103/jfmpc.jfmpc_440_19

AshooriM.WeiszJ. D. (2019). In AI We Trust? Factors That Influence Trustworthiness of AI-infused Decision-Making Processes. doi:10.48550/ARXIV.1912.02675

Baidoo-Anu, D., & Owusu Ansah, L. (2023). Education in the Era of Generative Artificial Intelligence (AI): Understanding the Potential Benefits of ChatGPT in Promoting Teaching and Learning. SSRN Electronic Journal. doi:10.2139/ssrn.4337484

Benlian, A., Klumpe, J., & Hinz, O. (2020). Mitigating the intrusive effects of smart home assistants by using anthropomorphic design features: A multimethod investigation. *Information Systems Journal*, *30*(6), 1010–1042. doi:10.1111/isj.12243

Briganti, G., & Le Moine, O. (2020). Artificial Intelligence in Medicine: Today and Tomorrow. *Frontiers in Medicine*, *7*, 27. doi:10.3389/fmed.2020.00027 PMID:32118012

Ferrer, X., Nuenen, T. V., Such, J. M., Cote, M., & Criado, N. (2021). Bias and Discrimination in AI: A Cross-Disciplinary Perspective. *IEEE Technology and Society Magazine*, *40*(2), 72–80. doi:10.1109/MTS.2021.3056293

Gunning, D., & Aha, D. (2019). DARPA's Explainable Artificial Intelligence (XAI). *AI Magazine*, *40*(2), 44–58. doi:10.1609/aimag.v40i2.2850

Gupta, R., Tanwar, S., Al-Turjman, F., Italiya, P., Nauman, A., & Kim, S. W. (2020). Smart Contract Privacy Protection Using AI in Cyber-Physical Systems: Tools, Techniques and Challenges. *IEEE Access : Practical Innovations, Open Solutions*, *8*, 24746–24772. doi:10.1109/ACCESS.2020.2970576

Hacker, P., Engel, A., & Mauer, M. (2023). Regulating ChatGPT and other Large Generative AI Models. *2023 ACM Conference on Fairness, Accountability, and Transparency*, 1112–1123. 10.1145/3593013.3594067

Hancock, J. T., Naaman, M., & Levy, K. (2020). AI-Mediated Communication: Definition, Research Agenda, and Ethical Considerations. *Journal of Computer-Mediated Communication*, *25*(1), 89–100. doi:10.1093/jcmc/zmz022

Kaul, V., Enslin, S., & Gross, S. A. (2020). History of artificial intelligence in medicine. *Gastrointestinal Endoscopy*, *92*(4), 807–812. doi:10.1016/j.gie.2020.06.040 PMID:32565184

Kaur, G., Sinha, R., Tiwari, P. K., Yadav, S. K., Pandey, P., Raj, R., Vashisth, A., & Rakhra, M. (2022). Face mask recognition system using CNN model. *Neuroscience Informatics (Online)*, *2*(3), 100035. doi:10.1016/j.neuri.2021.100035 PMID:36819833

Kumar, S., Talukder, M. B., Kabir, F., & Kaiser, F. (2024). Challenges and Sustainability of Green Finance in the Tourism Industry: Evidence from Bangladesh. In S. Taneja, P. Kumar, S. Grima, E. Ozen, & K. Sood (Eds.), Advances in Finance, Accounting, and Economics. IGI Global. doi:10.4018/979-8-3693-1388-6.ch006

Larsson, S., & Heintz, F. (2020). Transparency in artificial intelligence. *Internet Policy Review*, *9*(2). Advance online publication. doi:10.14763/2020.2.1469

Liao, Q. V., Gruen, D., & Miller, S. (2020). Questioning the AI: Informing Design Practices for Explainable AI User Experiences. *Proceedings of the 2020 CHI Conference on Human Factors in Computing Systems,* 1–15. 10.1145/3313831.3376590

Mehrabi, N., Morstatter, F., Saxena, N., Lerman, K., & Galstyan, A. (2022). A Survey on Bias and Fairness in Machine Learning. *ACM Computing Surveys*, *54*(6), 1–35. doi:10.1145/3457607

Misra, N. N., Dixit, Y., Al-Mallahi, A., Bhullar, M. S., Upadhyay, R., & Martynenko, A. (2022). IoT, Big Data, and Artificial Intelligence in Agriculture and Food Industry. *IEEE Internet of Things Journal*, *9*(9), 6305–6324. doi:10.1109/JIOT.2020.2998584

Mutascu, M. (2021). Artificial intelligence and unemployment: New insights. *Economic Analysis and Policy*, *69*, 653–667. doi:10.1016/j.eap.2021.01.012

Ntoutsi, E., Fafalios, P., Gadiraju, U., Iosifidis, V., Nejdl, W., Vidal, M., Ruggieri, S., Turini, F., Papadopoulos, S., Krasanakis, E., Kompatsiaris, I., Kinder-Kurlanda, K., Wagner, C., Karimi, F., Fernandez, M., Alani, H., Berendt, B., Kruegel, T., Heinze, C., ... Staab, S. (2020). Bias in data-driven artificial intelligence systems—An introductory survey. *Wiley Interdisciplinary Reviews. Data Mining and Knowledge Discovery*, *10*(3), e1356. Advance online publication. doi:10.1002/widm.1356

Pillai, R., Sivathanu, B., & Dwivedi, Y. K. (2020). Shopping intention at AI-powered automated retail stores (AIPARS). *Journal of Retailing and Consumer Services*, *57*, 102207. doi:10.1016/j.jretconser.2020.102207

Ristiandy, R. (2020). Bureaucratic disrupsion and threats of unemployment in the Indsutri 4.0 revolution. *Journal of Local Government Issues*, *3*(1). Advance online publication. doi:10.22219/logos.v3i1.10923

Schiliro, F., Moustafa, N., & Beheshti, A. (2020). Cognitive Privacy: AI-enabled privacy using EEG Signals in the Internet of Things. *2020 IEEE 6th International Conference on Dependability in Sensor, Cloud and Big Data Systems and Application (DependSys),* 73–79. 10.1109/DependSys51298.2020.00019

ShenY.SongK.TanX.LiD.LuW.ZhuangY. (2023). HuggingGPT: Solving AI Tasks with ChatGPT and its Friends in Hugging Face. doi:10.48550/ARXIV.2303.17580

Singh, S., Sharma, P. K., Yoon, B., Shojafar, M., Cho, G. H., & Ra, I.-H. (2020). Convergence of blockchain and artificial intelligence in IoT network for the sustainable smart city. *Sustainable Cities and Society*, *63*, 102364. doi:10.1016/j.scs.2020.102364

Talukder, M., Shakhawat Hossain, M., & Kumar, S. (2022). Blue Ocean Strategies in Hotel Industry in Bangladesh: A Review of Present Literatures' Gap and Suggestions for Further Study. SSRN *Electronic Journal*. doi:10.2139/ssrn.4160709

Talukder, M. B. (2020a). An Appraisal of the Economic Outlook for the Tourism Industry, Specially Cox's Bazar in Bangladesh. *I-Manager's Journal on Economics & Commerce*, *1*(2), 24–35.

Talukder, M. B. (2020b). The Future of Culinary Tourism: An Emerging Dimension for the Tourism Industry of Bangladesh. I-Manager's. *Journal of Management*, *15*(1), 27. doi:10.26634/jmgt.15.1.17181

Talukder, M. B. (2021). An assessment of the roles of the social network in the development of the Tourism Industry in Bangladesh. *International Journal of Business, Law, and Education*, *2*(3), 85–93. doi:10.56442/ijble.v2i3.21

Talukder, M. B., & Hossain, M. M. (2021). Prospects of Future Tourism in Bangladesh: An Evaluative Study. I-Manager's. *Journal of Management*, *15*(4), 1–8. doi:10.26634/jmgt.15.4.17495

Talukder, M. B., Kabir, F., Kaiser, F., & Lina, F. Y. (2024). Digital Detox Movement in the Tourism Industry: Traveler Perspective. In Business Drivers in Promoting Digital Detoxification (pp. 91-110). IGI Global.

Talukder, M. B., Kumar, S., Sood, K., & Grima, S. (2023). Information Technology, Food Service Quality and Restaurant Revisit Intention. *International Journal of Sustainable Development and Planning*, *18*(1), 295–303. doi:10.18280/ijsdp.180131

Tikhamarine, Y., Souag-Gamane, D., Najah Ahmed, A., Kisi, O., & El-Shafie, A. (2020). Improving artificial intelligence models accuracy for monthly streamflow forecasting using grey Wolf optimization (GWO) algorithm. *Journal of Hydrology (Amsterdam)*, *582*, 124435. doi:10.1016/j.jhydrol.2019.124435

Tussyadiah, I. (2020). A review of research into automation in tourism: Launching the Annals of Tourism Research Curated Collection on Artificial Intelligence and Robotics in Tourism. *Annals of Tourism Research*, *81*, 102883. doi:10.1016/j.annals.2020.102883

Vaishya, R., Javaid, M., Khan, I. H., & Haleem, A. (2020). Artificial Intelligence (AI) applications for COVID-19 pandemic. *Diabetes & Metabolic Syndrome*, *14*(4), 337–339. doi:10.1016/j.dsx.2020.04.012 PMID:32305024

Vasquez, D., Okal, B., & Arras, K. O. (2014). Inverse Reinforcement Learning algorithms and features for robot navigation in crowds: An experimental comparison. *2014 IEEE/RSJ International Conference on Intelligent Robots and Systems*, 1341–1346. 10.1109/IROS.2014.6942731

Walsh, T. (2023). Will AI end privacy? How do we avoid an Orwellian future. *AI & Society*, *38*(3), 1239–1240. doi:10.1007/s00146-022-01433-y

WanW.KubendranR.SchaeferC.EryilmazS. B.ZhangW.WuD.DeissS.RainaP. QianH.GaoB.JoshiS.WuH.WongH.-S. P.CauwenberghsG. (2021). Edge AI without Compromise: Efficient, Versatile and Accurate Neurocomputing in Resistive Random-Access Memory. doi:10.48550/ARXIV.2108.07879

Whyte, C. (2020). Deepfake news: AI-enabled disinformation as a multi-level public policy challenge. *Journal of Cyber Policy*, *5*(2), 199–217. doi:10.1080/23738871.2020.1797135

Zhang, C., & Lu, Y. (2021). Study on artificial intelligence: The state of the art and future prospects. *Journal of Industrial Information Integration*, *23*, 100224. doi:10.1016/j.jii.2021.100224

Zhang, Y., Wu, M., Tian, G. Y., Zhang, G., & Lu, J. (2021). Ethics and privacy of artificial intelligence: Understandings from bibliometrics. *Knowledge-Based Systems*, *222*, 106994. doi:10.1016/j.knosys.2021.106994

Zhao, S., Blaabjerg, F., & Wang, H. (2021). An Overview of Artificial Intelligence Applications for Power Electronics. *IEEE Transactions on Power Electronics*, *36*(4), 4633–4658. doi:10.1109/TPEL.2020.3024914

Chapter 6
Beyond the Hype:
Unveiling the Harms Caused by AI in Society

Jaskiran Kaur
https://orcid.org/0000-0002-4452-1807
Lovely Professional University, India

Pretty Bhalla
Lovely Professional University, India

Sanjeet Singh
Chandigarh University, India

Amit Dutt
Lovely Professional University, India

Geetika Madaan
https://orcid.org/0000-0001-8141-9935
Chandigarh University, India

ABSTRACT

Artificial intelligence (AI) is a highly disruptive innovation in the 21st century that has gotten a lot of attention from professionals and academicians. AI offers numerous, and previously unheard-of, prospects for significant enhancements and fundamental changes in a variety of industries. Amazing things like driverless vehicles, face recognition payment, guide robots, etc. are now possible because of disruptive technology. More specifically, AI energizes digital business, supports the creation of smart services, and encourages digital transformation. The favourable features of AI, however, are given a lot of attention, whereas the negative aspects of AI, particularly among academia, are little discussed. Given the significance and universality of AI, greater research is warranted to examine the considerable negative effects that AI has on people, organizations, and society. Given the paucity of study on AI's negative aspects, this chapter's goal is to shed light on the possible harm AI could do to society.

DOI: 10.4018/979-8-3693-0724-3.ch006

"Despite the fact that information technology has many advantages for businesses, many researchers have cautioned against its negative aspects. This is also true with AI technologies. It is acknowledged that AI has the potential to create risks for individuals, organizations, and society. Stephen Hawking, a renowned physicist, issued this scary caution: "Success in creating effective AI could be the biggest event in the history of our civilisation. Or the worst. So we cannot know if we will be infinitely helped by AI or ignored by it and side-lined, or conceivably destroyed by it." AI significantly impacts the loss of human decision-making and makes humans lazy. It also impacts security and privacy. 68.9% of laziness in humans, 68.6% in personal privacy and security issues, and 27.7% in the loss of decision-making are due to the impact of artificial intelligence as concluded by a study done in recent times. As AI replaces the need for people to meet face to face for idea exchange, human closeness will gradually diminish. As personal gatherings are no longer required for communication, AI will stand in the gap."

The favourable features of AI, however, are given a lot of attention, whereas the negative aspects of AI, particularly among academia, are little discussed. Given the significance and universality of AI, greater research is warranted to examine the considerable negative effects that AI has on people, organizations, and society. Given the paucity of study on AI's negative aspects, this chapter's goal is to shed light on the possible harm AI could do to society. The methodology for the same would be literature review, case studies, conversations with individuals representing diverse industries through interviews.

1. INTRODUCTION

The decision to travel to a new location doesn't take much contemplation anymore. We no longer need to rely on perplexing address directions; instead, we can just open the map application on our phone and enter our destination.

How does the app discover the best route, the correct directions, and even the existence of obstacles and traffic jams? A few years ago, the only navigation method available was GPS (satellite-based navigation). However, consumers can now have a much better experience in their particular circumstances thanks to artificial intelligence (AI).

"You've probably dealt with one of the most prevalent types of artificial intelligence if you've ever asked Siri to help you find your AirPods or instructed Amazon Alexa to turn out the lights."

There are many definitions of artificial intelligence (AI), but John McCarthy (2007) proposes the following one: "It is the science and engineering of making intelligent machines, especially intelligent computer programs." "Although it is related to the related job of utilizing computers to comprehend human intellect, AI should not be limited to techniques that can be observed by biological means."

The ground-breaking book "Computing Machinery and Intelligence" by Alan Turing, which was released in 1950, however, marks the beginning of the artificial intelligence debate decades before this term. "Father of computer science" Turing poses the following query in this essay: "Can machines think?" Then he proposes a test that has become commonly known as the "Turing Test", in which a human interrogator would attempt to differentiate between a computer-generated and a human-written text response. "Although this test has been under intense criticism since it was published, it nonetheless contributes significantly to the history of AI and continues to be a topic of discussion in philosophy because it makes use of linguistic concepts."

"After that, Stuart Russell and Peter Norvig published Artificial Intelligence: A Modern Approach, which went on to become one of the most influential works on the subject. In it, they explore four potential objectives or definitions of AI, differentiating between computer systems based on their reasoning and thinking vs acting:"

Human approach:

- "Systems that think like humans"
- "Systems that act like humans"

Ideal approach:

- "Systems that think rationally"
- "Systems that act rationally"

Alan Turing's definition would have fallen under the category of "systems that act like humans."

"Artificial intelligence is a topic that, in its most basic form, combines computer science and substantial datasets to facilitate problem-solving. Additionally, it includes the branches of artificial intelligence known as deep learning and machine learning, which are commonly addressed together. These fields use AI algorithms to build expert systems that make predictions or categorize information based on incoming data."

Even to skeptics, "the launch of OpenAI's ChatGPT appears to signal a turning point in the hype cycle that artificial intelligence has seen over the years. The advancements were in computer vision the last time generative AI was this significant, but today it is in natural language processing. Additionally, generative models may also learn the grammar of software code, chemicals, natural photographs, and many other sorts of data in addition to language."

The "potential uses for this technology are still being investigated, but they are expanding daily. But as the excitement surrounding the application of AI in business picks up, discussions about ethics become essential importance."

Artificial intelligence (AI) is a highly disruptive innovation in the twenty-first century that has gotten a lot of attention from professionals and academicians. AI offers numerous, and previously unheard-of, prospects for significant enhancements and fundamental changes in a variety of industries. Amazing things like driverless vehicles, face recognition payment, guide robots, etc. are now possible because of disruptive technology.

More specifically, AI energizes digital business, supports the creation of smart services, and encourages digital transformation. Currently, when businesses seek to apply the digital first approach, AI is regarded as one of the top five developing technologies. Due to the rising sophistication and accessibility of AI technology, it is anticipated that 70% of enterprises will create AI architectures (Goasduff, 2021). There is no doubt that the AI era is upon us. Recently, AI has captured the interest of numerous academics in their respective domains. Numerous researchers have looked into the use of AI in a variety of settings, including information systems (Gursoy et al., 2019), tourism and hospitality (Li et al., 2019), marketing (Syam & Sharma, 2018), and financial management (Culkin & Das, 2017). According to research findings, AI has the ability to alter how businesses connect with their customers and offers greater business benefits (such as boosting efficiency, enhancing effectiveness, and lowering cost).

Despite the fact that information technology has many advantages for businesses, Tarafdar et al. (2013) have cautioned against its negative aspects. This is also true with AI technologies. It is acknowledged that AI has the potential to create risks for individuals, organizations, and society (Alt, 2018). Stephen Hawking, a renowned physicist, issued this scary caution: "Success in creating effective AI could be the biggest event in the history of our civilisation. Or the worst. So we cannot know if we will be infinitely helped by AI or ignored by it and side-lined, or conceivably destroyed by it."

The favourable features of AI, however, are given a lot of attention, whereas the negative aspects of AI, particularly among academia, are little discussed. Given the significance and universality of AI, greater research is warranted to examine the considerable negative effects that AI has on people, organizations, and society.

Given the paucity of study on AI's negative aspects, this chapter's goal is to shed light on the possible harm AI could do to society. The methodology for the same would be literature review, case studies, conversations with individuals representing diverse industries through interviews.

2. HISTORY OF ARTIFICIAL INTELLIGENCE

Are Machines Capable of Thinking?

The idea of artificially intelligent robots became popular in science fiction during the first part of the 20th century. It started with the Wizard of Oz's "heartless" Tin Man and carried on with the humanoid robot that played Maria in Metropolis. By the 1950s, a generation of mathematicians, physicists, and philosophers had become culturally familiar with the idea of artificial intelligence (AI). Alan Turing was a British polymath who studied artificial intelligence and its potential through mathematics. Turing posited that humans solve issues and make decisions by combining reason and accessible information; why can't robots do the same? This served as the rationale for his 1950 study, Computing Machinery and Intelligence, which covered the development of intelligent machines as well as methods for evaluating their intelligence.

"Ancient Greece is when the concept of "a machine that thinks" first appeared. However, significant occasions and turning points in the development of artificial intelligence since the invention of electronic computing (and in relation to some of the subjects covered in this article) include the Table 1."

3. APPLICATIONS OF ARTIFICIAL INTELLIGENCE

"There are numerous, real-world applications of AI systems today. Below are some of the most common use cases:"

- ***"Speech recognition***: It is a capability that employs natural language processing (NLP) to convert spoken words into written ones. It is also known as automatic speech recognition (ASR), computer speech recognition, or speech-to-text. Many mobile devices have speech recognition built into their operating systems to enable voice search (like Siri) and to increase messaging accessibility."
- ***"Customer service***: Along the client journey, online virtual agents are replacing human agents. They provide individualized advise, respond to

Table 1.

1950	Publishing Computing Machinery and Intelligence is done by Alan Turing. Turing, who gained notoriety during World War II by cracking the Nazi ENIGMA code, proposes in the paper to address the subject of "Can machines think?" and introduces the Turing Test to ascertain whether a computer can exhibit the same intelligence (or the outcomes of the same intelligence) as a person. Since then, people have argued over the Turing test's usefulness."
1956	The phrase "artificial intelligence" is first used by John McCarthy at the inaugural AI conference at Dartmouth College. (McCarthy later created the Lisp language.) Allen Newell, J.C. Shaw, and Herbert Simon develop the Logic Theorist later that year, which is the first functioning AI software ever."
1962	Publishing Computing Machinery and Intelligence is done by Alan Turing. Turing, who gained notoriety during World War II by cracking the Nazi ENIGMA code, proposes in the paper to address the subject of "Can machines think?" and introduces the Turing Test to ascertain whether a computer can exhibit the same intelligence (or the outcomes of the same intelligence) as a person. Since then, people have argued over the Turing test's usefulness."
1968	The phrase "artificial intelligence" is first used by John McCarthy at the inaugural AI conference at Dartmouth College. (McCarthy later created the Lisp language.) Allen Newell, J.C. Shaw, and Herbert Simon develop the Logic Theorist later that year, which is the first functioning AI software ever."
1974	Publishing Computing Machinery and Intelligence is done by Alan Turing. Turing, who gained notoriety during World War II by cracking the Nazi ENIGMA code, proposes in the paper to address the subject of "Can machines think?" and introduces the Turing Test to ascertain whether a computer can exhibit the same intelligence (or the outcomes of the same intelligence) as a person. Since then, people have argued over the Turing test's usefulness."
1980	The phrase "artificial intelligence" is first used by John McCarthy at the inaugural AI conference at Dartmouth College. (McCarthy later created the Lisp language.) Allen Newell, J.C. Shaw, and Herbert Simon develop the Logic Theorist later that year, which is the first functioning AI software ever."
1986	Publishing Computing Machinery and Intelligence is done by Alan Turing. Turing, who gained notoriety during World War II by cracking the Nazi ENIGMA code, proposes in the paper to address the subject of "Can machines think?" and introduces the Turing Test to ascertain whether a computer can exhibit the same intelligence (or the outcomes of the same intelligence) as a person. Since then, people have argued over the Turing test's usefulness."
1992	The phrase "artificial intelligence" is first used by John McCarthy at the inaugural AI conference at Dartmouth College. (McCarthy later created the Lisp language.) Allen Newell, J.C. Shaw, and Herbert Simon develop the Logic Theorist later that year, which is the first functioning AI software ever."
1998	Publishing Computing Machinery and Intelligence is done by Alan Turing. Turing, who gained notoriety during World War II by cracking the Nazi ENIGMA code, proposes in the paper to address the subject of "Can machines think?" and introduces the Turing Test to ascertain whether a computer can exhibit the same intelligence (or the outcomes of the same intelligence) as a person. Since then, people have argued over the Turing test's usefulness."

frequently asked questions (FAQs) regarding subjects like shipping, or cross-sell products or make size recommendations to users, altering the way we view user interaction on websites and social media. Examples include virtual agent-equipped messaging bots on e-commerce websites, chat programs like Slack and Facebook Messenger, and jobs often carried out by virtual assistants and voice assistants."

- ***"Computer vision***: With the aid of artificial intelligence (AI), computers and other systems are now capable of extracting useful information from digital photos, movies, and other visual inputs and acting accordingly. It differs from picture recognition jobs in that it can make recommendations. With the use of convolutional neural networks, computer vision is used for radiological imaging in healthcare, photo tagging in social media, and self-driving automobiles in the automotive sector."
- ***"Recommendation engines***: AI algorithms can assist in finding data trends that can be leveraged to create more effective cross-selling strategies by using

historical consumption behaviour data. Online shops utilize this to suggest pertinent add-ons to customers during the checkout process."

- ***"Automated stock trading***: AI-driven high-frequency trading platforms execute hundreds or even millions of deals every day without the need for human participation in order to optimize stock portfolios."

4. "ADVANTAGES AND DISADVANTAGES OF ARTIFICIAL INTELLIGENCE"

"A software that has the capacity for learning and thought is said to have artificial intelligence. Anything that involves a program carrying out a task that we would typically believe a human would carry out qualifies as artificial intelligence. Let's start with artificial intelligence's benefits."

Advantages of Artificial Intelligence

- Reduction in Human Error

"The ability of artificial intelligence to drastically minimize errors and improve accuracy and precision is one of its main benefits. Every decision made by AI is based on data that has already been obtained and a certain set of algorithms. When properly coded, these errors can be eliminated completely."

"Robotic surgery systems, which can carry out complex procedures with precision and accuracy, reduce the risk of human error and improve patient safety in healthcare, are an example of how AI reduces human error."

- Zero Risks

"Another significant benefit of AI is that it allows people to avoid many dangers by delegating certain tasks to AI robots. Machines with metal bodies are resistant by nature and can survive hostile environments, making them ideal for defusing bombs, traveling to space, and exploring the deepest reaches of oceans. Additionally, they can deliver accurate work with more responsibility and durability."

"A fully automated production line in a manufacturing plant is an illustration of zero risks. All work is done by robots, which eliminates the possibility of human error and injury in dangerous situations."

- 24x7 Availability

"Numerous studies have shown that people only work productively for three to four hours each day on average. To balance their personal and professional lives, people also require breaks and vacation time. However, AI can operate continuously without rest. They can multitask with accuracy and think far more quickly than humans can. With the aid of AI algorithms, they can even do difficult repetitive tasks without difficulty.

Example: Online customer care chatbots are an illustration of this, as they may offer customers immediate assistance whenever and wherever they need it. Chatbots may respond to routine inquiries, address difficulties, and refer complex issues to human agents using AI and natural language processing, enabling seamless customer support around-the-clock."

- Digital Assistance

"Digital assistants are used by some of the most technologically advanced businesses to interact with customers, negating the need for human staff. Digital assistants are widely used by websites to deliver content that users have requested. We can have a dialogue with them about our search. Some chatbots are designed in such a way that it is challenging to distinguish between speaking with a human and a chatbot."

"As an illustration, everyone is aware that companies have a customer service team that must respond to questions and issues raised by customers. AI can be used by businesses to develop a chatbot or voice bot that can respond to all of their clients' inquiries."

- New Inventions

"AI is the driving force behind several developments that will help humans solve the bulk of difficult problems in virtually every sector."

"For instance, recent developments in AI-based technology have made it possible for medical professionals to identify breast cancer in a woman at an earlier stage."

"Self-driving cars are a another example of recent discoveries. These vehicles employ a combination of cameras, sensors, and AI algorithms to manage highways and traffic without the need for human input. Self-driving cars have the potential to expand accessibility for those with impairments or restricted mobility while also enhancing

traffic flow and road safety. They are intended to revolutionize transportation and are currently being developed by a number of businesses, including Tesla, Google, and Uber."

- Unbiased Decisions

"Whether we like it or not, emotions are what steer human beings. AI, on the other hand, is emotionless and approaches problems in a very practical and logical way. Artificial intelligence has the enormous benefit of being impartial, allowing for more precise decision-making."

"Example: AI-powered recruitment systems are an illustration of this, which assess job candidates based on their abilities and qualifications rather than their demographics. By removing bias from the hiring process, a more inclusive and diverse workforce is produced."

- Perform Repetitive Jobs

"As part of our regular work, we will perform numerous repetitive duties, such as proofreading documents for errors and mailing thank-you notes, among other things. Artificial intelligence may be used to effectively automate these mundane operations and even remove "boring" work from people's jobs so they may concentrate on becoming more creative."

Example: "An illustration of this is the use of robots in manufacturing assembly lines, which can quickly and accurately execute repetitive operations like welding, painting, and packaging, lowering costs and boosting efficiency."

- Daily Applications

"Today, the internet and mobile gadgets are absolutely necessary for our daily activities. We use several different programs, such as Google Maps, Alexa, Siri, Cortana on Windows, OK Google, as well as other tools like snapping selfies, making calls, and reacting to emails. Using a variety of AI-based methods, we can also predict the weather for the present day and the coming days."

"Example: When you were planned a trip about twenty years ago, you must have gotten directions from someone who had already been there. You only need to ask Google where Bangalore is right now. Bangalore's location and the best path between you and Bangalore will be shown on a Google map."

- AI in Risky Situations

"This is one of the key advantages of artificial intelligence. We can overcome many of the severe limitations that humans encounter by developing an AI robot that can carry out dangerous jobs on our behalf. Whether it is used for traveling to Mars, disarming a bomb, penetrating the deepest parts of the oceans, or mining for coal and oil, it may be used efficiently in every form of natural or man-made catastrophe."

"Take the explosion at the Chernobyl nuclear power plant in Ukraine as an example. At the time, there were no AI-powered robots that could help us lessen the impacts of radiation by managing the fire in its early stages because anyone who came close to the core would have perished in a matter of minutes."

- Faster Decision-Making

"Another advantage of AI is quicker decision-making. AI can assist enterprises in making quicker and more informed decisions by automating some tasks and offering real-time insights. This can be especially helpful in high-stakes situations where decisions need to be made fast and precisely to avoid expensive mistakes or save lives. Example: Using AI-powered predictive analytics in financial trading is an example of a speedier decision-making process. Algorithms can evaluate enormous volumes of data in real time and make well-informed investment decisions more quickly than human traders, which improves returns and lowers risks."

- Pattern Identification

"Another application for AI is pattern recognition. AI may assist companies and organizations in understanding consumer behavior, market trends, and other crucial elements by analyzing enormous volumes of data and identifying patterns and trends. Making better judgments and achieving better business results can be done using this information."

"Example: Machine learning algorithms may find patterns and abnormalities in transaction data to detect and prevent fraudulent conduct, boosting security and minimizing financial losses for people and businesses. This is an example of pattern identification in action."

- Medical Applications

"With applications in everything from drug development and clinical trials to diagnosis and therapy, AI has significantly advanced the field of medicine. Doctors and researchers may evaluate patient data, spot potential health hazards, and create individualized treatment plans with the use of AI-powered tools. Patients may have improved health as a result, and new medical technologies and therapies may develop more quickly."

Let us now look at what are the main disadvantages that Artificial intelligence holds.

Disadvantages of Artificial Intelligence

- High Costs

"It is an impressive achievement when a machine can mimic human intelligence. It can be very expensive and takes a lot of time and resources. AI is highly expensive because it requires the newest hardware and software to function in order to stay current and meet criteria."

- No Creativity

"The inability of AI to learn to think creatively beyond the box is a significant drawback. With pre-fed data and prior experiences, AI is able to learn over time, but it is not capable of taking a novel method. The robot Quill, which can write Forbes earnings reports, is a prime example. Only information that has already been sent to the bot is contained in these reports. The fact that a bot can create an essay on its own is astounding, yet it lacks the human touch found in other Forbes articles."

- Unemployment

"Robots are one use of artificial intelligence that, in some situations, are replacing jobs and raising unemployment. As a result, some assert that there is always a possibility of job loss as a result of chatbots and robots taking the place of people."

"For instance, in certain more technologically advanced countries like Japan, robots are regularly used to replace human resources in industrial enterprises. This is not always the case, though, since it can also give humans more opportunity to work while also displacing them to boost productivity."

- Make People Lazy

"The majority of laborious and repetitive operations are automated by AI technologies. We tend to use our brains less and less because we do not need to memorize information or solve puzzles to complete tasks. Future generations may experience issues as a result of this AI addiction."

- No Morals

"Morality and ethics are significant human traits that can be challenging to include into an AI. Numerous people are worried that as AI develops quickly, humans will one day become completely exterminated by it. The AI singularity is this point in time."

- Emotionless

"We have been taught from a young age that neither machines nor computers have feelings. Humans work as a team, and leading a team is crucial to accomplishing objectives. There is no doubting that when working successfully, robots are superior to humans, but it is also true that human connections, the cornerstone of teams, cannot be substituted by computers."

- No Progress

"Artificial intelligence is a technology that cannot be created by humans since it is pre-programmed with knowledge and experience. AI is good at performing the same work repeatedly, but if we want any modifications or enhancements, we must manually change the codes. AI can store a limitless amount of data, but it cannot be accessed or used in the same way as human intellect."

5. NEGATIVE IMPACT OF AI TO HUMAN EXISTENCE

One saying goes, "Don't feed the snake that can bite you." We are cultivating, accepting, and advancing AI beyond what is essential despite the fact that it is seen to be dangerous for humans. AI poses a threat to people, interpersonal connections, society, and global challenges. According to a research by an expert group led by a professor at Brown, AI has recently made a significant transition from the lab to everyday life, which enhances the need to comprehend any potential drawbacks.

- ***Jobless after AI automation***

There is significant concern regarding AI-powered job automation as AI is adopted in industries like marketing, manufacturing, and healthcare. 85 million jobs are projected to be lost to automation between 2020 and 2025, with Black and Latino workers being particularly vulnerable.

As AI computers become more intelligent and skilled, fewer people will be needed to perform the same tasks. Furthermore, even though 97 million new jobs will be created by AI by 2025, many people won't have the technical skills required for these professions and run the risk of falling behind if companies don't upskill their workforce.

- ***Manipulation of social activities by AI algorithms***

"Anyone who rules the media, rules the mind" An study of the hazards of artificial intelligence's potential abuse from 2018 identified social manipulation as one of the major risks. This concern has materialized as politicians rely more on platforms to push their objectives. For instance, in the most recent election, Ferdinand Marcos Jr. utilized a troll army on TikTok to gain the support of younger Filipinos.

TikTok makes use of an AI algorithm that constantly saturates users' newsfeeds with content associated with previously viewed video on the platform. Criticism of the app focuses on this process and the algorithm's incapacity to sift out harmful and deceptive information, raising questions about TikTok's ability to protect its users from such content. Online media and news have become even murkier in light of deepfakes infiltrating political and social spheres.

- ***Application of AI to social surveillance***

In addition to the greater grave threat posed by AI, revolutionaries are focusing on how it will badly affect privacy and security. A notable example is how face recognition technology is used in China's companies, schools, and other contexts. "In addition to tracking a person's travels, the Chinese government may be able to gather enough data to maintain tabs on their relationships, political beliefs, and activities."

"Another illustration is how U.S. police departments employ predictive policing algorithms to identify crime hotspots. The problem is that these algorithms are impacted by arrest rates, which disproportionately affect Black areas. The outcome is over policing and questions about whether self-declared democracies can thwart the emergence of AI as a tool of authoritarian rule. Police agencies then step up their efforts in these neighbourhoods."

- ***Artificial intelligence-related bias***

"Prejudice of various kinds against AI is also detrimental. In an interview with the New York Times, Olga Russakovsky, a professor of computer science at Princeton, asserted that bias in AI goes far beyond racial and gender issues. AI was developed by people, and people are biased by nature. Algorithmic bias may "amplify" the consequences of data bias."

"A.I. researchers are primarily people who are male, who come from certain racial demographics, who grew up in high socioeconomic areas, and are predominantly people without disabilities," said Russakovsky. "Because of our relatively homogeneous population, it can be difficult to think broadly about global issues."

"The lack of expertise among AI developers may be the reason why speech-recognition AI often struggles to recognize certain dialects and accents, or why businesses neglect to take into account the repercussions of a chatbot mimicking prominent characters from human history. Businesses and developers should take more precautions to prevent the reproduction of strong biases and prejudices that endanger minority communities."

- ***Increasing socioeconomic inequity due to AI***

"If businesses do not acknowledge the prejudices ingrained in AI algorithms, they risk jeopardizing their hiring goals. The idea that AI can assess a candidate's qualities through speech and visual analysis is nonetheless tainted by racial preconceptions, mirroring the discriminatory hiring practices that businesses claim to be doing away with."

"Another cause for concern is the growing social divide brought on by employment losses caused by AI, which highlights the class biases of AI use. The income of blue-collar workers who perform more repetitive, manual tasks has reduced by up to 70% as a result of automation. On the other hand, white-collar workers have largely experienced no change, and some are even earning more."

"Claims that AI has reduced social barriers or promoted employment in some way are too broad to encompass all of its effects. Variations based on race, class, and other characteristics must be taken into account. Otherwise, it becomes more challenging to pinpoint how automation and AI benefit some individuals and businesses at the expense of others."

- ***Ethics and good will weakening due to AI***

"Religious leaders have joined engineers, journalists, and politicians in raising concerns about the possible socio-economic drawbacks of AI. Pope Francis cautioned about AI's propensity to "circulate tendentious opinions and false data" at a 2019 Vatican summit themed, "The Common Good in the Digital Age," and emphasized the broad repercussions of allowing this technology to evolve without sufficient monitoring or constraint."

He said, "This would unfortunately result in a regression to a form of barbarism determined by the law of the strongest if mankind's so-called technological progress were to become an enemy of the common good."

"Due to ChatGPT's rapid expansion, these concerns have gained more significance. Technology has been widely used by users to get out of writing assignments, threatening both originality and academic integrity. OpenAI employed poor Kenyan employees at cheap rates to do the assignment even though there were attempts to make the device less hazardous."

"Some individuals are concerned that if there is money to be made, we will keep pushing the limits of artificial intelligence regardless of how many powerful people warn of its dangers."

"If we can do it, let's try it; let's see what happens," Messina remarked of the approach. "And if we can profit from it, we'll do a lot of it." It's not only technology, however. That has been occurring for ages.

- ***Artificial intelligence-powered autonomous weapons***

"Technology developments have been used in conflict, as is all too often the case. Some people are eager to take action on AI before it's too late: Over 30,000 people, including AI and robotics academics, protested the funding of autonomous weapons in a 2016 open letter."

"The most important decision facing mankind right now is whether to begin a global AI weapons competition or to stop it from happening, they argued." "The outcome of this technological trajectory is clear: autonomous weapons will become the norm. "Lethal Autonomous Weapon Systems, which autonomously find and kill targets while following by few rules, are proof that my prediction was accurate. If any major military power pursues the development of AI weapons, a global arms race is essentially inevitable. Due to the creation of powerful and sophisticated

weapons, some of the most powerful nations in the world have caved in to anxieties and contributed to a technical cold war."

"When autonomous weapons fall into the wrong hands, the threat grows, yet many of these modern weapons present serious risks to ground dwellers. It's not hard to imagine a bad actor hacking into autonomous weapons and wreaking complete havoc because hackers have perfected a range of cyberattack strategies."

If political rivalries and aggressive tendencies are not reined in, artificial intelligence may end up being utilized for the worst purposes.

- ***AI algorithms' role in financial crises***

The financial industry has become more amenable to using AI technology in everyday banking and trading activities. As a result, algorithmic trading may be to blame for our next major financial market disaster.

AI algorithms do not take into consideration settings, market interconnectedness, or factors like human trust and fear, despite the fact that they are unaffected by human emotions or judgment. Then, at a dizzying pace, these algorithms carry out hundreds of transactions with the goal of short-term selling for minor gains. Selling tens of thousands of transactions might scare away investors, who would then follow suit, leading to sharp drops and extremely turbulent markets.

Not that AI won't benefit the banking sector in some way. Actually, AI algorithms may help investors make wiser and more informed market decisions. However, financial businesses need to be certain that they are aware of their AI algorithms and the thought processes that went into them. To avoid triggering investor concern and a financial crisis, enterprises should evaluate if AI boosts or diminishes their confidence before incorporating the technology.

AI still offers several benefits, like the ability to organize health data and develop self-driving cars. Others, however, claim that significant regulation is necessary in order to properly capitalize on this potential technology.

Harms to Society

While artificial intelligence (AI) has the potential to significantly improve technology, there are worries about the possible negative effects on society that come with its broad use. The effect on employment is one important concern. There is a chance that employment will be lost as AI systems advance, especially in repetitive and routine work. When a portion of the population finds it difficult to adjust to the shifting work market, this can result in unemployment and economic disparity as some professions become outdated.

An other grave worry is the possibility of partiality in decision-making. Since AI systems are educated on historical data, they may reinforce or even worsen preexisting socioeconomic disparities if that data contains biases. Hiring procedures, criminal justice systems, and financial services are just a few areas where this prejudice might appear and produce unjust and discriminatory results.

Concerns about privacy are also quite real. Because AI systems frequently require enormous volumes of data to function well, there are worries over the unlawful gathering and usage of personal data. People's privacy rights could be violated when AI apps become more pervasive in daily life, which could result in problems with surveillance and the possibility of sensitive data being misused.

Another issue is security risks. AI systems are becoming more and more common, which makes them desirable targets for cyberattacks. When AI is used in critical infrastructure, malicious actors may be able to use its weaknesses to influence the system for evil intent, such as disseminating false information, committing financial fraud, or even causing physical harm.

The creation and application of artificial intelligence raises ethical questions, especially when it comes to potentially deadly autonomous weapons and self-driving cars. When mishaps or moral quandaries happen, questions regarding accountability and responsibility surface. Liability for AI-related occurrences is a complicated issue for legal and ethical frameworks, particularly when AI functions without direct human participation.

In conclusion, even though AI has a great deal of potential to benefit society, it is imperative to recognise and reduce any potential risks. This necessitates giving significant thought to problems like employment displacement, biassed decision-making, invasions of privacy, security threats, and moral ramifications. AI development and use require a thorough and responsible approach to guarantee that the positive effects of this technology are maximised while limiting the negative effects on society.

Ways to Mitigate Risks of Artificial Intelligence

Limiting AI risks is essential for ensuring safety, encouraging trust, addressing ethical concerns, foreseeing future barriers, conforming to laws, generating positive social effects, and forging international collaboration. By taking preventative measures, we can harness the power of AI while lowering risks and raising benefits.

- Create international and domestic regulations.
- Create organizational standards for using AI.

- Effective data governance.
- Mitigation and detection of bias.

6. CONCLUSION

In summary, exploring "Beyond the Hype: Unveiling the Harms Caused by AI in Society" exposes a complex environment in which major obstacles coexist alongside the promises of artificial intelligence. Our attention and proactive mitigation are required due to the potential hazards that AI poses as it infiltrate all facets of our existence.

The threat of automation-related unemployment highlights the need for strong social safety nets and reskilling. Because uncorrected bias reinforces societal imbalances, addressing biases in AI systems is not only a technological difficulty but also a moral obligation. Data governance and user rights must be reevaluated in light of privacy issues in order to guarantee that the convenience provided by AI does not come at the expense of personal freedoms.

Security flaws highlight the necessity of strong cybersecurity defences against the malevolent use of AI systems. Clear frameworks for accountability and responsibility are necessary in light of ethical concerns surrounding the deployment of AI, particularly in the areas of autonomy and decision-making.

As we navigate the difficult landscape of AI integration, it is obvious that a balanced approach is required. While aggressively attempting to reduce its negative consequences, we also need to fully utilise AI's transformational potential. We can properly negotiate this technical frontier by setting ethical principles, encouraging interdisciplinary collaboration, and regularly reevaluating regulatory frameworks. This will ensure that the potential benefits of AI are maximised and the potential drawbacks are carefully managed.

REFERENCES

Ahmad, S. F., Han, H., Alam, M. M., Rehmat, M., Irshad, M., Arraño-Muñoz, M., & Ariza-Montes, A. (2023). Impact of artificial intelligence on human loss in decision making, laziness and safety in education. *Humanities & Social Sciences Communications*, *10*(1), 1–14. doi:10.1057/s41599-023-01787-8 PMID:37325188

Alt, R. (2018). Electronic markets and current general research. *Electronic Markets*, *28*(2), 123–128. doi:10.1007/s12525-018-0299-0

Culkin, R., & Das, S. R. (2017). Machine learning in finance: The case of deep learning for option pricing. *Journal of Investment Management, 15*(4), 92–100.

Goasduff, L. (2021). *While advances in machine learning, computer vision, chatbots and edge artificial intelligence (AI) drive adoption, it's these trends that dominate this year's Hype Cycle*. Retrieved October 8, 2021, from https://www.gartner.com/en/articles/the–4–trends–that–prevail–on–the–gartner–hype–cycle–for–ai–2021

Gursoy, D., Chi, O. H., Lu, L., & Nunkoo, R. (2019). Consumers acceptance of artificially intelligent (AI) device use in service delivery. *International Journal of Information Management, 49*, 157–169. doi:10.1016/j.ijinfomgt.2019.03.008

Kamath, S. (2022). A Study on the Impact of Artificial Intelligence on Society. *International Journal of Applied Science and Engineering, 10*(1). Advance online publication. doi:10.30954/2322-0465.2.2021.3

Li, J., Bonn, M. A., & Ye, B. H. (2019). Hotel employee's artificial intelligence and robotics awareness and its impact on turnover intention: The moderating roles of perceived organizational support and competitive psychological climate. *Tourism Management, 73*, 172–181. doi:10.1016/j.tourman.2019.02.006

McCarthy, J. (2007). *What is artificial intelligence*. Academic Press.

Russell, S. J., & Norvig, P. (2014). Artificial Intelligence: A Modern Approach. *Industrial Marketing Management, 69*, 135–146. doi:10.1016/j.indmarman.2017.12.019

Tarafdar, M., Gupta, A., & Turel, O. (2013). The dark side of information technology use. *Information Systems Journal, 23*(3), 269–275. doi:10.1111/isj.12015

Top Advantages and Disadvantages of Artificial Intelligence. (2021, February 25). Simplilearn.com. https://www.simplilearn.com/advantages-and-disadvantages-of-artificial-intelligence-article

Turing, A. M. (2009). *Computing machinery and intelligence*. Springer Netherlands.

Chapter 7
Cyber Security Challenges and Dark Side of AI:
Review and Current Status

Nitish Kumar Ojha
https://orcid.org/0000-0002-2236-0766
Amity University, Noida, India

Archana Pandita
https://orcid.org/0000-0003-2927-637X
Amity University, Dubai, UAE

J. Ramkumar
https://orcid.org/0000-0001-9639-0899
Sri Krishna Arts and Science College, India

ABSTRACT

Experts believe that cyber security is a field in which trust is a volatile phenomenon because of its agnostic nature, and in this era of advanced technology, where AI is behaving like a human being, when both meet, everything is not bright. Still, things are scarier in the next upcoming wave of AI. In a time when offensive AI is inevitable, can we trust AI completely? In this chapter, the negative impact of AI has been reviewed.

INTRODUCTION

Reminiscent of the year 1982 science fiction film '*Blade Runner*', in which the protagonist is dismayed to discover that the one he loves is not a human but a mutant. It was just a glimpse of what and how technology can do and up to which

DOI: 10.4018/979-8-3693-0724-3.ch007

level. One vector of IT is Artificial Intelligence (AI) which is leading these days and has become the driving force of technology. AI is changing each segment of our daily life be it financial operation content writing online games or entertainment, no area of human life is untouched by the enormous growth of AI. This growth is so enormous that every age group is touched by AI in real life. The problem starts here as it is leading like a double-edged sword posing algorithms for better learning, production, prediction, detection, decision making, designing, planning, etc. but with negative impact in every sector where it is leading. Most of us encounter artificial intelligence in some way or the other almost every day. From the moment you wake up to check your smartphone, you start experimenting and experiencing AI. But what exactly is AI? Will this benefit mankind in the future? Well, Artificial Intelligence has lots of advantages and disadvantages. At the same time. Artificial intelligence is one of the best technologies in the world. It is made up of two words 'Artificial' and 'Intelligence'. It means "human-made thinking power. With the help of this technology, such a system can be created, which will be equal to human intelligence i.e., intelligence. Through this technology, learning algorithms, recognition, problem-solving, language, logical reasoning, Digital data processing, bioinformatics, and machine biology can be easily understood. Apart from this, this technology itself is capable of thinking, understanding, and working (Linardatos et al., 2020).

Artificial Intelligence Was Created in 1955

In 1955, John McCarthy officially introduced this technology. Artificial Intelligence was named. Let us tell you that John McCarthy was an American computer scientist. He defined Artificial Intelligence to make machines smart.

According to a study by Statista, the global AI market is set to grow by 54 percent every year [Statista Report 2022]. A report by Kaspersky Lab brings up the fact that technology and its negative effects go hand in hand and will grow in the future as the trends indicate (Rangone, 2023).

Type of AI

Reactive machines-based AI - These robots cannot retain historical data and do not base their judgments on previous experiences. It reacts by storing a small amount of data. For instance, IBM's "Deep Blue" chess-playing supercomputer upset legendary chess champion Garry Kasparov in 1997. The supercomputer could not store memory. Deep Blue controlled the game by observing the opponent's current move. (De Mántaras et al., 2023)

Limited Memory-supported AI - This type of artificial intelligence saves information from the past and utilizes it to predict future actions. Interestingly, this system has the capacity for independent learning and decision-making.

Theory of Mind-based AI - Machines using this form of artificial intelligence have surpassed the human brain's capabilities. Many machines are currently employed as voice assistants. This kind, of work, is currently being done at a high level in industries.

Self-Conscious sourced AI - The development of this kind of artificial intelligence is ongoing. According to scientists, Robots will eventually understand what life is like for humans once this system is in place. There won't be any distinction between humans and machines after this (Varriale et al., 2023).

How AI Works

Machine learning includes artificial intelligence. This method is supported by both hardware and software, making the algorithm simple to comprehend. AI does not equate to any particular programming language. Three abilities are the basis of artificial intelligence.

1. **Learning Process –** The main goal of artificial intelligence is to take data and create rules to turn it into accurate knowledge. Algorithms are what we call them. The computer system uses these algorithms to do tasks.
2. **Reasoning Process –** Artificial intelligence uses this ability to choose the best algorithm to provide the intended outcome.
3. **Self-Correction Process –** The algorithm is automatically corrected by Artificial Intelligence using this expertise, ensuring that consumers receive accurate results (Yan et al., 2023).

Benefits of AI

The medical sector of the country is going to benefit the most from Artificial Intelligence technology. With this technology, all the work like X-ray reading will become easy. Doctors will get help in research. Not only this but patients can also be treated in a better way with artificial intelligence. The field of sports will also benefit a lot with the help of artificial intelligence. Players will be able to keep an eye on their performance through this technology. Apart from this, people will get the facility to understand the game easily with technology. Artificial intelligence will benefit a lot from schools and colleges for people in the field of agriculture. On the one hand, artificial intelligence (AI) has the potential to automate time-consuming and repetitive jobs, freeing humans to concentrate on harder and more creative work. with fields like health care and transportation, it may aid with decision-making, error prevention, and safety (Berényi & Deutsch, 2023).

However, as more organizations automate routine work, uncontrolled AI adoption might potentially result in employment losses. Economic inequality may result from this, particularly in sectors where technology is replacing human labor.

Additionally, privacy and civil rights issues are brought up by the use of AI in fields like surveillance and face recognition. We must think about how AI will affect society as it advances and gets more sophisticated. To guarantee that it is, consider it and establish rules, in this way, AI is making people aware of their rights too. Not only this but there are also many segments where AI is playing a key role in a very beneficial manner. Compared to manual labor, artificial intelligence has a lower error rate since these machines are well-coded and leave no space for mistakes. Contrary to humans, machines can work continuously without needing a break. they can operate more quickly and efficiently than humans by continually performing the same activity. AI can better assist us by anticipating our needs and assisting us accordingly. performs and facilitates labor, for instance; When we type on smartphones, predictive text and auto-correcting grammar are shown. We can simply organize our data and methodically maintain our records with the use of AI so that we can check them back (Kushal, 2023).

The Dark Side of AI

We have been reading many fiction stories from the last few decades that the day will come when computers rule humans. Machines are mindless, if they get into the wrong hands, they can cause havoc and prove dangerous to the community. With the advent of artificial intelligence, unemployment will increase the most, because, in the coming times, work will be done by machines instead of humans.

Thankfully, just as there are chatbots that generate text, there are programs that verify whether a text is written by a human or an AI. But as Large Language Models (LLMs) become more powerful, this gap is bound to close sooner or later. Such a situation may also come that we cannot tell who what is and who has written what. Wouldn't then the distinction between humans and machines also completely disappear? This is the paradox and conundrum of AI (Taylor, 2023).

Will it become more human than humans and eventually take our place? The way concerns have been raised on the question of artificial intelligence over the past few months, and the way 30,000 netizens wrote a letter in March demanding a halt to giant AI experiments, forces us to confront this question. Can AI become a challenge to the future of humanity? Geoffrey Hinton, who is called the Godfather of AI, warned about the dangers of fast-growing AI. The challenge, he said, is not whether AI's human-like capabilities can compete with us. The main concern is that it would be a very different kind of intelligence than ours, one that might challenge what it means to be human. In his letter, Hinton wrote, that AI labs are more involved than ever in a blind race to create powerful digital brains that even their creators can neither understand nor control (Schmidt, 2023).

We could not have predicted how quickly artificial intelligence (AI) would advance. Technology experts have frequently stated that developments in AI are advancing in a very fast manner and things that are anticipated to occur in the future are already taking place. According to some experts, the rapid development of AI is advantageous and will facilitate our ability to learn and adapt. Some caution against AI's risks and assert that society may not be ready for it yet. Artificial intelligence will resemble human intelligence by 2030, according to Ray Kurzweil. Next comes 2045 after this self-decision-making capability can be expected in AI-supported technologies (Buttazzo, 2023).

By doing this, we can multiply the intelligence of our civilization—the intelligence of the human biological machine—billions of times".

LITERATURE REVIEW

The severity and effect of AI in a negative direction have been a serious concern of the scientific community for a long time. The very relevant work was reported by Solon et al. where it was pointed out that algorithms must be used only for ethical purposes but at the same time this is also a challenging task to define ethics it it is a relative phenomenon in many aspects (Leaver & Srdarov, 2023). Michal et al. raised ethical concerns about the potential misuse of AI in predicting sensitive personal attributes from facial images. Moving further, Gorwa et al. explored the privacy challenges in machine learning systems and the potential risks to individuals' data privacy (Gorwa et al., 2020). Data and its related issues such as privacy, integrity, and availability has been an issue of discussion too because it can be misused and abused and has multifold effect in many terms on its users. Few papers highlighted how AI systems can inherit and perpetuate biases present in the data they are trained on, leading to ethical concerns about fairness and discrimination (Boulianne et al., 2023). Few works have been observed in the field of wrong or malicious forecasting too. Potential malicious uses of AI, including cybersecurity threats, autonomous weapons, and social manipulation are quite possible and its negative effect has been noted down in the research world. Going ahead, a highly talked about topic is job replacement by AI and in this field the work done by Katija et al. reports the potential impacts of AI on employment, job displacement, and societal implications, raising concerns about economic inequality (Katija et al., 2022). In another similar paper, expert opinions were also explored when AI might surpass human capabilities across various tasks and the societal implications of such advancements. There are other papers in this direction and on a larger canvas, they shed light on different facets of the ethical, societal, and potential risks associated with AI and machine learning systems. They underscore the importance of responsible AI development and the need for ethical guidelines to govern their use.

It can be classified into two categories where AI is affecting in an unethical manner which can be termed as areas of the dark side –

TECHNOLOGY-RELATED AREAS

These can be classified into the following categories:

1. **Risk in data dependency and Decision Making –** These academics have attempted to define AI as a threat to humanity in the same way as pandemics and nuclear war are. The Centre for AI Safety has also provided instances to illustrate the potential dangers of AI in the future. One can create an AI weapon. For instance, chemical weapons can be made using drug discovery technologies. AI has the potential to spread false information and undermine civilization. There is a significant chance that this will impede our capacity for making group judgments. Another risk is that just a small number of individuals will be able to use artificial intelligence's full potential. The risk of this is that in such circumstances, a small number of people can impose their beliefs using oppressive means ("Money, Power," 2023). It can be further divided into two categories -
    a. **Data Security-related challenges** – can be classified into the following categories.
        i. **People-based risks generated by AI:** There are two examples where AI-based risk is involved when a wrong decision is made. The first case includes the wrong identification of a cancerous patient by Watson's computer. IBM's Watson, a medical tool, was repurposed to recommend cancer treatments, but its claims were unfounded due to biased training data, insufficient development time, and AI failure (Elish & Boyd, 2017).
        ii. **Process-based risks generated by AI**: A very famous case study includes the decision-making by AI-based systems in Amazon computers. Amazon, a leading eCommerce company, introduced an AI-based recruitment tool in 2014 to assess applicant resumes

and recommend the best candidates. However, the tool was found to favor male candidates over female ones, reflecting the skewed sex ratio in the IT industry. Amazon discontinued the project a few years after its launch due to its negative impact on the company's reputation. The tool's introduction was a significant setback for Amazon (Jiang et al., 2017).

b. **Network Security related challenges** – In cyber security, lots of data exchange is possible using different channels such s Zigbee, Bluetooth, IEEE 802.11X, etc. and because of their vulnerabilities, these devices and channels pose different issues which attract different attacks and hackers can learn about its pattern using AI. These risks can be further classified as:

   i. **Privacy-based risks generated by AI:** Work is becoming easier with the help of Artificial Intelligence, for which we use Alexa Siri and Google Assistant to collect the private data of all the users. When AI collects personal data, it is necessary to ensure that the collection, use, and processing of such data comply with the GDPR, which is highly unlikely because the use of this data varies across applications, making each level of monitoring of data is not possible and the possibility of its misuse increases (Li et al., 2019).

   ii. **Attack on Stored Data and use of AI:** With the ability to analyze large amounts of data, AI can be used to monitor individuals in ways that were previously impossible, including tracking their movements, monitoring their social media activity, and even That also includes analyzing their facial expressions and other biometric data. This was a problem with the old technology that the cameras used to do only passive recording i.e. the data footage was used only as evidence whereas now along with storing the data for a long time, it is completely analyzed which is why this The point is to identify which person is suspicious and what are the patterns of other people. There is also a big danger regarding the storage of data, which also includes the rate that the possibility of attack on the stored data is very high (Ansari et al., 2022).

   iii. **Monitoring and Surveillance involving AI:** Another area of concern is the use of AI for surveillance and monitoring purposes. For example, facial recognition technology has been used by law enforcement agencies to identify suspects and track individuals in public places. This raises questions about the right to privacy and the possibility of misuse of these technologies. There is also a concern that AI systems could perpetuate existing biases and discrimination.

That is, which person is collecting what type of data for which purpose and whether permission is being taken from the person whose data is being collected or not. If the data used to train an AI system contains preference biases, the system may learn and retain those biases. This could have serious consequences, especially in areas like employment, where AI algorithms can be used and misused to make hiring decisions.

iv. **Ignorance of Consent while using AI:** Whenever data is collected in any monitoring device, the user's consent is taken and is generally followed, but when that data is analyzed and that data is sold to a third party, then many of the rules are kept relaxed so that user data can be thoroughly analyzed. Due to various variations and changes in analysis levels, a word like consent loses its meaning and the user has gone far away from that data. Consent is no longer as powerful a tool as one might be led to believe, even though the requirements for consent are that it be informed and freely given. The Clearview AI example shows that consent was not sought as often as it should have been, but after a point that data was used in a variety of ways consent no longer meant anything. As a similar example, Microsoft deleted its database of 10 million facial photographs – which was being used by organizations such as IBM, Panasonic, Alibaba, military researchers, and Chinese surveillance firms – because the faces of the people in the dataset were Most of them had no idea that their images were included and what is also important here is that if Microsoft did remove but what did the groups that took this data from Microsoft remove? These are all such questions that need to be addressed and it is extremely important to give more freedom to the users so that their trust in consent remains intact even in this era of AI (Wahl et al., 2018).

v. **Risk because of Generative AI:** In general, the concept of personal information depends on the idea of identification, i.e. how is the individual being identified? Now it depends on what type of credentials the person has used to connect to that system. If an email ID has been used, then a person's profile can be created very easily by linking it to the email ID and the person is using the same email ID at many places, which can make his tracking very easy. However, the distinction between what is 'personal' and what is not considered 'personal' is being challenged by the increasing ability to link and match data from individuals, even where initially ' It was considered 'de-identified' or non-identified, but now almost all

> the applications are asking for email ID. This means that a digital profile of every person is being created which will be used by these companies as per their choice, which is a threat. As the amount of data available increases, and the techniques of processing and combining it improve, it becomes increasingly difficult to assess whether a given piece of data is 'identifiable' or not; And where has that user's information been used in shorter or encrypted form? This is not a true reflection of whether or not it can be considered 'personal information' (Brynjolfsson et al., 2023).

All kinds of risks can be depicted in the Figure 1.

Figure 1. Different types of risk associated with generative AI

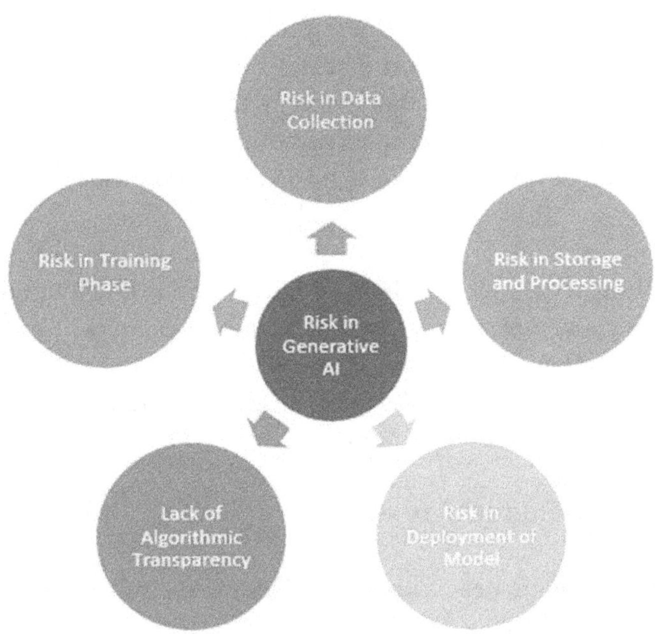

a. **Categorical Risk 1 -** Generative AI systems require large datasets to train on. The collection of this data may involve personal information and could be subject to privacy concerns.
b. **Categorical Risk 2 -** Once collected, the data needs to be stored and processed. This step carries the risk of unauthorized access, data breaches, or mishandling of personal information.

c. **Categorical Risk 3 -** During the development and deployment of generative AI models, there may be instances where the data needs to be accessed or shared with third parties. This increases the risk of data exposure and potential privacy violations.
d. **Categorical Risk 4 -** The training and fine-tuning process involves using the collected data to train the generative AI models. If the data contains personal information, there is a risk that the model may inadvertently learn and generate content that compromises privacy.
e. **Categorical Risk 5 -** The output or generated content of generative AI models may contain sensitive or private information. This raises concerns about the appropriate usage and dissemination of such content.
f. **Categorical Risk 6 –** Lack of Algorithmic Transparency - ChatGPT and other Large Language Models (LLMs) primarily rely on predicting the most likely word, phrase, or sentence a user will input based on their prompt. These models are trained on vast amounts of text data, including news articles, papers, and various other sources, to make these predictions. However, the lack of hard evidence or citations to support its claims poses a significant risk. This can lead to the repetition of potentially inaccurate or false information, which can be harmful. Moreover, the repeated use of the same material may contribute to the de-anonymization of users, further compromising their privacy and security.

All these AI decision-making blunders have certain things in common, such as hurried training and development, a lack of inclusiveness while algorithms are being created, and a few other things.

Businesses frequently overlook the fact that AI models require time and patience to "learn" and complete jobs with few errors.

Non-Technology-Based Areas

Non-technologies-based issues can be classified into the following categories –

a. Society-based cyber-risk generated by AI: These are the following risks generated by AI creating serious issues for society:
   i. **Automation-spurred job loss:** One of the primary concerns is the potential issue generated by AI is job displacement, due to automation. As AI systems become more capable, certain tasks and jobs may be automated, leading to unemployment or a shift in the job market. This can particularly impact jobs that involve repetitive or routine tasks.

ii. **Privacy violations:** The widespread use of AI often involves collecting and analyzing large amounts of data. This raises concerns about the privacy of individuals, as personal information may be used without proper consent or safeguards. AI applications such as facial recognition can be especially invasive as most people are not aware of their rights.

iii. **Bias and Fairness:** AI systems are trained on data, and if the data used for training contains biases, the AI models may perpetuate and even amplify those biases. This can result in discriminatory outcomes, affecting certain groups more than others, and raising ethical concerns, many types of research have been performed however more intensive is needed.

iv. **Ethical Dilemmas:** The development of AI raises ethical questions about the responsible use of technology which is utterly lacking according to the current reports received by agencies. Issues such as the use of AI in autonomous weapons, decision-making processes with significant societal impact, and accountability for AI-related errors are important ethical considerations. As reported by BBC, A man in his 40s was crushed to death by a robot in South Korea after it failed to differentiate him from the boxes of food it was handling. The robot was responsible for lifting pepper boxes and transferring them onto pallets. The man was sent to the hospital but later died. This kind of case raised concern about the ethical and acceptable use of AI (Hagendorff, 2020).

v. **Lack of Regulation and Standards:** The rapid advancement of AI technology has outpaced the development of regulatory frameworks and standards. This can lead to a lack of accountability and oversight, increasing the potential for misuse or unintended consequences. Not only in Western countries but at the global level governments are planning seriously to form guidelines and regulations to control people's rights wherever AI is coming into the picture (Chatterjee, 2019).

IT Security Policy-Based Risks Generated by AI

The integration of AI technologies into society raises a range of policy-related risks. Policymakers face the challenge of developing and implementing regulations that foster innovation, protect public interests, and address ethical concerns. There are the following concerns:

a. **Lack of Regulation:** The rapid development of AI has often raised the issue of regulatory frameworks. This lack of regulation can result in a policy vacuum, leaving the technology to advance without adequate safeguards in place. This may lead to potential misuse or unintended consequences.

b. **Inadequate Ethical Guidelines:** The absence of clear ethical guidelines and laws for the development and deployment of AI can result in ethical lapses at a technical level. These issues have generated a serious concern in social media. Policies should address issues such as bias, transparency, accountability, and the responsible use of AI to ensure that these technologies match the needs and societal values.

c. **International Policy Disparities:** AI development occurs on a global scale, and disparities in regulatory approaches between countries create challenges at the global level and pose a risk between two countries. Divergent policies may lead to issues related to data protection, privacy, and standards for AI systems, hindering international collaboration between two countries and creating friction in mutual relations involving cross-border applications.

d. **Security and Cybersecurity Policies:** As AI systems become more integrated into critical infrastructure and decision-making processes, policies must address security risks at a global level. Immature cybersecurity and e-governance policies may expose AI systems to vulnerabilities, potentially leading to data breaches, manipulation, or misuse by malicious actors and sometimes it is the outcome of espionage between two countries.

e. **Methodological Standardization Challenges:** The lack of standardized practices and interoperability among AI systems in different fields can create challenges for users and the deployer. Policies that promote industry collaboration, the development of common standards, and interoperability frameworks can facilitate a more cohesive and efficient AI ecosystem however standard policy creates a bigger risk for data operations, data migration, data integrity, data usability, and storage.

f. **Accountability Mechanisms:** Policies drafted at different levels in any organization at the logical level should establish mechanisms for holding individuals, organizations, and AI systems accountable for their actions. This includes defining responsibilities in the event of AI-related errors, biases, or adverse outcomes.

Operational IT Risks Generated by AI

Operational risk changes its face and scope according to different organizations. These risks are associated with the day-to-day implementation and use of AI technologies. Here are some operational risks generated by AI in the case of expert systems-based applications:

g. **Data Quality and Bias:** AI systems heavily rely on data for training and decision-making. If the data used is of poor quality or contains biases, it can lead to inaccurate or unfair outcomes. Operational challenges arise when organizations struggle to ensure the quality and representativeness of their training data.

h. **Algorithmic Complexity:** Highly complex AI algorithms can be challenging to understand, interpret, and troubleshoot. Operational teams may face difficulties in managing and maintaining intricate models, especially when trying to diagnose and address issues related to performance or unexpected behavior.
i. **Scalability Challenges:** As organizations deploy AI systems at scale, they may encounter challenges related to scalability issues in the organization. Operational issues may arise when attempting to expand AI applications across diverse use cases, large datasets, or complex infrastructures.
j. **Integration With Existing Systems:** Because General AI is still in its infancy, there are still numerous misconceptions regarding its capabilities and limits while integrating it into different business processes. Vague goals and inflated expectations contribute to many initiatives failing before their time. Integrating AI into existing business processes and systems can be complex. Operational risks emerge when organizations struggle with the seamless integration of AI technologies with legacy systems, potentially causing disruptions or inefficiencies.
k. **Continuous Monitoring and Maintenance:** Deployment of AI models in business processes at the initial level is again challenging. AI models require continuous monitoring and maintenance to ensure they remain effective over time. Operational challenges arise when organizations struggle to establish robust monitoring processes and fail to address issues such as model drift or evolving data distributions.

Cyber Security Linked Physical Security Risks Generated by AI

While artificial intelligence (AI) technologies offer numerous benefits, they also introduce unique physical security risks. It's important to be aware of these risks to implement appropriate safeguards. Here are some potential physical security risks associated with AI:

l. **Easy Penetration:** AI systems, including those used in security applications, may be susceptible to adversarial attacks. These attacks involve manipulating input data to mislead AI algorithms, potentially allowing unauthorized access.
m. **AI can be used as a tool:** Malicious actors may use AI to enhance the effectiveness of traditional cyber-attacks, such as brute-force attacks or password cracking, leading to unauthorized access.

n. **Biometric Spoofing:** AI-based security systems that rely on biometrics (such as facial recognition) may be vulnerable to spoofing attacks using manipulated or synthetic biometric data.

Societal Challenges Posed by AI

As artificial intelligence (AI) becomes increasingly sophisticated and pervasive, the concerns regarding its potential hazards amplify. The issues vary from the automation of specific jobs to the presence of gender and racial biases in algorithms, and the development of autonomous weapons devoid of human oversight, among others. These challenges evoke a sense of unease on multiple fronts. Moreover, we are only at the initial stages of understanding the true extent of AI capabilities, and because of malicious intent, it has been observed that it may be wrong. There are following risks that may arise are the following:

a. **Risk of Fake News:** The proliferation of fake news is on the rise in every part of the world. Most of the fake news is rising mostly because of social media. Misinformation, often disseminated to mislead or deceive the public, is becoming more prevalent. A high number of false narratives are being made through social media i.e., Facebook, Twitter, and Instagram (see Fig 2) .

Figure 2. How fake news is touching people through different channels (World Economic Forum Report, 2017)

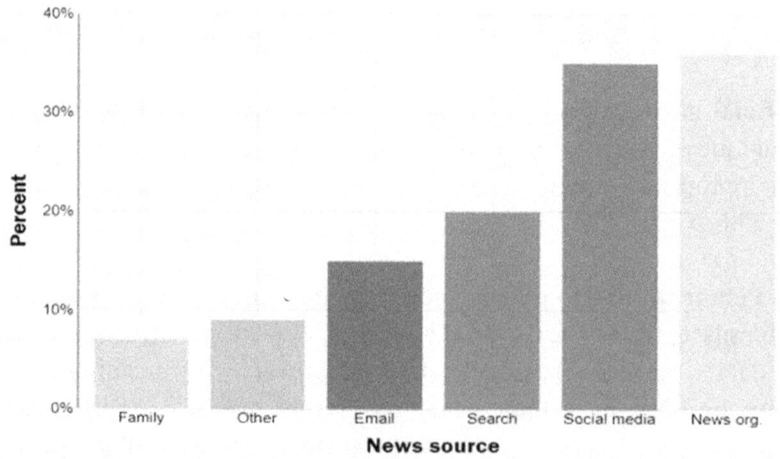

This trend poses a significant challenge as false narratives and distorted information can quickly spread through various online platforms, influencing public opinion and eroding trust in reliable sources. Addressing the growth of fake news requires concerted efforts from both technology platforms and society to promote media literacy, fact-checking, and responsible information sharing. Many research studies have been reported along with several frameworks to handle this situation however the situation is still not under control (*Global AI Software Market Growth 2019-2025 | Statista*, 2022).

b. **Risk of Deepfake Videos:** The risk of deepfake videos is a growing concern in various domains. Deepfakes involve the use of artificial intelligence (AI) to create highly convincing, manipulated videos or audio recordings that appear authentic but are entirely synthetic. Deepfake videos can be used to spread false information, creating misleading narratives and potentially influencing public opinion. Deepfake technology can be exploited to create videos that falsely depict individuals engaging in inappropriate or harmful activities. Deepfakes can be employed for political manipulation by creating forged videos of public figures making statements or engaging in activities that never occurred. To mitigate the risks associated with deepfake videos, efforts are underway to develop advanced detection methods, promote media literacy, and establish legal frameworks to address the malicious use of AI-generated content. Ongoing vigilance, education, and technological advancements are crucial in combating the negative consequences of deepfake technology.

c. **Manipulating elections through social media:** Manipulating elections through social media, often facilitated by the misuse of artificial intelligence (AI), is a serious concern. The use of AI in this context typically involves targeted and sophisticated strategies to spread misinformation, influence public opinion, and manipulate the democratic process. AI algorithms can be used to identify vulnerable demographics and strategically spread false or misleading information to influence voter perceptions. This can create a distorted view of candidates or issues, potentially swaying public opinion in favor of a particular agenda. Addressing the misuse of AI in election manipulation requires a multi-faceted approach involving technological solutions, legislative measures, and public awareness. Efforts to enhance transparency in political advertising, regulate the use of AI in election campaigns, and improve digital literacy are crucial steps in safeguarding the integrity of democratic processes in the era of AI and social media.

d. **Bias Content on social media:** The presence of biased content on social media can indeed be influenced by artificial intelligence (AI) algorithms. AI algorithms used by social media platforms may inadvertently reflect biases present in the training data used to develop them. If the training data contains biases, the algorithms can perpetuate and amplify those biases in content recommendations. Users may be exposed to content that aligns with existing biases, contributing to the formation of echo chambers and reinforcing pre-existing beliefs. Social media platforms often employ AI-driven personalization algorithms to curate content tailored to individual user preferences. If these algorithms are not designed to account for diversity and fairness, they can inadvertently reinforce existing biases. Users may be shown content that aligns with their existing viewpoints, limiting exposure to diverse perspectives and contributing to a narrowing of worldviews. Addressing bias in AI on social media requires a concerted effort from platform developers, policymakers, and the wider community. Steps can include improving transparency in algorithmic decision-making, diversifying training data, regularly auditing and refining algorithms, and implementing ethical guidelines for the use of AI in content recommendation and moderation. Additionally, user education and awareness are crucial to promoting critical thinking and mitigating the impact of biased content on social media.

e. **Socioeconomic economic inequality:** The impact of artificial intelligence (AI) on socioeconomic inequality is a complex and debated topic. While AI has the potential to bring about positive changes, it also can exacerbate existing inequalities. Automation driven by AI can lead to job displacement in certain industries, affecting lower-skilled workers more profoundly. Additionally, the demand for highly skilled workers in AI-related fields can widen the gap between those with and without advanced technical skills. Job loss among lower-skilled workers can contribute to income inequality, while the demand for specialized skills may result in a growing economic divide not only this, but AI is creating in the field of education too. Access to quality education and training in AI-related fields may be limited, creating disparities in the ability of individuals to acquire the skills needed for jobs in the AI-driven economy.

f. **Degrading of social ethics:** AI itself is a tool, and its impact on morality depends on how it is used and governed. It can be used both for nefarious purposes and to enhance ethical behavior. The responsibility for maintaining moral values lies with individuals and the broader societal framework that governs AI use. It is a big concern if people are using platforms like YouTube to learn unethical behaviors such as cheating. YouTube, like many other online platforms, contains a wide range of content, some of which may not align with ethical standards. Promoting ethical behavior and values, both in real life and online, is essential. Parents, educators, and guardians can play a significant role in teaching young people about ethical conduct, critical thinking, and the consequences of unethical actions [15].

g. **Autonomous weapons based on AI:** AI-based weapons, also known as autonomous weapons or lethal autonomous weapons systems (LAWS), refer to military systems that leverage artificial intelligence to identify, select, and engage targets without direct human intervention. The development and deployment of AI-based weapons raise various ethical, legal, and strategic concerns.

Case Study 1: Use of AI in Deepfake

Deepfakes involve the use of artificial intelligence to create manipulated videos or images that appear real but are fabricated. It's important to recognize the potential harm and ethical concerns associated with deepfakes. They can be used to spread misinformation, damage reputations, and violate individuals' privacy. Creating or sharing deepfakes without consent is both unethical and often illegal. According to the news reports, most of the obscene videos are made using deepfakes. This is the same deepfake from which a video of actress and national award winner Rashmika Mandanna was created. Rashmika's face was put on the body of another woman, and it was posted on social media. Rashmika herself also saw this video on social media, after which she said that it was quite scary.

Figure 3, is the photo cropped from that video shows an example, of Deepfake:

Figure 3. Rashmika Mandana viral video's instance where deepfake-based AI was used

Deepfake came into discussion for the first time in the year 2017. A social media user named his Reddit account Deepfake and created obscene videos using the faces of celebrities from around the world, including people like Vladimir Putin. Because deepfakes require videos and photos of any person, celebs or big personalities are its biggest victims, whose videos and photos are easily available on social media.

Deepfakes are also used in many films. Deepfake technology has been used in Hollywood and some Bollywood films. However, this technology is being misused more and more. The trend of deepfakes has increased rapidly in things like porn industry, sextortion, fake news, cyber fraud etc.

Case Study 2: Use of AI for Political Rivalry: Technology can also be used to cause political instability. A viral video made with AI technology shows a Malaysian political aide having sex with a cabinet minister. The video, which was released in 2019, also demands an investigation of the cabinet minister for alleged corruption. In particular, as a result of the release of this video, the coalition government became unstable, which also proved the potential political impact of deepfakes. Another such example involves a UK-based energy firm, which was compromised by a malicious individual using deepfake audio technology to impersonate the voice of the firm's CEO. AI-based technologies can also enable us to address a wide range of digital, physical, and political threats. To remain safe from malicious manifestations that misuse AI, enterprises and individual users alike need to recognize and understand the risks and potential malicious exploitation of AI systems.

Future Framework for AI

In each rapid pace of advancements in AI, there may be new considerations and frameworks but in practical sense it is beyond prediction because these trends evolve over time. One of the directions where government is working is developing regulatory framework. Governments and organizations are working on establishing regulatory frameworks for AI to address ethical, legal, and societal implications. These frameworks aim to ensure responsible AI development and deployment. Future AI frameworks will likely focus on enhancing collaboration between humans and AI systems. This involves creating interfaces that are user-friendly, promoting effective communication between humans and AI, and integrating AI as a supportive tool in various tasks. The next phase of development may include the merger of AI with subjects. Collaboration between AI researchers and experts in other domains, such as medicine, biology, and social sciences, is becoming more common. This interdisciplinary approach helps to address complex challenges and ensures that AI solutions are more contextually relevant. The last direction which has to be focused is maturing AI on its ethical part. Ethical considerations in AI have gained prominence. Efforts are being made to ensure that AI systems are developed and deployed in ways that are fair, unbiased, and align with ethical standards. This involves addressing issues such as algorithmic bias, fairness, and accountability.

CONCLUSION

The advent of Artificial Intelligence may increase data misuse with implications for privacy, the economy, and the distribution of information. Some scientists and philosophers have said that AI is a threat to the survival of the human species. Still, its promise in terms of revolutionizing various industries and opening human endeavors to new, more creative possibilities cannot be ignored. Therefore, it is essential to strike a balance between promoting innovation and ensuring ethical use. Globally, several initiatives have been taken by private players to create a framework to limit the negative impact of AI. Nowadays, artificial intelligence is used for many good purposes, including helping us make better medical diagnoses, finding new ways to treat cancer, and making our cars safer. Unfortunately, as our AI capabilities expand, we will also see it used for dangerous or malicious purposes. Because AI technology is advancing so rapidly, we need to develop the best ways to positively adapt to AI while reducing its destructive potential. Policymakers and technology researchers now need to work together to understand and prepare for its potential misuse.

REFERENCES

Ansari, M. F., Sharma, P. K., & Dash, B. (2022). Prevention of phishing attacks using AI-based cybersecurity awareness training. *International Journal of Smart Sensors and Ad Hoc Networks*, 61–72. doi:10.47893/IJSSAN.2022.1221

Berényi, L., & Deutsch, N. (2023). Technology adoption among higher education students. *Vezetéstudomány*, 28–39. doi:10.14267/VEZTUD.2023.11.03

Boulianne, E., Lecompte, A., & Fortin, M. (2023). Technology, Ethics, and the Pandemic: Responses from Key Accounting Actors. *Accounting and the Public Interest*, *23*(1), 177–194. doi:10.2308/API-2022-009

Brynjolfsson, E., Li, D., & Raymond, L. (2023). *Generative AI at work*. doi:10.3386/w31161

Buttazzo, G. (2023). Rise of artificial general intelligence: Risks and opportunities. *Frontiers in Artificial Intelligence*, *6*, 1226990. Advance online publication. doi:10.3389/frai.2023.1226990 PMID:37693010

Chatterjee, S. (2019). Impact of AI regulation on intention to use robots. *International Journal of Intelligent Unmanned Systems*, *8*(2), 97–114. doi:10.1108/IJIUS-09-2019-0051

De Mántaras, R. L., Gibert, K., Forment, M. A., Cortés, U., Hernández-Fernández, A., Balas, D. F., Carreras, A., Calle, A. M. T., & Domenjó, C. S. (2023). Creativitat digital. In Iniciativa Digital Politècnica. Oficina de Publicacions Acadèmiques Digitals de la UPC eBooks. doi:10.5821/ebook-9788410008090

Elish, M. C., & Boyd, D. (2017). Situating methods in the magic of Big Data and AI. *Communication Monographs*, *85*(1), 57–80. doi:10.1080/03637751.2017.1375130

Global AI software market growth 2019-2025 | Statista. (2022, June 27). Statista. https://www.statista.com/statistics/607960/worldwide-artificial-intelligence-market-growth/

Gorwa, R., Binns, R., & Katzenbach, C. (2020). Algorithmic content moderation: Technical and political challenges in the automation of platform governance. *Big Data & Society*, *7*(1). doi:10.1177/2053951719897945

Hagendorff, T. (2020). The Ethics of AI Ethics: An Evaluation of Guidelines. *Minds and Machines*, *30*(1), 99–120. doi:10.1007/s11023-020-09517-8

Jiang, F., Jiang, Y., Zhi, H., Dong, Y., Li, H., Ma, S., Wang, Y., Dong, Q., Shen, H., & Wang, Y. (2017). Artificial intelligence in healthcare: Past, present and future. *Stroke and Vascular Neurology*, *2*(4), 230–243. doi:10.1136/svn-2017-000101 PMID:29507784

Katija, K., Orenstein, E. C., Schlining, B., Lundsten, L., Barnard, K., Sainz, G., Boulais, O., Cromwell, M., Butler, E. E., Woodward, B., & Bell, K. L. (2022). FathomNet: A global image database for enabling artificial intelligence in the ocean. *Scientific Reports*, *12*(1), 15914. Advance online publication. doi:10.1038/s41598-022-19939-2 PMID:36151130

KushalP. (2023). AI as a Tool, Not a Master: Ensuring Human Control of Artificial Intelligence. Authorea *(*Authorea*)*. doi:10.22541/au.170000968.86867344/v1

Leaver, T., & Srdarov, S. (2023). ChatGPT isn't magic. *M/C Journal, 26*(5). doi:10.5204/mcj.3004

Li, J., Zhao, Z., Li, R., & Zhang, H. (2019). AI-Based Two-Stage intrusion detection for software defined IoT networks. *IEEE Internet of Things Journal*, *6*(2), 2093–2102. doi:10.1109/JIOT.2018.2883344

Linardatos, P., Papastefanopoulos, V., & Kotsiantis, S. (2020). Explainable AI: A review of Machine Learning Interpretability Methods. *Entropy (Basel, Switzerland)*, *23*(1), 18. doi:10.3390/e23010018 PMID:33375658

Money, Power, and AI. (2023). In *Cambridge University Press eBooks*. doi:10.1017/9781009334297

Rangone, N. (2023). Artificial intelligence challenging core State functions. *Revista De Derecho PúBlico, 8*, 95–126. doi:10.37417/RDP/vol_8_2023_1949

Schmidt, R. N. (2023). Technology, Ethics, and the Pandemic: Responses from Key Accounting Actors. *Accounting and the Public Interest, 23*(1), 195–203. doi:10.2308/API-2023-010

Taylor, I. (2023). Justice by Algorithm: The limits of AI in criminal Sentencing. *Criminal Justice Ethics, 42*(3), 1–21. doi:10.1080/0731129X.2023.2275967

The Global Competitiveness Report 2017-2018. (2023, November 9). World Economic Forum. https://www.weforum.org/publications/the-global-competitiveness-report-2017-2018/

Varriale, V., Cammarano, A., Michelino, F., & Caputo, M. (2023). Critical analysis of the impact of artificial intelligence integration with cutting-edge technologies for production systems. *Journal of Intelligent Manufacturing*. Advance online publication. doi:10.1007/s10845-023-02244-8

Wahl, B., Cossy-Gantner, A., Germann, S., & Schwalbe, N. (2018). Artificial intelligence (AI) and global health: How can AI contribute to health in resource-poor settings? *BMJ Global Health, 3*(4), e000798. doi:10.1136/bmjgh-2018-000798 PMID:30233828

Yan, L., Echeverría, V., Fernandez-Nieto, G., Jin, Y., Swiecki, Z., Zhao, L., Gašević, D., & Martínez-Maldonado, R. (2023). Human-AI Collaboration in Thematic Analysis using ChatGPT: A User Study and Design Recommendations. *arXiv (Cornell University)*. https://doi.org//arxiv.2311.03999 doi:10.48550

Chapter 8
Dark Gamification:
A Tale of Consumer Exploitation and Unfair Competition

Pooja Khanna
Lovely Professional University, India

ABSTRACT

Gamification has captivated the interest of consumers from all spheres of life, and marketing holds a dominant position. It enhances customer engagement and loyalty through non-gaming context like social media marketing, e-mail marketing, and customer relationship management. Gamification's growing use in the service environment has caught the attention of practitioners and marketers alike. However, everything has a positive and negative aspect, and gamification is no exception. Although there are many studies on gamification in the marketing arena, there are very few primary and secondary studies that focus on the negative side of gamification. In this chapter, the authors explore this lesser attended side of gamification with focus on addiction, exploitation, manipulation, and unfair competition. To address these issues, gamification designers must employ game design aspects that limit overuse and remove focus solely on extrinsic incentives. The authors feel that this study can help gamification specialists and marketers prevent harmful consequences by minimizing certain game design aspects.

INTRODUCTION

Gamification has grown in popularity and pervasiveness in a variety of areas, including healthcare, education, marketing and staff management. Firms are increasingly relying on gamification to keep people engaged with their offers, which is roughly defined as seeking to create motivational experiences by augmenting non-game services

DOI: 10.4018/979-8-3693-0724-3.ch008

with game-like affordances such as badges or leaderboards (Huotari and Hamari, 2017). Using game mechanics in a non-gaming context is an innovative approach in retail. While various studies have focused on the good results of technology, its uses, and possible benefits, we would like to take a different approach and investigate its potential negative repercussions on people and society, with focus on ethical problems also (Rapp, A et al., 2019). Designers should be aware that the technology they devised to have one specific influence on people's behaviour may have unintended consequences that must be considered, and users should be conscious of the technology they are investing in. The game element is very significant in the eventual outcome of gamification on customer behaviour. The negative aspects of gamification come when insufficient game features are used to engage the user in the gamified situation (Toda et al., 2017). Harry Brignull coined the term "dark patterns" when he identified several forms of interfaces that manipulate users into doing things that are not in their best interests (Brignull. H, 2018). As a result, dark pattern design might be defined as the craft of purposely developing patterns that harm the users' well-being. Negative player experiences are likely to occur without their consent and against their best interests. There is a need for investigation into dark gamification because it has the potential to be unethical. Our goal with this study is to reinforce the need of investigating any negative consequences of gamification. This study will also add to the body of existing literature by revealing the dark side of gamification.

LITERATURE REVIEW

Gamification

Gamification is a marketing and business strategy applied to increase customer engagement and loyalty, influence customer engagement and encourage behaviours, supporting and motivating users to the task (Hsu et al., 2018). When merchants want to include gamified mechanisms into their mobile retailing applications, they should do it through challenge levels, just as in video games (Aydınlıyurt et al.,2021). The app like WeChat, is gradually expanding its functions, thus enabling the app to become China's first multipurpose app, with users spending more than 360 minutes each day on it. Gamification is a marketing and business strategy applied to increase customer engagement and loyalty while influencing customer engagement thus supporting and motivating them to the task (Hollabeak et al., 2021). Gamification enhances consumers' knowledge, has an impact on their attitudes, and behaviour. Organisations can use serious game elements to promote desirable and sustainable behaviour as reward-based game elements enhance the same. There is also a need to thoroughly understand the relationship between elements of gamification in changing consumer behaviour in the marketing literature and the impact of reward-based game elements in marketing (Whittaker, L et al.,2021).

Gamified motivators lead to psychological outcome that changes consumer behaviour (Gatautis et al., 2021). Gamification technology can change desired behaviour by increasing consumer loyalty awareness and developing an eco-friendly mindset. It also aims to encourage sustainable behaviour (Vakaliuk, T. A, et al.,2020). Game design enhances the efficiency to change behaviour. Sometimes, if game design is inappropriate, it reduces replay ability or brings a lack of fun. For applying games, every aspect and mechanism needs to be considered to achieve desired behaviour change outcomes (Haque et al., 2017). For designing a game, a person who needs the context and target players well game should be tested in the real world to lead to better outcomes. For engagement, consider the fun and engagement of players because, without engagement, there will be no desired result (Epstein. D et al., 2021). A gamification platform is developed to motivate behavioural changes, by increasing awareness and consumer engagement using a pervasive application that analyses context, sends personalised messages, and manages[1] gamification peer competition feedback (Nerves et al., 2021). Gamification contributes to the value creation of customers in the retail context. When Gamification is applied in an activity, it affects the hedonic value, which is positive thus contributing towards value creation of customers in retail context. The satisfaction of hedonic value is better than reward as it provides better-continued engagement of customers. Gamification with continued engagement is positively associated with brand engagement (Bitrián et al., 2019).

Dark Side of Gamification

Gamification may be a strong technique in marketing to attract and retain customers, establish brand loyalty, and increase engagement with products or services. Harry Brignull introduced Dark patterns when he catalogued, on darkpatterns.org, the different types of user interfaces that trick users into doing things that are not in the user's best interest (Bringull. H., 2018). Dark gamification could be defined as the craft of purposefully designing gamification elements that do not have the well-being of the user in mind.

Yet, there are also possible drawbacks to using gamification in marketing, particularly when it comes to the "evil side" of gamification. Here are a few examples:

Manipulation: Gamification can be used to manipulate users into doing activities or behaviours that are not in their best interests. For example, a firm may employ gamification to persuade customers to spend more money on their products or services, even if they cannot afford it.

Addiction: Gamification can be designed to be addictive in order to keep users engaged for as long as possible. As a result, users may spend an inordinate amount of time and money on the platform or product, potentially developing addictive behaviors.

Lack of Transparency: Gamification can be used to hide some characteristics of a product or service from users, to manipulate them into performing activities they would not have taken otherwise. This lack of transparency might be troublesome for users who are not entirely aware of the repercussions of their choices.

Inequality: Gamification can also be used to create an unequal playing field in which some users have an unfair edge over others. For example, a firm may utilise gamification to reward certain people with special advantages or bonuses while leaving others behind.

Dehumanization: Gamification can be intended to treat users as mere game pieces rather than as human beings with their own thoughts and feelings. As a result of this, users may experience a lack of empathy and a loss of personal autonomy.

It is critical for businesses to use gamification in marketing in an ethical and transparent manner, and to prioritise their users' well-being and autonomy. Researchers should address the ethical function of gamification and persuasive designs in general (Benner, D et al.,2021). Failure to consider the ethical aspect might result in counterproductive effects, such as gamification concepts that encourage the opposite behaviour, such as procrastination or ignorance (Diefenbach and Mussig, 2019). Gone are the days when gamification was primarily viewed as a beneficial technique; more and more researchers have recently begun to highlight the negative aspects of gamification, including addiction. Gamification can be demoralising when users have unfavourable experiences, such as unjust behaviour or exaggerated punishment in the gamified system. Games often contain competition, but employing it in a professional environment has potential disadvantages. In such a situation, employees may feel unwanted or even abused in their jobs (Humlung and Haddara, 2019). Kim and Werbach (2016) identified various challenges that must be addressed while designing gamification. These challenges are classified into four categories: exploitation, manipulation, harm, and character. The bad experiences for gamers are likely to happen without their consent and against their best interest. Dark patterns are design methods that favour developers rather than the intended audience, for example, employing unethical applications such as coercion, deception, and fraud (Nyström and Stribe, 2020). According to researchers, when gamification relies too much on extrinsic motivation from traditional award systems, it undermines users' intrinsic motivation for a specific targeted behaviour, resulting in a detrimental influence on users' motivation in the long run. The emphasis on extrinsic rewards should be maintained to a minimal because such prizes are frequently ineffective in real life, regardless of their capacity to promote self-confidence or perceived prestige. While gamification is fashionable, marketers began using it without fully comprehending the fundamentals of game mechanics, flow, immersion, and story. Table 1 provides a brief description of the findings on the dark side of Gamifiactions.

Table 1. Findings from previous literature

Title	Author	Objective	Findings	Test & Techniques
The Bright and Dark Sides of Gamification	Fernando R. H. Andrade, Riichiro Mizoguchi, Seiji Isotani[1]	It discuss some of the problems of gamification, namely, addiction, undesired competition, and off-task behavior.	Authors identified addiction as the dark side of gamification and addressed the elements used in gamification that related to this phenomenon and how it occurs in gamified environments	Review
The dark side of gamification: An overview of negative effects of gamification in education	Armando M. Toda, Pedro H. D. Valle, and Seiji Isotani	What are the negative effects that can occur in gamification when applied to educational contexts?	Authors found that the game design may lead to a negative impact. For instance, Leaderboards are strongly associated to many negative effects mapped in this work.	Systematic Mapping
Uncovering the Dark Side of Gamification at Work: Impacts on Engagement and Well-Being	Wafa Hammedia, Thomas Leclercqb,c, Ingrid Poncind and Linda Alkire	investigating the role of gamification and its effect on employee engagement and well-being	The results highlight the negative impacts of gamified work on employee engagement and well-being, although the willingness of employees to participate in such gamified work moderates these negative impacts	Interviews and Experiments
The Dark Side of Narrow Gamification: Negative Impact of Assessment Gamification on Student Perceptions and Content Knowledge	Hee Yoon Kwon, Koray Özpolat	explored the effects of assessment gamification on students' content knowledge and perceptions of satisfaction, course experience, learning, and impact of teaching techniques	Ggamifying assessment activities resulted in significantly lower content knowledge, satisfaction, and course experience. Difference in perceived learning was not significant	T test, Anova
Examining the dark side of using gamification elements in online community engagement: an application of PLS-SEM and ANN modeling	Gautam Srivastav, Surajit Bag, Mohammad Osman Gani	The study examines the adverse effects of gamification during engaging in online communities.	This research presents a theoretical contribution by providing critical insights into online gamers' mental and emotional health. It implies that gamification can even bring mental and emotional disturbance. The resulting situation might lead to undesirable social consequences.	PLS- SEM

continued on following page

Table 1. Continued

Title	Author	Objective	Findings	Test & Techniques
Another dark side of gamification? How and when gamified service use triggers information disclosure	Simon Trang and Welf H. Weiger	To investigate whether engaging with gamified services can lead to increased information disclosure.	The findings contribute to the nascent research on dark sides of gamification in that they show that experiences in social comparison during gamified service usage can trigger information disclosure through loss of self-consciousness	SEM
Exploring the Darkness of Gamification – You Want It Darker?	Tobias Nystr¨om	to explore the negative aspects of the Gamification	Develop better frameworks for designing gamification. Iand also reignite the call to conduct more research about negative sides of gamification in order to improve the gamification experience.	Systematic Literature Review
The Shades of Grey: Datenherrschaft in Data-Driven Gamification	Sami Hyrynsalmi	This study surveys possible ethical problems of data-driven gamification	The study shows that there are clearly ethical issues, different shades of grey, related to the data-driven gamification and future work is needed in order assess, analyze and answer the presented problems	Case Study
Gamification: An Instructional Strategy to Engage Learners	Ms. R.K. Dixit, Mrs. M.A. Nirgude, Dr. Ms. P.S. Yalagi	The study presents the integration of' Gamification' instructional strategy along with traditional teaching modes for the course I&CS to increase the engagement of students teaching	The study observed that 80% of students found blending of gamification with traditional classroom teaching are appropriate and useful for course. It increased students' interest in the class. It increases student's engagement and attention span. To make class more active, gamification can be applied.	Experiments
Bright-side and Dark-side Effects of Gamification on Consumers' Adoption of Gamified Recommendation.	Lu, J., Chen, G., Wang, X., & Feng, Y.	this study explores both bright-side and dark-side effects of gamification on consumers adoption of gamified recommendation	entertainment and social interaction are positively associated with consumers' favorable attitude toward gamification, while perceived cost, social anxiety and ambiguity confusion are dark sides of gamification causing more consumer fatigue	SEM

continued on following page

Table 1. Continued

Title	Author	Objective	Findings	Test & Techniques
Gamifying the gig: transitioning the dark side to bright side of online engagement	Abhishek Behl, Pratima Sheorey	investigating digital platform gig work dropouts through the moderating impact of gamified interventions on online platforms	Results confirm that gamifying the online platform would enhance job satisfaction and productivity of gig employees, thereby reducing their chances of quitting gig work.	PLS-SEM
Theoretical Evidence of Addictive Nature of Gamification and Identification of Addictive Game Elements Used in Mobile Application Design	Bushra Qazi Abbasi and Samrah Awais	investigates which game elements used in mobile application design are addictive in nature, using a self-reporting surve	the results of the survey show highly addictive nature of Scrolling and relatively for tapping	CHI Square Analysis

CONCLUSION

The exploration of dark gamification in this chapter has shed light on a complex and often controversial aspect of human behaviour and technology integration. Dark gamification, while undeniably effective in driving user engagement and achieving specific goals, raises ethical and moral concerns that cannot be ignored. As we have seen, its manipulation tactics can lead to unintended consequences, including addiction, stress, and the erosion of personal privacy. Dark gamification raises important questions about the balance between using gamification techniques for positive outcomes, such as increasing productivity or encouraging healthy habits, and exploiting these techniques for profit or control. It highlights the need for a critical and ethical approach to the design and implementation of gamification systems, where careful consideration is given to the potential harm they may cause.

It is imperative that we approach dark gamification with caution and mindfulness. While it may offer short-term gains for businesses and organizations, the long-term consequences on individuals and society as a whole warrant a critical examination. Striking a balance between the benefits of gamification and the potential harms of dark gamification is essential for creating a sustainable and ethical approach to game design and user engagement.

Furthermore, it is our responsibility as designers, developers, and users to advocate for transparency, ethical design, and regulation in this rapidly evolving field. By fostering a culture of ethical gamification and being aware of the psychological triggers at play, we can harness the positive aspects of gamification while mitigating the negative impacts associated with dark gamification.

Ultimately, the future of gamification lies in our ability to navigate the fine line between motivation and manipulation, ensuring that our technological advancements serve the best interests of individuals and society as a whole. As we move forward, it is incumbent upon us to prioritize the well-being and autonomy of users, embracing a brighter and more ethical path in the world of gamification.

REFERENCES

Abbasi, B. Q., & Awais, S. (2022). *Playing mind gamification: Theoretical evidence of addictive nature of gamification and identification of addictive game elements used in mobile application design*. Academic Press.

Andrade, F. R., Mizoguchi, R., & Isotani, S. (2016). The bright and dark sides of gamification. *Intelligent Tutoring Systems: 13th International Conference, ITS 2016, Zagreb, Croatia, June 7-10, 2016 Proceedings*, *13*, 176–186.

Aydınlıyurt, E. T., Taşkın, N., Scahill, S., & Toker, A. (2021). Continuance intention in gamified mobile applications: A study of behavioral inhibition and activation systems. *International Journal of Information Management*, *61*, 102414. doi:10.1016/j.ijinfomgt.2021.102414

Behl, A., Sheorey, P., Jain, K., Chavan, M., Jajodia, I., & Zhang, Z. J. (2021). Gamifying the gig: Transitioning the dark side to bright side of online engagement. *AJIS. Australasian Journal of Information Systems*, *25*, 1–34. doi:10.3127/ajis.v25i0.2979

Benner, D., Schöbel, S., & Janson, A. (2021, August). It is only for your own good, or is it? Ethical Considerations for Designing Ethically Conscious Persuasive Information Systems. AMCIS.

Bitrián, P., Buil, I., & Catalán, S. (2021). Enhancing user engagement: The role of gamification in mobile apps. *Journal of Business Research*, *132*, 170–185. doi:10.1016/j.jbusres.2021.04.028

Diefenbach, S., & Müssig, A. (2019). Counterproductive effects of gamification: An analysis on the example of the gamified task manager Habitica. *International Journal of Human-Computer Studies*, *127*, 190–210. doi:10.1016/j.ijhcs.2018.09.004

Dixit, R. K., Nirgude, M. A., & Yalagi, P. S. (2018, December). Gamification: an instructional strategy to engage learner. In *2018 IEEE Tenth International Conference on Technology for Education (T4E)* (pp. 138-141). IEEE. 10.1109/T4E.2018.00037

Epstein, D. S., Zemski, A., Enticott, J., & Barton, C. (2021). Tabletop board game elements and gamification interventions for health behavior change: Realist review and proposal of a game design framework. *JMIR Serious Games*, *9*(1), e23302. doi:10.2196/23302 PMID:33787502

Gatautis, R., Banytė, J., & Vitkauskaitė, E. (2021). *Gamification and Consumer Engagement*. Progress in IS. doi:10.1007/978-3-030-54205-4

Hammedi, W., Leclercq, T., Poncin, I., & Alkire, L. (2021). Uncovering the dark side of gamification at work: Impacts on engagement and well-being. *Journal of Business Research*, *122*, 256–269. doi:10.1016/j.jbusres.2020.08.032

Haque, M. S., O'Broin, D., & Kehoe, J. (2017). To Gamify or not to Gamify? Analysing the Effect of Game Elements to foster Progression and Social Connectedness. *18th Annual European GAME-ON Conference 2020*.

Hollebeek, L. D., Das, K., & Shukla, Y. (2021). Game on! How gamified loyalty programs boost customer engagement value. *International Journal of Information Management*, *61*, 102308. doi:10.1016/j.ijinfomgt.2021.102308

Hsu, T. C., Chang, S. C., & Hung, Y. T. (2018). How to learn and how to teach computational thinking: Suggestions based on a review of the literature. *Computers & Education*, *126*, 296–310. doi:10.1016/j.compedu.2018.07.004

Humlung, O., & Haddara, M. (2019). The hero's journey to innovation: Gamification in enterprise systems. *Procedia Computer Science*, *164*, 86–95. doi:10.1016/j.procs.2019.12.158

Huotari, K., & Hamari, J. (2017). A definition for gamification: Anchoring gamification in the service marketing literature. *Electronic Markets*, *27*(1), 21–31. doi:10.1007/s12525-015-0212-z

Kim, T. W., & Werbach, K. (2016). More than just a game: Ethical issues in gamification. *Ethics and Information Technology*, *18*(2), 157–173. doi:10.1007/s10676-016-9401-5

Kwon, H. Y., & Özpolat, K. (2021). The dark side of narrow gamification: Negative impact of assessment gamification on student perceptions and content knowledge. *Transactions on Education*, *21*(2), 67–81. doi:10.1287/ited.2019.0227

Lu, J., Chen, G., Wang, X., & Feng, Y. (2022). *Bright-side and Dark-side Effects of Gamification on Consumers' Adoption of Gamified Recommendation*. Academic Press.

Neves, J. C., Melo, A., Soares, F. M., & Frade, J. (2021). A Bilingual in-Game Tutorial: Designing Videogame Instructions Accessible to Deaf Students. In *Advances in Design and Digital Communication: Proceedings of the 4th International Conference on Design and Digital Communication, Digicom 2020, November 5–7, 2020, Barcelos, Portugal* (pp. 58-67). Springer International Publishing.

Nyström, T., & Stibe, A. (2020, November). When persuasive technology gets dark? In *European, Mediterranean, and Middle Eastern Conference on Information Systems* (pp. 331-345). Cham: Springer International Publishing. 10.1007/978-3-030-63396-7_22

Rapp, A., Hopfgartner, F., Hamari, J., Linehan, C., & Cena, F. (2019). Strengthening gamification studies: Current trends and future opportunities of gamification research. *International Journal of Human-Computer Studies*, *127*, 1–6. doi:10.1016/j.ijhcs.2018.11.007

Srivastava, G., Bag, S., Rahman, M. S., Pretorius, J. H. C., & Gani, M. O. (2022). Examining the dark side of using gamification elements in online community engagement: an application of PLS-SEM and ANN modeling. *Benchmarking: An International Journal.*

Toda, A. M., Valle, P. H., & Isotani, S. (2017, March). The dark side of gamification: An overview of negative effects of gamification in education. In *Researcher links workshop: higher education for all* (pp. 143–156). Springer International Publishing.

Trang, S., & Weiger, W. H. (2019). Another dark side of gamification? How and when gamified service use triggers information disclosure. In GamiFIN (pp. 142-153). Academic Press.

Vakaliuk, T. A., Shevchuk, L. D., & Shevchuk, B. V. (2020). Possibilities of using AR and VR technologies in teaching mathematics to high school students. *Universal Journal of Educational Research*, *8*(11B), 6280–6288. doi:10.13189/ujer.2020.082267

Whittaker, L., Mulcahy, R., & Russell-Bennett, R. (2021). 'Go with the flow' for gamification and sustainability marketing. *International Journal of Information Management*, *61*, 102305. doi:10.1016/j.ijinfomgt.2020.102305

Chapter 9
Future Perspectives of Artificial Intelligence in Various Applications

Kannadhasan Suriyan
https://orcid.org/0000-0001-6443-9993
Study World College of Engineering, India

R. Nagarajan
https://orcid.org/0000-0002-4990-5869
Gnanamani College of Technology, India

B. Sundaravadivazhagan
University of Technology and Applied Sciences-Al Mussana, Oman

ABSTRACT

AI technology has a lengthy history and is continually evolving and expanding. It focuses on intelligent agents, which are composed of gadgets that observe their surroundings and then take appropriate action to increase the likelihood that a goal will be achieved. In this chapter, the authors discuss the fundamentals of contemporary AI as well as a number of illustrative applications. Artificial intelligence (AI) is the ability of computers, computer programmes, and other systems to mimic human intelligence and creativity, autonomously come up with solutions to issues, be able to reach judgements, and make choices. Additionally, there are ways in which existing artificial intelligence outsmarts humans. Additionally, it will examine the forecasts for artificial intelligence and provide viable solutions to address them in the next decades.

DOI: 10.4018/979-8-3693-0724-3.ch009

1. INTRODUCTION

Today's artificial intelligence (robotics) is capable of mimicking human intellect by carrying out a variety of activities that call for learning and reasoning, solving issues, and reaching different conclusions. Robots, computers, and other similar devices that have artificial intelligence software or programmes installed in them to give them the essential thinking capabilities. However, a lot of the present robotic artificial intelligence systems are still up for discussion since their methods for tackling problems still need more study. Artificial intelligence systems or robots should thus be able to do the necessary tasks without making mistakes. Robotics should also be able to carry out a variety of activities without any guidance from or aid from humans. With high performance skills like traffic management and speed minimization, today's artificial intelligence is quickly advancing, resulting in anything from self-driving vehicles to the SIRI. This includes robotic automobiles as well. The current focus on presenting artificial intelligence in robots for them to gain human-like traits significantly increases human dependency on technology. The capacity of artificial intelligence (AI) to successfully carry out any specific cognitive activity also significantly increases people's dependency on technology. Artificial intelligence (AI) techniques that can handle massive volumes of data on computers may provide users access to and analysis of all the data.

Due to the danger that this poses today, it is much easier for someone to collect and analyse large amounts of data. In recent years, artificial intelligence has been defined as the artificial representation of the human brain that strives to emulate the human learning process. Everyone has to be reassured that artificial intelligence that is equivalent to that of the human brain cannot be produced. We have just used a portion of our powers thus far. Since information is now expanding quickly, just a small portion of the human brain is required. Because of how much more capable the human brain is than we can now comprehend or demonstrate (De Vito, 2014; Huynh, 2023). There are roughly 100 trillion electrically conducting cells, or neurons, in the human brain, giving it an extraordinary computational ability to carry out tasks quickly and effectively. According to studies, computers are now capable to multiplying in an effective way, but they are still unable to accomplish tasks like learning and altering one's understanding of the world and recognising human features. Artificial intelligence has led to a number of advances, such as robotic automobiles that don't need a driver to steer or keep an eye on them. Robotic technology (artificial intelligence) also includes intelligent devices that analyse vast amounts of data in ways that humans are not capable of doing. Robotics are already taking on routine tasks that call for intelligence and ingenuity.

Additionally, Artificial Intelligence (AI) is a confluence of many technologies that gives robots the ability to comprehend, pick up on, observe, or carry out human actions on their own. In this situation, artificial intelligence (AI) programmes (robots) are created with certain goals in mind, such as learning, acting, and understanding, but human intelligence is primarily concerned with many multitasking skills. An artificial intelligence tool is often more interested in emphasising robotics that simulates human behaviours. However, because of differences between the human brain and computers, artificial intelligence may sometimes falter. In a nutshell, artificial intelligence has the ability to emulate human behaviour or character. Furthermore, artificial intelligence is still only partly developed, lacking sophisticated capacities for independent learning and instead relying on directives to carry out actions. Artificial intelligence will finally reach its zenith when robots can recognise human behaviour and emotions. Our everyday lives are being infiltrated by artificial intelligence thanks to GPS navigation and check-scanning devices (Ciregan, 2012; Wang, 2016).

The potentialization of several aspects of everyday life, including customer service, finance, sales and marketing, administration, and technical operations in different industries, is facilitated by the application of artificial intelligence (AI) in business. The use of technologies like AI at all levels and operations of businesses will become a reality to boost their competitiveness over the next years, and digital endeavours won't be isolated projects or initiatives in firms anymore. AI is starting to permeate company operations. It is crucial to keep in mind that it has not developed to take over human jobs, but to complement them and enable individuals to fully express their potential and creativity. The introduction of new technologies is a tool for the prevention and combat of corruption, and the management of them is made more secure by the traceability of electronic operations and the security that surrounds them. This article will demonstrate how artificial intelligence might increase productivity among workers, aid in employment growth, and start to make our society safer for kids. Massive research is now being done on artificial intelligence, which will considerably improve the future in which the bulk of work will be carried out by machines and people will only have control over them. This raises the issue of whether artificial intelligence is capable of doing tasks better than humans and more quickly, efficiently, and inexpensively. The study discusses artificial intelligence technologies in the present and the future and contrasts it with human intellect. The purpose of this article is to examine where AI technology is now and what its ultimate future may be if it were to be used consistently across all industries. We will also examine various AI methods and how they can enhance the system in the future (Chenz, 2017; Goldin, 2010).

AI and human intelligence have numerous similarities but also significant disparities. Every autonomous system that engages in interaction with a dynamic environment has to build and maintain a world model. This implies that before the computer 'brain' can make judgements, the environment must first be viewed (or felt by cameras, microphones, and/or tactile sensors) and then rebuilt in such a manner that it has an accurate and up-to-date picture of the world it is in. An efficient autonomous system depends on a world model that is accurate and updated on time. For instance, autonomous UAV navigation is rather simple since the world model on which it relies only comprises of maps that show preferred routes, height impediments, and no-fly zones. This model is enhanced in real time by radars, which show which altitudes are free of obstructions. GPS coordinates tell the UAV where it needs to travel, with the main objective of the GPS coordinate plan being to keep the aircraft from entering a no-fly zone or crashing into anything.In contrast, automated automobile navigation is far more challenging. In addition to comparable mapping capabilities, cars also need to be able to identify any adjacent vehicles, pedestrians, and bicycles, as well as where they are and where they are heading in the next few seconds. This is accomplished by driverless automobiles (and certain drones) using a mix of LIDAR (Light Detection And Ranging), conventional radars, and stereo computer vision sensors. Because of the complexity of the operational environment, the world model of a driverless automobile is far more developed than that of a normal UAV.

A computer in a driverless automobile must continuously calculate all probable locations of interaction, monitor all neighbouring vehicle dynamics, and predict how traffic will behave before making a choice about how to respond. Humans accomplish this with minimal cognitive effort, but it is a crucial aspect of how they drive—guessing or anticipating what other drivers will do. To keep track of all these variables while simultaneously attempting to maintain and update its current world model, a computer needs a lot of calculation power. A autonomous automobile will make optimal assumptions based on probability distributions in order to ensure safe execution durations for action given this enormous processing challenge. Therefore, the automobile is essentially assuming the optimum course of action given a certain confidence interval. In order to handle the complexity of diverse jobs, pilots heavily depend on procedures, to continue with the example of aviation. For instance, pilots are instructed to stabilise the aircraft first (a skill) and then consult the handbook to identify the appropriate course of action (rule following) when a fire-light shines or another subsystem signals a problem. Since there are too many answers to potential issues to memorise, such standardised processes are required. In many situations, especially when uncertainty and complexity rise, some interpretation of the techniques is necessary. This is especially true when dealing with numerous and compound issues.

When a predetermined set of rules does not necessarily apply to the present circumstance and quick mental simulations may be required to resolve the issue, knowledge-based reasoning is used. Building up over time, mental models—cognitive representations of the outside world—help people build and choose plans, especially when faced with ambiguity. It reflects a high level of uncertainty, necessitating the captain to create a mental model of the surroundings and the condition of the aircraft. This is the classic knowledge-based situation. The quick mental simulation that followed led him to successfully choose the option of abandoning. The reasoning behaviours that are built on knowledge-based reasoning are guided by expert behaviour. Expertise makes use of judgement, intuition, and fast situational analysis, particularly in a time-sensitive circumstance like a weapon discharge. Since analysing all potential plan alternatives takes time, especially in the face of uncertainty, experts often make tough judgements quickly and economically. One of the characteristics of a real expert in humans is their capacity to deal with the greatest levels of ambiguity, while in contrast, computers find it extremely challenging to mimic such conduct. Skill-based jobs are the simplest to automate since they are by definition extremely repetitive and have built-in feedback loops that can be managed using mathematical representations. However, the presence of the proper sensors is a crucial presumption. Rule-based behaviours are also potentially strong candidates for automation due to their if-then-else nature. However, when uncertainty grows, rule-based reasoning gives way to knowledge-based reasoning, necessitating good uncertainty management and genuine expertise (Gordon, 2016; Quillian, 2017).

The difference between the necessity for automated vs autonomous behaviours begins to show up at the rule-based level of reasoning. Here, some higher-level reasoning starts to take shape, but uncertainty is also beginning to increase - particularly in the context of an incomplete rule set. For instance, the Global Hawk military unmanned aerial vehicle (UAV) operates at a rule-based level and can land on its own if contact is lost, but it has not yet been shown that such an aircraft can reason in all the circumstances it may meet. The latter would need for more sophisticated logic. Knowledge-based behaviours and the associated competence constitute the most sophisticated types of cognitive reasoning and are frequently seen in fields with the greatest levels of uncertainty. Rule-based reasoning may help decision-makers (human or machine) choose amongst different options. However, it is sometimes difficult to determine which set of rules applies when there is a lot of ambiguity. Algorithms may not be able to comprehend the solution space in these uncertain settings, which are by definition imprecise and ambiguous, much less arrive at a workable answer. Any autonomous system performing a safety-critical operation, such as releasing weapons, must determine if it can resolve ambiguity to provide results that are acceptable. It is possible that an autonomous drone may be assigned the task of hitting a stationary target with a high chance of success on a military facility. Indeed, a lot of nations have missiles that are capable of doing that. However, could an autonomous drone that is looking for a particular person be able to tell from its real-time images that they has been located and that using a weapon on them would kill just them and not any innocent bystanders? Right now, the answer to this query is "no." When visual and moral judgement and reasoning are needed, human induction, or the capacity to derive general principles from particular bits of evidence, is crucial.

2. ARTIFICIAL INTELLIGENCE

Humans must use induction to make these judgements in order to deal with uncertainty. Computer algorithms are inherently brittle, which means that they can only take into account the quantifiable variables identified early on in the design stages when the algorithms are originally. This is especially true for data-driven algorithms like typical algorithms that fall under the category of AI. Computers are now unable to replicate the abstract ideas of intuition, knowledge-based reasoning, and actual expertise. There is a lot of research being done to fix this right now, especially in the machine learning/AI sector, but it is moving slowly.Such systems need engineers with both strong hardware and software skills. However, there is intense competition for highly trained workers since there are few colleges that graduate students in robotics, controls, mechatronics, and similar subjects with the technical acumen for such positions.

The aerospace and military industry, whose financing lags behind, is less enticing to the best qualified employees because of the fierce competition for roboticists and allied experts across these sectors. As a consequence, as the finest and brightest engineers go to the commercial sector, the global military industry is lagging behind its commercial counterparts in terms of technological innovation. Because of this relative lack of experience, military autonomous systems that are finally deployed may be inadequate or lack the necessary testing and safeguards. Therefore, although the discussion over whether autonomous weapons should be outlawed is undoubtedly relevant, a more pressing concern is the military industry' capacity to develop safe semi-autonomous systems, much alone completely autonomous ones. While some may argue that the current distribution of R&D and expertise is an inevitable result of competition and a free market, this argument fails to fully recognise the reality of a fundamental shift in technology prowess where militaries will begin to significantly lag behind commercial systems in terms of autonomous system capabilities. Before troops on the front lines, the typical American is more likely to own a driverless car, and terrorists may soon be able to purchase drones online with capabilities on par with or perhaps surpassing those of the military. Without a question, this disparity in access to technology will bring up brand-new, unexpected, and disruptive aspects for military operations. For instance, if security firms and governments continue on their current course of relative AI ignorance, might this result in a possible power shift wherein crucial AI services are leased via

Google, Amazon, or Facebook? In addition to purchasing extremely sophisticated robotics businesses and letting their previous military contracts expire, Google has long distanced itself from partnerships with the military.

AI technology has a lengthy history and is continually evolving and expanding. It focuses on intelligent agents, which have tools for observing the environment and acting accordingly in order to increase the likelihood that a goal will be achieved. In this essay, we will discuss the fundamentals of contemporary AI as well as a number of illustrative applications. Artificial intelligence (AI) is the ability of computers, computer programmes, and systems to carry out a person's intellectual and creative tasks, autonomously come up with solutions to issues, be able to draw conclusions, and make judgements in the context of the current digitalized world. The majority of artificial intelligence systems have the capacity to learn, which enables individuals to gradually increase their performance. The most current research on artificial intelligence (AI) techniques, such as machine learning, deep learning, and predictive analysis, aimed to improve the capacity for planning, learning, reasoning, thinking, and acting. In order to solve it within the next several decades, it will also examine future expectations for artificial intelligence. The capacity to learn and use a variety of abilities and information to address a particular issue is referred to as intelligence. Additionally, using one's broad mental abilities to reason through problems and learn new things is another aspect of intelligence. Multiple cognitive processes, including language, attention, planning, memory, and perception, are interwoven with intelligence. In the last 10 years, there has essentially been a lot of research on the development of intelligence. Both human and artificial intelligence are components of intelligence. Critical human intelligence in this context is concerned with problem-solving, thinking, and learning. Humans may also quickly learn basic complicated behaviours during their lifetime.

To-days Robotics and artificial intelligence (AI) are able to mimic human intellect in a variety of ways, including problem-solving, learning, and making judgement calls. Robots, computers, and other similar systems that have artificial intelligence software or programmes installed in them to give them the requisite thinking power. However, a lot of the present robotic artificial intelligence systems are still up for discussion since their methods for tackling problems still need more study. Artificial intelligence systems or robots should thus be able to do the necessary tasks without making mistakes. Robotics should also be able to carry out a variety of tasks independently of human direction or aid. With high performance skills like traffic management and speed minimization, today's artificial intelligence, including robotic automobiles, is quickly advancing. This includes SIRI and self-driving cars. The current focus on presenting artificial intelligence in robots for them to gain human-like traits significantly increases human dependency on technology. The capacity of artificial intelligence (AI) to efficiently carry out any specific cognitive activity also significantly increases people's reliance on technology. Artificial intelligence (AI) solutions that can handle massive volumes of data on computers may provide users with access to all the data for analysis. As a result, the danger posed by someone being able to collect and analyse data in a significant manner has increased significantly today. In recent years, artificial intelligence has been defined as the artificial representation of the human brain that strives to emulate the human learning process. It is important to convince everyone that it is impossible to construct artificial intelligence that is on par with the human brain. We have just used a portion of our powers thus far. Since information is now expanding quickly, just a small portion of the human brain is required. Because of how much more capable the human brain is than we can now comprehend or demonstrate. There are roughly 100 trillion electrically conducting cells, or neurons, in the human brain, which gives it an enormous computational ability to carry out tasks quickly and effectively.

Robots with human intellectual traits, behaviours, the capacity to learn from the past, detect, predict the future, and understand the significance of a given scenario are being developed using artificial intelligence. Current society is heavily influenced by robotic technology, which is becoming more and more popular in a variety of fields including business, healthcare, education, the military, entertainment, quantum physics, and many more. Artificial intelligence is a powerful tool that enables computers and software to govern robotic thought, using expert systems that clearly demonstrate intelligent behaviour, learn from experience, and provide users with useful advice. In general, artificial intelligence (AI) is understood to be the capacity for robots to think, make decisions, and solve problems. Artificial intelligence has led to a number of advances, such as robotic automobiles that don't need a driver to steer or keep an eye on them. Robotic technology (artificial intelligence) also includes intelligent devices that analyse vast amounts of data in ways that humans are not equipped to do. Robotics are already taking on routine tasks that call for intelligence and ingenuity. Additionally, artificial intelligence (AI) is the synthesis of a number of technologies that enables robots to comprehend, pick up knowledge, perceive, or carry out human tasks on their own. In this situation, artificial intelligence (AI) programmes (robots) are created with certain goals in mind, such as learning, acting, and understanding, but human intelligence is primarily concerned with many multitasking skills. An artificial intelligence tool's main focus often is on emphasising robotics that simulates human behaviours. However, because of differences between the human brain and computers, artificial intelligence may sometimes falter. In a nutshell, artificial intelligence has the capacity to replicate human personality or behaviour. Furthermore, artificial intelligence is now only partly developed, lacking sophisticated capacities for independent learning and relying instead on orders to execute actions. Artificial intelligence will eventually reach a point where it can recognise human behaviour and emotions and train its neural networks accordingly.

3. FUTURE TRENDS IN ARTIFICIAL INTELLIGENCE

Generally speaking, there are several ways to create intelligent machines that allow humans to create super-intelligent ones and give machines the ability to redesign their own software to boost their intelligence, a process known as the "intelligence explosion." In contrast, the primary component of the protected hu-man hunt is emotion. The development of AI technology has the potential to terrify people in ways that machines are unable to do. Therefore, there may be a chance that AI may assist humans with jobs and processes that often don't entail emotions or emotion. AI machines now lack the intellect and mind of humans in order to manage their processes. However, if AI growth continues at the same rate, mankind may be in danger since AI devices have the potential to learn harmful things via self-learning. This might lead to the abrupt extinction of humanity. In general, there are a number of traits that set human level intelligence apart from artificial intelligence, and these traits include the following. Due to the presence of emotions, which AI computers lack, thinking ability may be both beneficial and harmful. When emotions are needed, the absence of machine emotion might have negative consequences. According to Russell Stuart, machines would be able to reason in a limited way. In general, there are certain things that computers just cannot perform, regardless of the programming they are given, and some approaches to creating intelligent programmes are destined to fail eventually. A computer should be able to communicate for five minutes before being questioned, according to what would eventually become known as the Turing Test, and in reality, this goal was only partially met by the year 2000. Therefore, it may be said that robots are capable of thinking, despite the fact that they will never be able to laugh at themselves, fall in love, gain experience, tell good from evil, or exhibit other human traits. The last chapter of Artificial Intelligence: A Modern Approach wonders what might happen if computers with minds were created.

The relevance of AI has recently been discussed much more, which will likely lead to future arguments regarding whether artificial intelligence really exists. The goal of AI development is to simplify human existence. However, there is still much disagreement over the benefits and drawbacks of AI as a whole. Many global sectors are already benefiting from higher profitability thanks to the development and effective use of artificial intelligence (AI) technologies, and they will continue to have strong economic growth rates. Additionally, prospects for artificial intelligence will focus on innovation. The majority of businesses must take a more active role in development if these prospects are to be realised. The development of different artificial intelligence systems will assist the industrial sector globally in assuming the symbolic representations of things like reason and knowledge. Additionally, there will be worries about societal and political upheaval when artificial intelligence reaches an intellect higher than or equal to that of humans.In this situation, it is more possible that advancements in artificial intelligence will manifest themselves forcefully in the foreseeable future. Due to its many potential applications, artificial intelligence may make significant discoveries and breakthroughs for mankind in this manner. The majority of artificial intelligence systems have the capacity to learn, which enables individuals to gradually increase their performance. Outside of the IT industry, AI adoption is still in its early or experimental stages. The data indicates that AI may add genuine value to our lives.AI based its operation on acquiring enormous volumes of information, digesting it, and analysing it before performing tasks to address specific issues in accordance with its operation algorithms.

4. CONCLUSION

The future of AI will focus on enhancing speech, voice, video conferencing, and facial recognition in the next decades. Artificial intelligence will also help with personal support and completely automated systems that will help with heavy workloads, monitoring, and surveillance, among other things. Additionally, self-driving vehicles, delivery robots, and many other innovations will be made possible by artificial intelligence technologies such as robotics in the future. Robots inside surroundings will become more useful and aid in agriculture and other service settings as a result of the significant advancements in computer versions and legged movement. Additionally, robots will enhance service delivery, resulting in a decrease in household tasks. The enhancement of information quality and major information synthesis will result from the growth of search engines. Additionally, the advancement of the medical and biological systems via the use of artificial intelligence tools will lessen the complexity and amount of information difficulties that affect human skills. The algorithm that materialises numerous systems and programmes will employ artificial intelligence. Artificial intelligence will be made up of specialised hardware and software that aims to mimic how the human brain functions. Recent research on AI has significantly increased our understanding of the potential effects on organisations and industries. The use of AI technologies in product manufacturing processes will promote employment, flexibility, and a responsive supply chain.

REFERENCES

Chen, Z., Wang, G., & Li, L. L. (2017). Recurrent attentional reinforcement learning for multi-label image recognition. *arXiv:1712.07465.*

Ciregan, D., Meier, U., & Schmidhuber, J. (2017). Multi-column deep neural networks for image classification. *arXiv:1202.2745.*

De Vito, C., Angeloni, C., De Feo, E., Marzuillo, C., Lattanzi, A., Ricciardi, W., Villari, P., & Boccia, S. (2014). A large cross-sectional survey investigating the knowledge of cervical cancer risk etiology and the predictors of the adherence to cervical cancer screening related to mass media campaign. *BioMed Research International.* doi:10.1155/2014/304602 PMID:25013772

Goldin, C., & Katz, L. (2010). *The Race Between Education and Tech-nology.* Belknap Press for Harvard University Press. doi:10.2307/j.ctvjf9x5x

Gordon, R. J. (2016). The Rise and Fall of American Growth The U.S. Standard of Living since the Civil War. Princeton University Press.

Huynh, T., Pham, Q. V., Pham, X. Q., Nguyen, T. T., Han, Z., & Dong-Seong, K. (2023). Artificial intelligence for the metaverse: A survey. *Engineering Applications of Artificial Intelligence, 117,* 105581. doi:10.1016/j.engappai.2022.105581

Quillian, L., Pager, D., Hexel, O., & Midtboen, A. (2017). Meta-analysis of Field Experiments Shows No Change in Racial Discrimination in Hiring Over Time. *Proceedings of the National Academy of Sciences of the United States of America, 114*(41), 10870–10875. doi:10.1073/pnas.1706255114 PMID:28900012

Wang, J., Yang, J. H., Mao, Z. H., Huang, C., & Huang, W. X. (2016). CNN-RNN: A unified framework for multi-label image classification. *Proceedings of the 2016 IEEE Conference on Computer Vision and Pattern Recognition (CVRP).* 10.1109/CVPR.2016.251

Chapter 10
Impact of Negative Aspects of Artificial Intelligence on Customer Purchase Intention:
An Empirical Study of Online Retail Customers Towards AI-Enabled E-Retail Platforms

Arun Mittal
https://orcid.org/0000-0003-0602-8066
Birla Institute of Technology, India

Saumya Chaturvedi
Sri Guru Nanak Dev Khalsa College, India

Deen Dayal Chaturvedi
Sri Guru Gobind Singh College of Commerce, India

Priyank Kumar Singh
Doon University, India

ABSTRACT

The growing adoption of artificial intelligence (AI) in the retail industry has triggered a significant evolution in the shopping experience. However, concerns have surfaced regarding their potential psychological effects on consumers, which can sometimes lead to stress and confusion. As retailers continue to harness AI technology to enhance customer engagement and optimize their operations, it becomes increasingly important to confront and manage the potential risks and uncertainties that come with its swift deployment. The study considered 237 online retail customers to know the factors that determine the negative aspects of artificial intelligence and their impact on the purchase intention of online retail customers towards AI-enabled e-retail platforms. Financial information and security, consumer trust and AI autonomy, reliability issues due to novelty of the concept, and malfunctioning of systems are the factors that negatively impact the purchase intention of online retail customers towards AI-enabled e-retail platforms.

DOI: 10.4018/979-8-3693-0724-3.ch010

INTRODUCTION

The increasing integration of Artificial Intelligence (AI) in the retail sector has brought about a transformation in the shopping experience, introducing both opportunities and challenges. While AI-driven digital humans have been instrumental in enhancing the overall shopping journey, concerns have emerged regarding the psychological impact on consumers, leading to stress and confusion (Moore et al., 2022). As retailers strive to leverage AI technology to improve customer interactions and streamline operations, there is a growing need to address the potential risks and uncertainties associated with its rapid implementation.

In recent years, AI has become an integral part of the retail industry, offering a range of capabilities from chatbots and recommendation engines to cashier-less stores and personalised shopping experiences. These innovations have been widely celebrated for their potential to enhance operational efficiency, provide personalised services, and optimise decision-making processes. Beneath the surface of these advancements lie complex challenges that need to be recognized and addressed.

Acknowledging the transformative potential of AI, scholars have raised alarm about the uncontrolled advancement of Artificial General Intelligence (AGI) and the consequent risks to humanity. This has prompted calls for proactive regulatory measures to ensure that AI development aligns with ethical standards and societal well-being (Mahmoud et al., 2020). Despite the promise of AI-driven innovations in retail, a cautious approach is advised to avoid excessive dependence on AI systems. Emphasising the importance of a balanced approach, experts suggest that AI should complement human capabilities rather than replace them entirely (Guha et al., 2021). This consideration underscores the significance of non-customer-facing AI applications and the necessity of integrating AI with existing retail processes.

In addition to the practical challenges associated with AI implementation, there are also critical ethical and governance concerns that need to be addressed. The lack of transparency in AI decision-making processes calls for comprehensive policy frameworks and ethical guidelines (Dwivedi et al., 2019). The potential displacement of jobs due to increased automation has ignited discussions about the future of work and the coexistence of humans and AI in the retail industry as well.

As the retail landscape evolves, with online platforms becoming increasingly dominant, it's crucial to understand how AI's negative aspects influence the intentions of online retail customers. The choices consumers make and the level of trust they place in AI-enabled e-retail platforms can have a significant impact on the industry's future direction. In light of these complexities, this study aims to delve into the negative aspects of AI integration in the retail sector, focusing on its impact on the purchase intention of online retail customers towards AI-enabled e-retail platforms.

LITERATURE REVIEW

Financial Information and Security

The integration of AI-driven business analytics can compromise decision-making due to opacity, deficient governance, and data quality issues. This not only escalates perceived risks but also leads to operational inefficiencies, hampering sales growth and employee satisfaction. Implementing stringent AI governance, ensuring high-quality data, and providing comprehensive employee training are vital. At the same time, fostering a culture of adaptability to technological changes and building dynamic contingency plans can bolster a firm's resilience and sustained competitiveness (Rana et al., 2022).

The rapid integration of AI and robotics in the retail and service sectors necessitates a robust approach to privacy protection and consumer data ownership. Apart from regulatory measures, proactive steps by businesses and consumers are imperative in mitigating potential privacy breaches. Encouraging responsible data-sharing practices and promoting transparent consumer-robot interactions can uphold consumer trust while harnessing the transformative potential of AI and robotics for enhanced customer experiences and operational efficiencies (Noble & Mende, 2023).

The seamless integration of AI technologies in e-commerce has intensified concerns about data security and privacy breaches. Strengthening consumer awareness regarding data protection and cultivating a culture of data transparency and accountability within e-commerce platforms are crucial. And, advocating for comprehensive regulatory frameworks and industry standards can reinforce consumer confidence, thereby fostering sustainable growth and a secure online retail environment conducive to healthy customer-business relationships (Wang et al., 2021).

The proliferation of AI-driven products has magnified ethical dilemmas surrounding bias, privacy infringement, and the broader societal impact of AI adoption. While promoting corporate social responsibility is essential, a deeper exploration of potential adverse effects stemming from AI integration is critical. Developing comprehensive ethical guidelines for AI development and usage can help foster a more sustainable and equitable business landscape, fostering trust and promoting the responsible deployment of AI technologies for the benefit of all stakeholders (Du & Xie, 2020).

The rapidly evolving landscape of e-commerce poses a significant challenge in safeguarding consumer privacy. Addressing the widening gap between technological advancements and privacy protection measures necessitates continuous research efforts. Putting more focus on the importance of consumer education on data privacy, coupled with proactive measures to address emerging privacy concerns, can aid businesses in building consumer trust and enhancing their market positioning. Adopting robust privacy management strategies and staying attuned to evolving consumer privacy expectations are imperative for sustained growth and success in the digital marketplace (Bandara et al., 2019).

Consumer Trust and AI autonomy

Consumer scepticism towards highly autonomous AI services challenges the conventional assumption that trust is sufficient for widespread AI adoption. Establishing transparency and building trust are crucial to mitigating negative perceptions and fostering greater acceptance of AI-powered solutions, especially those with higher autonomy levels (Frank et al., 2023).

The integration of humanoid Retail Service Robots (RSRs) in retail encounters consumer unease, impacting the effectiveness of these robots despite their perceived usefulness and social capability. Addressing consumer anxieties is imperative to promote favourable acceptance and enhance the Human-Robot Interaction (HRI) experience (Song & Kim, 2022).

Consumer behaviour in digital retail is significantly shaped by perceived risks and privacy apprehensions. While acknowledging the pivotal role of these factors, the need for further empirical research arises to bridge existing gaps, especially in understanding the dynamics of trust and risk in mobile shopping environments. Identifying and addressing the barriers encountered across various stages of the online shopping journey can help fortify customer confidence and drive greater acceptance of e-commerce platforms (Marriott et al., 2017).

Despite the positive influence of various factors on consumer shopping intentions, persistent consumer insecurity and distrust regarding AI-powered retail environments present challenges. Ensuring consumer privacy and security in AI-driven retail environments is crucial for fostering trust and confidence among customers (Pillai et al., 2020).

Ameen et al. (2021) highlights that while consumer trust is pivotal, engaging with AI-driven services may entail significant sacrifices such as the loss of privacy and control. The need for a comprehensive understanding of the potential trade-offs and challenges in AI-driven services underscores the importance of addressing consumer concerns and ensuring a balanced approach to AI integration in the retail sector.

Nicolescu & Tudorache (2022) found that privacy concerns and unmet expectations from anthropomorphic features can lead to distrust and inconvenience in customer interactions with AI chatbots. While task-oriented chatbots excel in handling simple tasks, they might lack suitability in more complex scenarios, affecting customer behaviour and their continued use of the service.

Sivathanu et al. (2023) highlights the adverse impact of perceived deception in AI-generated "deep fake" advertisements on customer shopping intent, emphasising the importance of transparency and authenticity in marketing practices to foster consumer trust.

While the perceived friendliness and empathy of AI-based chatbots positively impact consumer trust, the relationship weakens during complex tasks. Additionally, the disclosure of the chatbot's identity can influence consumer perceptions, indicating potential challenges in implementing AI-based chatbots in e-commerce (Cheng et al., 2021).

Reliability Issues Due to Novelty of the Concept

Implementing AI in the retail industry can overlook critical operational and environmental implications, potentially leading to security vulnerabilities and data breaches, especially in less-prepared technological environments. Understanding the challenges posed by AI adoption is crucial for implementing robust security measures and ensuring organisational preparedness (Fu et al., 2023).

Gursoy et al. (2019) identified the factors influencing customers' acceptance of AI device use in service encounters but underscores the need for broader cross-national studies to ensure the generalizability of findings. Its limited scope restricts the applicability of the model, indicating uncertainties regarding the broader implications of AI adoption on customer behaviour across various sectors.

While AI-enabled checkouts enhance store experiences, neglecting potential concerns like privacy issues and impacts on traditional employment limits the understanding of AI integration in retail settings (Cui et al., 2022).

Implementing artificial empathy in AI marketing must be balanced, considering situations where its use may be unnecessary or detrimental. Ensuring meaningful and effective customer interactions with AI agents is crucial for fostering trust and enhancing customer experiences (Liu-Thompkins et al., 2022).

Trawnih et al. (2022) explored the potential trade-offs customers may face, including the loss of human connection and control, as well as the potential for irritability, in utilising AI services and cautions businesses about the potential drawbacks and challenges associated with incorporating AI in customer services, urging them to consider these implications for customer experiences.

While GAN technology positively influences consumer evaluations of fashion products, disclosing its use can lead to scepticism and lower purchase intentions. Educating consumers and managing their expectations is crucial for fostering trust and acceptance of AI technologies in product development (Sohn et al., 2020).

Malfunctioning of Systems

While AI has the potential to enhance tourist experiences through personalised services and integrated technological networks, its implementation poses risks, such as diminished social interactions and overpowering technological dominance. Grundner & Neuhofer (2021) emphasised the necessity for careful planning to maximise AI's positive potential and mitigate adverse impacts on the authentic autonomy of tourist experiences.

Consumer moral behaviour shows a notable decline when interacting with AI checkout and self-service technologies compared to human counterparts in the retail industry. This decline is linked to reduced feelings of guilt, indicating distinct perceptions of social and moral norms in human-technology interactions. Recognizing and addressing these ethical challenges is crucial for fostering responsible and ethical practices in the retail environment (Giroux et al., 2022).

The escalating integration of intelligent automation in the travel and tourism sector calls for a comprehensive research agenda focused on identifying pitfalls, examining barriers to adoption, assessing negative consequences, and ensuring responsible AI implementation. This approach is vital to inform policy interventions and guide stakeholders in the conscientious and sustainable deployment of AI technologies in the tourism industry (Tussyadiah, 2020).

While consumers favour the efficiency of chatbots in handling basic inquiries, their implementation can negatively impact human agents. This shift in consumer expectations highlights the complexities faced by retailers in balancing chatbot benefits with maintaining satisfactory human-agent experiences, particularly concerning service responsiveness and customer satisfaction (Tran et al., 2021).

Aytekin et al. (2021) underscores potential security, privacy, and ethical risks stemming from AI integration in the wholesale and retail trade sectors. Concerns include the potential malfunctioning of AI-driven robots, privacy violations through data collection, and the possibility of AI systems replacing human workers. Implementing stringent safety protocols and regulatory limits are necessary to manage and mitigate these risks.

Conceptual Framework of the Study

Figure 1. Conceptual Framework of the Study

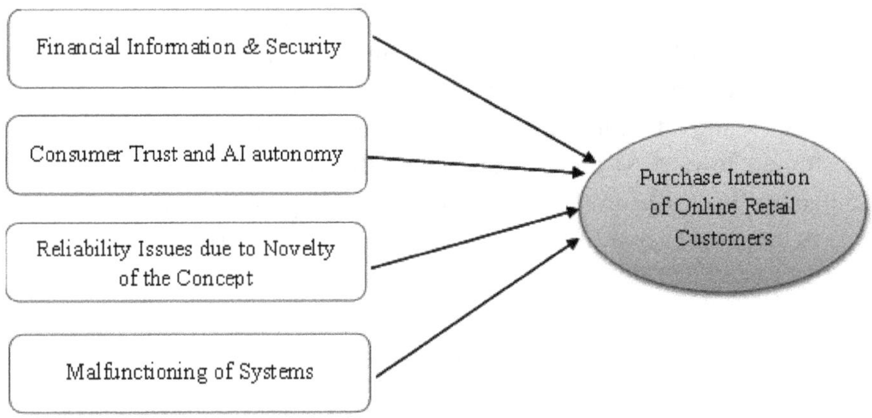

Objectives of the Study

1. To determine factors constituting the negative aspects of Artificial Intelligence in the context of online retailing customers' experience.
2. To measure the impact negative aspects of AI on purchase intention of online retail customers towards AI enabled e-retail platforms.

Methodology

Research Design: Primary data is collected from online retail customers. Survey method has been used to collect the data. The nature of research is quantitative.

Sample Size and Source of Data: In this study, we applied both "Exploratory Factor Analysis" and "Multiple Regression Analysis." It is generally assumed that for factor analysis, the sample size should consist of at least 10 respondents per item or statement (Hair et al., 2006). In the case of Multiple Regression, the minimum sample size required can be calculated using $N \geq 104 + m$, where m represents the number of predictors (Green, 1991). In our research, we have identified four predictors through factor analysis, so the minimum sample size required is $104 + 4$, which equals 108 (Burmeister & Aitken, 2012). As per the criteria stated in statement

(18), the sample size requirement is either 180 respondents or 108 respondents. We collected data from 237 customers, which fulfills the minimum requirements for conducting Exploratory Factor Analysis. Only those respondents who had experienced AI-based online retail shopping were included in the final questionnaire. To ensure this, we included five qualifying statements in the questionnaire.

Data Analysis Techniques: In this study, we initially employed Exploratory Factor Analysis (EFA) for data reduction. Subsequently, Multiple Regression Analysis was utilized to assess the influence of various factors on the purchase intention of online retail customers toward AI-enabled e-retail platforms. The independent variables, represented by "Factor Scores" derived from the EFA process, were included in the analysis. A comprehensive list of these variables, along with their corresponding codes, is presented in Table 1:

Table 1. Details of the Dependent and Independent Variables

Variables	Type of Variables	Denotation
Financial Information & Security	IDV	β1
Consumer Trust and AI autonomy	IDV	β2
Reliability Issues due to Novelty of the Concept	IDV	β3
Malfunctioning of Systems	IDV	β4
Purchase Intention of Online Retail Customers	DV	Y
Constant		α

Note: IDV- Independent Variable, DV – Dependent Variable

Multiple Regression Equation proposed:

$$Y = \text{“}\alpha\ (\text{Constant}) + \beta1^*\ (X1) + \beta2^*\ (X2) + \beta3^*\ (X3) + \beta4^*\ (X4) + \epsilon\text{”}$$

Y = Dependent Variable
α = Constant or Intercept
β1 to β4 = Parameters to be estimated
ϵ = Error Term or Residual

Findings

General demographic information regarding respondents indicated that 58.6% are males are rest 41.4% are female. 36.3% of them are below 28 years of age, 40.9% are from the age group of 28-40 years and the rest 22.8% are above 40 years of age. 34.2% of the respondents are students, 41.3% are homemakers, 37.6% are salaried, 29.1% are self-employed/business, 32.9% are professionals. 24.9% of the respondents have a monthly income of Below Rs. 51,000, 33.8% are earning Rs. 51,000-1,00000 every month and the remaining 41.3% are having a monthly income of Above Rs. 1,00000.

The factor analysis implied for main factors (See table 10.2 and table 10.3) .

Table 2 shows that 18 variables form 4 Factor, and the factors explained the variance of 23.889%, 22.229%, 16.601% and 16.243% respectively and the total variance explained is 78.961%.

Table 2. Total Variance Explained

Component	"Initial Eigen Values"			"Rotation Sums of Squared Loadings"		
	Total	% of Variance	Cumulative %	Total	% of Variance	Cumulative %
1	8.162	45.342	45.342	4.300	**23.889**	23.889
2	2.488	13.820	59.162	4.001	**22.229**	46.118
3	1.994	11.076	70.238	2.988	**16.601**	62.719
4	1.570	8.724	78.961	2.924	**16.243**	**78.961**
5	.622	3.456	82.417			
6	.541	3.005	85.422			
7	.455	2.526	87.948			
8	.370	2.056	90.004			
9	.339	1.882	91.886			
10	.273	1.518	93.404			
11	.232	1.291	94.695			
12	.209	1.159	95.854			
13	.183	1.014	96.868			
14	.159	.886	97.754			
15	.141	.782	98.536			
16	.114	.635	99.171			
17	.082	.455	99.626			
18	.067	.374	100.000			

Table 3 shows different factors and its variables that determines the negative aspects of Artificial Intelligence where first factor is "Financial Information & Security" which includes the variables like AI systems susceptible to cyberattacks, AI technologies in e-commerce has intensified concerns about data security and privacy breaches, Promotes robust regulatory frameworks and established industry

Table 3. Rotated Component Matrix

S. No.		Factor Loading	Factor Reliability
	Financial Information & Security		**.957**
1	AI systems susceptible to cyberattacks	.865	
2	AI technologies in e-commerce has intensified concerns about data security and privacy breaches	.860	
3	Promotes robust regulatory frameworks and established industry standards	.853	
4	AI-driven business analytics compromise decision-making due to opacity and deficient governance	.847	
5	Misuse or mishandling of data by AI systems lead to legal consequences	.792	
	Consumer Trust and AI autonomy		**.925**
6	Lack of transparency can erode consumer trust	.892	
7	AI systems can get biases from training data, which lead to unfair outcomes	.884	
8	Consumer doubt towards autonomous AI services challenges the conventional assumptions	.860	
9	Privacy concerns and unmet expectations from humanlike features	.853	
10	Concerns about how decisions are made and whether they align with customer's values and interests	.712	
	Reliability Issues due to Novelty of the Concept		**.887**
11	AI in the retail industry overlook critical operational and environmental implications	.888	
12	Loss of human connection and control, as well as the potential for irritability	.873	
13	AI systems struggle to provide reliable outcomes where traditional data sources are limited	.858	
14	Understanding the challenges posed by AI adoption is crucial for ensuring organizational preparedness	.670	
	Malfunctioning of Systems		**.866**
15	AI implementation poses risks like reduced social interactions and overpowering technological dominance	.847	
16	Consumer behavior shows notable decline while interacting with AI checkout and self-services	.838	
17	Diminished feelings of guilt suggest a separate interpretation of societal and ethical standards	.790	
18	Shift in consumer expectations shows complexities faced by retailers in balancing chatbot benefits	.747	
DV	Purchase Intention of Online Retail Customers towards AI Enabled E-Retail Platforms		

standards, AI-driven business analytics compromise decision-making due to opacity and deficient governance and Misuse or mishandling of data by AI systems lead to legal consequences. Second factor is "Consumer Trust and AI autonomy" and its associated variables are Lack of transparency can erode consumer trust, AI systems can get biases from training data, which lead to unfair outcomes, Consumer doubt towards autonomous AI services challenges the conventional assumptions, Privacy concerns and unmet expectations from humanlike features and Concerns about how decisions are made and whether they align with customer's values and interests. Third factor is "Reliability Issues due to Novelty of the Concept" which includes the variables like AI in the retail industry overlook critical operational and environmental implications, Loss of human connection and control, as well as the potential for irritability, AI systems struggle to provide reliable outcomes where traditional data sources are limited and understanding the challenges posed by AI adoption is crucial for ensuring organizational preparedness. Fourth factor is "Malfunctioning of Systems" and its associated variables are AI implementation poses risks like reduced social interactions and overpowering technological dominance, Consumer behavior shows notable decline while interacting with AI checkout and self-services, Diminished feelings of guilt suggest a separate interpretation of societal and ethical standards and Shift in consumer expectations shows complexities faced by retailers in balancing chatbot benefits.

The Multiple Regression Analysis:

Multiple regressions show that the model explained is 52% of the variance and R Square is .521 and the linear regression model is valid (Anova sig 0.000).

Table 4 shows that all the factors namely Financial Information & Security, Consumer Trust and AI autonomy, Reliability Issues due to Novelty of the Concept and Malfunctioning of Systems are showing negatively significant impact on "Purchase Intention of Online Retail Customers towards AI Enabled E-Retail Platforms". It is also found that highest impact is shown by Consumer Trust and

Table 4. Coefficients Results of Hypotheses Testing

Predictors	B*	Std. B*	Sig.	Results of Hypotheses Testing
(Constant)	3.101		.000	.....
Financial Information & Security	-.099	-.123	.008	Supported
Consumer Trust and AI autonomy	-.560	-.694	.000	Supported
Reliability Issues due to Novelty of the Concept	-.079	-.098	.032	Supported
Malfunctioning of Systems	-.099	-.123	.007	Supported

AI autonomy with beta value -0.694 followed by Financial Information & Security and Malfunctioning of Systems with beta value -0.123 and Reliability Issues due to Novelty of the Concept with beta value -0.098.

Figure 2. Impact of Negative Aspects of AI on Customer Purchase Intention

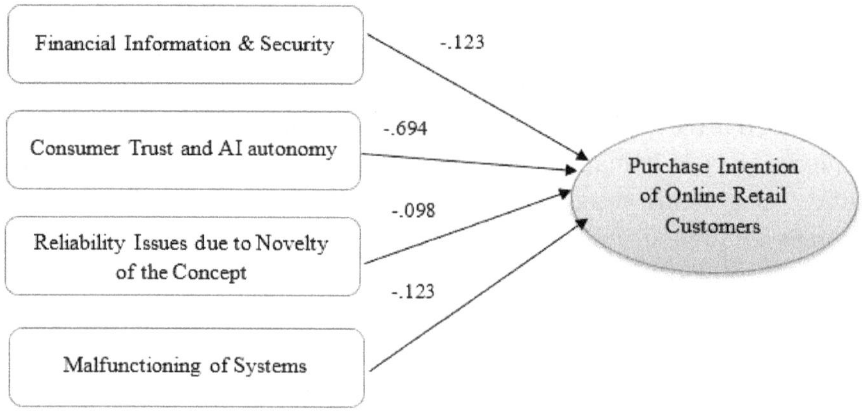

CONCLUSION

The study was conducted to know the factors that determines the negative aspects of Artificial Intelligence and the impact of different factors on purchase intention of online retail customers towards AI enabled e-retail platforms. It is found that Financial Information & Security, Consumer Trust and AI autonomy, Reliability Issues due to Novelty of the Concept and Malfunctioning of Systems are the factors that determines the negative aspects of Artificial Intelligence and there is negatively significant impact of different factors on purchase intention of online retail customers towards AI enabled e-retail platforms.

REFERENCES

Ameen, N., Tarhini, A., Reppel, A., & Anand, A. (2021). Customer experiences in the age of artificial intelligence. *Computers in Human Behavior*, *114*, 1–14. doi:10.1016/j.chb.2020.106548 PMID:32905175

Aytekin, P., Virlanuta, F. O., Guven, H., Stanciu, S., & Bolakca, I. (2021). Consumers Perception of Risk Towards Artificial Intelligence Technologies Used in Trade: A Scale Development Study. *Amfiteatru Economic*, *23*(56), 65–86. doi:10.24818/EA/2021/56/65

Bandara, R., Fernando, M., & Akter, S. (2019). Privacy Concerns in E-commerce: A Taxonomy and a Future Research Agenda. *Electronic Markets, 30*(3), 629–647. doi:10.1007/s12525-019-00375-6

Burmeister, E., & Aitken, L. M. (2012). Sample size: how many is enough? *Australian Critical Care: Official Journal of the Confederation of Australian Critical Care Nurses, 25*(4), 271– 274. doi:10.1016/j.aucc.2012.07.002

Cheng, X., Bao, Y., Zarifis, A., Gong, W., & Mou, J. (2021). Exploring consumers' response to text-based chatbots in e-commerce: The moderating role of task complexity and chatbot disclosure. *Internet Research, 32*(2), 496–517. doi:10.1108/INTR-08-2020-0460

Cui, Y. (Gina), van Esch, P., & Jain, S. P. (2022). Just walk out: The effect of AI-enabled checkouts. *European Journal of Marketing, 56*(6), 1650–1683.

Du, S., & Xie, C. (2020). Paradoxes of Artificial Intelligence in Consumer markets: Ethical Challenges and Opportunities. *Journal of Business Research, 129*, 1–14.

Dwivedi, Y. K., Hughes, L., Ismagilova, E., Aarts, G., Coombs, C., Crick, T., Duan, Y., Dwivedi, R., Edwards, J., Eirug, A., Galanos, V., Ilavarasan, P. V., Janssen, M., Jones, P., Kar, A. K., Kizgin, H., Kronemann, B., Lal, B., Lucini, B., & Medaglia, R. (2019). Artificial Intelligence (AI): Multidisciplinary perspectives on emerging challenges, opportunities, and agenda for research, practice, and policy. *International Journal of Information Management, 57*, 1–47.

Frank, D.-A., Jacobsen, L. F., Søndergaard, H. A., & Otterbring, T. (2023). In companies we trust consumer adoption of artificial intelligence services and the role of trust in companies and AI autonomy. *Information Technology & People, 36*(8), 155–173. doi:10.1108/ITP-09-2022-0721

Fu, H.-P., Chang, T.-H., Lin, S.-W., Teng, Y.-H., & Huang, Y.-Z. (2023). Evaluation and adoption of artificial intelligence in the retail industry. *International Journal ofRetail & Distribution Management, 51*(6), 773–790. doi:10.1108/IJRDM-12-2021-0610

Giroux, M., Kim, J., Lee, J. C., & Park, J. (2022). Artificial Intelligence and Declined Guilt: Retailing Morality Comparison Between Human and AI. *Journal of Business Ethics, 178*(4), 1027–1041. doi:10.1007/s10551-022-05056-7 PMID:35194275

Green, S. B. (1991). How many subjects does it take to do a regression analysis? *Multivariate Behavioral Research, 1991*(26), 499–510. doi:10.1207/s15327906mbr2603_7 PMID:26776715

Grundner, L., & Neuhofer, B. (2021). The bright and dark sides of artificial intelligence: A futures perspective on tourist destination experiences. *Journal of Destination Marketing & Management, 19*, 1–25. doi:10.1016/j.jdmm.2020.100511

Guha, A., Grewal, D., Kopalle, P. K., Haenlein, M., Schneider, M. J., Jung, H., Moustafa, R., Hegde, D. R., & Hawkins, G. (2021). How Artificial Intelligence Will Affect the Future of Retailing. *Journal of Retailing*, *97*(1), 28–41. doi:10.1016/j.jretai.2021.01.005

Gursoy, D., Chi, O. H., Lu, L., & Nunkoo, R. (2019). Consumers acceptance of artificially intelligent (AI) device use in service delivery. *International Journal of Information Management*, *49*(49), 157–169. doi:10.1016/j.ijinfomgt.2019.03.008

Hair, J. F., Black, W. C., Babin, B. J., Anderson, R. E., & Tatham, R. L. (2006). Multivariate data analysis (6th ed.). Pearson Prentice Hall.

Liu-Thompkins, Y., Okazaki, S., & Li, H. (2022). Artificial empathy in marketing interactions: Bridging the human-AI gap in affective and social customer experience. *Journal of the Academy of Marketing Science*, *50*(6), 1198–1218. doi:10.1007/s11747-022-00892-5

Mahmoud, A. B., Tehseen, S., & Fuxman, L. (2020). The Dark Side of Artificial Intelligence in Retail Innovation. *Retail Futures*, 165–180.

Marriott, H. R., Williams, M. D., & Dwivedi, Y. K. (2017). Risk, privacy and security concerns in digital retail. *The Marketing Review*, *17*(3), 337–365. doi:10.1362/146934717X14909733966254

Moore, S., Bulmer, S., & Elms, J. (2022). The social significance of AI in retail on customer experience and shopping practices. *Journal of Retailing and Consumer Services*, *64*(1), 1–8. doi:10.1016/j.jretconser.2021.102755

Nicolescu, L., & Tudorache, M. T. (2022). Human-Computer Interaction in Customer Service: The Experience with AI Chatbots—A Systematic Literature Review. *Electronics (Basel)*, *11*(10), 1–24. doi:10.3390/electronics11101579

Noble, S. M., & Mende, M. (2023). The future of artificial intelligence and robotics in the retail and service sector: Sketching the field of consumer-robot-experiences. *Journal of the Academy of Marketing Science*, *51*(4), 747–756. doi:10.1007/s11747-023-00948-0 PMID:37359262

Pillai, R., Sivathanu, B., & Dwivedi, Y. K. (2020). Shopping intention at AI-powered automated retail stores (AIPARS). *Journal of Retailing and Consumer Services*, *57*, 1–15. doi:10.1016/j.jretconser.2020.102207

Rana, N. P., Chatterjee, S., Dwivedi, Y. K., & Akter, S. (2022). Understanding Dark Side of Artificial Intelligence (AI) Integrated Business analytics: Assessing Firm's Operational Inefficiency and Competitiveness. *European Journal of Information Systems, 31*(3), 364–387. doi:10.1080/0960085X.2021.1955628

Sivathanu, B., Pillai, R., & Metri, B. (2023). Customers' online shopping intention by watching AI-based deepfake advertisements. *International Journal of Retail & Distribution Management, 51*(1), 124–145. doi:10.1108/IJRDM-12-2021-0583

Sohn, K., Sung, C. E., Koo, G., & Kwon, O. (2020). Artificial intelligence in the fashion industry: Consumer responses to generative adversarial network (GAN) technology. *International Journal of Retail & Distribution Management, 49*(1), 61–80. doi:10.1108/IJRDM-03-2020-0091

Song, C. S., & Kim, Y.-K. (2022). The role of the human-robot interaction in consumers' acceptance of humanoid retail service robots. *Journal of Business Research, 146*, 489–503. doi:10.1016/j.jbusres.2022.03.087

Tran, A. D., Pallant, J. I., & Johnson, L. W. (2021). Exploring the impact of chatbots on consumer sentiment and expectations in retail. *Journal of Retailing and Consumer Services, 63*, 1–10. doi:10.1016/j.jretconser.2021.102718

Trawnih, A., Al-Masaeed, S., Alsoud, M., & Alkufahy, A. M. (2022). Understanding artificial intelligence experience: A customer perspective. *International Journal of Data and Network Science, 6*(4), 1471–1484. doi:10.5267/j.ijdns.2022.5.004

Tussyadiah, I. (2020). A review of research into automation in tourism: Launching the Annals of Tourism Research Curated Collection on Artificial Intelligence and Robotics in Tourism. *Annals of Tourism Research, 81*, 1–13. doi:10.1016/j.annals.2020.102883

Wang, S., Chen, Z., Xiao, Y., & Lin, C. (2021). Consumer Privacy Protection with the Growth of AI-Empowered Online Shopping Based on the Evolutionary Game Model. *Frontiers in Public Health, 9*, 1–9. doi:10.3389/fpubh.2021.705777 PMID:34307290

Chapter 11
Sustainable Development and AI:
Navigating Safety and Ethical Challenges

Sohail Verma
https://orcid.org/0000-0002-2271-0455
Lovely Professional University, India

Pretty Bhalla
Lovely Professional University, India

ABSTRACT

This chapter delves into the fusion of artificial intelligence (AI) and Sustainable Development Goals (SDGs), emphasizing the need to navigate safety risks and ethical concerns. AI offers substantial potential in addressing sustainability challenges across various domains, such as energy conservation, workplace management, and advertising. However, its integration may influence employee well-being and data privacy. To effectively achieve SDGs, organizations must adopt proactive strategies to manage these inherent risks, ensuring a harmonious integration of AI and sustainability for a promising and equitable future.

INTRODUCTION

United Nations: Sustainable Development Goals

The United Nations overwhelmingly endorsed the Sustainable Development Goals (SDGs), often known as the Global Goals, in 2015, representing a universal call to action. By 2030, this revolutionary agenda seeks to alleviate poverty, safeguard the

DOI: 10.4018/979-8-3693-0724-3.ch011

environment, and advance peace and prosperity for all. These objectives lay forth a big vision for eradicating AIDS, gender prejudice, hunger, and poverty, with a special emphasis on improving the position of women and girls. Attaining these goals will necessitate the collective commitment and participation of our whole community, drawing upon our creativity, knowledge, technological advancements, and financial resources. The SDGs serve as a guiding compass, urging governments, organizations, and individuals to align their efforts and and collaboratively craft a world that thrives sustainably and welcomes all. It is a call to leverage the power of innovation, collaboration, and compassion to bring about meaningful change in every context and for every individual, ultimately shaping a brighter future for generations to come. These objectives provide a thorough framework to direct activities made in the name of sustainable development worldwide. Following are the 17 SDGs:

Zero Hunger, Good Health and Well-being, Quality Education, Gender Equality, Clean Water and Sanitation, Affordable and Clean Energy, Decent Work and Economic Growth, Industry, Innovation, and Infrastructure, Reduced Inequalities, Sustainable Cities and Communities, Responsible Consumption and Production, Climate Action, Life on Land, Peace, Justice, and Strong Institutions, Partnerships for the Goals, No Poverty, Life Below Water.

In addition to these ambitious objectives, it is crucial to consider the safety risks associated with the integration of Artificial Intelligence (AI) into the pursuit of these goals. The introduction of AI in various sectors can potentially introduce safety risks that need careful consideration and management to ensure the well-being of all stakeholders (Aliman et al., 2019; UN, 2015).

Research Questions

- How does the integration of Artificial Intelligence (AI) contribute to the advancement of Sustainable Development Goals (SDGs) in diverse sectors, including energy conservation, workplace management, and advertising?
- What safety risks are inherent in the deployment of AI across different domains, particularly in the workplace, energy conservation initiatives, and advertising strategies? How do these risks manifest, and what potential consequences do they pose to individuals and organizations?
- In what ways can organizations effectively safeguard ethical practices during the implementation of AI, considering concerns such as data privacy, algorithmic biases, and the overall impact on individual well-being? What regulatory frameworks and proactive strategies can be proposed to mitigate these ethical challenges and ensure responsible AI deployment?

Balancing Sustainable Development and AI Advancements: Achieving SDG 9 While Managing AI Safety Risks

In recent times, there has been a growing focus on Sustainable Development, which has become a prominent theme in conferences, research articles, and various developmental and environmental activities. Desire for progress that meets present requirements without jeopardizing the ability of forthcoming generations to meet their own necessities is often described as sustainable development and has origins in the 18th century (World Commission on Environment and growth, 1987). Sustainability has emerged as a key objective, aiming to address the demands of the present generation while protecting those of future generations and making optimal use of available resources. Under the auspices of Agenda 2030, the United Nations approved the SDGs in 2015 with the intention of advancing world peace, raising standards of living, preserving the environment, and creating prosperity for everyone. (Ionescu et al., 2020). Achieving the SDGs requires collective efforts from various stakeholders, including governments, businesses, educational institutions, healthcare providers, and the general public (Cai & Choi, 2020).

The 17 SDGs, comprising a total of 169 targets, encompass a wide range of goals that cover aspects such as workplaces, health, education, markets, and more. These objectives encompass eradicating famine and poverty, ensuring access to top-notch education and healthcare, and nurturing gender parity., ensuring access to hygienic water and sanitation, working to develop affordable, sustainable energy, fostering inclusive workplaces, encouraging equitable utilisation of natural resources, combating climate change, protecting marine resources, and forming international partnerships. (Ionescu et al., 2020). SDG 9 specifically recognizes the significance of developing sustainable and resilient industries and infrastructure, as well as utilizing environmentally friendly technologies. It is closely linked to enhancing economic and social development and promoting progress in the industrial sector. Effective management plays a paramount role in achieving SDG 9. Society, culture, and the economy have experienced significant changes, largely driven by technology (Ivaldi et al., 2022).

The beginning of the fourth industrial revolution, characterized by a surge in the usage of cutting-edge technology like artificial intelligence (AI), the internet of things (IoT), machine learning, and virtual reality, has brought about transformative changes across various domains (Kwiotkowska et al., 2021; Jeon & Suh, 2017). As organizations adapt to these changes, they require consistent support and guidance from management, along with the effective utilization of employees and technology for smooth operations. AI, in particular, has emerged as a prominent element of the

4th Industrial Revolution, capturing the attention of organizations for its potential to drive development and innovation (Hassani et al., 2020; Vinuesa et al., 2020).

However, alongside the incredible potential of AI, there are also safety risks to consider. AI, as a rapidly advancing field that mimics human thought processes, has applications spanning multiple sectors, including education, healthcare, science, law, engineering, and more (Votto et al., 2021). It introduces new dynamics in workplaces, affecting employees' stress levels, work-life balance, quality of life, and physical and mental health (Fukumura et al., 2021). Organizations recognize the importance of creating a conducive work environment and are adopting strategies to promote employee health, well-being, and productivity (Litchfield et al., 2016).

However, the integration of AI in the workplace can also pose safety risks, including concerns related to data privacy, algorithmic biases, and the potential for AI systems to make critical errors that impact employees' well-being and the organization's overall effectiveness. Ensuring the safe and responsible deployment of AI in the workplace is crucial in achieving the goals of SDG 9 while mitigating these associated risks (Smith et al., 2022).

Through encouraging sustainability and the effective use of resources in an ecologically responsible way, employers play a crucial role in attaining SDG 9 in society, all while safeguarding against the potential safety risks introduced by AI (Smith et al., 2022).

Fostering Sustainable Development With AI: Navigating Safety Risks in Transforming Industries

Artificial intelligence (AI) has gained increasing recognition and prominence across various fields, thanks to continuous advancements. As a potent and promising instrument for achieving the SDGs (Vinuesa et al., 2020), AI is increasingly recognized as a major facilitator for sustainable development in a variety of fields, including transportation, the environment, agriculture, and the economy. Its potential lies in addressing complex sustainability challenges, including waste management, efficient resource utilization, cost savings, land planning, crop evaluation, weather prediction, air pollution forecasting, and monitoring of water resources and energy demands (Vinuesa et al., 2020).

However, it's essential to acknowledge that with the vast potential AI offers, there are also safety risks that demand attention. The integration of AI into various sectors introduces unique challenges, including data security, algorithmic fairness, and the need to ensure that AI systems do not inadvertently harm individuals or communities. For instance, in agriculture, AI-driven decisions must consider not only crop evaluation but also ethical practices to avoid potential environmental damage (Smith & Johnson, 2021). The adoption of AI in industries has the potential to revolutionize operations with concepts like the "smart factory." However, this technological shift also requires a closer look at potential safety risks. Ensuring that AI-driven automation processes are secure, resilient, and error-free is crucial to prevent accidents, data breaches, or financial losses (Jones et al., 2022). As a result, implementing AI at work brings creative management techniques and has a favorable influence on staff members, workers, and other employees while also necessitating a careful evaluation of safety concerns (Smith & Johnson, 2021; Jones et al., 2022).

Adopting AI in the Workplace: Ensuring Safety and Ethical Practices

The dynamic interaction between humans and machines has revolutionized the division of work, with artificial intelligence (AI) playing a pivotal role. It is crucial for AI implementation to allocate mundane tasks to machines and technological systems, while reserving creative endeavors for human beings (Jarrahi, 2018).

While AI brings a host of advantages in organizational settings, such as increased efficiency and reduced repetitive tasks, it also raises significant concerns regarding safety and ethics. Responsible AI deployment involves the proactive addressal of these concerns to ensure a safe and equitable working environment. It is essential that organizations and policymakers collaborate to develop and enhance rules and legislation aimed at protecting the welfare of organizations and their employees from any potential negative effects associated with the deployment of AI (Brendel et al., 2021). Ensuring the safety of human-machine interactions is paramount in this evolving workplace. Issues related to data privacy, algorithmic biases, and the potential for AI to make harmful decisions must be addressed through robust safety measures, including data protection protocols and ethical AI frameworks (García et al., 2023). AI's transformative power in the workplace is undeniable, but it should be harnessed with a clear focus on safety and ethics to maximize its benefits while minimizing potential risks.

Optimizing HRM With AI: Ethical Considerations and Safety Measures

Human resource management (HRM) plays a pivotal role in organizations, focusing on personnel and overall performance. The integration of technological advancements into HRM processes offers a transformative opportunity for organizations to reassess and enhance the utilization of their workforce as valuable assets. AI-based applications have gained prominence in HRM functions, providing a wide range of capabilities, including candidate sourcing, screening, task assignment, and activity monitoring.

AI's utilization in HRM streamlines HR tasks, allowing HR staff to concentrate on more strategic aspects of their roles (Votto et al., 2021).

While AI brings significant benefits to HRM, it also introduces safety risks and ethical considerations. The use of algorithms for personnel selection, hiring, and training necessitates a vigilant approach to ensure fairness and minimize biases. Organizations must implement safeguards to prevent discriminatory practices and protect employee data privacy when utilizing AI in HR processes. AI-driven HR systems offer a powerful tool for informed decision-making, simplifying complex tasks and providing precise predictions. Strategic planning is essential for the effective execution of HRM functions, contributing to an organization's growth, sustainability, and competitiveness. Managers must navigate the incorporation of AI into HR processes to maximize the benefits while mitigating potential safety and ethical risks.

The integration of AI into HRM is crucial for organizational development and optimization. It enhances operational efficiency while also bolstering the workforce for innovative projects. However, organizations must be diligent in addressing safety concerns and ethical considerations to ensure a fair and equitable work environment.

AI-Driven Workplace Transformation: Balancing Well-Being and Safety

The evolving landscape of organizations brings about substantial changes that span various dimensions, from socio-economic and environmental to technological and political. These transformations have a profound impact on the well-being and health of the workforce, necessitating innovative approaches to safeguard and improve their overall welfare, both within and outside of working hours. The workplace environment plays a pivotal role in influencing well-being, quality of life, and overall health. Artificial intelligence (AI) emerges as a key enabler of fostering a positive workplace atmosphere, thanks to its applications in infrastructure, lighting systems, temperature control, personalized comfort devices, and the promotion of beneficial work-related behaviors, such as maintaining proper posture. Moreover, AI extends its reach to monitor human health activities through wearable smart devices, prioritizing the health and well-being of employees (Fukumura et al., 2021). The concept of smart offices, empowered by AI and the Internet of Things (IoT), acts as a preventive and control mechanism to counteract the adverse effects of work on health and overall wellness. Workplace stress, a significant predictor of health outcomes, has an inverse relationship with job satisfaction, well-being, and work productivity. Technological advancements, particularly AI, play a pivotal role in addressing workplace stress. Smartphones, for instance, assist in reducing stress by aiding in task organization and completion, leading to improved work productivity.

However, alongside these advancements, it is crucial to address safety risks associated with AI in the workplace. The integration of AI and IoT devices for health monitoring requires robust data security measures to protect employees' sensitive information. Additionally, there is a need to ensure that AI-driven workplace interventions prioritize the ethical use of data and do not infringe upon employees' privacy. As organizations transition into a new workplace culture centered around AI, strategic planning, continuous monitoring, and a steadfast commitment to prioritizing safety, health, and well-being are essential. While AI has the potential to enhance workplace well-being, its implementation must be accompanied by stringent safeguards to protect employees and their data.

Harnessing AI for Sustainable Energy: Mitigating Safety Risks

The cultivation of a green corporate culture plays a pivotal role in driving progress towards the achievement of the Sustainable Development Goals (SDGs). Energy conservation stands out as a crucial aspect of this culture, with its benefits extending beyond the organization itself to contribute to environmental preservation (Thakur et al., 2022). Within this context, the integration of AI in the workplace takes on particular significance, as it empowers energy conservation practices, including the automatic powering off of electronic devices, lights, and fans when employees are absent (Dua et al., 2022).

While AI holds the potential to revolutionize energy conservation, it is imperative to consider the associated safety risks. AI-driven systems that control energy usage need to be robust and secure. Vulnerabilities in these systems could lead to unauthorized access and manipulation, potentially causing disruptions, and, in some cases, posing safety hazards. Ensuring the safety and integrity of AI systems is paramount, particularly when they are responsible for critical functions such as managing energy resources. Organizations that embrace sustainable energy use not only address pressing concerns related to energy crises and climate change but also safeguard their own operations and the planet (Razak et al., 2020). The integration of AI and the Internet of Things (IoT) further enhances the transformation of enterprises, reshaping the economic landscape and offering new opportunities for sustainable growth (Shah et al., 2020). Through the convergence of AI and energy conservation efforts, organizations have the potential to foster a sustainable organizational culture that contributes to their own success and the global pursuit of sustainable development. While the combination of AI and energy conservation is a promising avenue for achieving sustainability, it necessitates a rigorous focus on ensuring the safety and security of AI systems. Proactive measures must be in place to protect against potential risks, thereby enabling organizations to reap the full benefits of sustainable efficiency.

AI-Driven Advertising: Navigating Safety and Ethical Challenges

In the quest to introduce new products and services to the market, companies rely on advertising techniques to generate public awareness and stimulate consumer purchases. The effectiveness and quality of advertising campaigns significantly impact an organization's profits, serving as a fundamental cornerstone for building product popularity among consumers (Shah et al., 2020). Recent years have witnessed the emergence of artificial intelligence (AI) and machine learning as transformative tools in the advertising domain. Enterprises are increasingly embracing AI for advertising, harnessing its capabilities to gain profound insights into consumer preferences, identify target audiences, and disseminate product information through appropriate communication channels. AI technology opens up avenues for product promotion through various advertising mediums, including email, websites, and search engines. Notably, personalized advertisements, tailored based on online data collection, wield substantial influence over product sales, with AI playing a pivotal role in both data acquisition and advertisement design (Shah et al., 2020). However, it is essential to address the safety risks and ethical considerations associated with AI in advertising. AI's ability to collect and analyze vast amounts of consumer data raises concerns about privacy and data security. There is a need for robust safeguards and regulatory frameworks to ensure that consumer data is handled responsibly and ethically. Unauthorized access to or misuse of this data could lead to breaches in privacy and potential harm to individuals. The responsible and ethical deployment of machine learning and AI in advertising necessitates the implementation of clear and strategic rules and regulations to uphold ethical boundaries and protect consumers' interests. It is essential to strike a balance between leveraging AI for marketing advantage and safeguarding individual privacy and data security. Through the amalgamation of AI and advertising, organizations have the potential to revolutionize their marketing strategies, enabling them to connect with consumers in a more targeted and impactful manner. However, it is imperative that this transformation occurs within the framework of ethical guidelines and data security measures to mitigate potential safety risks and protect consumer privacy.

CONCLUSION

In the pursuit of Sustainable Development Goals (SDGs), the integration of Artificial Intelligence (AI) stands as a powerful enabler, offering the potential to address complex sustainability challenges in areas such as energy conservation, workplace management, and advertising. However, this transformative potential is accompanied by notable safety risks and ethical considerations. As AI becomes deeply embedded in the workplace, organizations must proactively address concerns related to data privacy, algorithmic biases, and the potential for AI systems to make errors that could impact employees' well-being and overall effectiveness. For instance, AI in the workplace may influence employee stress levels, work-life balance, and the quality of life, raising concerns about safety and well-being (Fukumura et al., 2021). Likewise, in the realm of energy conservation, rigorous safeguards are essential to protect against vulnerabilities that could compromise the integrity and security of AI-driven systems, particularly with the automatic control of electronic devices (Dua et al., 2022). In the advertising domain, the promise of personalized marketing campaigns powered by AI must be balanced with robust regulations and ethical frameworks to ensure individual privacy and data security, as unauthorized access and misuse of data can lead to breaches in privacy (Shah et al., 2020). It is by acknowledging and addressing these safety risks and ethical considerations that the symbiotic relationship between AI and the pursuit of SDGs can truly thrive, contributing to a sustainable and equitable future.

REFERENCES

Abdul Razak, M. A., Othman, M. M., Musirin, I., Yahya, M. A., & Zakaria, Z. (2020). Significant implication of optimal capacitor placement and sizing for a sustainable electrical operation in a building. *Sustainability (Basel)*, *12*(13), 5399. doi:10.3390/su12135399

Albayrak, N., Özdemir, A., & Zeydan, E. (2019). An artificial intelligence enabled data analytics platform for digital advertisement. In *22nd Conference on Innovation in Clouds, Internet and Networks and Workshops (ICIN)* (pp. 239–241). IEEE. 10.1109/ICIN.2019.8685870

Aliman, N. M., Kester, L., Werkhoven, P., & Ziesche, S. (2019). Sustainable AI safety? Delphi, 2, 226.

Anjum, A., Ming, X., Siddiqi, A. F., & Rasool, S. F. (2018). An empirical study analyzing job productivity in toxic workplace environments. *International Journal of Environmental Research and Public Health*, *15*(5), 1035. doi:10.3390/ijerph15051035 PMID:29883424

Azadeh, A., Yazdanparast, R., Zadeh, S. A., & Keramati, A. (2018). An intelligent algorithm for optimizing emergency department job and patient satisfaction. *International Journal of Health Care Quality Assurance*, *31*(5), 374–390. doi:10.1108/IJHCQA-06-2016-0086 PMID:29865961

Brendel, A. B., Mirbabaie, M., Lembcke, T. B., & Hofeditz, L. (2021). Ethical management of artificial intelligence. *Sustainability (Basel)*, *13*(4), 1974. doi:10.3390/su13041974

Cai, Y. J., & Choi, T. M. (2020). A United Nations' Sustainable Development Goals perspective for sustainable textile and apparel supply chain management. *Transportation Research Part E, Logistics and Transportation Review*, *141*, 102010. doi:10.1016/j.tre.2020.102010 PMID:32834741

Dua, S., Kumar, S. S., Albagory, Y., Ramalingam, R., Dumka, A., Singh, R., Rashid, M., Gehlot, A., Alshamrani, S. S., & AlGhamdi, A. S. (2022). Developing a Speech Recognition System for Recognizing Tonal Speech Signals Using a Convolutional Neural Network. *Applied Sciences (Basel, Switzerland)*, *12*(12), 6223. doi:10.3390/app12126223

Fukumura, Y. E., Gray, J. M., Lucas, G. M., Becerik-Gerber, B., & Roll, S. C. (2021). Worker perspectives on incorporating artificial intelligence into office workspaces: Implications for the future of office work. *International Journal of Environmental Research and Public Health*, *18*(4), 1690. doi:10.3390/ijerph18041690 PMID:33578736

Hassani, H., Silva, E. S., Unger, S., TajMazinani, M., & Mac Feely, S. (2020). Artificial intelligence (AI) or intelligence augmentation (IA): What is the future? *AI*, *1*(2), 8. doi:10.3390/ai1020008

Ionescu, G. H., Firoiu, D., Tănasie, A., Sorin, T., Pîrvu, R., & Manta, A. (2020). Assessing the Achievement of the SDG Targets for Health and Well-Being at EU Level by 2030. *Sustainability (Basel)*, *12*(14), 5829. doi:10.3390/su12145829

Ivaldi, S., Scaratti, G., & Fregnan, E. (2022). Dwelling within the fourth industrial revolution: Organizational learning for new competences, processes and work cultures. *Journal of Workplace Learning*, *34*(1), 1–26. doi:10.1108/JWL-07-2020-0127

Jarrahi, M. H. (2018). Artificial intelligence and the future of work: Human-AI symbiosis in organizational decision making. *Business Horizons*, *61*(4), 577–586. doi:10.1016/j.bushor.2018.03.007

Jeon, J., & Suh, Y. (2017). Analyzing the Major Issues of the 4 th Industrial Revolution. *Asian Journal of Innovation & Policy*, *6*(3).

Kwiotkowska, A., Gajdzik, B., Wolniak, R., Vveinhardt, J., & Gębczyńska, M. (2021). Leadership competencies in making Industry 4.0 effective: The case of Polish heat and power industry. *Energies*, *14*(14), 4338. doi:10.3390/en14144338

Litchfield, P., Cooper, C., Hancock, C., & Watt, P. (2016). Work and wellbeing in the 21st century. *International Journal of Environmental Research and Public Health*, *13*(11), 1065. doi:10.3390/ijerph13111065 PMID:27809265

Shah, N., Engineer, S., Bhagat, N., Chauhan, H., & Shah, M. (2020). Research trends on the usage of machine learning and artificial intelligence in advertising. *Augmented Human Research*, *5*(1), 1–15. doi:10.1007/s41133-020-00038-8

Thakur, A. K., Singh, R., Gehlot, A., Kaviti, A. K., Aseer, R., Suraparaju, S. K., Natarajan, S. K., & Sikarwar, V. S. (2022). Advancements in solar technologies for sustainable development of agricultural sector in India: A comprehensive review on challenges and opportunities. *Environmental Science and Pollution Research International*, *29*(29), 43607–43634. doi:10.1007/s11356-022-20133-0 PMID:35419684

United Nations Development Programme. (2015). *Sustainable Development Goals*. https://www.undp.org/sustainable-development-goals

Vinuesa, R., Azizpour, H., Leite, I., Balaam, M., Dignum, V., Domisch, S., Felländer, A., Langhans, S. D., Tegmark, M., & Fuso Nerini, F. (2020). The role of artificial intelligence in achieving the Sustainable Development Goals. *Nature Communications*, *11*(1), 1–10. doi:10.1038/s41467-019-14108-y PMID:31932590

Votto, A. M., Valecha, R., Najafirad, P., & Rao, H. R. (2021). Artificial intelligence in tactical human resource management: A systematic literature review. *International Journal of Information Management Data Insights*, *1*(2), 100047. doi:10.1016/j.jjimei.2021.100047

Chapter 12
Unmasking the Shadows:
Exploring Unethical AI Implementation

Dwijendra Nath Dwivedi
https://orcid.org/0000-0001-7662-415X
Krakow University of Economics, Poland

Ghanashyama Mahanty
https://orcid.org/0000-0002-6560-2825
Utkal University, India

ABSTRACT

In the rapidly evolving landscape of artificial intelligence (AI), the ethical ramifications of its implementation have become a pressing concern. This chapter delves into the darker facets of AI deployment, examining cases where technology has been used in ways that defy established ethical norms. It identifies common patterns and motivations behind unethical AI applications through a comprehensive review of real-world instances. Additionally, the research underscores the potential societal consequences of these actions, emphasizing the importance of transparency, accountability, and ethical frameworks in AI development and deployment. This chapter serves as a clarion call for the AI community to prioritize ethics in every AI research and application phase, ensuring that the technology is harnessed for the greater good rather than misused in the shadows.

1. INTRODUCTION

In recent years, the growth of artificial intelligence (AI) has been nothing short of meteoric, transforming myriad facets of our daily lives and the global economy. Advances in machine learning and deep learning drive this rapid evolution. Vast amounts of data have empowered industries from healthcare to finance. It is

DOI: 10.4018/979-8-3693-0724-3.ch012

enhancing efficiency and spawning entirely new business models. Innovations such as personalized medicine, autonomous vehicles and smart home devices directly result from this AI revolution. AI promises unprecedented opportunities, such as economic growth and improved quality of life. At the same time, it also presents significant challenges. Concerns over job displacement, privacy infringements and algorithmic biases have sparked global debates. Ethical considerations surrounding AI's decision-making processes and its broader societal implications have come to the forefront. In the history of human achievement, the advent of artificial intelligence (AI) stands as one of the most transformative. Like all powerful tools, AI is not immune to misuse. For instance, the case of 'Deepfake' technology is built upon advanced neural networks. Deepfakes allow for the creation of hyper-realistic but entirely fake content. While it's marveled at as an impressive feat of AI, it has also been weaponized to produce misleading videos. It is causing defamation and spreading disinformation as well. Another example is the use of AI in surveillance. Cities like Beijing have implemented facial recognition systems that can identify any one of its millions of residents in seconds. While touted as a means for enhanced security, it also raises severe concerns about individual privacy and the potential for state control. In the realm of commerce, companies have been caught using AI-driven algorithms that perpetuate bias. An infamous instance is a job recruitment tool that trained on historical hiring data and started favouring male candidates over female ones for tech jobs. It amplified gender bias. The autonomous weapons sector, often termed as "killer robots", also poses an ethical dilemma. AI powers these machines and can make life-or-death decisions without human intervention. The moral implications of a machine deciding the fate of a human being are profound and unsettling.

Even in simple things like suggesting movies or shopping items, AI can accidentally make people only see things they already agree with. This can make people more polarized and exacerbate inequality as opposed to eliminating it. Many examples like this show we need to think about how we use AI in the right way. As we move into a future with more AI, we need to make sure we use it fairly. There are many examples of of historical failure while using AI (please see table 1)

Background and Estimations Negative Consequences while using AI

The research and media stories evidence a number of potential negative consequences of the use of AI. Estimating the precise negative impact on mankind is challenging due to the multifaceted consequences of AI failures, but we have tried to summarise the same from available reports (see Table 2 and Figure 1).

AI systems face many of the same pitfalls as any system; AI is no exception. As more sophisticated tasks and manual processes become automated through AI,

Table 1. illustrates some well-known instances of AI failures in history.

Year	Incident	Description
2019-2021	Clearview AI Privacy Concerns	Clearview AI scraped billions of images from the internet, leading to significant privacy concerns.
2020	Twitter's Image Cropping Algorithm Bias	Twitter's image cropping algorithm seemed to favor white faces over Black faces.
2020	Zoom Virtual Background Issues	Zoom's virtual background feature had difficulty recognizing people with darker skin tones.
2020	AI in COVID-19 Predictions	Many AI models produced inconsistent or inaccurate results in predicting the spread and impact of COVID-19.
2020	OpenAI's GPT-3 Controversies	GPT-3 produced biased, sexist, or inappropriate outputs in certain scenarios.
2016	Microsoft's Tay Chatbot	Microsoft released a Twitter-based chatbot named Tay. It quickly began producing racist and offensive tweets after manipulation by users.
2015	Google Photos Misclassification	Google Photos' image recognition mistakenly classified African Americans as 'gorillas'.
Unknown	Amazon's Recruitment Tool Bias	Amazon's AI recruitment tool was biased against female candidates, favoring male resumes.
2018	Uber Self-driving Car Accident	An autonomous car from Uber failed to recognize a pedestrian, leading to a fatal accident in Arizona.
2019	Apple Card Gender Bias	Apple Card offered higher credit limits to men than women with similar financial backgrounds.
2018	IBM Watson for Oncology	Watson for Oncology gave incorrect and unsafe treatment advice for cancer patients.

Table 2. Background and estimation of AI failures

AI Failure Category	Background	Source of Estimate
Deepfakes & Misinformation	The proliferation of deepfake technology and other AI-driven misinformation tools can significantly distort the truth, leading to public confusion, mistrust, and potentially harmful actions based on false information.	Pew Research survey conducted in 2016 found that 64% of Americans believe fake news has caused a great deal of confusion about basic facts of current events.
AI-driven Surveillance	Advanced surveillance systems, especially those equipped with AI-driven facial recognition, can monitor vast populations, leading to privacy concerns and potential misuse by authorities.	Various reports and articles, such as those from BBC, have highlighted China's extensive surveillance system, which is believed to contain over 20 million cameras.
Algorithmic Bias	AI algorithms, when trained on biased data, can reinforce and perpetuate existing societal biases, leading to unfair or discriminatory outcomes in areas like recruitment, law enforcement, and lending.	A study by NIST found that some commercial facial recognition systems had higher misidentification rates for African-American and Asian faces compared to Caucasian faces.
Autonomous Vehicle Accidents	While autonomous vehicles promise safer roads by eliminating human error, they aren't infallible. Early-stage testing and real-world implementations have seen accidents, some of which were fatal.	Various reports on self-driving car accidents, such as those from RAND Corporation, have discussed the safety concerns surrounding autonomous vehicles.
Healthcare AI Misdiagnoses	AI in healthcare aims to aid doctors in diagnosis and treatment. However, if not properly trained or tested, these systems can provide incorrect recommendations, potentially harming patients.	Issues with IBM Watson's treatment recommendations were reported in various publications, including STAT News, which detailed how the system sometimes gave unsafe and incorrect treatment recommendations.

Figure 1. Estimated percentage age of cases showing type of Impact of AI

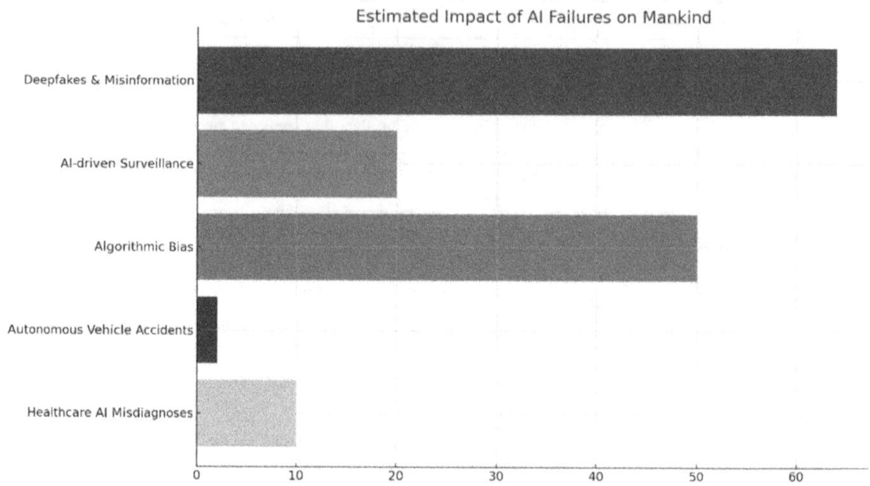

they too become vulnerable to these risks - AI bias, potential job replacement by AI technologies, privacy concerns and their misuse to deceive or manipulate being among these. This paper proposed a KPI-based framework to detect one of the ten reasons that could drive unethical AI implementations.

2. LITERATURE REVIEW

Our literature review encompasses three primary themes: the ethical dilemmas and risks associated with AI, sentiment analysis derived from Twitter data and other sources, and standard methodologies employed in the realm of sentiment analysis.

Dwijendra and Mahanty (2021) explored the AI incident database, identifying prominent areas of AI risk from recent incidents. Hagendorf (2020) analysed 22 ethical guidelines, revealing overlapping themes and areas lacking attention. This analysis is instrumental in refining the practical aspects of AI ethical standards. Maas's 2018 research suggests that AI systems can lead to extensive, cascading mistakes. Box & Data (2019) centred on the impact of human biases on machine learning models. Martinho (2020) integrated both theoretical and empirical approaches to explore ethical decision-making within AI. Tamboli (2019) highlighted the evolving challenges from changing data trends, underlining the "concept drift" phenomenon. Bolander (2019) expressed reservations about AI's implications and technical hurdles in replacing human tasks. Andreas Holzinger (2019) paper underscored the need for diverse, high-calibre data to address critical medical issues, advocating for combining clinical, imaging, and molecular datasets to unravel intricate illnesses."

Oneto and Chaippa (2020) paper discussed fairness in machine learning and the challenges in quantifying and assessing fairness metrics, which is relevant for ethical AI assessment. Boehmke and Greenwell (2020) explored techniques for making machine learning models more interpretable, a crucial aspect of ethical AI assessment. Bostrom and Yudkowsky (2014) addressed a wide range of ethical issues in AI, providing valuable insights into the ethical dimensions that should be considered in assessment. Aïvodji et.al (2019) highlighted the potential for "fairwashing" in AI ethics, where biased AI systems are presented as unbiased. It offers insights into the challenges of assessing fairness in AI. Bellamy et al. (2019) provided a practical resource for assessing and mitigating bias in AI systems, a critical aspect of ethical AI assessment. Doshi-Velez et al. (2017) discussed AI accountability's legal and ethical implications and the importance of explanation in AI systems. Barocas et al. (2017) introduce various metrics for measuring bias in machine learning models, which can be valuable for ethical AI assessment. Hanson(2016) explored future scenarios in a world dominated by AI and discussed ethical considerations related to AI systems. d'Amato et al. (2017) explored trust-related concepts in computer science and the semantic web. In their study, Yogarajan et al. (2022) examined the implementation of artificial intelligence (AI) in the healthcare sector and highlighted the possible biases and inequalities that could emerge, particularly with regards to underrepresented indigenous communities in New Zealand. Their research sought to investigate equality and fairness metrics in artificial intelligence for healthcare in New Zealand. In their study, Peng, A. et al. (2022) investigated the interplay between a model's prediction accuracy and its bias on human decision-making in the context of ML-assisted hiring. They examined the dynamics of this relationship in a recommendation-aided decision task. In their study, Katare, D. et. al (2022) examined the potential prejudices present in AI algorithms, with a particular focus on the field of autonomous driving. Kwasniewska and Szankin (2022) discovered that although AI has demonstrated encouraging outcomes in enhancing accuracy, throughput, and minimizing latency, it still faces persistent obstacles such as inadequate explainability, data imbalance, and bias. Belenguer, L. (2022) introduces a new method for tackling prejudiced prejudice in artificial intelligence. In their study, Ayesha Nadeem et al. (2022) performed a comprehensive analysis of existing literature to examine the presence of gender bias in decision-making systems that utilize artificial intelligence (AI). Norori, N et al. (2021) examined the capacity of artificial intelligence (AI) in the field of healthcare and addressed the obstacles posed by algorithmic bias. In their study, D. Newman-Griffis et al. (2022) emphasized the potential for bias in artificial intelligence (AI) systems, particularly when it comes to those with disabilities. The text explores the emergence of bias resulting from certain design choices and the potential for diverse interpretations of disability to give rise to varying biases. Alzamil, H. et al.(2020) discovered disparities in the utilization of distinct diagnostic criteria among the two groups. The study emphasizes the necessity of establishing uniform diagnostic criteria for PCOS. The paper by Dash, B, et al. (2022) provides an analysis of the risks and advantages linked to AI-driven intrusion detection systems in the field of cybersecurity. O'Sullivan, M. E. et al. (2021) examined the difficulties involved in creating artificial intelligence systems for the purpose of monitoring the fetal heart rate during the process of birthing. Dwivedi et.al(2022) performed sentiment mining for AI ethics and shared key concerns.

3. EXISTING FRAMEWORKS TO DETECT UNETHICAL AI IMPLEMENTATIONS:

3.1 Fairness and Accountability Toolkits

- Fairness Indicators: An open-source toolkit by Google to evaluate and improve fairness in machine learning models.
- AI Fairness 360 (AIF360): An extensible open-source toolkit by IBM Research that can help examine, report, and mitigate discrimination and bias in machine learning models.

3.2 Transparency and Interpretability Tools

- LIME (Local Interpretable Model-agnostic Explanations): It's a project dedicated to providing a way to understand the decisions made by machine learning models.
- SHAP (Shapley Additive exPlanations): A method to explain the output of any machine learning model using game theory concepts.

3.3 Auditing and Evaluation Frameworks

- Model Cards: Introduced by Google, these are short documents accompanying trained machine learning models that provide a benchmarked evaluation in a variety of conditions.
- Algorithmic Impact Assessments (AIA): A framework to help organizations evaluate the social impact of the algorithms they deploy.

3.4 Bias Detection and Mitigation Tools

- Biasly.ai: A platform for detecting and mitigating bias in AI.
- Manifold: A model-agnostic visual debugging tool for machine learning developed by Uber.

3.5 Ethics Guidelines and Checklists

- The Ethics Guidelines for Trustworthy AI: Developed by the European Commission's High-Level Expert Group on AI, these guidelines provide a list of requirements that AI systems should meet to be deemed trustworthy.
- The Toronto Declaration focuses on the right to equality and non-discrimination in machine learning systems.

3.6 Community and Research Initiatives

- Partnership on AI: A coalition of companies, academics, and NGOs working together to understand AI's societal impacts better and to set best practices.
- OpenAI's Charter: A document outlining the commitment of OpenAI to ensure that artificial general intelligence benefits all of humanity.

3.7 Certification Programs

- AI Ethics Certification: Some organizations and institutions offer certification programs assessing AI projects' ethical considerations.

3.8 Public Scrutiny and Open Source

- Open-sourcing AI models and algorithms can allow the broader community to review, critique, and assess the ethical implications of an AI implementation.

4. KPI-BASED FRAMEWORKS TO DETECT UNETHICAL AI IMPLEMENTATIONS

A KPI (Key Performance Indicator) based framework can be invaluable in this endeavour. Table 3 shows KPI based framework to detect unethical AI implementations. Such a framework would define explicit metrics that quantify ethical behaviour in AI systems. For instance, fairness metrics could be employed to measure and ensure that AI models do not disproportionately favour one group

Table 3. KPI based framework to detect unethical AI implementations

Area	KPI 1	KPI 2
Transparency and Explainability	Percentage of Decisions Explained	Average Explanation Clarity Score
Bias and Fairness	Disparity Ratio	Bias Incident Reports
Privacy and Data Protection	Data Breach Incidents	Percentage of Anonymized Data
Accountability and Responsibility	Incident Response Time	Number of Accountability Trainings
Robustness and Security	System Uptime	Number of Security Audits
Economic and Social Impact	Job Impact Ratio	User Satisfaction Score
Environmental Impact	Energy Consumption Rate	Carbon Footprint
Stakeholder Inclusion	Stakeholder Engagement Score	Number of Stakeholder Meetings
Continuous Monitoring and Feedback	Feedback Collection Frequency	System Update Frequency
Regulatory and Legal Compliance	Compliance Audit Pass Rate	Number of Legal Violations
Area	**KPI 3**	**KPI 4**
Transparency and Explainability	Number of User Queries Answered	Frequency of Documentation Updates
Bias and Fairness	Percentage of Diverse Data Sources	Bias Audit Frequency
Privacy and Data Protection	Data Retention Compliance Rate	User Consent Rate
Accountability and Responsibility	Stakeholder Communication Frequency	Percentage of Decisions Reviewed
Robustness and Security	Incident Recovery Time	Percentage of Secure Data Transfers
Economic and Social Impact	Economic Benefit Analysis	Social Impact Assessment
Environmental Impact	Resource Utilization Efficiency	Sustainability Audit Frequency
Stakeholder Inclusion	Feedback Implementation Rate	Diversity of Stakeholder Groups
Continuous Monitoring and Feedback	User Report Resolution Time	Feedback Implementation Rate
Regulatory and Legal Compliance	Regulatory Update Frequency	User Rights Violation Reports

over another. Transparency metrics could gauge the explainability of AI decisions, ensuring stakeholders understand the logic behind AI outputs. Moreover, privacy metrics could assess how AI systems protect user data. By continuously monitoring these KPIs, organizations can detect deviations from ethical norms and take corrective actions. A well-defined, KPI-based framework safeguards against unethical AI practices and instils greater trust among users and stakeholders, reinforcing the responsible and transparent use of AI technologies.

5. THE ROLE OF THE GOVERNMENT AND INDUSTRY

Governments play a crucial role in shaping AI development and deployment trajectory. Through well-thought-out policies, governments can reduce AI's negative impacts and ensure its benefits are widespread and equitable. Table 4 summarises some policy recommendations that governments can consider.

Table 4. Government Role In Detecting And Control Unethical AI Implementations

Policy Recommendation	Description
Clear AI Ethics Framework	Establish a national framework on AI ethics emphasizing fairness, accountability, and transparency. This framework can guide organizations and researchers in ethical AI development.
Data Privacy Regulations	Strengthen data protection and privacy laws, ensuring that AI systems respect user privacy and adhere to data handling standards.
Transparency and Disclosure	Mandate transparency for AI systems, particularly those in public sectors. Companies should disclose AI functionalities, data sources, and potential biases.
Research and Development Support	Allocate government funding for research into AI safety, bias mitigation, and ethical AI practices. Support academic institutions and independent research entities.
AI Literacy and Training	Promote AI literacy within government agencies. Offer training programs to ensure that policymakers are informed about AI's capabilities and limitations.
Independent AI Audits	Encourage or mandate third-party audits for high-stakes AI applications. This ensures an unbiased evaluation of AI systems.
Public Engagement	Host public consultations on AI developments, deployments, and regulations. Public input ensures policies align with societal values.
International Collaboration	Collaborate with other nations on AI standards, research, and best practices. International cooperation can lead to more comprehensive and cohesive policies.
Continuous Monitoring	Establish mechanisms to monitor the effects of AI in various sectors regularly. Policies should be updated based on new findings and technological advancements.
Redressal Mechanisms	Set up legal frameworks to address AI-related grievances. Ensure individuals have avenues to seek redress in case of AI-induced harm.

Recommendations for Industry Controlling AI based Failures: As the primary driver behind AI development and deployment, the industry bears a significant responsibility in ensuring the ethical use of these technologies. Businesses, research institutions, and AI developers must work towards detecting and mitigating unethical AI practices actively. This involves integrating ethical considerations into the AI design process and implementing rigorous testing and validation stages to identify biases, inaccuracies, and other potential pitfalls. Collaborative efforts, including partnerships with external auditors and the broader AI community, can further ensure unbiased evaluations and the sharing of best practices. Moreover, fostering a culture of continuous learning, transparency, and open dialogue within the industry is crucial. This will enable timely identification of ethical concerns and drive proactive measures to address them. Ultimately, it is the industry's role to prioritize ethical AI as a standard practice, ensuring that as AI technologies advance, they align with societal values and promote fairness, accountability, and transparency. Table 5, shows a description of some Recommendations for the Industry.

Table 5. Industry role to detect and control unethical AI implementations

Recommendation	Description
Robust Testing and Validation	Undertake rigorous testing and validation of AI systems before deployment, especially for high-stakes applications to ensure their reliability.
Ethical AI Teams	Establish dedicated teams focused on ethical AI development, responsible for regular audits, bias assessments, and ethical considerations of AI products.
Diverse Data Sets	Use diverse datasets for training to ensure models are representative and less prone to biases. Regularly update datasets to reflect current trends.
Open Source Collaboration	Engage in open-source communities to share, review, and collaboratively improve AI algorithms and methodologies.
Stakeholder Engagement	Regularly engage with stakeholders, including end-users, to gather feedback, understand potential issues, and make necessary adjustments.
Continuous Learning and Adaptation	Design AI systems for continuous learning and adaptation. Regularly update models based on new data and feedback.
Transparency and Explainability	Strive for AI models that are explainable, ensuring stakeholders can understand the decision-making processes.
Employee Training	Invest in continuous training for employees to stay updated on ethical considerations, potential biases, and best practices in AI development.
Third-party Audits	Seek third-party audits, especially for critical AI systems, to ensure an unbiased evaluation and adherence to best practices.
Feedback Mechanisms	Implement robust feedback loops, allowing users to report issues or biases they encounter, leading to iterative improvements.

6. CONCLUSION

This article introduces a new way to look at key performance indicators (KPIs) by using several ethical criteria, such as justice, transparency, and reducing bias. It gives a thorough score system for figuring out whether an AI system is ethically successful or unsuccessful. This method provides a structured way for AI makers and other interested parties to evaluate and compare AI systems from an ethical point of view. This piece stresses how important it is for responsible artificial intelligence development in today's business world by using case studies that show how it can be used in real life. Artificial intelligence (AI) is becoming more and more common in business. This framework focuses on values like openness and responsibility, which are important for integrating AI in a way that is responsible for businesses. This approach also makes sure that AI will grow in a way that is good for society. Paper thoroughly analyzes case studies in which AI has been employed in manners that violate ethical limits, including privacy infringements, decision-making biases, and lack of transparency. The article utilizes key performance indicators (KPIs) to objectively evaluate the effects of unethical actions. These KPIs include metrics for public trust, rates of bias incidents, and indices for transparency.

Further research can look into how new rules can change to keep up with how quickly AI is changing, and suggest ways that AI ethics can be standardized around the world. Also it can explore the techniques to Reduce Bias: Test new ways to find and reduce bias in AI systems using real-world data, especially in areas with a lot at stake, like healthcare and criminal justice. Further use of longitudinal studies can be dexplored to see how people's views on AI change over time, especially when it comes to trusting and accepting automatic systems. Privacy-Preserving AI Technologies must be looked into how privacy-preserving AI technologies like collaborative learning and differential privacy have been developed and what is stopping people from using them.

Conflict of Interest

The authors whose names are listed immediately below certify that they have NO affiliations with or involvement in any organization or entity with any financial interest (such as honoraria; educational grants; participation in speakers' bureaus; membership, employment, consultancies, stock ownership, or other equity interest; and expert testimony or patent-licensing arrangements), or non-financial interest (such as personal or professional relationships, affiliations, knowledge or beliefs) in the subject matter or materials discussed in this manuscript.

REFERENCES

Aïvodji, U., Arai, H., Fortineau, O., Gambs, S., Hara, S., & Tapp, A. (2019). Fairwashing: the risk of rationalization. In *International Conference on Machine Learning* (pp. 161-170). PMLR.

Alzamil, H., Aloraini, K., AlAgeel, R., Ghanim, A., Alsaaran, R., Alsomali, N., Albahlal, R. A., & Alnuaim, L. (2020). Disparity among Endocrinologists and Gynaecologists in the Diagnosis of Polycystic Ovarian Syndrome. *Sultan Qaboos University Medical Journal.*

Belenguer, L. (2022). AI bias: Exploring discriminatory algorithmic decision-making models and the application of possible machine-centric solutions adapted from the pharmaceutical industry. *AI and Ethics*, *2*(4), 771–787. doi:10.1007/s43681-022-00138-8 PMID:35194591

Bellamy, R. K., Dey, K., Hind, M., Hoffman, S. C., Houde, S., Kannan, K., Lohia, P., Martino, J., Mehta, S., Mojsilovic, A., Nagar, S., Ramamurthy, K. N., Richards, J., Saha, D., Sattigeri, P., Singh, M., Varshney, K. R., & Zhang, Y. (2019). AI Fairness 360: An extensible toolkit for detecting and mitigating algorithmic bias. *IBM Journal of Research and Development*, *63*(4/5), 4–1. doi:10.1147/JRD.2019.2942287

Boehmke, B. C., & Greenwell, B. M. (2019). *Interpretable Machine Learning*. Hands-On Machine Learning with R. doi:10.1201/9780367816377-16

Bolander, T. (2019). What do we loose when machines take the decisions? *The Journal of Management and Governance*, *23*(4), 849–867. doi:10.1007/s10997-019-09493-x

Bostrom, N., & Yudkowsky, E. (2014). The ethics of artificial intelligence. The Cambridge handbook of artificial intelligence, 1, 316-334.

Box, J., & Data, P. (2019). Do You Know What Your Model is Doing ? How Human Bias Influences Machine Learning. *PHUSE EU Connect 2019.*

C. d'Amato, M. Fernandez, V. Tamma, F. Lecue, P. Cudré-Mauroux, J. Sequeda, & J. Heflin (Eds.). (2017). The Semantic Web–ISWC 2017*: 16th International Semantic Web Conference,* Vienna, Austria, October 21–25, 2017*, Proceedings, Part I* (Vol. 10587). Springer.

Dash, B., Ansari, M. M., Sharma, P., & Ali, A. (2022). Threats and Opportunities with AI-based Cyber Security Intrusion Detection: A Review. *International Journal of Software Engineering and Its Applications*, *13*(5).

Doshi-Velez, F., Kortz, M., Budish, R., Bavitz, C., Gershman, S., O'Brien, D., . . . Wood, A. (2017). Accountability of AI under the law: The role of explanation. *arXiv preprint arXiv:1711.01134*.

Dwijendra, D. N., & Mahanty, G. (2021). A text mining-based approach for accessing AI risk incidents. *International Conference on Artificial Intelligence*.

Dwivedi, D., Batra, S., & Pathak, Y. K. (2023). A machine learning based approach to identify key drivers for improving corporate's esg ratings. *Journal of Law and Sustainable Development*, *11*(1), e0242. doi:10.37497/sdgs.v11i1.242

Dwivedi, D. N. (2024). The Use of Artificial Intelligence in Supply Chain Management and Logistics. In D. Sharma, B. Bhardwaj, & M. Dhiman (Eds.), *Leveraging AI and Emotional Intelligence in Contemporary Business Organizations* (pp. 306–313). IGI Global. doi:10.4018/979-8-3693-1902-4.ch018

Dwivedi, D. N., & Mahanty, G. (2024). AI-Powered Employee Experience: Strategies and Best Practices. In M. Rafiq, M. Farrukh, R. Mushtaq, & O. Dastane (Eds.), *Exploring the Intersection of AI and Human Resources Management* (pp. 166–181). IGI Global. doi:10.4018/979-8-3693-0039-8.ch009

Dwivedi, D. N., Mahanty, G., & Pathak, Y. K. (2023). AI Applications for Financial Risk Management. In M. Irfan, M. Elmogy, M. Shabri Abd. Majid, & S. El-Sappagh (Eds.), The Impact of AI Innovation on Financial Sectors in the Era of Industry 5.0 (pp. 17-31). IGI Global. doi:10.4018/979-8-3693-0082-4.ch002

Dwivedi, D. N., Mahanty, G., & Vemareddy, A. (2022). How Responsible Is AI?: Identification of Key Public Concerns Using Sentiment Analysis and Topic Modeling. *International Journal of Information Retrieval Research*, *12*(1), 1–14. doi:10.4018/IJIRR.298646

Dwivedi, D. N., Pandey, A. K., & Dwivedi, A. D. (2023). Examining the emotional tone in politically polarized Speeches in India: An In-Depth analysis of two contrasting perspectives. *South India Journal of Social Sciences, 21*(2), 125-136. https://journal.sijss.com/index.php/home/article/view/65

Dwivedi, D. N., Tadoori, G., & Batra, S. (2023). Impact of women leadership and ESG ratings and in organizations: A time series segmentation study. *Academy of Strategic Management Journal*, *22*(S3), 1–6.

Gupta, A., Dwivedi, D. N., & Shah, J. (2023a). Overview of Money Laundering. In Artificial Intelligence Applications in Banking and Financial Services. Future of Business and Finance. Springer. doi:10.1007/978-981-99-2571-1_1

Gupta, A., Dwivedi, D. N., & Shah, J. (2023g). Financial Crimes Management and Control in Financial Institutions. In Artificial Intelligence Applications in Banking and Financial Services. Future of Business and Finance. Springer. doi:10.1007/978-981-99-2571-1_2

Gupta, A., Dwivedi, D. N., & Shah, J. (2023c). Overview of Technology Solutions. In Artificial Intelligence Applications in Banking and Financial Services. Future of Business and Finance. Springer. doi:10.1007/978-981-99-2571-1_3

Gupta, A., Dwivedi, D. N., & Shah, J. (2023d). Data Organization for an FCC Unit. In Artificial Intelligence Applications in Banking and Financial Services. Future of Business and Finance. Springer. doi:10.1007/978-981-99-2571-1_4

Gupta, A., Dwivedi, D. N., & Shah, J. (2023e). Planning for AI in Financial Crimes. In Artificial Intelligence Applications in Banking and Financial Services. Future of Business and Finance. Springer. doi:10.1007/978-981-99-2571-1_5

Gupta, A., Dwivedi, D. N., & Shah, J. (2023f). Applying Machine Learning for Effective Customer Risk Assessment. In Artificial Intelligence Applications in Banking and Financial Services. Future of Business and Finance. Springer. doi:10.1007/978-981-99-2571-1_6

Gupta, A., Dwivedi, D. N., & Shah, J. (2023g). Artificial Intelligence-Driven Effective Financial Transaction Monitoring. In Artificial Intelligence Applications in Banking and Financial Services. Future of Business and Finance. Springer. doi:10.1007/978-981-99-2571-1_7

Gupta, A., Dwivedi, D. N., & Shah, J. (2023h). Machine Learning-Driven Alert Optimization. In Artificial Intelligence Applications in Banking and Financial Services. Future of Business and Finance. Springer. doi:10.1007/978-981-99-2571-1_8

Gupta, A., Dwivedi, D. N., & Shah, J. (2023i). Applying Artificial Intelligence on Investigation. In Artificial Intelligence Applications in Banking and Financial Services. Future of Business and Finance. Springer. doi:10.1007/978-981-99-2571-1_9

Gupta, A., Dwivedi, D. N., & Shah, J. (2023j). Ethical Challenges for AI-Based Applications. In Artificial Intelligence Applications in Banking and Financial Services. Future of Business and Finance. Springer. doi:10.1007/978-981-99-2571-1_10

Gupta, A., Dwivedi, D. N., & Shah, J. (2023k). Setting up a Best-In-Class AI-Driven Financial Crime Control Unit (FCCU). In Artificial Intelligence Applications in Banking and Financial Services. Future of Business and Finance. Springer. doi:10.1007/978-981-99-2571-1_11

Hagendorff, T. (2020). The Ethics of AI Ethics: An Evaluation of Guidelines. *Minds and Machines*, *30*(1), 99–120. doi:10.1007/s11023-020-09517-8

Hanson, R. (2016). The age of. In *Work, love, and life when robots rule the Earth*. Oxford University Press.

Holzinger, A., Haibe-Kains, B., & Jurisica, I. (2019). Why imaging data alone is not enough: AI-based integration of imaging, omics, and clinical data. *European Journal of Nuclear Medicine and Molecular Imaging*, *46*(13), 2722–2730. doi:10.1007/s00259-019-04382-9 PMID:31203421

Katare, D., Kourtellis, N., Park, S., Perino, D., Janssen, M., & Ding, A. (2022). Bias Detection and Generalization in AI Algorithms on Edge for Autonomous Driving. *Proceedings of the IEEE International Conference on Edge Computing*. 10.1109/SEC54971.2022.00050

Kwasniewska, A., & Szankin, M. (2022). Can AI See Bias in X-ray Images? *International Journal of New Developments in Imaging*.

Maas, M. M. (2018). *Regulating for "Normal AI Accidents."* doi:10.1145/3278721.3278766

Martinho, A., Kroesen, M., & Chorus, C. (2020). *An Empirical Approach to Capture Moral Uncertainty in AI*. doi:10.1145/3375627.3375805

Newman-Griffis, D., Rauchberg, J., Alharbi, R., Hickman, L., & Hochheiser, H. (2022). Definition drives design: Disability models and mechanisms of bias in AI technologies. *First Monday*.

Norori, N., Hu, Q., Aellen, F., Faraci, F., & Tzovara, A. (2021). Addressing bias in big data and AI for health care: A call for open science. *Patterns (New York, N.Y.)*, *2*(10), 100347. doi:10.1016/j.patter.2021.100347 PMID:34693373

O'Sullivan, M. E., Considine, E. C., O'Riordan, M., Marnane, W., Rennie, J., & Boylan, G. (2021). Challenges of Developing Robust AI for Intrapartum Fetal Heart Rate Monitoring. *Frontiers in Artificial Intelligence*, *4*, 4. doi:10.3389/frai.2021.765210 PMID:34765970

Oneto, L., & Chiappa, S. (2020). *Fairness in Machine Learning*. ArXiv, abs/2012.15816.

Pozzi, F. A., & Dwivedi, D. (2023). ESG and IoT: Ensuring Sustainability and Social Responsibility in the Digital Age. In S. Tiwari, F. Ortiz-Rodríguez, S. Mishra, E. Vakaj, & K. Kotecha (Eds.), *Artificial Intelligence: Towards Sustainable Intelligence. AI4S 2023. Communications in Computer and Information Science* (Vol. 1907). Springer. doi:10.1007/978-3-031-47997-7_2

Tamboli, A. (2019). Evaluating Risks of the AI Solution. *Keeping Your AI Under Control*, 31–42. doi:10.1007/978-1-4842-5467-7_4

Ziska Fields, . (Ed.). (2023). *Human Creativity vs. Machine Creativity: Innovations and Challenges. In Multidisciplinary Approaches in AI, Creativity, Innovation, and Green Collaboration* (pp. 19–28). Global. doi:10.4018/978-1-6684-6366-6.ch002

Compilation of References

2023 *SC US endreport AI and law*. (n.d.). www.supremecourt.gov. https://www.supremecourt.gov/publicinfo/year-end/2023year-endreport.pdf

Abbasi, B. Q., & Awais, S. (2022). *Playing mind gamification: Theoretical evidence of addictive nature of gamification and identification of addictive game elements used in mobile application design*. Academic Press.

Abdul Razak, M. A., Othman, M. M., Musirin, I., Yahya, M. A., & Zakaria, Z. (2020). Significant implication of optimal capacitor placement and sizing for a sustainable electrical operation in a building. *Sustainability (Basel)*, *12*(13), 5399. doi:10.3390/su12135399

Ahmad, S. F., Han, H., Alam, M. M., Rehmat, M., Irshad, M., Arraño-Muñoz, M., & Ariza-Montes, A. (2023). Impact of artificial intelligence on human loss in decision making, laziness and safety in education. *Humanities & Social Sciences Communications*, *10*(1), 1–14. doi:10.1057/s41599-023-01787-8 PMID:37325188

AI technology and justice system. (n.d.). https://lordslibrary.parliament.uk/ai-technology-and-the-justice-system-lords-committee-report/

Aïvodji, U., Arai, H., Fortineau, O., Gambs, S., Hara, S., & Tapp, A. (2019). Fairwashing: the risk of rationalization. In *International Conference on Machine Learning* (pp. 161-170). PMLR.

Alam, A. (2021). Possibilities and Apprehensions in the Landscape of Artificial Intelligence in Education. *2021 International Conference on Computational Intelligence and Computing Applications (ICCICA),* 1–8. 10.1109/ICCICA52458.2021.9697272

Alami, H., Lehoux, P., Denis, J. L., Motulsky, A., Petitgand, C., Savoldelli, M., Rouquet, R., Gagnon, M. P., Roy, D., & Fortin, J. P. (2021). Organizational readiness for artificial intelligence in health care: Insights for decision-making and practice. *Journal of Health Organization and Management*, *35*(1), 106–114. doi:10.1108/JHOM-03-2020-0074 PMID:33258359

Albayrak, N., Özdemir, A., & Zeydan, E. (2019). An artificial intelligence enabled data analytics platform for digital advertisement. In *22nd Conference on Innovation in Clouds, Internet and Networks and Workshops (ICIN)* (pp. 239–241). IEEE. 10.1109/ICIN.2019.8685870

Albrecht, W. S., Albrecht, C. O., Albrecht, C. C., & Zimbelman, M. F. (2018). *Fraud Examination. Cengage Learning.*

Aliman, N. M., Kester, L., Werkhoven, P., & Ziesche, S. (2019). Sustainable AI safety? Delphi, 2, 226.

Alt, R. (2018). Electronic markets and current general research. *Electronic Markets*, *28*(2), 123–128. doi:10.1007/s12525-018-0299-0

Alzahrani, R. A., & Aljabri, M. (2022). AI-Based Techniques for Ad Click Fraud Detection and Prevention: Review and Research Directions. *Journal of Sensor and Actuator Networks*, *12*(1), 4. doi:10.3390/jsan12010004

Alzamil, H., Aloraini, K., AlAgeel, R., Ghanim, A., Alsaaran, R., Alsomali, N., Albahlal, R. A., & Alnuaim, L. (2020). Disparity among Endocrinologists and Gynaecologists in the Diagnosis of Polycystic Ovarian Syndrome. *Sultan Qaboos University Medical Journal.*

Ameen, N., Tarhini, A., Reppel, A., & Anand, A. (2021). Customer experiences in the age of artificial intelligence. *Computers in Human Behavior*, *114*, 1–14. doi:10.1016/j.chb.2020.106548 PMID:32905175

Amisha, N., Malik, P., Pathania, M., & Rathaur, V. K. (2019). Overview of artificial intelligence in medicine. *Journal of Family Medicine and Primary Care, 8*(7), 2328–2331. doi:10.4103/jfmpc.jfmpc_440_19

Andini, N. P. (2014). Pengaruh viral marketing terhadap kepercayaan pelanggan dan keputusan pembelian (Studi pada Mahasiswa Fakultas Ilmu Administrasi Universitas Brawijaya angkatan 2013 yang melakukan pembelian online melalui media sosial instagram). *Jurnal Administrasi Bisnis, 11*(1).

Andrade, F. R., Mizoguchi, R., & Isotani, S. (2016). The bright and dark sides of gamification. *Intelligent Tutoring Systems: 13th International Conference, ITS 2016, Zagreb, Croatia, June 7-10, 2016 Proceedings*, *13*, 176–186.

Anjum, A., Ming, X., Siddiqi, A. F., & Rasool, S. F. (2018). An empirical study analyzing job productivity in toxic workplace environments. *International Journal of Environmental Research and Public Health*, *15*(5), 1035. doi:10.3390/ijerph15051035 PMID:29883424

Ansari, M. F., Sharma, P. K., & Dash, B. (2022). Prevention of phishing attacks using AI-based cybersecurity awareness training. *International Journal of Smart Sensors and Ad Hoc Networks*, 61–72. doi:10.47893/IJSSAN.2022.1221

Artificiallawyer. (2017, February 12). *AL Interview: Ravel and the AI revolution in legal research.* ArtificialLawyer. https://www.artificiallawyer.com/2017/01/23/al-interview-ravel-and-the-ai-revolution-in-legal-research/

AshooriM.WeiszJ. D. (2019). In AI We Trust? Factors That Influence Trustworthiness of AI-infused Decision-Making Processes. doi:10.48550/ARXIV.1912.02675

Aslam, F., Hunjra, A. I., Ftiti, Z., Louhichi, W., & Shams, T. (2022). Insurance fraud detection: Evidence from artificial intelligence and machine learning. *Research in International Business and Finance, 62*, 101744.

Aydınlıyurt, E. T., Taşkın, N., Scahill, S., & Toker, A. (2021). Continuance intention in gamified mobile applications: A study of behavioral inhibition and activation systems. *International Journal of Information Management, 61*, 102414. doi:10.1016/j.ijinfomgt.2021.102414

Aytekin, P., Virlanuta, F. O., Guven, H., Stanciu, S., & Bolakca, I. (2021). Consumers Perception of Risk Towards Artificial Intelligence Technologies Used in Trade: A Scale Development Study. *Amfiteatru Economic, 23*(56), 65–86. doi:10.24818/EA/2021/56/65

Azadeh, A., Yazdanparast, R., Zadeh, S. A., & Keramati, A. (2018). An intelligent algorithm for optimizing emergency department job and patient satisfaction. *International Journal of Health Care Quality Assurance, 31*(5), 374–390. doi:10.1108/IJHCQA-06-2016-0086 PMID:29865961

Babich, V., Birge, J. R., & Hilary, G. (Eds.), *Innovative Technology at the Interface of Finance and Operations. Springer Series in Supply Chain Management* (Vol. 11). Springer.

Baidoo-Anu, D., & Owusu Ansah, L. (2023). Education in the Era of Generative Artificial Intelligence (AI): Understanding the Potential Benefits of ChatGPT in Promoting Teaching and Learning. SSRN Electronic Journal. doi:10.2139/ssrn.4337484

Bandara, R., Fernando, M., & Akter, S. (2019). Privacy Concerns in E-commerce: A Taxonomy and a Future Research Agenda. *Electronic Markets, 30*(3), 629–647. doi:10.1007/s12525-019-00375-6

Baowaly, M. K., Lin, C.-C., Liu, C.-L., & Chen, K.-T. (2019). Synthesizing electronic health records using improved generative adversarial networks. *Journal of the American Medical Informatics Association : JAMIA, 26*(3), 228–241. doi:10.1093/jamia/ocy142 PMID:30535151

Bao, Y., Hilary, G., & Ke, B. (2022). Artificial intelligence and fraud detection. *Innovative Technology at the Interface of Finance and Operations, I*, 223–247. doi:10.1007/978-3-030-75729-8_8

Bar & Bench. (2023). Law student develops Law Bot Pro, a free legal AI app. *Bar And Bench - Indian Legal News*. https://www.barandbench.com/apprentice-lawyer/law-student-develops-indias-first-free-legal-ai-app

Behl, A., Sheorey, P., Jain, K., Chavan, M., Jajodia, I., & Zhang, Z. J. (2021). Gamifying the gig: Transitioning the dark side to bright side of online engagement. *AJIS. Australasian Journal of Information Systems, 25*, 1–34. doi:10.3127/ajis.v25i0.2979

Belenguer, L. (2022). AI bias: Exploring discriminatory algorithmic decision-making models and the application of possible machine-centric solutions adapted from the pharmaceutical industry. *AI and Ethics, 2*(4), 771–787. doi:10.1007/s43681-022-00138-8 PMID:35194591

Bellamy, R. K., Dey, K., Hind, M., Hoffman, S. C., Houde, S., Kannan, K., Lohia, P., Martino, J., Mehta, S., Mojsilovic, A., Nagar, S., Ramamurthy, K. N., Richards, J., Saha, D., Sattigeri, P., Singh, M., Varshney, K. R., & Zhang, Y. (2019). AI Fairness 360: An extensible toolkit for detecting and mitigating algorithmic bias. *IBM Journal of Research and Development*, *63*(4/5), 4–1. doi:10.1147/JRD.2019.2942287

Benlian, A., Klumpe, J., & Hinz, O. (2020). Mitigating the intrusive effects of smart home assistants by using anthropomorphic design features: A multimethod investigation. *Information Systems Journal*, *30*(6), 1010–1042. doi:10.1111/isj.12243

Benner, D., Schöbel, S., & Janson, A. (2021, August). It is only for your own good, or is it? Ethical Considerations for Designing Ethically Conscious Persuasive Information Systems. AMCIS.

Berényi, L., & Deutsch, N. (2023). Technology adoption among higher education students. *Vezetéstudomány*, 28–39. doi:10.14267/VEZTUD.2023.11.03

Binz, M., & Schulz, E. (2023). Using cognitive psychology to understand GPT-3. *Proceedings of the National Academy of Sciences of the United States of America*, *120*(6). Advance online publication. doi:10.1073/pnas.2218523120 PMID:36730192

Bitrián, P., Buil, I., & Catalán, S. (2021). Enhancing user engagement: The role of gamification in mobile apps. *Journal of Business Research*, *132*, 170–185. doi:10.1016/j.jbusres.2021.04.028

Boehmke, B. C., & Greenwell, B. M. (2019). *Interpretable Machine Learning*. Hands-On Machine Learning with R. doi:10.1201/9780367816377-16

Bolander, T. (2019). What do we loose when machines take the decisions? *The Journal of Management and Governance*, *23*(4), 849–867. doi:10.1007/s10997-019-09493-x

Bostrom, N., & Yudkowsky, E. (2014). The ethics of artificial intelligence. The Cambridge handbook of artificial intelligence, 1, 316-334.

Boulianne, E., Lecompte, A., & Fortin, M. (2023). Technology, Ethics, and the Pandemic: Responses from Key Accounting Actors. *Accounting and the Public Interest*, *23*(1), 177–194. doi:10.2308/API-2022-009

Box, J., & Data, P. (2019). Do You Know What Your Model is Doing ? How Human Bias Influences Machine Learning. *PHUSE EU Connect 2019.*

Brendel, A. B., Mirbabaie, M., Lembcke, T. B., & Hofeditz, L. (2021). Ethical management of artificial intelligence. *Sustainability (Basel)*, *13*(4), 1974. doi:10.3390/su13041974

Briganti, G., & Le Moine, O. (2020). Artificial Intelligence in Medicine: Today and Tomorrow. *Frontiers in Medicine*, *7*, 27. doi:10.3389/fmed.2020.00027 PMID:32118012

Brown, R., Rocha, A., & Cowling, M. (2020). Financing entrepreneurship in times of crisis: Exploring the impact of COVID-19 on the market for entrepreneurial finance in the United Kingdom. *International Small Business Journal*, *38*(5), 380–390. doi:10.1177/0266242620937464

Brynjolfsson, E., Li, D., & Raymond, L. (2023). *Generative AI at work.* doi:10.3386/w31161

Burmeister, E., & Aitken, L. M. (2012). Sample size: how many is enough? *Australian Critical Care: Official Journal of the Confederation of Australian Critical Care Nurses, 25*(4), 271– 274. doi:10.1016/j.aucc.2012.07.002

Buttazzo, G. (2023). Rise of artificial general intelligence: Risks and opportunities. *Frontiers in Artificial Intelligence, 6*, 1226990. Advance online publication. doi:10.3389/frai.2023.1226990 PMID:37693010

Cai, Y. J., & Choi, T. M. (2020). A United Nations' Sustainable Development Goals perspective for sustainable textile and apparel supply chain management. *Transportation Research Part E, Logistics and Transportation Review, 141*, 102010. doi:10.1016/j.tre.2020.102010 PMID:32834741

Cao, L. (2022). Ai in finance: Challenges, Techniques, and Opportunities. *ACM Computing Surveys, 55*(3), 1–38. doi:10.1145/3502289

Capraş, I. L., & Achim, M. V. (2023). An Overview of Forensic Accounting and Its Effectiveness in the Detection and Prevention of Fraud. *Economic and Financial Crime, Sustainability and Good Governance*, 319-346.

Caron, M. S. (2019). The transformative effect of AI on the banking industry. *Banking & Finance Law Review, 34*(2), 169–214.

Case text's open AI. GPT-4 version . (n.d.). Case Text.

Chan, H. C. S., Shan, H., Dahoun, T., Vogel, H., & Yuan, S. (2019). Advancing Drug Discovery via Artificial Intelligence. *Trends in Pharmacological Sciences, 40*(8), 592–604. doi:10.1016/j.tips.2019.06.004 PMID:31320117

Chaquet-Ulldemolins, J. (2022). On the black-box challenge for fraud detection using machine learning (ii): nonlinear analysis through interpretable autoencoders. *Applied Sciences, 12*(8), 3856.

Chatterjee, S. (2019). Impact of AI regulation on intention to use robots. *International Journal of Intelligent Unmanned Systems, 8*(2), 97–114. doi:10.1108/IJIUS-09-2019-0051

Chen, Z., Wang, G., & Li, L. L. (2017). Recurrent attentional reinforcement learning for multi-label image recognition. *arXiv:1712.07465.*

Cheng, X., Bao, Y., Zarifis, A., Gong, W., & Mou, J. (2021). Exploring consumers' response to text-based chatbots in e-commerce: The moderating role of task complexity and chatbot disclosure. *Internet Research, 32*(2), 496–517. doi:10.1108/INTR-08-2020-0460

Choi, D., & Lee, K. (2018). An artificial intelligence approach to financial fraud detection under IoT environment: A survey and implementation. *Security and Communication Networks.* doi:10.1155/2018/5483472

Ciregan, D., Meier, U., & Schmidhuber, J. (2017). Multi-column deep neural networks for image classification. *arXiv:1202.2745.*

Cirqueira, D., Helfert, M., & Bezbradica, M. (2021). Towards design principles for user-centric explainable AI in fraud detection. In *International Conference on Human-Computer Interaction*. Cham: Springer International Publishing. 10.1007/978-3-030-77772-2_2

Cruciger, O., Schildhauer, T. A., Meindl, R. C., Tegenthoff, M., Schwenkreis, P., Citak, M., & Aach, M. (2016a). Impact of locomotion training with a neurologic controlled hybrid assistive limb (HAL) exoskeleton on neuropathic pain and health related quality of life (HRQoL) in chronic SCI: A case study. *Disability and Rehabilitation. Assistive Technology*, *11*(6), 529–534. doi:10.3109/17483107.2014.981875 PMID:25382234

Cui, Y. (Gina), van Esch, P., & Jain, S. P. (2022). Just walk out: The effect of AI-enabled checkouts. *European Journal of Marketing*, *56*(6), 1650–1683.

Culkin, R., & Das, S. R. (2017). Machine learning in finance: The case of deep learning for option pricing. *Journal of Investment Management*, *15*(4), 92–100.

C. d'Amato, M. Fernandez, V. Tamma, F. Lecue, P. Cudré-Mauroux, J. Sequeda, & J. Heflin (Eds.). (2017). The Semantic Web–ISWC 2017*: 16th International Semantic Web Conference,* Vienna, Austria, October 21–25, 2017*, Proceedings, Part I* (Vol. 10587). Springer.

Damschroder, L. J., Aron, D. C., Keith, R. E., Kirsh, S. R., Alexander, J. A., & Lowery, J. C. (2009). Fostering implementation of health services research findings into practice: A consolidated framework for advancing implementation science. *Implementation Science : IS*, *4*(1), 1–15. doi:10.1186/1748-5908-4-50 PMID:19664226

Dash, B., Ansari, M. M., Sharma, P., & Ali, A. (2022). Threats and Opportunities with AI-based Cyber Security Intrusion Detection: A Review. *International Journal of Software Engineering and Its Applications*, *13*(5).

Davenport, T., & Kalakota, R. (2019). The potential for artificial intelligence in healthcare. *Future Healthcare Journal*, *6*(2), 94–98. doi:10.7861/futurehosp.6-2-94 PMID:31363513

de Deus Chaves, R., Chiarion Sassi, F., Davison Mangilli, L., Jayanthi, S. K., Cukier, A., Zilberstein, B., & Furquim de Andrade, C. R. (2014). Swallowing transit times and valleculae residue in stable chronic obstructive pulmonary disease. *BMC Pulmonary Medicine*, *14*(1), 1–9. doi:10.1186/1471-2466-14-62 PMID:24739506

De Mántaras, R. L., Gibert, K., Forment, M. A., Cortés, U., Hernández-Fernández, A., Balas, D. F., Carreras, A., Calle, A. M. T., & Domenjó, C. S. (2023). Creativitat digital. In Iniciativa Digital Politècnica. Oficina de Publicacions Acadèmiques Digitals de la UPC eBooks. doi:10.5821/ebook-9788410008090

De Vito, C., Angeloni, C., De Feo, E., Marzuillo, C., Lattanzi, A., Ricciardi, W., Villari, P., & Boccia, S. (2014). A large cross-sectional survey investigating the knowledge of cervical cancer risk etiology and the predictors of the adherence to cervical cancer screening related to mass media campaign. *BioMed Research International*. doi:10.1155/2014/304602 PMID:25013772

Deng, J., & Lin, Y. (2022). The benefits and challenges of ChatGPT: An overview. *Frontiers in Computing and Intelligent Systems*, *2*(2), 81–83. doi:10.54097/fcis.v2i2.4465

Denti, L., & Hemlin, S. (2012). *Leadership and innovation in organizations: A systematic review of factors that mediate or moderate the relationship.* doi:10.1142/S1363919612400075

Dentons - Regulating artificial intelligence in the EU: top 10 issues for businesses to consider. (n.d.). Retrieved December 19, 2023, from https://www.dentons.com/en/insights/articles/2021/june/28/regulating-artificial-intelligence-in-the-eu-top-10-issues-for-businesses-to-consider

Dharma, B., Syarbaini, A. M. B., Rahmah, M., & Hasby, M. (2023). Enhancing Literacy and Management of Productive Waqf at BKM Al Mukhlisin Towards a Mosque as a Center for Community Worship and Economics. *ABDIMAS: Jurnal Pengabdian Masyarakat*, *6*(1), 3246–3255.

Dhieb, N., Ghazzai, H., Besbes, H., & Massoud, Y. (2020). A secure AI-driven architecture for automated insurance systems: Fraud detection and risk measurement. *IEEE Access : Practical Innovations, Open Solutions*, *8*, 58546–58558. doi:10.1109/ACCESS.2020.2983300

Diamond, A. (2015). Effects of physical exercise on executive functions: going beyond simply moving to moving with thought. *Annals of Sports Medicine and Research, 2*(1), 1011.

Díaz, Ó., Dalton, J. A. R., & Giraldo, J. (2019). Artificial Intelligence: A Novel Approach for Drug Discovery. *Trends in Pharmacological Sciences*, *40*(8), 550–551. doi:10.1016/j.tips.2019.06.005 PMID:31279568

Diefenbach, S., & Müssig, A. (2019). Counterproductive effects of gamification: An analysis on the example of the gamified task manager Habitica. *International Journal of Human-Computer Studies*, *127*, 190–210. doi:10.1016/j.ijhcs.2018.09.004

Dixit, R. K., Nirgude, M. A., & Yalagi, P. S. (2018, December). Gamification: an instructional strategy to engage learner. In *2018 IEEE Tenth International Conference on Technology for Education (T4E)* (pp. 138-141). IEEE. 10.1109/T4E.2018.00037

Doshi-Velez, F., Kortz, M., Budish, R., Bavitz, C., Gershman, S., O'Brien, D., . . . Wood, A. (2017). Accountability of AI under the law: The role of explanation. *arXiv preprint arXiv:1711.01134.*

Dua, S., Kumar, S. S., Albagory, Y., Ramalingam, R., Dumka, A., Singh, R., Rashid, M., Gehlot, A., Alshamrani, S. S., & AlGhamdi, A. S. (2022). Developing a Speech Recognition System for Recognizing Tonal Speech Signals Using a Convolutional Neural Network. *Applied Sciences (Basel, Switzerland)*, *12*(12), 6223. doi:10.3390/app12126223

Du, S., & Xie, C. (2020). Paradoxes of Artificial Intelligence in Consumer markets: Ethical Challenges and Opportunities. *Journal of Business Research*, *129*, 1–14.

Dwijendra, D. N., & Mahanty, G. (2021). A text mining-based approach for accessing AI risk incidents. *International Conference on Artificial Intelligence.*

Dwivedi, D. N., Mahanty, G., & Pathak, Y. K. (2023). AI Applications for Financial Risk Management. In M. Irfan, M. Elmogy, M. Shabri Abd. Majid, & S. El-Sappagh (Eds.), The Impact of AI Innovation on Financial Sectors in the Era of Industry 5.0 (pp. 17-31). IGI Global. doi:10.4018/979-8-3693-0082-4.ch002

Dwivedi, D. N., Pandey, A. K., & Dwivedi, A. D. (2023). Examining the emotional tone in politically polarized Speeches in India: An In-Depth analysis of two contrasting perspectives. *South India Journal of Social Sciences, 21*(2), 125-136. https://journal.sijss.com/index.php/home/article/view/65

Dwivedi, D. N. (2024). The Use of Artificial Intelligence in Supply Chain Management and Logistics. In D. Sharma, B. Bhardwaj, & M. Dhiman (Eds.), *Leveraging AI and Emotional Intelligence in Contemporary Business Organizations* (pp. 306–313). IGI Global. doi:10.4018/979-8-3693-1902-4.ch018

Dwivedi, D. N., & Mahanty, G. (2024). AI-Powered Employee Experience: Strategies and Best Practices. In M. Rafiq, M. Farrukh, R. Mushtaq, & O. Dastane (Eds.), *Exploring the Intersection of AI and Human Resources Management* (pp. 166–181). IGI Global. doi:10.4018/979-8-3693-0039-8.ch009

Dwivedi, D. N., Mahanty, G., & Vemareddy, A. (2022). How Responsible Is AI?: Identification of Key Public Concerns Using Sentiment Analysis and Topic Modeling. *International Journal of Information Retrieval Research, 12*(1), 1–14. doi:10.4018/IJIRR.298646

Dwivedi, D. N., Tadoori, G., & Batra, S. (2023). Impact of women leadership and ESG ratings and in organizations: A time series segmentation study. *Academy of Strategic Management Journal, 22*(S3), 1–6.

Dwivedi, D., Batra, S., & Pathak, Y. K. (2023). A machine learning based approach to identify key drivers for improving corporate's esg ratings. *Journal of Law and Sustainable Development, 11*(1), e0242. doi:10.37497/sdgs.v11i1.242

Dwivedi, Y. K., Hughes, L., Ismagilova, E., Aarts, G., Coombs, C., Crick, T., Duan, Y., Dwivedi, R., Edwards, J., Eirug, A., Galanos, V., Ilavarasan, P. V., Janssen, M., Jones, P., Kar, A. K., Kizgin, H., Kronemann, B., Lal, B., Lucini, B., & Medaglia, R. (2019). Artificial Intelligence (AI): Multidisciplinary perspectives on emerging challenges, opportunities, and agenda for research, practice, and policy. *International Journal of Information Management, 57*, 1–47.

Dymitruk, M. (2019). Ethical artificial intelligence in judiciary. *ResearchGate*. https://www.researchgate.net/publication/333995919_Ethical_artificial_intelligence_in_judiciary

Elish, M. C., & Boyd, D. (2017). Situating methods in the magic of Big Data and AI. *Communication Monographs, 85*(1), 57–80. doi:10.1080/03637751.2017.1375130

Epstein, D. S., Zemski, A., Enticott, J., & Barton, C. (2021). Tabletop board game elements and gamification interventions for health behavior change: Realist review and proposal of a game design framework. *JMIR Serious Games, 9*(1), e23302. doi:10.2196/23302 PMID:33787502

Ethical principles on AI in courts by European union. (n.d.). https://www.coe.int/en/web/cepej/cepej-european-ethical-charter-on-the-use-of-artificial-intelligence-ai-in-judicial-systems-and-their-environment

Fadel, C., Holmes, W., & Bialik, M. (2019). *Artificial intelligence in education: Promises and implications for teaching and learning*. The Center for Curriculum Redesign.

Fawcett, T., Haimowitz, I., Provost, F., & Stolfo, S. (1998). AI approaches to fraud detection and risk management. *AI Magazine*, *19*(2), 107–107.

FDA permits marketing of artificial intelligence-based device to detect certain diabetes-related eye problems. (n.d.). Retrieved December 19, 2023, from https://www.fda.gov/news-events/press-announcements/fda-permits-marketing-artificial-intelligence-based-device-detect-certain-diabetes-related-eye

Fernandes, M., Vieira, S. M., Leite, F., Palos, C., Finkelstein, S., & Sousa, J. M. C. (2020). Clinical Decision Support Systems for Triage in the Emergency Department using Intelligent Systems: A Review. *Artificial Intelligence in Medicine*, *102*, 101762. doi:10.1016/j.artmed.2019.101762 PMID:31980099

Ferrer, X., Nuenen, T. V., Such, J. M., Cote, M., & Criado, N. (2021). Bias and Discrimination in AI: A Cross-Disciplinary Perspective. *IEEE Technology and Society Magazine*, *40*(2), 72–80. doi:10.1109/MTS.2021.3056293

Frank, D.-A., Jacobsen, L. F., Søndergaard, H. A., & Otterbring, T. (2023). In companies we trust consumer adoption of artificial intelligence services and the role of trust in companies and AI autonomy. *Information Technology & People*, *36*(8), 155–173. doi:10.1108/ITP-09-2022-0721

Fu, H.-P., Chang, T.-H., Lin, S.-W., Teng, Y.-H., & Huang, Y.-Z. (2023). Evaluation and adoption of artificial intelligence in the retail industry. *International Journal of Retail & Distribution Management*, *51*(6), 773–790. doi:10.1108/IJRDM-12-2021-0610

Fukumura, Y. E., Gray, J. M., Lucas, G. M., Becerik-Gerber, B., & Roll, S. C. (2021). Worker perspectives on incorporating artificial intelligence into office workspaces: Implications for the future of office work. *International Journal of Environmental Research and Public Health*, *18*(4), 1690. doi:10.3390/ijerph18041690 PMID:33578736

Gama, F., Tyskbo, D., Nygren, J., Barlow, J., Reed, J., & Svedberg, P. (2022). Implementation Frameworks for Artificial Intelligence Translation into Health Care Practice: Scoping Review. *Journal of Medical Internet Research*, *24*(1), e32215. doi:10.2196/32215 PMID:35084349

Gatautis, R., Banytė, J., & Vitkauskaitė, E. (2021). *Gamification and Consumer Engagement*. Progress in IS. doi:10.1007/978-3-030-54205-4

Ghandour, A. (2021). Opportunities and challenges of artificial intelligence in banking: Systematic literature review. *TEM Journal*, *10*(4), 1581–1587. doi:10.18421/TEM104-12

GhojoghB.GhodsiA. (2020). Attention Mechanism, Transformers, BERT, and GPT: Tutorial and Survey. *Research Gate*. https://doi.org/ doi:10.31219/osf.io/m6gcn

Giroux, M., Kim, J., Lee, J. C., & Park, J. (2022). Artificial Intelligence and Declined Guilt: Retailing Morality Comparison Between Human and AI. *Journal of Business Ethics*, *178*(4), 1027–1041. doi:10.1007/s10551-022-05056-7 PMID:35194275

Global AI software market growth 2019-2025 | Statista. (2022, June 27). Statista. https://www.statista.com/statistics/607960/worldwide-artificial-intelligence-market-growth/

Goasduff, L. (2021). *While advances in machine learning, computer vision, chatbots and edge artificial intelligence (AI) drive adoption, it's these trends that dominate this year's Hype Cycle*. Retrieved October 8, 2021, from https://www.gartner.com/en/articles/the–4–trends–that–prevail–on–the–gartner–hype–cycle–for–ai–2021

Goldin, C., & Katz, L. (2010). *The Race Between Education and Tech-nology*. Belknap Press for Harvard University Press. doi:10.2307/j.ctvjf9x5x

Gordon, R. J. (2016). The Rise and Fall of American Growth The U.S. Standard of Living since the Civil War. Princeton University Press.

Gorwa, R., Binns, R., & Katzenbach, C. (2020). Algorithmic content moderation: Technical and political challenges in the automation of platform governance. *Big Data & Society*, *7*(1). doi:10.1177/2053951719897945

Green, S. B. (1991). How many subjects does it take to do a regression analysis? *Multivariate Behavioral Research*, *1991*(26), 499–510. doi:10.1207/s15327906mbr2603_7 PMID:26776715

Grundner, L., & Neuhofer, B. (2021). The bright and dark sides of artificial intelligence: A futures perspective on tourist destination experiences. *Journal of Destination Marketing & Management*, *19*, 1–25. doi:10.1016/j.jdmm.2020.100511

Guha, A., Grewal, D., Kopalle, P. K., Haenlein, M., Schneider, M. J., Jung, H., Moustafa, R., Hegde, D. R., & Hawkins, G. (2021). How Artificial Intelligence Will Affect the Future of Retailing. *Journal of Retailing*, *97*(1), 28–41. doi:10.1016/j.jretai.2021.01.005

Gunning, D., & Aha, D. (2019). DARPA's Explainable Artificial Intelligence (XAI). *AI Magazine*, *40*(2), 44–58. doi:10.1609/aimag.v40i2.2850

Gupta, A., Dwivedi, D. N., & Shah, J. (2023a). Overview of Money Laundering. In Artificial Intelligence Applications in Banking and Financial Services. Future of Business and Finance. Springer. doi:10.1007/978-981-99-2571-1_1

Gupta, A., Dwivedi, D. N., & Shah, J. (2023c). Overview of Technology Solutions. In Artificial Intelligence Applications in Banking and Financial Services. Future of Business and Finance. Springer. doi:10.1007/978-981-99-2571-1_3

Gupta, A., Dwivedi, D. N., & Shah, J. (2023d). Data Organization for an FCC Unit. In Artificial Intelligence Applications in Banking and Financial Services. Future of Business and Finance. Springer. doi:10.1007/978-981-99-2571-1_4

Gupta, A., Dwivedi, D. N., & Shah, J. (2023e). Planning for AI in Financial Crimes. In Artificial Intelligence Applications in Banking and Financial Services. Future of Business and Finance. Springer. doi:10.1007/978-981-99-2571-1_5

Gupta, A., Dwivedi, D. N., & Shah, J. (2023f). Applying Machine Learning for Effective Customer Risk Assessment. In Artificial Intelligence Applications in Banking and Financial Services. Future of Business and Finance. Springer. doi:10.1007/978-981-99-2571-1_6

Gupta, A., Dwivedi, D. N., & Shah, J. (2023g). Artificial Intelligence-Driven Effective Financial Transaction Monitoring. In Artificial Intelligence Applications in Banking and Financial Services. Future of Business and Finance. Springer. doi:10.1007/978-981-99-2571-1_7

Gupta, A., Dwivedi, D. N., & Shah, J. (2023g). Financial Crimes Management and Control in Financial Institutions. In Artificial Intelligence Applications in Banking and Financial Services. Future of Business and Finance. Springer. doi:10.1007/978-981-99-2571-1_2

Gupta, A., Dwivedi, D. N., & Shah, J. (2023h). Machine Learning-Driven Alert Optimization. In Artificial Intelligence Applications in Banking and Financial Services. Future of Business and Finance. Springer. doi:10.1007/978-981-99-2571-1_8

Gupta, A., Dwivedi, D. N., & Shah, J. (2023i). Applying Artificial Intelligence on Investigation. In Artificial Intelligence Applications in Banking and Financial Services. Future of Business and Finance. Springer. doi:10.1007/978-981-99-2571-1_9

Gupta, A., Dwivedi, D. N., & Shah, J. (2023j). Ethical Challenges for AI-Based Applications. In Artificial Intelligence Applications in Banking and Financial Services. Future of Business and Finance. Springer. doi:10.1007/978-981-99-2571-1_10

Gupta, A., Dwivedi, D. N., & Shah, J. (2023k). Setting up a Best-In-Class AI-Driven Financial Crime Control Unit (FCCU). In Artificial Intelligence Applications in Banking and Financial Services. Future of Business and Finance. Springer. doi:10.1007/978-981-99-2571-1_11

Gupta, R., Tanwar, S., Al-Turjman, F., Italiya, P., Nauman, A., & Kim, S. W. (2020). Smart Contract Privacy Protection Using AI in Cyber-Physical Systems: Tools, Techniques and Challenges. *IEEE Access : Practical Innovations, Open Solutions*, *8*, 24746–24772. doi:10.1109/ACCESS.2020.2970576

Gursoy, D., Chi, O. H., Lu, L., & Nunkoo, R. (2019). Consumers acceptance of artificially intelligent (AI) device use in service delivery. *International Journal of Information Management*, *49*, 157–169. doi:10.1016/j.ijinfomgt.2019.03.008

Hacker, P., Engel, A., & Mauer, M. (2023). Regulating ChatGPT and other Large Generative AI Models. *2023 ACM Conference on Fairness, Accountability, and Transparency*, 1112–1123. 10.1145/3593013.3594067

Hagendorff, T. (2020). The Ethics of AI Ethics: An Evaluation of Guidelines. *Minds and Machines*, *30*(1), 99–120. doi:10.1007/s11023-020-09517-8

Hair, J. F., Black, W. C., Babin, B. J., Anderson, R. E., & Tatham, R. L. (2006). Multivariate data analysis (6th ed.). Pearson Prentice Hall.

Hamid, S. (2016). *The opportunities and risks of artificial intelligence in medicine and healthcare*. Academic Press.

Hammedi, W., Leclercq, T., Poncin, I., & Alkire, L. (2021). Uncovering the dark side of gamification at work: Impacts on engagement and well-being. *Journal of Business Research*, *122*, 256–269. doi:10.1016/j.jbusres.2020.08.032

Hancock, J. T., Naaman, M., & Levy, K. (2020). AI-Mediated Communication: Definition, Research Agenda, and Ethical Considerations. *Journal of Computer-Mediated Communication*, *25*(1), 89–100. doi:10.1093/jcmc/zmz022

Hanson, R. (2016). The age of. In *Work, love, and life when robots rule the Earth*. Oxford University Press.

Haque, M. S., O'Broin, D., & Kehoe, J. (2017). To Gamify or not to Gamify? Analysing the Effect of Game Elements to foster Progression and Social Connectedness. *18th Annual European GAME-ON Conference 2020.*

Hassani, H., Silva, E. S., Unger, S., TajMazinani, M., & Mac Feely, S. (2020). Artificial intelligence (AI) or intelligence augmentation (IA): What is the future? *AI*, *1*(2), 8. doi:10.3390/ai1020008

Hazizah, S. N., & Nasution, M. I. P. (2022). Peran Media Sosial Instagram Terhadap Minat Berwirausaha Mahasiswa. *Fair Value: Jurnal Ilmiah Akuntansi dan Keuangan, 5*(4).

Hidayat, T., & Suhairi, S. (2022). Pengaruh Persepsi Nilai, Harga dan Promosi Digital Marketing Terhadap Minat Beli Pasca Pandemi di Suzuya Mall Tanjung Morawa. *Cakrawala Repositori IMWI*, *5*(2), 607–615.

Hollebeek, L. D., Das, K., & Shukla, Y. (2021). Game on! How gamified loyalty programs boost customer engagement value. *International Journal of Information Management*, *61*, 102308. doi:10.1016/j.ijinfomgt.2021.102308

HolzingerA.BiemannC.PattichisC. S.KellD. B. (2017). What do we need to build explainable AI systems for the medical domain? https://arxiv.org/abs/1712.09923v1

Holzinger, A., Haibe-Kains, B., & Jurisica, I. (2019). Why imaging data alone is not enough: AI-based integration of imaging, omics, and clinical data. *European Journal of Nuclear Medicine and Molecular Imaging*, *46*(13), 2722–2730. doi:10.1007/s00259-019-04382-9 PMID:31203421

Hsu, T. C., Chang, S. C., & Hung, Y. T. (2018). How to learn and how to teach computational thinking: Suggestions based on a review of the literature. *Computers & Education*, *126*, 296–310. doi:10.1016/j.compedu.2018.07.004

Humlung, O., & Haddara, M. (2019). The hero's journey to innovation: Gamification in enterprise systems. *Procedia Computer Science*, *164*, 86–95. doi:10.1016/j.procs.2019.12.158

Hummel, P., & Braun, M. (2020). Just data? Solidarity and justice in data-driven medicine. *Life Sciences, Society and Policy*, *16*(1), 1–18. doi:10.1186/s40504-020-00101-7 PMID:32839878

Huotari, K., & Hamari, J. (2017). A definition for gamification: Anchoring gamification in the service marketing literature. *Electronic Markets*, *27*(1), 21–31. doi:10.1007/s12525-015-0212-z

Huynh, T., Pham, Q. V., Pham, X. Q., Nguyen, T. T., Han, Z., & Dong-Seong, K. (2023). Artificial intelligence for the metaverse: A survey. *Engineering Applications of Artificial Intelligence*, *117*, 105581. doi:10.1016/j.engappai.2022.105581

Ionescu, G. H., Firoiu, D., Tănasie, A., Sorin, T., Pîrvu, R., & Manta, A. (2020). Assessing the Achievement of the SDG Targets for Health and Well-Being at EU Level by 2030. *Sustainability (Basel)*, *12*(14), 5829. doi:10.3390/su12145829

Ivaldi, S., Scaratti, G., & Fregnan, E. (2022). Dwelling within the fourth industrial revolution: Organizational learning for new competences, processes and work cultures. *Journal of Workplace Learning*, *34*(1), 1–26. doi:10.1108/JWL-07-2020-0127

Jakšič, M., & Marinč, M. (2019). Relationship banking and information technology: The role of artificial intelligence and FinTech. *Risk Management*, *21*(1), 1–18. doi:10.1057/s41283-018-0039-y

Jarrahi, M. H. (2018). Artificial intelligence and the future of work: Human-AI symbiosis in organizational decision making. *Business Horizons*, *61*(4), 577–586. doi:10.1016/j.bushor.2018.03.007

Jeon, J., & Suh, Y. (2017). Analyzing the Major Issues of the 4 th Industrial Revolution. *Asian Journal of Innovation & Policy*, *6*(3).

Ji, S., Gu, Q., Weng, H., Liu, Q., Zhou, P., Chen, J., Li, Z., Beyah, R., & Wang, T. (2019). De-Health: All Your Online Health Information Are Belong to Us. *Proceedings - International Conference on Data Engineering,* 1609–1620. 10.1109/ICDE48307.2020.00143

Jiang, F., Jiang, Y., Zhi, H., Dong, Y., Li, H., Ma, S., Wang, Y., Dong, Q., Shen, H., & Wang, Y. (2017). Artificial intelligence in healthcare: Past, present and future. *Stroke and Vascular Neurology*, *2*(4), 230–243. doi:10.1136/svn-2017-000101 PMID:29507784

Jordan, M. I., & Mitchell, T. M. (2015). Machine learning: Trends, perspectives, and prospects. *Science*, *349*(6245), 255–260. doi:10.1126/science.aaa8415 PMID:26185243

Jubb, C. A., Nigrini, M. J., & Mulford, C. W. (2014). Artificial intelligence and the detection of fraud. *Journal of Emerging Technologies in Accounting*, *11*(1), 89–108.

Kamath, S. (2022). A Study on the Impact of Artificial Intelligence on Society. *International Journal of Applied Science and Engineering*, *10*(1). Advance online publication. doi:10.30954/2322-0465.2.2021.3

Katare, D., Kourtellis, N., Park, S., Perino, D., Janssen, M., & Ding, A. (2022). Bias Detection and Generalization in AI Algorithms on Edge for Autonomous Driving. *Proceedings of the IEEE International Conference on Edge Computing*. 10.1109/SEC54971.2022.00050

Katija, K., Orenstein, E. C., Schlining, B., Lundsten, L., Barnard, K., Sainz, G., Boulais, O., Cromwell, M., Butler, E. E., Woodward, B., & Bell, K. L. (2022). FathomNet: A global image database for enabling artificial intelligence in the ocean. *Scientific Reports*, *12*(1), 15914. Advance online publication. doi:10.1038/s41598-022-19939-2 PMID:36151130

KatzD.BommaritoM. J.BlackmanJ. (2014). Predicting the behavior of the Supreme Court of the United States: A General approach. *Social Science Research Network*. doi:10.2139/ssrn.2463244

Kaul, V., Enslin, S., & Gross, S. A. (2020). History of artificial intelligence in medicine. *Gastrointestinal Endoscopy*, *92*(4), 807–812. doi:10.1016/j.gie.2020.06.040 PMID:32565184

Kaur, D., Sahdev, S. L., Sharma, D., & Siddiqui, L. (2020). Banking 4.0:'The Influence of Artificial Intelligence on the Banking Industry & How AI Is Changing the Face of Modern-Day Banks. *International Journal of Management*, *11*(6). Advance online publication. doi:10.34218/IJM.11.6.2020.049

Kaur, G., Sinha, R., Tiwari, P. K., Yadav, S. K., Pandey, P., Raj, R., Vashisth, A., & Rakhra, M. (2022). Face mask recognition system using CNN model. *Neuroscience Informatics (Online)*, *2*(3), 100035. doi:10.1016/j.neuri.2021.100035 PMID:36819833

Kim, T. W., & Werbach, K. (2016). More than just a game: Ethical issues in gamification. *Ethics and Information Technology*, *18*(2), 157–173. doi:10.1007/s10676-016-9401-5

Kokina & Davenport. (2017). The Emergence of Artificial Intelligence: How Automation is Changing Auditing. *Journal of Emerging Technologies in Accounting, 14*(1), 115–122. doi:10.2308/jeta-51730

Königstorfer, F., & Thalmann, S. (2020). Applications of Artificial Intelligence in commercial banks–A research agenda for behavioural finance. *Journal of Behavioral and Experimental Finance*, *27*, 100352. doi:10.1016/j.jbef.2020.100352

Korteling, J. E. (2016). Determining training effectiveness. Paris: North Atlantic Treaty Organization (NATO) Research & Technology Organisation (RTO).

Kotler, P. (2009). *Marketing management: A south Asian perspective*. Pearson Education India.

Kranacher, M. J., & Riley, R. (2019). *Forensic accounting and fraud examination*. John Wiley & Sons.

Kranacher, M. J., Riley, R. A., & Wells, J. T. (2011). *Forensic Accounting and Fraud Examination*. John Wiley & Sons.

Kumar, S., Aishwarya Lakshmi, S., & Akalya, A. (2020). Impact and Challenges of Artificial Intelligence in Banking. *Journal of Information and Computational Science, 10*(2) 1101–1109.

Kumar, S., Talukder, M. B., Kabir, F., & Kaiser, F. (2024). Challenges and Sustainability of Green Finance in the Tourism Industry: Evidence from Bangladesh. In S. Taneja, P. Kumar, S. Grima, E. Ozen, & K. Sood (Eds.), Advances in Finance, Accounting, and Economics. IGI Global. doi:10.4018/979-8-3693-1388-6.ch006

KushalP. (2023). AI as a Tool, Not a Master: Ensuring Human Control of Artificial Intelligence. Authorea *(*Authorea*)*. doi:10.22541/au.170000968.86867344/v1

Kwasniewska, A., & Szankin, M. (2022). Can AI See Bias in X-ray Images? *International Journal of New Developments in Imaging*.

Kwiotkowska, A., Gajdzik, B., Wolniak, R., Vveinhardt, J., & Gębczyńska, M. (2021). Leadership competencies in making Industry 4.0 effective: The case of Polish heat and power industry. *Energies*, *14*(14), 4338. doi:10.3390/en14144338

Kwon, H. Y., & Özpolat, K. (2021). The dark side of narrow gamification: Negative impact of assessment gamification on student perceptions and content knowledge. *Transactions on Education*, *21*(2), 67–81. doi:10.1287/ited.2019.0227

Larsson, S., & Heintz, F. (2020). Transparency in artificial intelligence. *Internet Policy Review*, *9*(2). Advance online publication. doi:10.14763/2020.2.1469

Leaver, T., & Srdarov, S. (2023). ChatGPT isn't magic. *M/C Journal*, *26*(5). doi:10.5204/mcj.3004

Lee, S. I., Celik, S., Logsdon, B. A., Lundberg, S. M., Martins, T. J., Oehler, V. G., Estey, E. H., Miller, C. P., Chien, S., Dai, J., Saxena, A., Blau, C. A., & Becker, P. S. (2018). A machine learning approach to integrate big data for precision medicine in acute myeloid leukemia. *Nature Communications*, *9*(1), 1–13. doi:10.1038/s41467-017-02465-5

Liao, Q. V., Gruen, D., & Miller, S. (2020). Questioning the AI: Informing Design Practices for Explainable AI User Experiences. *Proceedings of the 2020 CHI Conference on Human Factors in Computing Systems*, 1–15. 10.1145/3313831.3376590

Li, J., Bonn, M. A., & Ye, B. H. (2019). Hotel employee's artificial intelligence and robotics awareness and its impact on turnover intention: The moderating roles of perceived organizational support and competitive psychological climate. *Tourism Management*, *73*, 172–181. doi:10.1016/j.tourman.2019.02.006

Li, J., Zhao, Z., Li, R., & Zhang, H. (2019). AI-Based Two-Stage intrusion detection for software defined IoT networks. *IEEE Internet of Things Journal*, *6*(2), 2093–2102. doi:10.1109/JIOT.2018.2883344

Linardatos, P., Papastefanopoulos, V., & Kotsiantis, S. (2020). Explainable AI: A review of Machine Learning Interpretability Methods. *Entropy (Basel, Switzerland)*, *23*(1), 18. doi:10.3390/e23010018 PMID:33375658

Litchfield, P., Cooper, C., Hancock, C., & Watt, P. (2016). Work and wellbeing in the 21st century. *International Journal of Environmental Research and Public Health*, *13*(11), 1065. doi:10.3390/ijerph13111065 PMID:27809265

Liu, H., Lin, C., & Chen, Y. (2019). Beyond State v Loomis: Artificial intelligence, government algorithmization and accountability. *International Journal of Law and Information Technology*, *27*(2), 122–141. doi:10.1093/ijlit/eaz001

Liu-Thompkins, Y., Okazaki, S., & Li, H. (2022). Artificial empathy in marketing interactions: Bridging the human-AI gap in affective and social customer experience. *Journal of the Academy of Marketing Science*, *50*(6), 1198–1218. doi:10.1007/s11747-022-00892-5

Lu, J., Chen, G., Wang, X., & Feng, Y. (2022). *Bright-side and Dark-side Effects of Gamification on Consumers' Adoption of Gamified Recommendation.* Academic Press.

Lubarsky, B. (2010). Re-identification of "anonymized data." *Georgetown Law Technology Review. Available Online:* Https://Www. Georgetownlawtechreview. Org/Re-Identification-of-Anonymized-Data/GLTR-04-2017 *(Accessed on 10 September 2021).*

Lui, A., & Lamb, G. W. (2018). Artificial intelligence and augmented intelligence collaboration: Regaining trust and confidence in the financial sector. *Information & Communications Technology Law*, *27*(3), 267–283. doi:10.1080/13600834.2018.1488659

Maas, M. M. (2018). *Regulating for "Normal AI Accidents."* doi:10.1145/3278721.3278766

Mahmoud, A. B., Tehseen, S., & Fuxman, L. (2020). The Dark Side of Artificial Intelligence in Retail Innovation. *Retail Futures*, 165–180.

Marr, B. (2019). *Artificial intelligence in practice: How 50 Successful Companies Used AI and Machine Learning to Solve Problems*. John Wiley & Sons.

Marriott, H. R., Williams, M. D., & Dwivedi, Y. K. (2017). Risk, privacy and security concerns in digital retail. *The Marketing Review*, *17*(3), 337–365. doi:10.1362/146934717X14909733966254

Martinho, A., Kroesen, M., & Chorus, C. (2020). *An Empirical Approach to Capture Moral Uncertainty in AI.* doi:10.1145/3375627.3375805

McCarthy, J. (2007). *What is artificial intelligence*. Academic Press.

McCarthy, H. D. (2006). Body fat measurements in children as predictors for the metabolic syndrome: Focus on waist circumference. *The Proceedings of the Nutrition Society*, *65*(4), 385–392. PMID:17181905

McCarthy, J., & Feigenbaum, E. A. (1990). In memoriam: Arthur Samuel: Pioneer in Machine learning. *AI Magazine*, *11*(3), 10–11. doi:10.1609/aimag.v11i3.840

McCarthy, J., Minsky, M., Rochester, N., & Shannon, C. E. (2006). A proposal for the Dartmouth Summer Research Project on Artificial Intelligence, August 31, 1955. *AI Magazine*, *27*(4), 12. doi:10.1609/aimag.v27i4.1904

Mehrabi, N., Morstatter, F., Saxena, N., Lerman, K., & Galstyan, A. (2022). A Survey on Bias and Fairness in Machine Learning. *ACM Computing Surveys*, *54*(6), 1–35. doi:10.1145/3457607

Mehta, K., Mittal, P., Gupta, P. K., & Tandon, J. K. (2022). Analyzing the impact of forensic accounting in the detection of financial fraud: The mediating role of artificial intelligence. In *International Conference on Innovative Computing and Communications: Proceedings of ICICC 2021,* Volume 2 (pp. 585–592). Springer Singapore. 10.1007/978-981-16-2597-8_50

Mhlanga, D. (2020). Industry 4.0 in finance: the impact of artificial intelligence (AI) on digital financial inclusion. *International Journal of Financial Studies, 8*(3), 45.

Mhlanga, D. (2020). Industry 4.0 in finance: The impact of artificial intelligence (AI) on digital financial inclusion. *International Journal of Financial Studies*, *8*(3), 45. doi:10.3390/ijfs8030045

Misra, N. N., Dixit, Y., Al-Mallahi, A., Bhullar, M. S., Upadhyay, R., & Martynenko, A. (2022). IoT, Big Data, and Artificial Intelligence in Agriculture and Food Industry. *IEEE Internet of Things Journal*, *9*(9), 6305–6324. doi:10.1109/JIOT.2020.2998584

Money, Power, and AI. (2023). In *Cambridge University Press eBooks*. doi:10.1017/9781009334297

Moore, S., Bulmer, S., & Elms, J. (2022). The social significance of AI in retail on customer experience and shopping practices. *Journal of Retailing and Consumer Services*, *64*(1), 1–8. doi:10.1016/j.jretconser.2021.102755

Mutascu, M. (2021). Artificial intelligence and unemployment: New insights. *Economic Analysis and Policy*, *69*, 653–667. doi:10.1016/j.eap.2021.01.012

Nabilah'Izzaturrahmah, A., Nhita, F., & Kurniawan, I. (2021, October). Implementation of Support Vector Machine on Text-based GERD Detection by using Drug Review Content. In *2021 International Conference Advancement in Data Science, E-learning and Information Systems (ICADEIS)* (pp. 1-6). IEEE.

Neill, D. B. (2013). Using artificial intelligence to improve hospital inpatient care. *IEEE Intelligent Systems*, *28*(2), 92–95. doi:10.1109/MIS.2013.51

Neves, J. C., Melo, A., Soares, F. M., & Frade, J. (2021). A Bilingual in-Game Tutorial: Designing Videogame Instructions Accessible to Deaf Students. In *Advances in Design and Digital Communication: Proceedings of the 4th International Conference on Design and Digital Communication, Digicom 2020, November 5–7, 2020, Barcelos, Portugal* (pp. 58-67). Springer International Publishing.

Newman-Griffis, D., Rauchberg, J., Alharbi, R., Hickman, L., & Hochheiser, H. (2022). Definition drives design: Disability models and mechanisms of bias in AI technologies. *First Monday*.

Newton, J. R., & Williams, M. C. (2022). Instagram as a special educator professional development tool: A guide to teachergram. *Journal of Special Education Technology*, *37*(3), 447–452. doi:10.1177/01626434211033596

Nicolescu, L., & Tudorache, M. T. (2022). Human-Computer Interaction in Customer Service: The Experience with AI Chatbots—A Systematic Literature Review. *Electronics (Basel)*, *11*(10), 1–24. doi:10.3390/electronics11101579

Noble, S. M., & Mende, M. (2023). The future of artificial intelligence and robotics in the retail and service sector: Sketching the field of consumer-robot-experiences. *Journal of the Academy of Marketing Science*, *51*(4), 747–756. doi:10.1007/s11747-023-00948-0 PMID:37359262

Norori, N., Hu, Q., Aellen, F., Faraci, F., & Tzovara, A. (2021). Addressing bias in big data and AI for health care: A call for open science. *Patterns (New York, N.Y.), 2*(10), 100347. doi:10.1016/j.patter.2021.100347 PMID:34693373

Ntoutsi, E., Fafalios, P., Gadiraju, U., Iosifidis, V., Nejdl, W., Vidal, M., Ruggieri, S., Turini, F., Papadopoulos, S., Krasanakis, E., Kompatsiaris, I., Kinder-Kurlanda, K., Wagner, C., Karimi, F., Fernandez, M., Alani, H., Berendt, B., Kruegel, T., Heinze, C., ... Staab, S. (2020). Bias in data-driven artificial intelligence systems—An introductory survey. *Wiley Interdisciplinary Reviews. Data Mining and Knowledge Discovery, 10*(3), e1356. Advance online publication. doi:10.1002/widm.1356

Nyström, T., & Stibe, A. (2020, November). When persuasive technology gets dark? In *European, Mediterranean, and Middle Eastern Conference on Information Systems* (pp. 331-345). Cham: Springer International Publishing. 10.1007/978-3-030-63396-7_22

O'Sullivan, M. E., Considine, E. C., O'Riordan, M., Marnane, W., Rennie, J., & Boylan, G. (2021). Challenges of Developing Robust AI for Intrapartum Fetal Heart Rate Monitoring. *Frontiers in Artificial Intelligence, 4*, 4. doi:10.3389/frai.2021.765210 PMID:34765970

Obiora, F. C., Onuora, J. K. J., & Amodu, O. A. (2022). Forensic accounting services and its effect on fraud prevention in Health Care Firms in Nigeria. *World Journal of Finance and Investment Research, 6*(1), 16–28.

Ogunode, O. A., & Dada, S. O. (2022). Fraud Prevention Strategies: An Integrative Approach on the Role of Forensic Accounting. *Archives of Business Research, 10*(7), 34–50. doi:10.14738/abr.107.12613

Okoye, E. I. (2009, November). The role of forensic accounting in fraud investigation and litigation support. In The Nigerian. *The Academy Forum, 17*(1).

Oladejo, M. T., & Jack, L. (2020). Fraud prevention and detection in a blockchain technology environment: Challenges posed to forensic accountants. *International Journal of Economics and Accounting, 9*(4), 315–335. doi:10.1504/IJEA.2020.110162

Olaoye, C. O., & Olanipekun, C. T. (2018). Impact of forensic accounting and investigation on corporate governance in Ekiti State. Journal of Accounting. *Business and Finance Research, 4*(1), 28–36.

Oneto, L., & Chiappa, S. (2020). *Fairness in Machine Learning*. ArXiv, abs/2012.15816.

OyedokunP.EmmanuelG. (2016). Forensic Accounting Investigation Techniques: Any Rationalization? *Available at* SSRN 2910318.

Pearson, T. A., & Singleton, T. W. (2008). Fraud and forensic accounting in the digital environment. *Issues in Accounting Education, 23*(4), 545–559. doi:10.2308/iace.2008.23.4.545

Pillai, R., Sivathanu, B., & Dwivedi, Y. K. (2020). Shopping intention at AI-powered automated retail stores (AIPARS). *Journal of Retailing and Consumer Services, 57*, 102207. doi:10.1016/j.jretconser.2020.102207

Pozzi, F. A., & Dwivedi, D. (2023). ESG and IoT: Ensuring Sustainability and Social Responsibility in the Digital Age. In S. Tiwari, F. Ortiz-Rodríguez, S. Mishra, E. Vakaj, & K. Kotecha (Eds.), *Artificial Intelligence: Towards Sustainable Intelligence. AI4S 2023. Communications in Computer and Information Science* (Vol. 1907). Springer. doi:10.1007/978-3-031-47997-7_2

Press Trust of India & Business Standard. (2023, February 22). *Union law minister Rijiju lauds use of AI to transcribe SC proceedings*. https://www.business-standard.com/article/current-affairs/union-law-minister-rijiju-lauds-use-of-ai-to-transcribe-sc-proceedings-123022201258_1.html

Puspitarini, D. S., & Nuraeni, R. (2019). Pemanfaatan media sosial sebagai media promosi. *Jurnal Common, 3*(1), 71–80. doi:10.34010/common.v3i1.1950

Quillian, L., Pager, D., Hexel, O., & Midtboen, A. (2017). Meta-analysis of Field Experiments Shows No Change in Racial Discrimination in Hiring Over Time. *Proceedings of the National Academy of Sciences of the United States of America, 114*(41), 10870–10875. doi:10.1073/pnas.1706255114 PMID:28900012

Rana, N. P., Chatterjee, S., Dwivedi, Y. K., & Akter, S. (2022). Understanding Dark Side of Artificial Intelligence (AI) Integrated Business analytics: Assessing Firm's Operational Inefficiency and Competitiveness. *European Journal of Information Systems, 31*(3), 364–387. doi:10.1080/0960085X.2021.1955628

Rangone, N. (2023). Artificial intelligence challenging core State functions. *Revista De Derecho PúBlico, 8*, 95–126. doi:10.37417/RDP/vol_8_2023_1949

Rapp, A., Hopfgartner, F., Hamari, J., Linehan, C., & Cena, F. (2019). Strengthening gamification studies: Current trends and future opportunities of gamification research. *International Journal of Human-Computer Studies, 127*, 1–6. doi:10.1016/j.ijhcs.2018.11.007

Reed, J. E., Howe, C., Doyle, C., & Bell, D. (2018). Simple rules for evidence translation in complex systems: A qualitative study. *BMC Medicine, 16*(1), 1–20. doi:10.1186/s12916-018-1076-9 PMID:29921274

Ristiandy, R. (2020). Bureaucratic disrupsion and threats of unemployment in the Indsutri 4.0 revolution. *Journal of Local Government Issues, 3*(1). Advance online publication. doi:10.22219/logos.v3i1.10923

Russell, S. J., & Norvig, P. (2014). Artificial Intelligence: A Modern Approach. *Industrial Marketing Management, 69*, 135–146. doi:10.1016/j.indmarman.2017.12.019

Ryman-Tubb, N. F., Krause, P., & Garn, W. (2018). *How Artificial Intelligence and machine learning research impacts payment card fraud detection: A survey and industry benchmark*. Engineering Applications of Artificial Intelligence.

SagarA. (2021). The Role of Judiciary in India and Pendency of Cases: an overall view. *Social Science Research Network*. doi:10.2139/ssrn.3798261

Sarker, I. H. (2022). Ai-based modeling: Techniques, applications and research issues towards automation, intelligent and smart systems. *SN Computer Science*, *3*(2), 158. doi:10.1007/s42979-022-01043-x PMID:35194580

Schiliro, F., Moustafa, N., & Beheshti, A. (2020). Cognitive Privacy: AI-enabled privacy using EEG Signals in the Internet of Things. *2020 IEEE 6th International Conference on Dependability in Sensor, Cloud and Big Data Systems and Application (DependSys),* 73–79. 10.1109/DependSys51298.2020.00019

Schmidt-Erfurth, U., Bogunovic, H., Sadeghipour, A., Schlegl, T., Langs, G., Gerendas, B. S., Osborne, A., & Waldstein, S. M. (2018). Machine Learning to Analyze the Prognostic Value of Current Imaging Biomarkers in Neovascular Age-Related Macular Degeneration. *Ophthalmology Retina*, *2*(1), 24–30. doi:10.1016/j.oret.2017.03.015 PMID:31047298

Schönberger, D. (2019). Artificial intelligence in healthcare: A critical analysis of the legal and ethical implications. *International Journal of Law and Information Technology*, *27*(2), 171–203. doi:10.1093/ijlit/eaz004

Shah, N., Engineer, S., Bhagat, N., Chauhan, H., & Shah, M. (2020). Research trends on the usage of machine learning and artificial intelligence in advertising. *Augmented Human Research*, *5*(1), 1–15. doi:10.1007/s41133-020-00038-8

Sharma, D., & Panigrahi, P. K. (2020). Forensic Accounting and Artificial Intelligence: A Review. *Journal of Forensic Accounting Research*, *5*(1), 1–28.

ShenY.SongK.TanX.LiD.LuW.ZhuangY. (2023). HuggingGPT: Solving AI Tasks with ChatGPT and its Friends in Hugging Face. doi:10.48550/ARXIV.2303.17580

Singh, S., Sharma, P. K., Yoon, B., Shojafar, M., Cho, G. H., & Ra, I.-H. (2020). Convergence of blockchain and artificial intelligence in IoT network for the sustainable smart city. *Sustainable Cities and Society*, *63*, 102364. doi:10.1016/j.scs.2020.102364

Singleton, T. W., Singleton, A. J., Bologna, J., & Lindquist, R. J. (2019). *Fraud Auditing and Forensic Accounting*. John Wiley & Sons.

Sivathanu, B., Pillai, R., & Metri, B. (2023). Customers' online shopping intention by watching AI-based deepfake advertisements. *International Journal of Retail & Distribution Management*, *51*(1), 124–145. doi:10.1108/IJRDM-12-2021-0583

Sohn, K., Sung, C. E., Koo, G., & Kwon, O. (2020). Artificial intelligence in the fashion industry: Consumer responses to generative adversarial network (GAN) technology. *International Journal of Retail & Distribution Management*, *49*(1), 61–80. doi:10.1108/IJRDM-03-2020-0091

Sondakh, R. A., Erawan, E., & Wibowo, S. E. (2019). Pemanfaatan Media Sosial Instagram Pada Akun@ Geprekexpress Dalam Mempromosikan Restoran Geprek Express. *Llmu Komunikasi*, *7*(1), 279–292.

SondhiS. (2023). Aspects of Dharma. *Available at* SSRN 4552530.

Song, C. S., & Kim, Y.-K. (2022). The role of the human-robot interaction in consumers' acceptance of humanoid retail service robots. *Journal of Business Research*, *146*, 489–503. doi:10.1016/j.jbusres.2022.03.087

Soviany, C. (2018). The benefits of artificial intelligence in payment fraud detection: A case study. *Journal of Payments Strategy & Systems*, *12*(2), 102–110.

Spathis, C., Doumpos, M., & Zopounidis, C. (2018). A survey on accounting and auditing approaches to prevent fraud in the era of artificial intelligence. *Journal of Financial Crime*, *25*(2), 429–448.

Srivastava, G., Bag, S., Rahman, M. S., Pretorius, J. H. C., & Gani, M. O. (2022). Examining the dark side of using gamification elements in online community engagement: an application of PLS-SEM and ANN modeling. *Benchmarking: An International Journal.*

Stoica, I., Song, D., Popa, R. A., Patterson, D., Mahoney, M. W., Katz, R., . . . Abbeel, P. (2017). A Berkeley view of systems challenges for AI. *arXiv preprint arXiv:1712.05855.*

Sulianta, F. (2021). Distictive Sport Youtube Channel Assesment Through The Methodological Approach Of Netnography. *Turkish Journal of Computer and Mathematics Education*, *12*(8), 381–386.

Susilawati, C., Miller, W., & Mardiasmo, D. (2017, August). Sustainable housing innovation toolkit. *12th World Congress on Engineering Asset Management and 13th International Conference on Vibration Engineering and Technology of Machinery.*

Tadi Beni, Y. (2016). Size-dependent electromechanical bending, buckling, and free vibration analysis of functionally graded piezoelectric nanobeams. *Journal of Intelligent Material Systems and Structures*, *27*(16), 2199–2215. doi:10.1177/1045389X15624798

Talukder, M. B., Kabir, F., Kaiser, F., & Lina, F. Y. (2024). Digital Detox Movement in the Tourism Industry: Traveler Perspective. In Business Drivers in Promoting Digital Detoxification (pp. 91-110). IGI Global.

Talukder, M., Shakhawat Hossain, M., & Kumar, S. (2022). Blue Ocean Strategies in Hotel Industry in Bangladesh: A Review of Present Literatures' Gap and Suggestions for Further Study. SSRN *Electronic Journal*. doi:10.2139/ssrn.4160709

Talukder, M. B. (2020a). An Appraisal of the Economic Outlook for the Tourism Industry, Specially Cox's Bazar in Bangladesh. *I-Manager's Journal on Economics & Commerce*, *1*(2), 24–35.

Talukder, M. B. (2020b). The Future of Culinary Tourism: An Emerging Dimension for the Tourism Industry of Bangladesh. I-Manager's. *Journal of Management*, *15*(1), 27. doi:10.26634/jmgt.15.1.17181

Talukder, M. B. (2021). An assessment of the roles of the social network in the development of the Tourism Industry in Bangladesh. *International Journal of Business, Law, and Education*, *2*(3), 85–93. doi:10.56442/ijble.v2i3.21

Talukder, M. B., & Hossain, M. M. (2021). Prospects of Future Tourism in Bangladesh: An Evaluative Study. I-Manager's. *Journal of Management*, *15*(4), 1–8. doi:10.26634/jmgt.15.4.17495

Talukder, M. B., Kumar, S., Sood, K., & Grima, S. (2023). Information Technology, Food Service Quality and Restaurant Revisit Intention. *International Journal of Sustainable Development and Planning*, *18*(1), 295–303. doi:10.18280/ijsdp.180131

Tamboli, A. (2019). Evaluating Risks of the AI Solution. *Keeping Your AI Under Control*, 31–42. doi:10.1007/978-1-4842-5467-7_4

Tarafdar, M., Gupta, A., & Turel, O. (2013). The dark side of information technology use. *Information Systems Journal*, *23*(3), 269–275. doi:10.1111/isj.12015

Taylor, I. (2023). Justice by Algorithm: The limits of AI in criminal Sentencing. *Criminal Justice Ethics*, *42*(3), 1–21. doi:10.1080/0731129X.2023.2275967

Teachers and Leaders in Vocational Education and Training. (2021). doi:10.1787/59d4fbb1-en

Thakur, A. K., Singh, R., Gehlot, A., Kaviti, A. K., Aseer, R., Suraparaju, S. K., Natarajan, S. K., & Sikarwar, V. S. (2022). Advancements in solar technologies for sustainable development of agricultural sector in India: A comprehensive review on challenges and opportunities. *Environmental Science and Pollution Research International*, *29*(29), 43607–43634. doi:10.1007/s11356-022-20133-0 PMID:35419684

The Global Competitiveness Report 2017-2018. (2023, November 9). World Economic Forum. https://www.weforum.org/publications/the-global-competitiveness-report-2017-2018/

The state of AI in 2021. (2021, December 8). McKinsey & Company. https://www.mckinsey.com/capabilities/quantumblack/our-insights/global-survey-the-state-of-ai-in-2021

Tikhamarine, Y., Souag-Gamane, D., Najah Ahmed, A., Kisi, O., & El-Shafie, A. (2020). Improving artificial intelligence models accuracy for monthly streamflow forecasting using grey Wolf optimization (GWO) algorithm. *Journal of Hydrology (Amsterdam)*, *582*, 124435. doi:10.1016/j.jhydrol.2019.124435

Toda, A. M., Valle, P. H., & Isotani, S. (2017, March). The dark side of gamification: An overview of negative effects of gamification in education. In *Researcher links workshop: higher education for all* (pp. 143–156). Springer International Publishing.

Top Advantages and Disadvantages of Artificial Intelligence. (2021, February 25). Simplilearn.com. https://www.simplilearn.com/advantages-and-disadvantages-of-artificial-intelligence-article

Tran, A. D., Pallant, J. I., & Johnson, L. W. (2021). Exploring the impact of chatbots on consumer sentiment and expectations in retail. *Journal of Retailing and Consumer Services*, *63*, 1–10. doi:10.1016/j.jretconser.2021.102718

Trang, S., & Weiger, W. H. (2019). Another dark side of gamification? How and when gamified service use triggers information disclosure. In GamiFIN (pp. 142-153). Academic Press.

Trawnih, A., Al-Masaeed, S., Alsoud, M., & Alkufahy, A. M. (2022). Understanding artificial intelligence experience: A customer perspective. *International Journal of Data and Network Science*, *6*(4), 1471–1484. doi:10.5267/j.ijdns.2022.5.004

Turing, A. M. (2009). *Computing machinery and intelligence*. Springer Netherlands.

Tussyadiah, I. (2020). A review of research into automation in tourism: Launching the Annals of Tourism Research Curated Collection on Artificial Intelligence and Robotics in Tourism. *Annals of Tourism Research*, *81*, 102883. doi:10.1016/j.annals.2020.102883

United Nations Development Programme. (2015). *Sustainable Development Goals*. https://www.undp.org/sustainable-development-goals

Vaishya, R., Javaid, M., Khan, I. H., & Haleem, A. (2020). Artificial Intelligence (AI) applications for COVID-19 pandemic. *Diabetes & Metabolic Syndrome*, *14*(4), 337–339. doi:10.1016/j.dsx.2020.04.012 PMID:32305024

Vakaliuk, T. A., Shevchuk, L. D., & Shevchuk, B. V. (2020). Possibilities of using AR and VR technologies in teaching mathematics to high school students. *Universal Journal of Educational Research*, *8*(11B), 6280–6288. doi:10.13189/ujer.2020.082267

Varriale, V., Cammarano, A., Michelino, F., & Caputo, M. (2023). Critical analysis of the impact of artificial intelligence integration with cutting-edge technologies for production systems. *Journal of Intelligent Manufacturing*. Advance online publication. doi:10.1007/s10845-023-02244-8

Vasquez, D., Okal, B., & Arras, K. O. (2014). Inverse Reinforcement Learning algorithms and features for robot navigation in crowds: An experimental comparison. *2014 IEEE/RSJ International Conference on Intelligent Robots and Systems*, 1341–1346. 10.1109/IROS.2014.6942731

Victor Nicholas, A. (2020). The Impact of Artificial Intelligence on Forensic Accounting and Testimony—Congress Should Amend "The Daubert Rule" to Include a New Standard. *Emory Law Journal Online*, *2039*, 1–26. https://scholarlycommons.law.emory.edu/elj-online/3

Vijai, D. C. (2019). Artificial intelligence in Indian banking sector: Challenges and opportunities. *International Journal of Advanced Research*, *7*(5), 1581–1587. doi:10.21474/IJAR01/8987

Vinuesa, R., Azizpour, H., Leite, I., Balaam, M., Dignum, V., Domisch, S., Felländer, A., Langhans, S. D., Tegmark, M., & Fuso Nerini, F. (2020). The role of artificial intelligence in achieving the Sustainable Development Goals. *Nature Communications*, *11*(1), 1–10. doi:10.1038/s41467-019-14108-y PMID:31932590

Votto, A. M., Valecha, R., Najafirad, P., & Rao, H. R. (2021). Artificial intelligence in tactical human resource management: A systematic literature review. *International Journal of Information Management Data Insights*, *1*(2), 100047. doi:10.1016/j.jjimei.2021.100047

Wahl, B., Cossy-Gantner, A., Germann, S., & Schwalbe, N. (2018). Artificial intelligence (AI) and global health: How can AI contribute to health in resource-poor settings? *BMJ Global Health*, *3*(4), e000798. doi:10.1136/bmjgh-2018-000798 PMID:30233828

Walsh, T. (2023). Will AI end privacy? How do we avoid an Orwellian future. *AI & Society*, *38*(3), 1239–1240. doi:10.1007/s00146-022-01433-y

Wang, J., Yang, J. H., Mao, Z. H., Huang, C., & Huang, W. X. (2016). CNN-RNN: A unified framework for multi-label image classification. *Proceedings of the 2016 IEEE Conference on Computer Vision and Pattern Recognition (CVRP).* 10.1109/CVPR.2016.251

Wang, S., Chen, Z., Xiao, Y., & Lin, C. (2021). Consumer Privacy Protection with the Growth of AI-Empowered Online Shopping Based on the Evolutionary Game Model. *Frontiers in Public Health*, *9*, 1–9. doi:10.3389/fpubh.2021.705777 PMID:34307290

WanW.KubendranR.SchaeferC.EryilmazS. B.ZhangW.WuD.DeissS.RainaP.QianH.GaoB. JoshiS.WuH.WongH.-S. P.CauwenberghsG. (2021). Edge AI without Compromise: Efficient, Versatile and Accurate Neurocomputing in Resistive Random-Access Memory. doi:10.48550/ARXIV.2108.07879

Wells, J. T. (2011). *Corporate Fraud Handbook: Prevention and Detection*. John Wiley & Sons.

Whittaker, L., Mulcahy, R., & Russell-Bennett, R. (2021). 'Go with the flow'for gamification and sustainability marketing. *International Journal of Information Management*, *61*, 102305. doi:10.1016/j.ijinfomgt.2020.102305

Whyte, C. (2020). Deepfake news: AI-enabled disinformation as a multi-level public policy challenge. *Journal of Cyber Policy*, *5*(2), 199–217. doi:10.1080/23738871.2020.1797135

Winston, P. H. (1992). *Artificial intelligence*. Addison-Wesley Longman Publishing Co., Inc.

Wolff, J., Pauling, J., Keck, A., & Baumbach, J. (2020). The economic impact of artificial intelligence in health care: Systematic review. *Journal of Medical Internet Research*, *22*(2), e16866. doi:10.2196/16866 PMID:32130134

Yan, L., Echeverría, V., Fernandez-Nieto, G., Jin, Y., Swiecki, Z., Zhao, L., Gašević, D., & Martínez-Maldonado, R. (2023). Human-AI Collaboration in Thematic Analysis using ChatGPT: A User Study and Design Recommendations. *arXiv (Cornell University)*. https://doi.org//arxiv.2311.03999 doi:10.48550

Zhang, C., & Lu, Y. (2021). Study on artificial intelligence: The state of the art and future prospects. *Journal of Industrial Information Integration*, *23*, 100224. doi:10.1016/j.jii.2021.100224

Zhang, Y., Wu, M., Tian, G. Y., Zhang, G., & Lu, J. (2021). Ethics and privacy of artificial intelligence: Understandings from bibliometrics. *Knowledge-Based Systems*, *222*, 106994. doi:10.1016/j.knosys.2021.106994

Zhao, S., Blaabjerg, F., & Wang, H. (2021). An Overview of Artificial Intelligence Applications for Power Electronics. *IEEE Transactions on Power Electronics*, *36*(4), 4633–4658. doi:10.1109/TPEL.2020.3024914

Zioviris, G., Kolomvatsos, K., & Stamoulis, G. (2022). Credit card fraud detection using a deep learning multistage model. *The Journal of Supercomputing*, *78*(12), 14571–14596. doi:10.1007/s11227-022-04465-9

Ziska Fields, . (Ed.). (2023). *Human Creativity vs. Machine Creativity: Innovations and Challenges. In Multidisciplinary Approaches in AI, Creativity, Innovation, and Green Collaboration* (pp. 19–28). Global. doi:10.4018/978-1-6684-6366-6.ch002

Zolbanin, H. M., Nabati, M., & Lee, T. S. (2019). Fraud detection in financial statements: A review of artificial intelligence-based approaches. *Computers & Industrial Engineering*, *136*, 621–635.

Related References

To continue our tradition of advancing information science and technology research, we have compiled a list of recommended IGI Global readings. These references will provide additional information and guidance to further enrich your knowledge and assist you with your own research and future publications.

Abdul Razak, R., & Mansor, N. A. (2021). Instagram Influencers in Social Media-Induced Tourism: Rethinking Tourist Trust Towards Tourism Destination. In M. Dinis, L. Bonixe, S. Lamy, & Z. Breda (Eds.), *Impact of New Media in Tourism* (pp. 135-144). IGI Global. https://doi.org/10.4018/978-1-7998-7095-1.ch009

Abir, T., & Khan, M. Y. (2022). Importance of ICT Advancement and Culture of Adaptation in the Tourism and Hospitality Industry for Developing Countries. In C. Ramos, S. Quinteiro, & A. Gonçalves (Eds.), *ICT as Innovator Between Tourism and Culture* (pp. 30–41). IGI Global. https://doi.org/10.4018/978-1-7998-8165-0.ch003

Abir, T., & Khan, M. Y. (2022). Importance of ICT Advancement and Culture of Adaptation in the Tourism and Hospitality Industry for Developing Countries. In C. Ramos, S. Quinteiro, & A. Gonçalves (Eds.), *ICT as Innovator Between Tourism and Culture* (pp. 30–41). IGI Global. https://doi.org/10.4018/978-1-7998-8165-0.ch003

Abtahi, M. S., Behboudi, L., & Hasanabad, H. M. (2017). Factors Affecting Internet Advertising Adoption in Ad Agencies. *International Journal of Innovation in the Digital Economy*, *8*(4), 18–29. doi:10.4018/IJIDE.2017100102

Afenyo-Agbe, E., & Mensah, I. (2022). Principles, Benefits, and Barriers to Community-Based Tourism: Implications for Management. In I. Mensah & E. Afenyo-Agbe (Eds.), *Prospects and Challenges of Community-Based Tourism and Changing Demographics* (pp. 1–29). IGI Global. doi:10.4018/978-1-7998-7335-8.ch001

Agbo, V. M. (2022). Distributive Justice Issues in Community-Based Tourism. In I. Mensah & E. Afenyo-Agbe (Eds.), *Prospects and Challenges of Community-Based Tourism and Changing Demographics* (pp. 107–129). IGI Global. https://doi.org/10.4018/978-1-7998-7335-8.ch005

Agrawal, S. (2017). The Impact of Emerging Technologies and Social Media on Different Business(es): Marketing and Management. In O. Rishi & A. Sharma (Eds.), *Maximizing Business Performance and Efficiency Through Intelligent Systems* (pp. 37–49). Hershey, PA: IGI Global. doi:10.4018/978-1-5225-2234-8.ch002

Ahmad, A., & Johari, S. (2022). Georgetown as a Gastronomy Tourism Destination: Visitor Awareness Towards Revisit Intention of Nasi Kandar Restaurant. In M. Valeri (Ed.), *New Governance and Management in Touristic Destinations* (pp. 71–83). IGI Global. https://doi.org/10.4018/978-1-6684-3889-3.ch005

Alkhatib, G., & Bayouq, S. T. (2021). A TAM-Based Model of Technological Factors Affecting Use of E-Tourism. *International Journal of Tourism and Hospitality Management in the Digital Age*, *5*(2), 50–67. https://doi.org/10.4018/IJTHMDA.20210701.oa1

Altinay Ozdemir, M. (2021). Virtual Reality (VR) and Augmented Reality (AR) Technologies for Accessibility and Marketing in the Tourism Industry. In C. Eusébio, L. Teixeira, & M. Carneiro (Eds.), *ICT Tools and Applications for Accessible Tourism* (pp. 277-301). IGI Global. https://doi.org/10.4018/978-1-7998-6428-8.ch013

Anantharaman, R. N., Rajeswari, K. S., Angusamy, A., & Kuppusamy, J. (2017). Role of Self-Efficacy and Collective Efficacy as Moderators of Occupational Stress Among Software Development Professionals. *International Journal of Human Capital and Information Technology Professionals*, *8*(2), 45–58. doi:10.4018/IJHCITP.2017040103

Aninze, F., El-Gohary, H., & Hussain, J. (2018). The Role of Microfinance to Empower Women: The Case of Developing Countries. *International Journal of Customer Relationship Marketing and Management*, *9*(1), 54–78. doi:10.4018/IJCRMM.2018010104

Antosova, G., Sabogal-Salamanca, M., & Krizova, E. (2021). Human Capital in Tourism: A Practical Model of Endogenous and Exogenous Territorial Tourism Planning in Bahía Solano, Colombia. In V. Costa, A. Moura, & M. Mira (Eds.), *Handbook of Research on Human Capital and People Management in the Tourism Industry* (pp. 282–302). IGI Global. https://doi.org/10.4018/978-1-7998-4318-4.ch014

Arsenijević, O. M., Orčić, D., & Kastratović, E. (2017). Development of an Optimization Tool for Intangibles in SMEs: A Case Study from Serbia with a Pilot Research in the Prestige by Milka Company. In M. Vemić (Ed.), *Optimal Management Strategies in Small and Medium Enterprises* (pp. 320–347). Hershey, PA: IGI Global. doi:10.4018/978-1-5225-1949-2.ch015

Aryanto, V. D., Wismantoro, Y., & Widyatmoko, K. (2018). Implementing Eco-Innovation by Utilizing the Internet to Enhance Firm's Marketing Performance: Study of Green Batik Small and Medium Enterprises in Indonesia. *International Journal of E-Business Research, 14*(1), 21–36. doi:10.4018/IJEBR.2018010102

Asero, V., & Billi, S. (2022). New Perspective of Networking in the DMO Model. In M. Valeri (Ed.), *New Governance and Management in Touristic Destinations* (pp. 105–118). IGI Global. https://doi.org/10.4018/978-1-6684-3889-3.ch007

Atiku, S. O., & Fields, Z. (2017). Multicultural Orientations for 21st Century Global Leadership. In N. Baporikar (Ed.), *Management Education for Global Leadership* (pp. 28–51). Hershey, PA: IGI Global. doi:10.4018/978-1-5225-1013-0.ch002

Atiku, S. O., & Fields, Z. (2018). Organisational Learning Dimensions and Talent Retention Strategies for the Service Industries. In N. Baporikar (Ed.), *Global Practices in Knowledge Management for Societal and Organizational Development* (pp. 358–381). Hershey, PA: IGI Global. doi:10.4018/978-1-5225-3009-1.ch017

Atsa'am, D. D., & Kuset Bodur, E. (2021). Pattern Mining on How Organizational Tenure Affects the Psychological Capital of Employees Within the Hospitality and Tourism Industry: Linking Employees' Organizational Tenure With PsyCap. *International Journal of Tourism and Hospitality Management in the Digital Age, 5*(2), 17–28. https://doi.org/10.4018/IJTHMDA.2021070102

Ávila, L., & Teixeira, L. (2018). The Main Concepts Behind the Dematerialization of Business Processes. In M. Khosrow-Pour, D.B.A. (Ed.), Encyclopedia of Information Science and Technology, Fourth Edition (pp. 888-898). Hershey, PA: IGI Global. https://doi.org/ doi:10.4018/978-1-5225-2255-3.ch076

Ayorekire, J., Mugizi, F., Obua, J., & Ampaire, G. (2022). Community-Based Tourism and Local People's Perceptions Towards Conservation: The Case of Queen Elizabeth Conservation Area, Uganda. In I. Mensah & E. Afenyo-Agbe (Eds.), *Prospects and Challenges of Community-Based Tourism and Changing Demographics* (pp. 56–82). IGI Global. https://doi.org/10.4018/978-1-7998-7335-8.ch003

Baleiro, R. (2022). Tourist Literature and the Architecture of Travel in Olga Tokarczuk and Patti Smith. In R. Baleiro & R. Pereira (Eds.), *Global Perspectives on Literary Tourism and Film-Induced Tourism* (pp. 202-216). IGI Global. https://doi.org/10.4018/978-1-7998-8262-6.ch011

Barat, S. (2021). Looking at the Future of Medical Tourism in Asia. *International Journal of Tourism and Hospitality Management in the Digital Age*, *5*(1), 19–33. https://doi.org/10.4018/IJTHMDA.2021010102

Barbosa, C. A., Magalhães, M., & Nunes, M. R. (2021). Travel Instagramability: A Way of Choosing a Destination? In M. Dinis, L. Bonixe, S. Lamy, & Z. Breda (Eds.), *Impact of New Media in Tourism* (pp. 173-190). IGI Global. https://doi.org/10.4018/978-1-7998-7095-1.ch011

Bari, M. W., & Khan, Q. (2021). Pakistan as a Destination of Religious Tourism. In E. Alaverdov & M. Bari (Eds.), *Global Development of Religious Tourism* (pp. 1-10). IGI Global. https://doi.org/10.4018/978-1-7998-5792-1.ch001

Bartens, Y., Chunpir, H. I., Schulte, F., & Voß, S. (2017). Business/IT Alignment in Two-Sided Markets: A COBIT 5 Analysis for Media Streaming Business Models. In S. De Haes & W. Van Grembergen (Eds.), *Strategic IT Governance and Alignment in Business Settings* (pp. 82–111). Hershey, PA: IGI Global. doi:10.4018/978-1-5225-0861-8.ch004

Bashayreh, A. M. (2018). Organizational Culture and Organizational Performance. In W. Lee & F. Sabetzadeh (Eds.), *Contemporary Knowledge and Systems Science* (pp. 50–69). Hershey, PA: IGI Global. doi:10.4018/978-1-5225-5655-8.ch003

Bechthold, L., Lude, M., & Prügl, R. (2021). Crisis Favors the Prepared Firm: How Organizational Ambidexterity Relates to Perceptions of Organizational Resilience. In A. Zehrer, G. Glowka, K. Schwaiger, & V. Ranacher-Lackner (Eds.), *Resiliency Models and Addressing Future Risks for Family Firms in the Tourism Industry* (pp. 178–205). IGI Global. https://doi.org/10.4018/978-1-7998-7352-5.ch008

Bedford, D. A. (2018). Sustainable Knowledge Management Strategies: Aligning Business Capabilities and Knowledge Management Goals. In N. Baporikar (Ed.), *Global Practices in Knowledge Management for Societal and Organizational Development* (pp. 46–73). Hershey, PA: IGI Global. doi:10.4018/978-1-5225-3009-1.ch003

Bekjanov, D., & Matyusupov, B. (2021). Influence of Innovative Processes in the Competitiveness of Tourist Destination. In J. Soares (Ed.), *Innovation and Entrepreneurial Opportunities in Community Tourism* (pp. 243–263). IGI Global. https://doi.org/10.4018/978-1-7998-4855-4.ch014

Bharwani, S., & Musunuri, D. (2018). Reflection as a Process From Theory to Practice. In M. Khosrow-Pour, D.B.A. (Ed.), Encyclopedia of Information Science and Technology, Fourth Edition (pp. 1529-1539). Hershey, PA: IGI Global. doi:10.4018/978-1-5225-2255-3.ch132

Bhatt, G. D., Wang, Z., & Rodger, J. A. (2017). Information Systems Capabilities and Their Effects on Competitive Advantages: A Study of Chinese Companies. *Information Resources Management Journal, 30*(3), 41–57. doi:10.4018/IRMJ.2017070103

Bhushan, M., & Yadav, A. (2017). Concept of Cloud Computing in ESB. In R. Bhadoria, N. Chaudhari, G. Tomar, & S. Singh (Eds.), *Exploring Enterprise Service Bus in the Service-Oriented Architecture Paradigm* (pp. 116–127). Hershey, PA: IGI Global. doi:10.4018/978-1-5225-2157-0.ch008

Bhushan, S. (2017). System Dynamics Base-Model of Humanitarian Supply Chain (HSCM) in Disaster Prone Eco-Communities of India: A Discussion on Simulation and Scenario Results. *International Journal of System Dynamics Applications, 6*(3), 20–37. doi:10.4018/IJSDA.2017070102

Binder, D., & Miller, J. W. (2021). A Generations' Perspective on Employer Branding in Tourism. In V. Costa, A. Moura, & M. Mira (Eds.), *Handbook of Research on Human Capital and People Management in the Tourism Industry* (pp. 152–174). IGI Global. https://doi.org/10.4018/978-1-7998-4318-4.ch008

Birch Freeman, A. A., Mensah, I., & Antwi, K. B. (2022). Smiling vs. Frowning Faces: Community Participation for Sustainable Tourism in Ghanaian Communities. In I. Mensah & E. Afenyo-Agbe (Eds.), *Prospects and Challenges of Community-Based Tourism and Changing Demographics* (pp. 83–106). IGI Global. https://doi.org/10.4018/978-1-7998-7335-8.ch004

Biswas, A., & De, A. K. (2017). On Development of a Fuzzy Stochastic Programming Model with Its Application to Business Management. In S. Trivedi, S. Dey, A. Kumar, & T. Panda (Eds.), *Handbook of Research on Advanced Data Mining Techniques and Applications for Business Intelligence* (pp. 353–378). Hershey, PA: IGI Global. doi:10.4018/978-1-5225-2031-3.ch021

Boragnio, A., & Faracce Macia, C. (2021). "Taking Care of Yourself at Home": Use of E-Commerce About Food and Care During the COVID-19 Pandemic in the City of Buenos Aires. In M. Korstanje (Ed.), *Socio-Economic Effects and Recovery Efforts for the Rental Industry: Post-COVID-19 Strategies* (pp. 45–71). IGI Global. https://doi.org/10.4018/978-1-7998-7287-0.ch003

Borges, V. D. (2021). Happiness: The Basis for Public Policy in Tourism. In A. Perinotto, V. Mayer, & J. Soares (Eds.), *Rebuilding and Restructuring the Tourism Industry: Infusion of Happiness and Quality of Life* (pp. 1–25). IGI Global. https://doi.org/10.4018/978-1-7998-7239-9.ch001

Bücker, J., & Ernste, K. (2018). Use of Brand Heroes in Strategic Reputation Management: The Case of Bacardi, Adidas, and Daimler. In A. Erdemir (Ed.), *Reputation Management Techniques in Public Relations* (pp. 126–150). Hershey, PA: IGI Global. doi:10.4018/978-1-5225-3619-2.ch007

Buluk Eşitti, B. (2021). COVID-19 and Alternative Tourism: New Destinations and New Tourism Products. In M. Demir, A. Dalgıç, & F. Ergen (Eds.), *Handbook of Research on the Impacts and Implications of COVID-19 on the Tourism Industry* (pp. 786–805). IGI Global. https://doi.org/10.4018/978-1-7998-8231-2.ch038

Bureš, V. (2018). Industry 4.0 From the Systems Engineering Perspective: Alternative Holistic Framework Development. In R. Brunet-Thornton & F. Martinez (Eds.), *Analyzing the Impacts of Industry 4.0 in Modern Business Environments* (pp. 199–223). Hershey, PA: IGI Global. doi:10.4018/978-1-5225-3468-6.ch011

Buzady, Z. (2017). Resolving the Magic Cube of Effective Case Teaching: Benchmarking Case Teaching Practices in Emerging Markets – Insights from the Central European University Business School, Hungary. In D. Latusek (Ed.), *Case Studies as a Teaching Tool in Management Education* (pp. 79–103). Hershey, PA: IGI Global. doi:10.4018/978-1-5225-0770-3.ch005

Camillo, A. (2021). *Legal Matters, Risk Management, and Risk Prevention: From Forming a Business to Legal Representation*. IGI Global. doi:10.4018/978-1-7998-4342-9.ch004

Căpusneanu, S., & Topor, D. I. (2018). Business Ethics and Cost Management in SMEs: Theories of Business Ethics and Cost Management Ethos. In I. Oncioiu (Ed.), *Ethics and Decision-Making for Sustainable Business Practices* (pp. 109–127). Hershey, PA: IGI Global. doi:10.4018/978-1-5225-3773-1.ch007

Chan, R. L., Mo, P. L., & Moon, K. K. (2018). Strategic and Tactical Measures in Managing Enterprise Risks: A Study of the Textile and Apparel Industry. In K. Strang, M. Korstanje, & N. Vajjhala (Eds.), *Research, Practices, and Innovations in Global Risk and Contingency Management* (pp. 1–19). Hershey, PA: IGI Global. doi:10.4018/978-1-5225-4754-9.ch001

Charlier, S. D., Burke-Smalley, L. A., & Fisher, S. L. (2018). Undergraduate Programs in the U.S: A Contextual and Content-Based Analysis. In J. Mendy (Ed.), *Teaching Human Resources and Organizational Behavior at the College Level* (pp. 26–57). Hershey, PA: IGI Global. doi:10.4018/978-1-5225-2820-3.ch002

Chumillas, J., Güell, M., & Quer, P. (2022). The Use of ICT in Tourist and Educational Literary Routes: The Role of the Guide. In C. Ramos, S. Quinteiro, & A. Gonçalves (Eds.), *ICT as Innovator Between Tourism and Culture* (pp. 15–29). IGI Global. https://doi.org/10.4018/978-1-7998-8165-0.ch002

Dahlberg, T., Kivijärvi, H., & Saarinen, T. (2017). IT Investment Consistency and Other Factors Influencing the Success of IT Performance. In S. De Haes & W. Van Grembergen (Eds.), *Strategic IT Governance and Alignment in Business Settings* (pp. 176–208). Hershey, PA: IGI Global. doi:10.4018/978-1-5225-0861-8.ch007

Damnjanović, A. M. (2017). Knowledge Management Optimization through IT and E-Business Utilization: A Qualitative Study on Serbian SMEs. In M. Vemić (Ed.), *Optimal Management Strategies in Small and Medium Enterprises* (pp. 249–267). Hershey, PA: IGI Global. doi:10.4018/978-1-5225-1949-2.ch012

Daneshpour, H. (2017). Integrating Sustainable Development into Project Portfolio Management through Application of Open Innovation. In M. Vemić (Ed.), *Optimal Management Strategies in Small and Medium Enterprises* (pp. 370–387). Hershey, PA: IGI Global. doi:10.4018/978-1-5225-1949-2.ch017

Daniel, A. D., & Reis de Castro, V. (2018). Entrepreneurship Education: How to Measure the Impact on Nascent Entrepreneurs. In A. Carrizo Moreira, J. Guilherme Leitão Dantas, & F. Manuel Valente (Eds.), *Nascent Entrepreneurship and Successful New Venture Creation* (pp. 85–110). Hershey, PA: IGI Global. doi:10.4018/978-1-5225-2936-1.ch004

David, R., Swami, B. N., & Tangirala, S. (2018). Ethics Impact on Knowledge Management in Organizational Development: A Case Study. In N. Baporikar (Ed.), *Global Practices in Knowledge Management for Societal and Organizational Development* (pp. 19–45). Hershey, PA: IGI Global. doi:10.4018/978-1-5225-3009-1.ch002

De Uña-Álvarez, E., & Villarino-Pérez, M. (2022). Fostering Ecocultural Resources, Identity, and Tourism in Inland Territories (Galicia, NW Spain). In G. Fernandes (Ed.), *Challenges and New Opportunities for Tourism in Inland Territories: Ecocultural Resources and Sustainable Initiatives* (pp. 1-16). IGI Global. https://doi.org/10.4018/978-1-7998-7339-6.ch001

Delias, P., & Lakiotaki, K. (2018). Discovering Process Horizontal Boundaries to Facilitate Process Comprehension. *International Journal of Operations Research and Information Systems, 9*(2), 1–31. doi:10.4018/IJORIS.2018040101

Denholm, J., & Lee-Davies, L. (2018). Success Factors for Games in Business and Project Management. In *Enhancing Education and Training Initiatives Through Serious Games* (pp. 34–68). Hershey, PA: IGI Global. doi:10.4018/978-1-5225-3689-5.ch002

Deshpande, M. (2017). Best Practices in Management Institutions for Global Leadership: Policy Aspects. In N. Baporikar (Ed.), *Management Education for Global Leadership* (pp. 1–27). Hershey, PA: IGI Global. doi:10.4018/978-1-5225-1013-0.ch001

Deshpande, M. (2018). Policy Perspectives for SMEs Knowledge Management. In N. Baporikar (Ed.), *Knowledge Integration Strategies for Entrepreneurship and Sustainability* (pp. 23–46). Hershey, PA: IGI Global. doi:10.4018/978-1-5225-5115-7.ch002

Dezdar, S. (2017). ERP Implementation Projects in Asian Countries: A Comparative Study on Iran and China. *International Journal of Information Technology Project Management, 8*(3), 52–68. doi:10.4018/IJITPM.2017070104

Domingos, D., Respício, A., & Martinho, R. (2017). Reliability of IoT-Aware BPMN Healthcare Processes. In C. Reis & M. Maximiano (Eds.), *Internet of Things and Advanced Application in Healthcare* (pp. 214–248). Hershey, PA: IGI Global. doi:10.4018/978-1-5225-1820-4.ch008

Dosumu, O., Hussain, J., & El-Gohary, H. (2017). An Exploratory Study of the Impact of Government Policies on the Development of Small and Medium Enterprises in Developing Countries: The Case of Nigeria. *International Journal of Customer Relationship Marketing and Management, 8*(4), 51–62. doi:10.4018/IJCRMM.2017100104

Durst, S., Bruns, G., & Edvardsson, I. R. (2017). Retaining Knowledge in Smaller Building and Construction Firms. *International Journal of Knowledge and Systems Science, 8*(3), 1–12. doi:10.4018/IJKSS.2017070101

Edvardsson, I. R., & Durst, S. (2017). Outsourcing, Knowledge, and Learning: A Critical Review. *International Journal of Knowledge-Based Organizations, 7*(2), 13–26. doi:10.4018/IJKBO.2017040102

Edwards, J. S. (2018). Integrating Knowledge Management and Business Processes. In M. Khosrow-Pour, D.B.A. (Ed.), Encyclopedia of Information Science and Technology, Fourth Edition (pp. 5046-5055). Hershey, PA: IGI Global. doi:10.4018/978-1-5225-2255-3.ch437

Eichelberger, S., & Peters, M. (2021). Family Firm Management in Turbulent Times: Opportunities for Responsible Tourism. In A. Zehrer, G. Glowka, K. Schwaiger, & V. Ranacher-Lackner (Eds.), *Resiliency Models and Addressing Future Risks for Family Firms in the Tourism Industry* (pp. 103–124). IGI Global. https://doi.org/10.4018/978-1-7998-7352-5.ch005

Eide, D., Hjalager, A., & Hansen, M. (2022). Innovative Certifications in Adventure Tourism: Attributes and Diffusion. In R. Augusto Costa, F. Brandão, Z. Breda, & C. Costa (Eds.), *Planning and Managing the Experience Economy in Tourism* (pp. 161-175). IGI Global. https://doi.org/10.4018/978-1-7998-8775-1.ch009

Ejiogu, A. O. (2018). Economics of Farm Management. In *Agricultural Finance and Opportunities for Investment and Expansion* (pp. 56–72). Hershey, PA: IGI Global. doi:10.4018/978-1-5225-3059-6.ch003

Ekanem, I., & Abiade, G. E. (2018). Factors Influencing the Use of E-Commerce by Small Enterprises in Nigeria. *International Journal of ICT Research in Africa and the Middle East*, *7*(1), 37–53. doi:10.4018/IJICTRAME.2018010103

Ekanem, I., & Alrossais, L. A. (2017). Succession Challenges Facing Family Businesses in Saudi Arabia. In P. Zgheib (Ed.), *Entrepreneurship and Business Innovation in the Middle East* (pp. 122–146). Hershey, PA: IGI Global. doi:10.4018/978-1-5225-2066-5.ch007

El Faquih, L., & Fredj, M. (2017). Ontology-Based Framework for Quality in Configurable Process Models. *Journal of Electronic Commerce in Organizations*, *15*(2), 48–60. doi:10.4018/JECO.2017040104

Faisal, M. N., & Talib, F. (2017). Building Ambidextrous Supply Chains in SMEs: How to Tackle the Barriers? *International Journal of Information Systems and Supply Chain Management*, *10*(4), 80–100. doi:10.4018/IJISSCM.2017100105

Fernandes, T. M., Gomes, J., & Romão, M. (2017). Investments in E-Government: A Benefit Management Case Study. *International Journal of Electronic Government Research*, *13*(3), 1–17. doi:10.4018/IJEGR.2017070101

Figueira, L. M., Honrado, G. R., & Dionísio, M. S. (2021). Human Capital Management in the Tourism Industry in Portugal. In V. Costa, A. Moura, & M. Mira (Eds.), *Handbook of Research on Human Capital and People Management in the Tourism Industry* (pp. 1–19). IGI Global. doi:10.4018/978-1-7998-4318-4.ch001

Gao, S. S., Oreal, S., & Zhang, J. (2018). Contemporary Financial Risk Management Perceptions and Practices of Small-Sized Chinese Businesses. In I. Management Association (Ed.), Global Business Expansion: Concepts, Methodologies, Tools, and Applications (pp. 917-931). Hershey, PA: IGI Global. doi:10.4018/978-1-5225-5481-3.ch041

Garg, R., & Berning, S. C. (2017). Indigenous Chinese Management Philosophies: Key Concepts and Relevance for Modern Chinese Firms. In B. Christiansen & G. Koc (Eds.), *Transcontinental Strategies for Industrial Development and Economic Growth* (pp. 43–57). Hershey, PA: IGI Global. doi:10.4018/978-1-5225-2160-0.ch003

Gencer, Y. G. (2017). Supply Chain Management in Retailing Business. In U. Akkucuk (Ed.), *Ethics and Sustainability in Global Supply Chain Management* (pp. 197–210). Hershey, PA: IGI Global. doi:10.4018/978-1-5225-2036-8.ch011

Gera, R., Arora, S., & Malik, S. (2021). Emotional Labor in the Tourism Industry: Strategies, Antecedents, and Outcomes. In V. Costa, A. Moura, & M. Mira (Eds.), *Handbook of Research on Human Capital and People Management in the Tourism Industry* (pp. 73–91). IGI Global. https://doi.org/10.4018/978-1-7998-4318-4.ch004

Giacosa, E. (2018). The Increasing of the Regional Development Thanks to the Luxury Business Innovation. In L. Carvalho (Ed.), *Handbook of Research on Entrepreneurial Ecosystems and Social Dynamics in a Globalized World* (pp. 260–273). Hershey, PA: IGI Global. doi:10.4018/978-1-5225-3525-6.ch011

Glowka, G., Tusch, M., & Zehrer, A. (2021). The Risk Perception of Family Business Owner-Manager in the Tourism Industry: A Qualitative Comparison of the Intra-Firm Senior and Junior Generation. In A. Zehrer, G. Glowka, K. Schwaiger, & V. Ranacher-Lackner (Eds.), *Resiliency Models and Addressing Future Risks for Family Firms in the Tourism Industry* (pp. 126–153). IGI Global. https://doi.org/10.4018/978-1-7998-7352-5.ch006

Glykas, M., & George, J. (2017). Quality and Process Management Systems in the UAE Maritime Industry. *International Journal of Productivity Management and Assessment Technologies*, *5*(1), 20–39. doi:10.4018/IJPMAT.2017010102

Glykas, M., Valiris, G., Kokkinaki, A., & Koutsoukou, Z. (2018). Banking Business Process Management Implementation. *International Journal of Productivity Management and Assessment Technologies*, *6*(1), 50–69. doi:10.4018/IJPMAT.2018010104

Gomes, J., & Romão, M. (2017). The Balanced Scorecard: Keeping Updated and Aligned with Today's Business Trends. *International Journal of Productivity Management and Assessment Technologies*, *5*(2), 1–15. doi:10.4018/IJPMAT.2017070101

Gomes, J., & Romão, M. (2017). Aligning Information Systems and Technology with Benefit Management and Balanced Scorecard. In S. De Haes & W. Van Grembergen (Eds.), *Strategic IT Governance and Alignment in Business Settings* (pp. 112–131). Hershey, PA: IGI Global. doi:10.4018/978-1-5225-0861-8.ch005

Goyal, A. (2021). Communicating and Building Destination Brands With New Media. In M. Dinis, L. Bonixe, S. Lamy, & Z. Breda (Eds.), *Impact of New Media in Tourism* (pp. 1-20). IGI Global. https://doi.org/10.4018/978-1-7998-7095-1.ch001

Grefen, P., & Turetken, O. (2017). Advanced Business Process Management in Networked E-Business Scenarios. *International Journal of E-Business Research*, *13*(4), 70–104. doi:10.4018/IJEBR.2017100105

Guasca, M., Van Broeck, A. M., & Vanneste, D. (2021). Tourism and the Social Reintegration of Colombian Ex-Combatants. In J. da Silva, Z. Breda, & F. Carbone (Eds.), *Role and Impact of Tourism in Peacebuilding and Conflict Transformation* (pp. 66-86). IGI Global. https://doi.org/10.4018/978-1-7998-5053-3.ch005

Haider, A., & Saetang, S. (2017). Strategic IT Alignment in Service Sector. In S. Rozenes & Y. Cohen (Eds.), *Handbook of Research on Strategic Alliances and Value Co-Creation in the Service Industry* (pp. 231–258). Hershey, PA: IGI Global. doi:10.4018/978-1-5225-2084-9.ch012

Hajilari, A. B., Ghadaksaz, M., & Fasghandis, G. S. (2017). Assessing Organizational Readiness for Implementing ERP System Using Fuzzy Expert System Approach. *International Journal of Enterprise Information Systems*, *13*(1), 67–85. doi:10.4018/IJEIS.2017010105

Haldorai, A., Ramu, A., & Murugan, S. (2018). Social Aware Cognitive Radio Networks: Effectiveness of Social Networks as a Strategic Tool for Organizational Business Management. In H. Bansal, G. Shrivastava, G. Nguyen, & L. Stanciu (Eds.), *Social Network Analytics for Contemporary Business Organizations* (pp. 188–202). Hershey, PA: IGI Global. doi:10.4018/978-1-5225-5097-6.ch010

Hall, O. P. Jr. (2017). Social Media Driven Management Education. *International Journal of Knowledge-Based Organizations*, *7*(2), 43–59. doi:10.4018/IJKBO.2017040104

Hanifah, H., Halim, H. A., Ahmad, N. H., & Vafaei-Zadeh, A. (2017). Innovation Culture as a Mediator Between Specific Human Capital and Innovation Performance Among Bumiputera SMEs in Malaysia. In N. Ahmad, T. Ramayah, H. Halim, & S. Rahman (Eds.), *Handbook of Research on Small and Medium Enterprises in Developing Countries* (pp. 261–279). Hershey, PA: IGI Global. doi:10.4018/978-1-5225-2165-5.ch012

Hartlieb, S., & Silvius, G. (2017). Handling Uncertainty in Project Management and Business Development: Similarities and Differences. In Y. Raydugin (Ed.), *Handbook of Research on Leveraging Risk and Uncertainties for Effective Project Management* (pp. 337–362). Hershey, PA: IGI Global. doi:10.4018/978-1-5225-1790-0.ch016

Hass, K. B. (2017). Living on the Edge: Managing Project Complexity. In Y. Raydugin (Ed.), *Handbook of Research on Leveraging Risk and Uncertainties for Effective Project Management* (pp. 177–201). Hershey, PA: IGI Global. doi:10.4018/978-1-5225-1790-0.ch009

Hawking, P., & Carmine Sellitto, C. (2017). Developing an Effective Strategy for Organizational Business Intelligence. In M. Tavana (Ed.), *Enterprise Information Systems and the Digitalization of Business Functions* (pp. 222–237). Hershey, PA: IGI Global. doi:10.4018/978-1-5225-2382-6.ch010

Hawking, P., & Sellitto, C. (2017). A Fast-Moving Consumer Goods Company and Business Intelligence Strategy Development. *International Journal of Enterprise Information Systems*, *13*(2), 22–33. doi:10.4018/IJEIS.2017040102

Hawking, P., & Sellitto, C. (2017). Business Intelligence Strategy: Two Case Studies. *International Journal of Business Intelligence Research*, *8*(2), 17–30. doi:10.4018/IJBIR.2017070102

Hee, W. J., Jalleh, G., Lai, H., & Lin, C. (2017). E-Commerce and IT Projects: Evaluation and Management Issues in Australian and Taiwanese Hospitals. *International Journal of Public Health Management and Ethics*, *2*(1), 69–90. doi:10.4018/IJPHME.2017010104

Hernandez, A. A. (2018). Exploring the Factors to Green IT Adoption of SMEs in the Philippines. *Journal of Cases on Information Technology*, *20*(2), 49–66. doi:10.4018/JCIT.2018040104

Hollman, A., Bickford, S., & Hollman, T. (2017). Cyber InSecurity: A Post-Mortem Attempt to Assess Cyber Problems from IT and Business Management Perspectives. *Journal of Cases on Information Technology*, *19*(3), 42–70. doi:10.4018/JCIT.2017070104

Ibrahim, F., & Zainin, N. M. (2021). Exploring the Technological Impacts: The Case of Museums in Brunei Darussalam. *International Journal of Tourism and Hospitality Management in the Digital Age*, *5*(1), 1–18. https://doi.org/10.4018/IJTHMDA.2021010101

Igbinakhase, I. (2017). Responsible and Sustainable Management Practices in Developing and Developed Business Environments. In Z. Fields (Ed.), *Collective Creativity for Responsible and Sustainable Business Practice* (pp. 180–207). Hershey, PA: IGI Global. doi:10.4018/978-1-5225-1823-5.ch010

Iwata, J. J., & Hoskins, R. G. (2017). Managing Indigenous Knowledge in Tanzania: A Business Perspective. In P. Jain & N. Mnjama (Eds.), *Managing Knowledge Resources and Records in Modern Organizations* (pp. 198–214). Hershey, PA: IGI Global. doi:10.4018/978-1-5225-1965-2.ch012

Jain, P. (2017). Ethical and Legal Issues in Knowledge Management Life-Cycle in Business. In P. Jain & N. Mnjama (Eds.), *Managing Knowledge Resources and Records in Modern Organizations* (pp. 82–101). Hershey, PA: IGI Global. doi:10.4018/978-1-5225-1965-2.ch006

James, S., & Hauli, E. (2017). Holistic Management Education at Tanzanian Rural Development Planning Institute. In N. Baporikar (Ed.), *Management Education for Global Leadership* (pp. 112–136). Hershey, PA: IGI Global. doi:10.4018/978-1-5225-1013-0.ch006

Janošková, M., Csikósová, A., & Čulková, K. (2018). Measurement of Company Performance as Part of Its Strategic Management. In R. Leon (Ed.), *Managerial Strategies for Business Sustainability During Turbulent Times* (pp. 309–335). Hershey, PA: IGI Global. doi:10.4018/978-1-5225-2716-9.ch017

Jean-Vasile, A., & Alecu, A. (2017). Theoretical and Practical Approaches in Understanding the Influences of Cost-Productivity-Profit Trinomial in Contemporary Enterprises. In A. Jean Vasile & D. Nicolò (Eds.), *Sustainable Entrepreneurship and Investments in the Green Economy* (pp. 28–62). Hershey, PA: IGI Global. doi:10.4018/978-1-5225-2075-7.ch002

Joia, L. A., & Correia, J. C. (2018). CIO Competencies From the IT Professional Perspective: Insights From Brazil. *Journal of Global Information Management*, *26*(2), 74–103. doi:10.4018/JGIM.2018040104

Juma, A., & Mzera, N. (2017). Knowledge Management and Records Management and Competitive Advantage in Business. In P. Jain & N. Mnjama (Eds.), *Managing Knowledge Resources and Records in Modern Organizations* (pp. 15–28). Hershey, PA: IGI Global. doi:10.4018/978-1-5225-1965-2.ch002

K., I., & A, V. (2018). Monitoring and Auditing in the Cloud. In K. Munir (Ed.), *Cloud Computing Technologies for Green Enterprises* (pp. 318-350). Hershey, PA: IGI Global. https://doi.org/ doi:10.4018/978-1-5225-3038-1.ch013

Kabra, G., Ghosh, V., & Ramesh, A. (2018). Enterprise Integrated Business Process Management and Business Intelligence Framework for Business Process Sustainability. In A. Paul, D. Bhattacharyya, & S. Anand (Eds.), *Green Initiatives for Business Sustainability and Value Creation* (pp. 228–238). Hershey, PA: IGI Global. doi:10.4018/978-1-5225-2662-9.ch010

Kaoud, M. (2017). Investigation of Customer Knowledge Management: A Case Study Research. *International Journal of Service Science, Management, Engineering, and Technology*, *8*(2), 12–22. doi:10.4018/IJSSMET.2017040102

Katuu, S. (2018). A Comparative Assessment of Enterprise Content Management Maturity Models. In N. Gwangwava & M. Mutingi (Eds.), *E-Manufacturing and E-Service Strategies in Contemporary Organizations* (pp. 93–118). Hershey, PA: IGI Global. doi:10.4018/978-1-5225-3628-4.ch005

Khan, M. Y., & Abir, T. (2022). The Role of Social Media Marketing in the Tourism and Hospitality Industry: A Conceptual Study on Bangladesh. In C. Ramos, S. Quinteiro, & A. Gonçalves (Eds.), *ICT as Innovator Between Tourism and Culture* (pp. 213–229). IGI Global. https://doi.org/10.4018/978-1-7998-8165-0.ch013

Kinnunen, S., Ylä-Kujala, A., Marttonen-Arola, S., Kärri, T., & Baglee, D. (2018). Internet of Things in Asset Management: Insights from Industrial Professionals and Academia. *International Journal of Service Science, Management, Engineering, and Technology*, *9*(2), 104–119. doi:10.4018/IJSSMET.2018040105

Klein, A. Z., Sabino de Freitas, A., Machado, L., Freitas, J. C. Jr, Graziola, P. G. Jr, & Schlemmer, E. (2017). Virtual Worlds Applications for Management Education. In L. Tomei (Ed.), *Exploring the New Era of Technology-Infused Education* (pp. 279–299). Hershey, PA: IGI Global. doi:10.4018/978-1-5225-1709-2.ch017

Kővári, E., Saleh, M., & Steinbachné Hajmásy, G. (2022). The Impact of Corporate Digital Responsibility (CDR) on Internal Stakeholders' Satisfaction in Hungarian Upscale Hotels. In M. Valeri (Ed.), *New Governance and Management in Touristic Destinations* (pp. 35–51). IGI Global. https://doi.org/10.4018/978-1-6684-3889-3.ch003

Kożuch, B., & Jabłoński, A. (2017). Adopting the Concept of Business Models in Public Management. In M. Lewandowski & B. Kożuch (Eds.), *Public Sector Entrepreneurship and the Integration of Innovative Business Models* (pp. 10–46). Hershey, PA: IGI Global. doi:10.4018/978-1-5225-2215-7.ch002

Kumar, J., Adhikary, A., & Jha, A. (2017). Small Active Investors' Perceptions and Preferences Towards Tax Saving Mutual Fund Schemes in Eastern India: An Empirical Note. *International Journal of Asian Business and Information Management, 8*(2), 35–45. doi:10.4018/IJABIM.2017040103

Latusi, S., & Fissore, M. (2021). Pilgrimage Routes to Happiness: Comparing the Camino de Santiago and Via Francigena. In A. Perinotto, V. Mayer, & J. Soares (Eds.), *Rebuilding and Restructuring the Tourism Industry: Infusion of Happiness and Quality of Life* (pp. 157–182). IGI Global. https://doi.org/10.4018/978-1-7998-7239-9.ch008

Lavassani, K. M., & Movahedi, B. (2017). Applications Driven Information Systems: Beyond Networks toward Business Ecosystems. *International Journal of Innovation in the Digital Economy, 8*(1), 61–75. doi:10.4018/IJIDE.2017010104

Lazzareschi, V. H., & Brito, M. S. (2017). Strategic Information Management: Proposal of Business Project Model. In G. Jamil, A. Soares, & C. Pessoa (Eds.), *Handbook of Research on Information Management for Effective Logistics and Supply Chains* (pp. 59–88). Hershey, PA: IGI Global. doi:10.4018/978-1-5225-0973-8.ch004

Lechuga Sancho, M. P., & Martín Navarro, A. (2022). Evolution of the Literature on Social Responsibility in the Tourism Sector: A Systematic Literature Review. In G. Fernandes (Ed.), *Challenges and New Opportunities for Tourism in Inland Territories: Ecocultural Resources and Sustainable Initiatives* (pp. 169–186). IGI Global. https://doi.org/10.4018/978-1-7998-7339-6.ch010

Lederer, M., Kurz, M., & Lazarov, P. (2017). Usage and Suitability of Methods for Strategic Business Process Initiatives: A Multi Case Study Research. *International Journal of Productivity Management and Assessment Technologies, 5*(1), 40–51. doi:10.4018/IJPMAT.2017010103

Lee, I. (2017). A Social Enterprise Business Model and a Case Study of Pacific Community Ventures (PCV). In V. Potocan, M. Ünğan, & Z. Nedelko (Eds.), *Handbook of Research on Managerial Solutions in Non-Profit Organizations* (pp. 182–204). Hershey, PA: IGI Global. doi:10.4018/978-1-5225-0731-4.ch009

Leon, L. A., Seal, K. C., Przasnyski, Z. H., & Wiedenman, I. (2017). Skills and Competencies Required for Jobs in Business Analytics: A Content Analysis of Job Advertisements Using Text Mining. *International Journal of Business Intelligence Research, 8*(1), 1–25. doi:10.4018/IJBIR.2017010101

Levy, C. L., & Elias, N. I. (2017). SOHO Users' Perceptions of Reliability and Continuity of Cloud-Based Services. In M. Moore (Ed.), *Cybersecurity Breaches and Issues Surrounding Online Threat Protection* (pp. 248–287). Hershey, PA: IGI Global. doi:10.4018/978-1-5225-1941-6.ch011

Levy, M. (2018). Change Management Serving Knowledge Management and Organizational Development: Reflections and Review. In N. Baporikar (Ed.), *Global Practices in Knowledge Management for Societal and Organizational Development* (pp. 256–270). Hershey, PA: IGI Global. doi:10.4018/978-1-5225-3009-1.ch012

Lewandowski, M. (2017). Public Organizations and Business Model Innovation: The Role of Public Service Design. In M. Lewandowski & B. Kożuch (Eds.), *Public Sector Entrepreneurship and the Integration of Innovative Business Models* (pp. 47–72). Hershey, PA: IGI Global. doi:10.4018/978-1-5225-2215-7.ch003

Lhannaoui, H., Kabbaj, M. I., & Bakkoury, Z. (2017). A Survey of Risk-Aware Business Process Modelling. *International Journal of Risk and Contingency Management, 6*(3), 14–26. doi:10.4018/IJRCM.2017070102

Li, J., Sun, W., Jiang, W., Yang, H., & Zhang, L. (2017). How the Nature of Exogenous Shocks and Crises Impact Company Performance?: The Effects of Industry Characteristics. *International Journal of Risk and Contingency Management, 6*(4), 40–55. doi:10.4018/IJRCM.2017100103

Lopez-Fernandez, M., Perez-Perez, M., Serrano-Bedia, A., & Cobo-Gonzalez, A. (2021). Small and Medium Tourism Enterprise Survival in Times of Crisis: "El Capricho de Gaudí. In D. Toubes & N. Araújo-Vila (Eds.), *Risk, Crisis, and Disaster Management in Small and Medium-Sized Tourism Enterprises* (pp. 103–129). IGI Global. doi:10.4018/978-1-7998-6996-2.ch005

Mahajan, A., Maidullah, S., & Hossain, M. R. (2022). Experience Toward Smart Tour Guide Apps in Travelling: An Analysis of Users' Reviews on Audio Odigos and Trip My Way. In R. Augusto Costa, F. Brandão, Z. Breda, & C. Costa (Eds.), *Planning and Managing the Experience Economy in Tourism* (pp. 255-273). IGI Global. https://doi.org/10.4018/978-1-7998-8775-1.ch014

Malega, P. (2017). Small and Medium Enterprises in the Slovak Republic: Status and Competitiveness of SMEs in the Global Markets and Possibilities of Optimization. In M. Vemić (Ed.), *Optimal Management Strategies in Small and Medium Enterprises* (pp. 102–124). Hershey, PA: IGI Global. doi:10.4018/978-1-5225-1949-2.ch006

Malewska, K. M. (2017). Intuition in Decision-Making on the Example of a Non-Profit Organization. In V. Potocan, M. Ünğan, & Z. Nedelko (Eds.), *Handbook of Research on Managerial Solutions in Non-Profit Organizations* (pp. 378–399). Hershey, PA: IGI Global. doi:10.4018/978-1-5225-0731-4.ch018

Maroofi, F. (2017). Entrepreneurial Orientation and Organizational Learning Ability Analysis for Innovation and Firm Performance. In N. Baporikar (Ed.), *Innovation and Shifting Perspectives in Management Education* (pp. 144–165). Hershey, PA: IGI Global. doi:10.4018/978-1-5225-1019-2.ch007

Marques, M., Moleiro, D., Brito, T. M., & Marques, T. (2021). Customer Relationship Management as an Important Relationship Marketing Tool: The Case of the Hospitality Industry in Estoril Coast. In M. Dinis, L. Bonixe, S. Lamy, & Z. Breda (Eds.), Impact of New Media in Tourism (pp. 39-56). IGI Global. https://doi.org/doi:10.4018/978-1-7998-7095-1.ch003

Martins, P. V., & Zacarias, M. (2017). A Web-based Tool for Business Process Improvement. *International Journal of Web Portals*, *9*(2), 68–84. doi:10.4018/IJWP.2017070104

Matthies, B., & Coners, A. (2017). Exploring the Conceptual Nature of e-Business Projects. *Journal of Electronic Commerce in Organizations*, *15*(3), 33–63. doi:10.4018/JECO.2017070103

Mayer, V. F., Fraga, C. C., & Silva, L. C. (2021). Contributions of Neurosciences to Studies of Well-Being in Tourism. In A. Perinotto, V. Mayer, & J. Soares (Eds.), *Rebuilding and Restructuring the Tourism Industry: Infusion of Happiness and Quality of Life* (pp. 108–128). IGI Global. https://doi.org/10.4018/978-1-7998-7239-9.ch006

McKee, J. (2018). Architecture as a Tool to Solve Business Planning Problems. In M. Khosrow-Pour, D.B.A. (Ed.), Encyclopedia of Information Science and Technology, Fourth Edition (pp. 573-586). Hershey, PA: IGI Global. doi:10.4018/978-1-5225-2255-3.ch050

McMurray, A. J., Cross, J., & Caponecchia, C. (2018). The Risk Management Profession in Australia: Business Continuity Plan Practices. In N. Bajgoric (Ed.), *Always-On Enterprise Information Systems for Modern Organizations* (pp. 112–129). Hershey, PA: IGI Global. doi:10.4018/978-1-5225-3704-5.ch006

Meddah, I. H., & Belkadi, K. (2018). Mining Patterns Using Business Process Management. In R. Hamou (Ed.), *Handbook of Research on Biomimicry in Information Retrieval and Knowledge Management* (pp. 78–89). Hershey, PA: IGI Global. doi:10.4018/978-1-5225-3004-6.ch005

Melian, A. G., & Camprubí, R. (2021). The Accessibility of Museum Websites: The Case of Barcelona. In C. Eusébio, L. Teixeira, & M. Carneiro (Eds.), *ICT Tools and Applications for Accessible Tourism* (pp. 234–255). IGI Global. https://doi.org/10.4018/978-1-7998-6428-8.ch011

Mendes, L. (2017). TQM and Knowledge Management: An Integrated Approach Towards Tacit Knowledge Management. In D. Jaziri-Bouagina & G. Jamil (Eds.), *Handbook of Research on Tacit Knowledge Management for Organizational Success* (pp. 236–263). Hershey, PA: IGI Global. doi:10.4018/978-1-5225-2394-9.ch009

Menezes, V. D., & Cavagnaro, E. (2021). Communicating Sustainable Initiatives in the Hotel Industry: The Case of the Hotel Jakarta Amsterdam. In F. Brandão, Z. Breda, R. Costa, & C. Costa (Eds.), *Handbook of Research on the Role of Tourism in Achieving Sustainable Development Goals* (pp. 224-234). IGI Global. https://doi.org/10.4018/978-1-7998-5691-7.ch013

Menezes, V. D., & Cavagnaro, E. (2021). Communicating Sustainable Initiatives in the Hotel Industry: The Case of the Hotel Jakarta Amsterdam. In F. Brandão, Z. Breda, R. Costa, & C. Costa (Eds.), *Handbook of Research on the Role of Tourism in Achieving Sustainable Development Goals* (pp. 224-234). IGI Global. https://doi.org/10.4018/978-1-7998-5691-7.ch013

Mitas, O., Bastiaansen, M., & Boode, W. (2022). If You're Happy, I'm Happy: Emotion Contagion at a Tourist Information Center. In R. Augusto Costa, F. Brandão, Z. Breda, & C. Costa (Eds.), *Planning and Managing the Experience Economy in Tourism* (pp. 122-140). IGI Global. https://doi.org/10.4018/978-1-7998-8775-1.ch007

Mnjama, N. M. (2017). Preservation of Recorded Information in Public and Private Sector Organizations. In P. Jain & N. Mnjama (Eds.), *Managing Knowledge Resources and Records in Modern Organizations* (pp. 149–167). Hershey, PA: IGI Global. doi:10.4018/978-1-5225-1965-2.ch009

Mokoqama, M., & Fields, Z. (2017). Principles of Responsible Management Education (PRME): Call for Responsible Management Education. In Z. Fields (Ed.), *Collective Creativity for Responsible and Sustainable Business Practice* (pp. 229–241). Hershey, PA: IGI Global. doi:10.4018/978-1-5225-1823-5.ch012

Monteiro, A., Lopes, S., & Carbone, F. (2021). Academic Mobility: Bridging Tourism and Peace Education. In J. da Silva, Z. Breda, & F. Carbone (Eds.), *Role and Impact of Tourism in Peacebuilding and Conflict Transformation* (pp. 275-301). IGI Global. https://doi.org/10.4018/978-1-7998-5053-3.ch016

Muniapan, B. (2017). Philosophy and Management: The Relevance of Vedanta in Management. In P. Ordóñez de Pablos (Ed.), *Managerial Strategies and Solutions for Business Success in Asia* (pp. 124–139). Hershey, PA: IGI Global. doi:10.4018/978-1-5225-1886-0.ch007

Murad, S. E., & Dowaji, S. (2017). Using Value-Based Approach for Managing Cloud-Based Services. In A. Turuk, B. Sahoo, & S. Addya (Eds.), *Resource Management and Efficiency in Cloud Computing Environments* (pp. 33–60). Hershey, PA: IGI Global. doi:10.4018/978-1-5225-1721-4.ch002

Mutahar, A. M., Daud, N. M., Thurasamy, R., Isaac, O., & Abdulsalam, R. (2018). The Mediating of Perceived Usefulness and Perceived Ease of Use: The Case of Mobile Banking in Yemen. *International Journal of Technology Diffusion*, *9*(2), 21–40. doi:10.4018/IJTD.2018040102

Naidoo, V. (2017). E-Learning and Management Education at African Universities. In N. Baporikar (Ed.), *Management Education for Global Leadership* (pp. 181–201). Hershey, PA: IGI Global. doi:10.4018/978-1-5225-1013-0.ch009

Naidoo, V., & Igbinakhase, I. (2018). Opportunities and Challenges of Knowledge Retention in SMEs. In N. Baporikar (Ed.), *Knowledge Integration Strategies for Entrepreneurship and Sustainability* (pp. 70–94). Hershey, PA: IGI Global. doi:10.4018/978-1-5225-5115-7.ch004

Naumov, N., & Costandachi, G. (2021). Creativity and Entrepreneurship: Gastronomic Tourism in Mexico. In J. Soares (Ed.), *Innovation and Entrepreneurial Opportunities in Community Tourism* (pp. 90–108). IGI Global. https://doi.org/10.4018/978-1-7998-4855-4.ch006

Nayak, S., & Prabhu, N. (2017). Paradigm Shift in Management Education: Need for a Cross Functional Perspective. In N. Baporikar (Ed.), *Management Education for Global Leadership* (pp. 241–255). Hershey, PA: IGI Global. doi:10.4018/978-1-5225-1013-0.ch012

Nedelko, Z., & Potocan, V. (2017). Management Solutions in Non-Profit Organizations: Case of Slovenia. In V. Potocan, M. Ünğan, & Z. Nedelko (Eds.), *Handbook of Research on Managerial Solutions in Non-Profit Organizations* (pp. 1–22). Hershey, PA: IGI Global. doi:10.4018/978-1-5225-0731-4.ch001

Nedelko, Z., & Potocan, V. (2017). Priority of Management Tools Utilization among Managers: International Comparison. In V. Wang (Ed.), *Encyclopedia of Strategic Leadership and Management* (pp. 1083–1094). Hershey, PA: IGI Global. doi:10.4018/978-1-5225-1049-9.ch075

Nedelko, Z., Raudeliūnienė, J., & Črešnar, R. (2018). Knowledge Dynamics in Supply Chain Management. In N. Baporikar (Ed.), *Knowledge Integration Strategies for Entrepreneurship and Sustainability* (pp. 150–166). Hershey, PA: IGI Global. doi:10.4018/978-1-5225-5115-7.ch008

Nguyen, H. T., & Hipsher, S. A. (2018). Innovation and Creativity Used by Private Sector Firms in a Resources-Constrained Environment. In S. Hipsher (Ed.), *Examining the Private Sector's Role in Wealth Creation and Poverty Reduction* (pp. 219–238). Hershey, PA: IGI Global. doi:10.4018/978-1-5225-3117-3.ch010

Obicci, P. A. (2017). Risk Sharing in a Partnership. In *Risk Management Strategies in Public-Private Partnerships* (pp. 115–152). Hershey, PA: IGI Global. doi:10.4018/978-1-5225-2503-5.ch004

Obidallah, W. J., & Raahemi, B. (2017). Managing Changes in Service Oriented Virtual Organizations: A Structural and Procedural Framework to Facilitate the Process of Change. *Journal of Electronic Commerce in Organizations*, *15*(1), 59–83. doi:10.4018/JECO.2017010104

Ojo, O. (2017). Impact of Innovation on the Entrepreneurial Success in Selected Business Enterprises in South-West Nigeria. *International Journal of Innovation in the Digital Economy*, *8*(2), 29–38. doi:10.4018/IJIDE.2017040103

Okdinawati, L., Simatupang, T. M., & Sunitiyoso, Y. (2017). Multi-Agent Reinforcement Learning for Value Co-Creation of Collaborative Transportation Management (CTM). *International Journal of Information Systems and Supply Chain Management*, *10*(3), 84–95. doi:10.4018/IJISSCM.2017070105

Olivera, V. A., & Carrillo, I. M. (2021). Organizational Culture: A Key Element for the Development of Mexican Micro and Small Tourist Companies. In J. Soares (Ed.), *Innovation and Entrepreneurial Opportunities in Community Tourism* (pp. 227–242). IGI Global. doi:10.4018/978-1-7998-4855-4.ch013

Ossorio, M. (2022). Corporate Museum Experiences in Enogastronomic Tourism. In R. Augusto Costa, F. Brandão, Z. Breda, & C. Costa (Eds.), Planning and Managing the Experience Economy in Tourism (pp. 107-121). IGI Global. https://doi.org/doi:10.4018/978-1-7998-8775-1.ch006

Ossorio, M. (2022). Enogastronomic Tourism in Times of Pandemic. In G. Fernandes (Ed.), *Challenges and New Opportunities for Tourism in Inland Territories: Ecocultural Resources and Sustainable Initiatives* (pp. 241–255). IGI Global. https://doi.org/10.4018/978-1-7998-7339-6.ch014

Özekici, Y. K. (2022). ICT as an Acculturative Agent and Its Role in the Tourism Context: Introduction, Acculturation Theory, Progress of the Acculturation Theory in Extant Literature. In C. Ramos, S. Quinteiro, & A. Gonçalves (Eds.), *ICT as Innovator Between Tourism and Culture* (pp. 42–66). IGI Global. https://doi.org/10.4018/978-1-7998-8165-0.ch004

Pal, K. (2018). Building High Quality Big Data-Based Applications in Supply Chains. In A. Kumar & S. Saurav (Eds.), *Supply Chain Management Strategies and Risk Assessment in Retail Environments* (pp. 1–24). Hershey, PA: IGI Global. doi:10.4018/978-1-5225-3056-5.ch001

Palos-Sanchez, P. R., & Correia, M. B. (2018). Perspectives of the Adoption of Cloud Computing in the Tourism Sector. In J. Rodrigues, C. Ramos, P. Cardoso, & C. Henriques (Eds.), *Handbook of Research on Technological Developments for Cultural Heritage and eTourism Applications* (pp. 377–400). Hershey, PA: IGI Global. doi:10.4018/978-1-5225-2927-9.ch018

Papadopoulou, G. (2021). Promoting Gender Equality and Women Empowerment in the Tourism Sector. In F. Brandão, Z. Breda, R. Costa, & C. Costa (Eds.), Handbook of Research on the Role of Tourism in Achieving Sustainable Development Goals (pp. 152-174). IGI Global. https://doi.org/ doi:10.4018/978-1-7998-5691-7.ch009

Papp-Váry, Á. F., & Tóth, T. Z. (2022). Analysis of Budapest as a Film Tourism Destination. In R. Baleiro & R. Pereira (Eds.), *Global Perspectives on Literary Tourism and Film-Induced Tourism* (pp. 257-279). IGI Global. https://doi.org/10.4018/978-1-7998-8262-6.ch014

Patiño, B. E. (2017). New Generation Management by Convergence and Individual Identity: A Systemic and Human-Oriented Approach. In N. Baporikar (Ed.), *Innovation and Shifting Perspectives in Management Education* (pp. 119–143). Hershey, PA: IGI Global. doi:10.4018/978-1-5225-1019-2.ch006

Patro, C. S. (2021). Digital Tourism: Influence of E-Marketing Technology. In M. Dinis, L. Bonixe, S. Lamy, & Z. Breda (Eds.), *Impact of New Media in Tourism* (pp. 234-254). IGI Global. https://doi.org/10.4018/978-1-7998-7095-1.ch014

Pawliczek, A., & Rössler, M. (2017). Knowledge of Management Tools and Systems in SMEs: Knowledge Transfer in Management. In A. Bencsik (Ed.), *Knowledge Management Initiatives and Strategies in Small and Medium Enterprises* (pp. 180–203). Hershey, PA: IGI Global. doi:10.4018/978-1-5225-1642-2.ch009

Pejic-Bach, M., Omazic, M. A., Aleksic, A., & Zoroja, J. (2018). Knowledge-Based Decision Making: A Multi-Case Analysis. In R. Leon (Ed.), *Managerial Strategies for Business Sustainability During Turbulent Times* (pp. 160–184). Hershey, PA: IGI Global. doi:10.4018/978-1-5225-2716-9.ch009

Perano, M., Hysa, X., & Calabrese, M. (2018). Strategic Planning, Cultural Context, and Business Continuity Management: Business Cases in the City of Shkoder. In A. Presenza & L. Sheehan (Eds.), *Geopolitics and Strategic Management in the Global Economy* (pp. 57–77). Hershey, PA: IGI Global. doi:10.4018/978-1-5225-2673-5.ch004

Pereira, R., Mira da Silva, M., & Lapão, L. V. (2017). IT Governance Maturity Patterns in Portuguese Healthcare. In S. De Haes & W. Van Grembergen (Eds.), *Strategic IT Governance and Alignment in Business Settings* (pp. 24–52). Hershey, PA: IGI Global. doi:10.4018/978-1-5225-0861-8.ch002

Pérez-Uribe, R. I., Torres, D. A., Jurado, S. P., & Prada, D. M. (2018). Cloud Tools for the Development of Project Management in SMEs. In R. Perez-Uribe, C. Salcedo-Perez, & D. Ocampo-Guzman (Eds.), *Handbook of Research on Intrapreneurship and Organizational Sustainability in SMEs* (pp. 95–120). Hershey, PA: IGI Global. doi:10.4018/978-1-5225-3543-0.ch005

Petrisor, I., & Cozmiuc, D. (2017). Global Supply Chain Management Organization at Siemens in the Advent of Industry 4.0. In L. Saglietto & C. Cezanne (Eds.), *Global Intermediation and Logistics Service Providers* (pp. 123–142). Hershey, PA: IGI Global. doi:10.4018/978-1-5225-2133-4.ch007

Pierce, J. M., Velliaris, D. M., & Edwards, J. (2017). A Living Case Study: A Journey Not a Destination. In N. Silton (Ed.), *Exploring the Benefits of Creativity in Education, Media, and the Arts* (pp. 158–178). Hershey, PA: IGI Global. doi:10.4018/978-1-5225-0504-4.ch008

Pipia, S., & Pipia, S. (2021). Challenges of Religious Tourism in the Conflict Region: An Example of Jerusalem. In E. Alaverdov & M. Bari (Eds.), *Global Development of Religious Tourism* (pp. 135-148). IGI Global. https://doi.org/10.4018/978-1-7998-5792-1.ch009

Poulaki, P., Kritikos, A., Vasilakis, N., & Valeri, M. (2022). The Contribution of Female Creativity to the Development of Gastronomic Tourism in Greece: The Case of the Island of Naxos in the South Aegean Region. In M. Valeri (Ed.), *New Governance and Management in Touristic Destinations* (pp. 246–258). IGI Global. https://doi.org/10.4018/978-1-6684-3889-3.ch015

Radosavljevic, M., & Andjelkovic, A. (2017). Multi-Criteria Decision Making Approach for Choosing Business Process for the Improvement: Upgrading of the Six Sigma Methodology. In J. Stanković, P. Delias, S. Marinković, & S. Rochhia (Eds.), *Tools and Techniques for Economic Decision Analysis* (pp. 225–247). Hershey, PA: IGI Global. doi:10.4018/978-1-5225-0959-2.ch011

Radovic, V. M. (2017). Corporate Sustainability and Responsibility and Disaster Risk Reduction: A Serbian Overview. In M. Camilleri (Ed.), *CSR 2.0 and the New Era of Corporate Citizenship* (pp. 147–164). Hershey, PA: IGI Global. doi:10.4018/978-1-5225-1842-6.ch008

Raghunath, K. M., Devi, S. L., & Patro, C. S. (2018). Impact of Risk Assessment Models on Risk Factors: A Holistic Outlook. In K. Strang, M. Korstanje, & N. Vajjhala (Eds.), *Research, Practices, and Innovations in Global Risk and Contingency Management* (pp. 134–153). Hershey, PA: IGI Global. doi:10.4018/978-1-5225-4754-9.ch008

Raman, A., & Goyal, D. P. (2017). Extending IMPLEMENT Framework for Enterprise Information Systems Implementation to Information System Innovation. In M. Tavana (Ed.), *Enterprise Information Systems and the Digitalization of Business Functions* (pp. 137–177). Hershey, PA: IGI Global. doi:10.4018/978-1-5225-2382-6.ch007

Rao, Y., & Zhang, Y. (2017). The Construction and Development of Academic Library Digital Special Subject Databases. In L. Ruan, Q. Zhu, & Y. Ye (Eds.), *Academic Library Development and Administration in China* (pp. 163–183). Hershey, PA: IGI Global. doi:10.4018/978-1-5225-0550-1.ch010

Ravasan, A. Z., Mohammadi, M. M., & Hamidi, H. (2018). An Investigation Into the Critical Success Factors of Implementing Information Technology Service Management Frameworks. In K. Jakobs (Ed.), *Corporate and Global Standardization Initiatives in Contemporary Society* (pp. 200–218). Hershey, PA: IGI Global. doi:10.4018/978-1-5225-5320-5.ch009

Rezaie, S., Mirabedini, S. J., & Abtahi, A. (2018). Designing a Model for Implementation of Business Intelligence in the Banking Industry. *International Journal of Enterprise Information Systems, 14*(1), 77–103. doi:10.4018/IJEIS.2018010105

Richards, V., Matthews, N., Williams, O. J., & Khan, Z. (2021). The Challenges of Accessible Tourism Information Systems for Tourists With Vision Impairment: Sensory Communications Beyond the Screen. In C. Eusébio, L. Teixeira, & M. Carneiro (Eds.), *ICT Tools and Applications for Accessible Tourism* (pp. 26–54). IGI Global. https://doi.org/10.4018/978-1-7998-6428-8.ch002

Rodrigues de Souza Neto, V., & Marques, O. (2021). Rural Tourism Fostering Welfare Through Sustainable Development: A Conceptual Approach. In A. Perinotto, V. Mayer, & J. Soares (Eds.), *Rebuilding and Restructuring the Tourism Industry: Infusion of Happiness and Quality of Life* (pp. 38–57). IGI Global. https://doi.org/10.4018/978-1-7998-7239-9.ch003

Romano, L., Grimaldi, R., & Colasuonno, F. S. (2017). Demand Management as a Success Factor in Project Portfolio Management. In L. Romano (Ed.), *Project Portfolio Management Strategies for Effective Organizational Operations* (pp. 202–219). Hershey, PA: IGI Global. doi:10.4018/978-1-5225-2151-8.ch008

Rubio-Escuderos, L., & García-Andreu, H. (2021). Competitiveness Factors of Accessible Tourism E-Travel Agencies. In C. Eusébio, L. Teixeira, & M. Carneiro (Eds.), *ICT Tools and Applications for Accessible Tourism* (pp. 196–217). IGI Global. https://doi.org/10.4018/978-1-7998-6428-8.ch009

Rucci, A. C., Porto, N., Darcy, S., & Becka, L. (2021). Smart and Accessible Cities?: Not Always – The Case for Accessible Tourism Initiatives in Buenos Aries and Sydney. In C. Eusébio, L. Teixeira, & M. Carneiro (Eds.), *ICT Tools and Applications for Accessible Tourism* (pp. 115–145). IGI Global. https://doi.org/10.4018/978-1-7998-6428-8.ch006

Ruhi, U. (2018). Towards an Interdisciplinary Socio-Technical Definition of Virtual Communities. In M. Khosrow-Pour, D.B.A. (Ed.), Encyclopedia of Information Science and Technology, Fourth Edition (pp. 4278-4295). Hershey, PA: IGI Global. doi:10.4018/978-1-5225-2255-3.ch371

Ryan, L., Catena, M., Ros, P., & Stephens, S. (2021). Designing Entrepreneurial Ecosystems to Support Resource Management in the Tourism Industry. In V. Costa, A. Moura, & M. Mira (Eds.), *Handbook of Research on Human Capital and People Management in the Tourism Industry* (pp. 265–281). IGI Global. https://doi.org/10.4018/978-1-7998-4318-4.ch013

Sabuncu, I. (2021). Understanding Tourist Perceptions and Expectations During Pandemic Through Social Media Big Data. In M. Demir, A. Dalgıç, & F. Ergen (Eds.), *Handbook of Research on the Impacts and Implications of COVID-19 on the Tourism Industry* (pp. 330–350). IGI Global. https://doi.org/10.4018/978-1-7998-8231-2.ch016

Safari, M. R., & Jiang, Q. (2018). The Theory and Practice of IT Governance Maturity and Strategies Alignment: Evidence From Banking Industry. *Journal of Global Information Management*, *26*(2), 127–146. doi:10.4018/JGIM.2018040106

Sahoo, J., Pati, B., & Mohanty, B. (2017). Knowledge Management as an Academic Discipline: An Assessment. In B. Gunjal (Ed.), *Managing Knowledge and Scholarly Assets in Academic Libraries* (pp. 99–126). Hershey, PA: IGI Global. doi:10.4018/978-1-5225-1741-2.ch005

Saini, D. (2017). Relevance of Teaching Values and Ethics in Management Education. In N. Baporikar (Ed.), *Management Education for Global Leadership* (pp. 90–111). Hershey, PA: IGI Global. doi:10.4018/978-1-5225-1013-0.ch005

Sambhanthan, A. (2017). Assessing and Benchmarking Sustainability in Organisations: An Integrated Conceptual Model. *International Journal of Systems and Service-Oriented Engineering*, *7*(4), 22–43. doi:10.4018/IJSSOE.2017100102

Sambhanthan, A., & Potdar, V. (2017). A Study of the Parameters Impacting Sustainability in Information Technology Organizations. *International Journal of Knowledge-Based Organizations*, *7*(3), 27–39. doi:10.4018/IJKBO.2017070103

Sánchez-Fernández, M. D., & Manríquez, M. R. (2018). The Entrepreneurial Spirit Based on Social Values: The Digital Generation. In P. Isaias & L. Carvalho (Eds.), *User Innovation and the Entrepreneurship Phenomenon in the Digital Economy* (pp. 173–193). Hershey, PA: IGI Global. doi:10.4018/978-1-5225-2826-5.ch009

Sanchez-Ruiz, L., & Blanco, B. (2017). Process Management for SMEs: Barriers, Enablers, and Benefits. In M. Vemić (Ed.), *Optimal Management Strategies in Small and Medium Enterprises* (pp. 293–319). Hershey, PA: IGI Global. doi:10.4018/978-1-5225-1949-2.ch014

Sanz, L. F., Gómez-Pérez, J., & Castillo-Martinez, A. (2018). Analysis of the European ICT Competence Frameworks. In V. Ahuja & S. Rathore (Eds.), *Multidisciplinary Perspectives on Human Capital and Information Technology Professionals* (pp. 225–245). Hershey, PA: IGI Global. doi:10.4018/978-1-5225-5297-0.ch012

Sarvepalli, A., & Godin, J. (2017). Business Process Management in the Classroom. *Journal of Cases on Information Technology, 19*(2), 17–28. doi:10.4018/JCIT.2017040102

Saxena, G. G., & Saxena, A. (2021). Host Community Role in Medical Tourism Development. In M. Singh & S. Kumaran (Eds.), *Growth of the Medical Tourism Industry and Its Impact on Society: Emerging Research and Opportunities* (pp. 105–127). IGI Global. https://doi.org/10.4018/978-1-7998-3427-4.ch006

Saygili, E. E., Ozturkoglu, Y., & Kocakulah, M. C. (2017). End Users' Perceptions of Critical Success Factors in ERP Applications. *International Journal of Enterprise Information Systems, 13*(4), 58–75. doi:10.4018/IJEIS.2017100104

Saygili, E. E., & Saygili, A. T. (2017). Contemporary Issues in Enterprise Information Systems: A Critical Review of CSFs in ERP Implementations. In M. Tavana (Ed.), *Enterprise Information Systems and the Digitalization of Business Functions* (pp. 120–136). Hershey, PA: IGI Global. doi:10.4018/978-1-5225-2382-6.ch006

Schwaiger, K. M., & Zehrer, A. (2021). The COVID-19 Pandemic and Organizational Resilience in Hospitality Family Firms: A Qualitative Approach. In A. Zehrer, G. Glowka, K. Schwaiger, & V. Ranacher-Lackner (Eds.), *Resiliency Models and Addressing Future Risks for Family Firms in the Tourism Industry* (pp. 32–49). IGI Global. https://doi.org/10.4018/978-1-7998-7352-5.ch002

Scott, N., & Campos, A. C. (2022). Cognitive Science of Tourism Experiences. In R. Augusto Costa, F. Brandão, Z. Breda, & C. Costa (Eds.), Planning and Managing the Experience Economy in Tourism (pp. 1-21). IGI Global. https://doi.org/ doi:10.4018/978-1-7998-8775-1.ch001

Seidenstricker, S., & Antonino, A. (2018). Business Model Innovation-Oriented Technology Management for Emergent Technologies. In M. Khosrow-Pour, D.B.A. (Ed.), Encyclopedia of Information Science and Technology, Fourth Edition (pp. 4560-4569). Hershey, PA: IGI Global. doi:10.4018/978-1-5225-2255-3.ch396

Selvi, M. S. (2021). Changes in Tourism Sales and Marketing Post COVID-19. In M. Demir, A. Dalgıç, & F. Ergen (Eds.), *Handbook of Research on the Impacts and Implications of COVID-19 on the Tourism Industry* (pp. 437–460). IGI Global. doi:10.4018/978-1-7998-8231-2.ch021

Senaratne, S., & Gunarathne, A. D. (2017). Excellence Perspective for Management Education from a Global Accountants' Hub in Asia. In N. Baporikar (Ed.), *Management Education for Global Leadership* (pp. 158–180). Hershey, PA: IGI Global. doi:10.4018/978-1-5225-1013-0.ch008

Sensuse, D. I., & Cahyaningsih, E. (2018). Knowledge Management Models: A Summative Review. *International Journal of Information Systems in the Service Sector, 10*(1), 71–100. doi:10.4018/IJISSS.2018010105

Seth, M., Goyal, D., & Kiran, R. (2017). Diminution of Impediments in Implementation of Supply Chain Management Information System for Enhancing its Effectiveness in Indian Automobile Industry. *Journal of Global Information Management, 25*(3), 1–20. doi:10.4018/JGIM.2017070101

Seyal, A. H., & Rahman, M. N. (2017). Investigating Impact of Inter-Organizational Factors in Measuring ERP Systems Success: Bruneian Perspectives. In M. Tavana (Ed.), *Enterprise Information Systems and the Digitalization of Business Functions* (pp. 178–204). Hershey, PA: IGI Global. doi:10.4018/978-1-5225-2382-6.ch008

Shaqrah, A. A. (2018). Analyzing Business Intelligence Systems Based on 7s Model of McKinsey. *International Journal of Business Intelligence Research, 9*(1), 53–63. doi:10.4018/IJBIR.2018010104

Sharma, A. J. (2017). Enhancing Sustainability through Experiential Learning in Management Education. In N. Baporikar (Ed.), *Management Education for Global Leadership* (pp. 256–274). Hershey, PA: IGI Global. doi:10.4018/978-1-5225-1013-0.ch013

Shetty, K. P. (2017). Responsible Global Leadership: Ethical Challenges in Management Education. In N. Baporikar (Ed.), *Innovation and Shifting Perspectives in Management Education* (pp. 194–223). Hershey, PA: IGI Global. doi:10.4018/978-1-5225-1019-2.ch009

Sinthupundaja, J., & Kohda, Y. (2017). Effects of Corporate Social Responsibility and Creating Shared Value on Sustainability. *International Journal of Sustainable Entrepreneurship and Corporate Social Responsibility, 2*(1), 27–38. doi:10.4018/IJSECSR.2017010103

Škarica, I., & Hrgović, A. V. (2018). Implementation of Total Quality Management Principles in Public Health Institutes in the Republic of Croatia. *International Journal of Productivity Management and Assessment Technologies, 6*(1), 1–16. doi:10.4018/IJPMAT.2018010101

Skokic, V. (2021). How Small Hotel Owners Practice Resilience: Longitudinal Study Among Small Family Hotels in Croatia. In A. Zehrer, G. Glowka, K. Schwaiger, & V. Ranacher-Lackner (Eds.), *Resiliency Models and Addressing Future Risks for Family Firms in the Tourism Industry* (pp. 50–73). IGI Global. doi:10.4018/978-1-7998-7352-5.ch003

Smuts, H., Kotzé, P., Van der Merwe, A., & Loock, M. (2017). Framework for Managing Shared Knowledge in an Information Systems Outsourcing Context. *International Journal of Knowledge Management, 13*(4), 1–30. doi:10.4018/IJKM.2017100101

Sousa, M. J., Cruz, R., Dias, I., & Caracol, C. (2017). Information Management Systems in the Supply Chain. In G. Jamil, A. Soares, & C. Pessoa (Eds.), *Handbook of Research on Information Management for Effective Logistics and Supply Chains* (pp. 469–485). Hershey, PA: IGI Global. doi:10.4018/978-1-5225-0973-8.ch025

Spremic, M., Turulja, L., & Bajgoric, N. (2018). Two Approaches in Assessing Business Continuity Management Attitudes in the Organizational Context. In N. Bajgoric (Ed.), *Always-On Enterprise Information Systems for Modern Organizations* (pp. 159–183). Hershey, PA: IGI Global. doi:10.4018/978-1-5225-3704-5.ch008

Steenkamp, A. L. (2018). Some Insights in Computer Science and Information Technology. In *Examining the Changing Role of Supervision in Doctoral Research Projects: Emerging Research and Opportunities* (pp. 113–133). Hershey, PA: IGI Global. doi:10.4018/978-1-5225-2610-0.ch005

Stipanović, C., Rudan, E., & Zubović, V. (2022). Reaching the New Tourist Through Creativity: Sustainable Development Challenges in Croatian Coastal Towns. In M. Valeri (Ed.), *New Governance and Management in Touristic Destinations* (pp. 231–245). IGI Global. https://doi.org/10.4018/978-1-6684-3889-3.ch014

Tabach, A., & Croteau, A. (2017). Configurations of Information Technology Governance Practices and Business Unit Performance. *International Journal of IT/Business Alignment and Governance, 8*(2), 1–27. doi:10.4018/IJITBAG.2017070101

Talaue, G. M., & Iqbal, T. (2017). Assessment of e-Business Mode of Selected Private Universities in the Philippines and Pakistan. *International Journal of Online Marketing, 7*(4), 63–77. doi:10.4018/IJOM.2017100105

Tam, G. C. (2017). Project Manager Sustainability Competence. In *Managerial Strategies and Green Solutions for Project Sustainability* (pp. 178–207). Hershey, PA: IGI Global. doi:10.4018/978-1-5225-2371-0.ch008

Tambo, T. (2018). Fashion Retail Innovation: About Context, Antecedents, and Outcome in Technological Change Projects. In I. Management Association (Ed.), Fashion and Textiles: Breakthroughs in Research and Practice (pp. 233-260). Hershey, PA: IGI Global. https://doi.org/ doi:10.4018/978-1-5225-3432-7.ch010

Tantau, A. D., & Frăţilă, L. C. (2018). Information and Management System for Renewable Energy Business. In *Entrepreneurship and Business Development in the Renewable Energy Sector* (pp. 200–244). Hershey, PA: IGI Global. doi:10.4018/978-1-5225-3625-3.ch006

Teixeira, N., Pardal, P. N., & Rafael, B. G. (2018). Internationalization, Financial Performance, and Organizational Challenges: A Success Case in Portugal. In L. Carvalho (Ed.), *Handbook of Research on Entrepreneurial Ecosystems and Social Dynamics in a Globalized World* (pp. 379–423). Hershey, PA: IGI Global. doi:10.4018/978-1-5225-3525-6.ch017

Teixeira, P., Teixeira, L., Eusébio, C., Silva, S., & Teixeira, A. (2021). The Impact of ICTs on Accessible Tourism: Evidence Based on a Systematic Literature Review. In C. Eusébio, L. Teixeira, & M. Carneiro (Eds.), *ICT Tools and Applications for Accessible Tourism* (pp. 1–25). IGI Global. doi:10.4018/978-1-7998-6428-8.ch001

Trad, A., & Kalpić, D. (2018). The Business Transformation Framework, Agile Project and Change Management. In M. Khosrow-Pour, D.B.A. (Ed.), Encyclopedia of Information Science and Technology, Fourth Edition (pp. 620-635). Hershey, PA: IGI Global. https://doi.org/ doi:10.4018/978-1-5225-2255-3.ch054

Trad, A., & Kalpić, D. (2018). The Business Transformation and Enterprise Architecture Framework: The Financial Engineering E-Risk Management and E-Law Integration. In B. Sergi, F. Fidanoski, M. Ziolo, & V. Naumovski (Eds.), *Regaining Global Stability After the Financial Crisis* (pp. 46–65). Hershey, PA: IGI Global. doi:10.4018/978-1-5225-4026-7.ch003

Trengereid, V. (2022). Conditions of Network Engagement: The Quest for a Common Good. In R. Augusto Costa, F. Brandão, Z. Breda, & C. Costa (Eds.), *Planning and Managing the Experience Economy in Tourism* (pp. 69-84). IGI Global. https://doi.org/10.4018/978-1-7998-8775-1.ch004

Turulja, L., & Bajgoric, N. (2018). Business Continuity and Information Systems: A Systematic Literature Review. In N. Bajgoric (Ed.), *Always-On Enterprise Information Systems for Modern Organizations* (pp. 60–87). Hershey, PA: IGI Global. doi:10.4018/978-1-5225-3704-5.ch004

Vargas-Hernández, J. G. (2017). Professional Integrity in Business Management Education. In N. Baporikar (Ed.), *Management Education for Global Leadership* (pp. 70–89). Hershey, PA: IGI Global. doi:10.4018/978-1-5225-1013-0.ch004

Varnacı Uzun, F. (2021). The Destination Preferences of Foreign Tourists During the COVID-19 Pandemic and Attitudes Towards: Marmaris, Turkey. In M. Demir, A. Dalgıç, & F. Ergen (Eds.), *Handbook of Research on the Impacts and Implications of COVID-19 on the Tourism Industry* (pp. 285–306). IGI Global. https://doi.org/10.4018/978-1-7998-8231-2.ch014

Vasista, T. G., & AlAbdullatif, A. M. (2017). Role of Electronic Customer Relationship Management in Demand Chain Management: A Predictive Analytic Approach. *International Journal of Information Systems and Supply Chain Management, 10*(1), 53–67. doi:10.4018/IJISSCM.2017010104

Vieru, D., & Bourdeau, S. (2017). Survival in the Digital Era: A Digital Competence-Based Multi-Case Study in the Canadian SME Clothing Industry. *International Journal of Social and Organizational Dynamics in IT, 6*(1), 17–34. doi:10.4018/IJSODIT.2017010102

Vijayan, G., & Kamarulzaman, N. H. (2017). An Introduction to Sustainable Supply Chain Management and Business Implications. In M. Khan, M. Hussain, & M. Ajmal (Eds.), *Green Supply Chain Management for Sustainable Business Practice* (pp. 27–50). Hershey, PA: IGI Global. doi:10.4018/978-1-5225-0635-5.ch002

Vlachvei, A., & Notta, O. (2017). Firm Competitiveness: Theories, Evidence, and Measurement. In A. Vlachvei, O. Notta, K. Karantininis, & N. Tsounis (Eds.), *Factors Affecting Firm Competitiveness and Performance in the Modern Business World* (pp. 1–42). Hershey, PA: IGI Global. doi:10.4018/978-1-5225-0843-4.ch001

Wang, C., Schofield, M., Li, X., & Ou, X. (2017). Do Chinese Students in Public and Private Higher Education Institutes Perform at Different Level in One of the Leadership Skills: Critical Thinking?: An Exploratory Comparison. In V. Wang (Ed.), *Encyclopedia of Strategic Leadership and Management* (pp. 160–181). Hershey, PA: IGI Global. doi:10.4018/978-1-5225-1049-9.ch013

Wang, J. (2017). Multi-Agent based Production Management Decision System Modelling for the Textile Enterprise. *Journal of Global Information Management, 25*(4), 1–15. doi:10.4018/JGIM.2017100101

Wiedemann, A., & Gewald, H. (2017). Examining Cross-Domain Alignment: The Correlation of Business Strategy, IT Management, and IT Business Value. *International Journal of IT/Business Alignment and Governance, 8*(1), 17–31. doi:10.4018/IJITBAG.2017010102

Wolf, R., & Thiel, M. (2018). Advancing Global Business Ethics in China: Reducing Poverty Through Human and Social Welfare. In S. Hipsher (Ed.), *Examining the Private Sector's Role in Wealth Creation and Poverty Reduction* (pp. 67–84). Hershey, PA: IGI Global. doi:10.4018/978-1-5225-3117-3.ch004

Yablonsky, S. (2018). Innovation Platforms: Data and Analytics Platforms. In *Multi-Sided Platforms (MSPs) and Sharing Strategies in the Digital Economy: Emerging Research and Opportunities* (pp. 72–95). Hershey, PA: IGI Global. doi:10.4018/978-1-5225-5457-8.ch003

Yaşar, B. (2021). The Impact of COVID-19 on Volatility of Tourism Stocks: Evidence From BIST Tourism Index. In M. Demir, A. Dalgıç, & F. Ergen (Eds.), *Handbook of Research on the Impacts and Implications of COVID-19 on the Tourism Industry* (pp. 23–44). IGI Global. https://doi.org/10.4018/978-1-7998-8231-2.ch002

Yusoff, A., Ahmad, N. H., & Halim, H. A. (2017). Agropreneurship among Gen Y in Malaysia: The Role of Academic Institutions. In N. Ahmad, T. Ramayah, H. Halim, & S. Rahman (Eds.), *Handbook of Research on Small and Medium Enterprises in Developing Countries* (pp. 23–47). Hershey, PA: IGI Global. doi:10.4018/978-1-5225-2165-5.ch002

Zacher, D., & Pechlaner, H. (2021). Resilience as an Opportunity Approach: Challenges and Perspectives for Private Sector Participation on a Community Level. In A. Zehrer, G. Glowka, K. Schwaiger, & V. Ranacher-Lackner (Eds.), *Resiliency Models and Addressing Future Risks for Family Firms in the Tourism Industry* (pp. 75–102). IGI Global. https://doi.org/10.4018/978-1-7998-7352-5.ch004

Zanin, F., Comuzzi, E., & Costantini, A. (2018). The Effect of Business Strategy and Stock Market Listing on the Use of Risk Assessment Tools. In *Management Control Systems in Complex Settings: Emerging Research and Opportunities* (pp. 145–168). Hershey, PA: IGI Global. doi:10.4018/978-1-5225-3987-2.ch007

Zgheib, P. W. (2017). Corporate Innovation and Intrapreneurship in the Middle East. In P. Zgheib (Ed.), *Entrepreneurship and Business Innovation in the Middle East* (pp. 37–56). Hershey, PA: IGI Global. doi:10.4018/978-1-5225-2066-5.ch003

About the Contributors

Sumesh Dadwal has 22 years of experience in research, teaching, e-Learning, quality management, and examination assessment in a wide range of business subjects. Currently, Sumesh is working as a Sr. Lecturer of Strategy and Course Director at LSBU Business School. Before joining LSBU, he worked as Sr. Lecturer, Dissertation Lead, and Programme Leader with Northumbria Universities London campus and also as an associate with London Graduate School and Regent College London (Bucks New University and the University of Bolton, UK). Dr Dawdal has also worked as an associate lecturer with Birkbeck College (UoL), University of West London, Plymouth University (GSM, London), Uni of Roehampton UK, and also worked as a Sr. lecturer and Programme Leader (MBA) at Glyndwr University London. Sumesh has hands-on experience in managing departments and in supporting the implementation of effective quality management systems. Previously, Dr Dawdal has also worked with QAA, UK, He has designed, developed, and supported for validation and review of the various programme. He has published in journals and books.

Shikha Goyal has extensive experience in teaching and her research interest includes Performance management, Emotional Intelligence, Workplace Diversity and Organisational Culture.

Pawan Kumar is working as a Professor in the Department of Marketing at Mittal School of Business, Lovely Professional University, Punjab, India. He has 17 years of experience in business academic research .His areas of interest in research include entrepreneurship, marketing, e-commerce, consumer behaviour, marketing research, etc. He is an avid researcher. He is active in Ph.D research supervision and has good number of publications in Q1 and Q2 Journals to his credit in various research papers published Scopus indexed journals namely: The TQM Journal from Emerald, Visions: Journal of Business Perspectives from Sage, International Journal of Business and Globalization, International Journal of Business Information Systems from Inderscience and other national/international journals of repute.

He has edited book on Opportunities and challenges in Business5.0 and drivers of SME Growth and Sustainability in Emerging Markets from IGI global.

Rajesh Verma is Sr. Dean and Professor of Strategy & Marketing at Mittal School of Business (NIRF Rank #34), Lovely Professional University, Punjab (India). His research & teaching interests entails areas like Business Models, Strategic Management & Political Marketing. He is a MBA from Utkal University, Bhubaneshwar (Orissa), Ph.D from Himachal Pradesh University, Shimla (HP) & has done an Executive Programme from IIM, Lucknow. He is also a Wiley Certified Design Thinking Practitioner and being a passionate trainer, he has conducted several training programmes on design thinking, selling skills, changing business models, brand building and customer orientation etc. for corporates like Indian Oil, Radington, TT Consultants etc. He has acted as resource person in more than 60 faculty training programmes focusing on new age teaching pedagogies, research, case writing etc. apart from being a regular speaker in national & international conferences. Being an avid learner himself, he has attended more than 50 relevant training & courses for continuous learning. He is recipient of Research Appreciation Award from Ms. Smriti Zubin Irani, Hon'ble Minister of Human Resource Development, Government of India. He has also received Junior Research Fellowship (JRF) from University Grant Commission (UGC) of India and other research grants from UK-India Education and Research Initiative (UKIERI); European Commission; and Department of Science & Technology (DST), Government of India. As ingenious researcher & writer, he has published 20 business case studies, 60+ research papers in Journals and 06 research papers/chapters in refereed edited books. He has authored 2 books and had edited 5 books. He has guided 7 Ph.D and 10 M.Phil research students. On different academic & administrative assignments he has travelled to countries like UK, Spain, Portugal, Sri Lanka, Nigeria, Thailand & Dubai.

* * *

Rohit Bansal is working as Associate Professor in Department of Management Studies in Vaish College of Engineering, Rohtak. He is a perseverant, passionate academician cum seasoned professional. He obtained Ph.D. in Management from Maharshi Dayanand University, Rohtak. With a rich experience of 15 years, he has achieved growth through robust and proactive academic initiatives. He has authored & edited 25 books with renowned national & international publishers including IGI Global USA, Scrivener-Wiley Publishing, De Gruyter, Weser Books, Scholar's Press, Germany etc. In addition to, Dr. Rohit has published 150 research papers and chapters in journals of repute including Scopus indexed as well as edited books. He has also presented papers in 50 conferences and seminars. His area of interest includes marketing management, organizational behaviour, services marketing, customer engagement, digital marketing, human resource management and organizational development. He is on Editorial Advisory Board as a member in 125 national and international peer reviewed journals. He has acted as session chair in many international conferences.

Pretty Bhalla is a Professor of Marketing at Mittal School of Business, Lovely Professional University, Punjab. Her research & teaching interests entail areas like organizational culture, stress, retail, workplace romance, happiness, emotional intelligence. She is the recipient of a Red Cross Society scholarship. As a researcher she has published, 25+ research papers and 03 edited books. She has acted as a resource person in many Happittude training programs in schools, colleges, universities, and corporate houses. She has conducted sessions for the University of Saudi Arabia and for Women in Technology, USA corporate House EPI-USE. She has developed a Value Added Course on Happittude and believes the true essence of living is to be happy.

D. D. Chaturvedi is on the guest faculty of several technical as well as management institutes, including Delhi Technological University as well as Delhi School of Economics. He has many publications to his credit besides some papers in leading journals. Prof. Chaturvedi has written numerous books on Microeconomics, Macro Economics, Indian Economy, Industrial Economics, Statistics, International Trade, International Business, Business Environment, Foreign Exchange Management, Environmental Studies, Business Economics, Managerial Economics, Banking, and Insurance. He was accorded international felicitation during the Sixth World Environment Congress for his contribution in nation building, planning, and environment protection. Prof. Chaturvedi had earlier been conferred the State Honour by the Delhi Government for his contribution in the academic, literary, and social fields. Later, the International Council for Human Welfare honoured him twice for his outstanding contributions in diversified fields. He was also conferred 'Clean up the Earth Award' jointly sponsored by the Global Peace University (Netherlands) and the Indian Institute of Ecology and Environment. Prof. Chaturvedi has also presented papers in several conferences at different levels in India and abroad. Apart from being an acclaimed author of books, he has obtained patents from India and abroad. Prof. Chaturvedi earlier served as Director, Rukmini Devi Institute of Advanced Studies, affiliated to Guru Gobind Singh Indraprastha University on deputation basis.

Saumya Chaturvedi is currently working with SGND Khalsa College, University of Delhi. She has completed her Master's in Commerce and is an Actuarial Expert. With an experience of about 7 years in teaching, Ms. Saumya Chaturvedi has an expertise in Financial Management, Accounting for Managers and Indian Financial Markets & Services. She has 6 research papers to her credit of which 3 are in SCOPUS indexed journals, who co-authored about 25 books. Ms. Chaturvedi also has 3 patents to her credit of which 1 is registered in Australia.

Saumendra Das is presently working as an Associate Professor at the School of Management Studies, GIET University, Gunupur, Odisha. He has more than 20 years of teaching, research, and industry experience. He has published more than 52 articles in national and international journals, conference proceedings, and book chapters. He also authored one book on advertising effectiveness. Dr Das has participated and presented many papers in seminars, conferences, and workshops in India and abroad. He has organized many FDPs and workshops in his career. He is an academician, author, and editor. He has also published two patents also. He is an active member of various professional bodies such as ICA, ISTE and RFI. In the year 2023, he has been awarded as the best teacher by Research Foundation India.

Sabyasachi Dey has a Doctorate degree from Utkal University, Odisha in Business Administration. Dr. Dey has his interest areas in the field of Marketing Management, Services Marketing, Retail Management, Sales & Distribution Management, Marketing Analytics, Quantitative Techniques and Research Methodology. During his academic experience of 11 years, Prof. Dey has been a part of reputed management institutions like Trident Academy of Creative Technology (Currently working), Centurion University, DRIEMS (Cuttack), Ravenshaw University (Cuttack), College of IT and Management Education (CIME) Bhubaneswar and International School of Business Management (ISBM). As an academician, Dr. Dey has to his credit published numerous articles in Journals of National & International repute. He has also cleared UGC-NET in Management subject for the eligibility of Assistant Professor.

Amit Dutt is a Professor and Associate Dean, in Lovely Professional University. As a tenured professor at Lovely Professional University, he has made indelible contributions to the academic landscape. His research spans a wide array of topics within operations management, His work has been published in prestigious journals. His research is characterized by its innovative thinking, rigorous empirical methodologies, and real-world applicability. Their publications have not only advanced theoretical frameworks but have also provided actionable insights for organizations seeking to enhance their operational efficiency and effectiveness.

Dwijendra Nath Dwivedi is a professional with 20+ years of subject matter expertise creating right value propositions for analytics and AI. He currently heads the EMEA+AP AI and IoT team at SAS, a worldwide frontrunner in AI technology.

He is a post-Graduate in Economics from Indira Gandhi Institute of Development and Research and currently perusing PHD from crackow university of economics Poland. He has presented his research in more than 20 international conference and published several Scopus indexed paper on AI adoption in many areas. As an author he has contributed to more than 8 books and has more than 25 publications in high impact journals. He conducts AI Value seminars and workshops for the executive audience and for power users.

Ramkumar Jaganathan is an Associate Professor, Sri Krishna Arts and Science College at Sri Krishna Arts and Science College based in Coimbatore Ukkadam, Tamil Nadu. Sri Krishna Arts and Science College, also known as the SKASC Coimbatore, was established by the V.L.B. Trust in 1997 and is an ISO certified co-educational institution. SKASC has 24-hour internet access. It has science labs equipped with IBM servers.

Fahmida Kaiser is a Lecturer of Department of Tourism and Hospitality Management of Daffodil Institute of IT. A former student of University of Dhaka, Bangladesh. She has done her BBA and MBA in Tourism and Hospitality management from University of Dhaka with CGPA 3.65 and 3.73 out of 4 with Dhaka university merit award. She was very careful, studious and investigative during the completion of the book chapters. She has checked the authenticity of every sphere of the writing. By reading this book people's knowledge about Artificial Intelligence will increase.

Sanjeev Kumar has pursued Ph.D. from Amity University Rajasthan Jaipur. He is currently associated with Lovely Professional University. His areas of interests are data analysis, LR in Hospitality area, Food and Beverages.

Geetika Madaan is working as Assistant Professor, at the University centre for research and development Chandigarh University, Mohali, India.

Ghana Mahanty leads MENA Data science, UAE and Global Data Science Center of Excellent, India for Visa Inc. He is a data enthusiast with expertise in mobilizing the organization to deliver value out of data and specializing in business management, data transformation strategy, and machine learning and artificial intelligence solutions for Retail Banking and Payment industry. He has worked extensively across North America, Asia, Europe and Middle East regions. Currently pursuing PhD. in Economics from Department of Analytical and Applied Economics, Utkal University, Bhubaneswar, India. His research area of interests are machine learning, artificial intelligence, macro econometric and structural data modelling, panel modelling, money, banking and payments.

Arun Mittal is presently working as Assistant Professor (III), Birla Institute of Technology, Mesra Ranchi (Deemed University), Off Campus Noida. He holds Ph.D. & MBA in M.Phil., and ECPDM (IIM-Kashipur). He has 16 years of experience of teaching Consumer Behaviour, Marketing Research, Marketing Analytics and Multivariate Data Analysis. He has published about 20 research papers SCOPUS, SSCI indexed, ranked by ABDC and UGC CARE approved Journals. He has also presented papers in around 25 conferences and seminars and authored and co-authored five books in the field of management. He has successfully supervised 4 Ph.D., and 3 are currently under supervision. Dr. Mittal has conducted many FDPs, MDPs and Workshops on Digital Marketing, Self-help, Business Analytics and Research Methodology. Dr. Mittal is a Project Director and Co-Director in the Projects sponsored by ICSSR and MGNCRE. He is a life member of Indian Commerce Association and International Society for Training and Development.

R. Nagarajan received his B.E. in Electrical and Electronics Engineering from Madurai Kamarajar University, Madurai, India, in 1997. He received his M.E. in Power Electronics and Drives from Anna University, Chennai, India, in 2008. He received his Ph.D in Electrical Engineering from Anna University, Chennai, India, in 2014. He has worked in the industry as an Electrical Engineer. He is currently working as Professor of Electrical and Electronics Engineering at Gnanamani College of Technology, Namakkal, Tamilnadu, India. His current research interest includes Power Electronics, Power System, Network Security, Cloud Computing, Wireless Sensor Communication, Digital Image Processing, Data Mining, Soft Computing Techniques and Renewable Energy Sources. He is published more than 120 Research Articles in various referred International Journals and he is published more than 60 Books & Book Chapter in various referred international Publications.

Nitish Ojha is a distinguished scholar, researcher, and mentor having rich Industrial experience as well as varied experience in Teaching and Research. He has academic experience of over 15 years with renowned universities like American University of Europe, University of Stirling UK, and others where he worked in the capacity of Assistant Professor, also worked as a Core Member of Research and Development in Indian Universities i.e., Chandigarh University, LPU, Amity University. He has worked as a software engineer in Nokia Siemens Network, India. He served in several research projects in different profiles of researchers funded by DST/MCIT/MOHFW Govt. of India having National and International importance at IIT Delhi and in AIIMS.

Pramod Ranjan Panda (PhD) is presently working as an Assistant Professor at the School of Management Studies GIET University Gunupur Odisha. He has more than 14 years of teaching, research and industry experience. He has more than 11 articles published in The International Journal of analytical and experimental model analysis and Journal of Interdisciplinary Cycle Research, Indian council of social science and research few book chapters and few National and International Patents. He has attended many FDPs, national and international seminars, paper presented in conferences, attended in international webinars and some workshops he teaches marketing specialization subjects, Strategic Management, Entrepreneurship development. His research area is Consumer Behavior.

Archana Pandita is a dedicated and goal-driven professional educator, currently serving as an Assistant Professor at Amity University Dubai. With over 12 years of international teaching experience in Computer Science, she has worked as an Associate Professor at Westford University College, Program Director at the University of Stirling, RAK campus, UAE, and Head of Department at Birla Institute of Technology RAK Campus. Dr. Pandita has three years of industry experience in Web Applications and Databases and holds a strong academic background, including a Doctor of Philosophy, Master of Technology, and Bachelor of Engineering in relevant fields. She is also an Associate Fellow of the Higher Education Academy (AFHEA), UK. Her expertise extends to being an IBM-certified educator for security analysts and Big Data Engineers and certified in Python for Data Science.

Nayan Deep S. Kanwal's life traces an international pathway that makes him an asset to any organisation, especially an academic institution, which can only gain from his broad outlook, considerable cultural exposure and vast life experience. Born in India in 1958, Nayan left the country at the young age of 11 for a stint in Kenya, where his father served a United Nations (UNDP/ILO) Chief Technical Adviser. Upon his return to India to begin secondary school, Nayan was enrolled in one of the country's best schools in the capital city, the Delhi Public School. While Nayan's academic background is in agriculture management, he has accumulated extensive professional experience in publishing. In 1982, he obtained his Bachelor's degree in agriculture from the University of Papua New Guinea/Queensland University, Australia. He went on to receive his Master's degree, also in Agriculture, in 1985 from the same university, and worked there as a research associate for a year. In 1987, he went freelance to work in Singapore. He later obtained his doctorate in 2005 from France. Nayan lays claim to almost 36 years of professional experience primarily in Communication, Scholarly Journal publishing and Research and Development Management & Administration. His research expertise is in the following areas: Languages, Linguistics, Management, Environmental sciences, etc Nayan is an experienced senior Executive Editor, Editor-in-Chief, Author, Reviewer and a Professor, with a demonstrated history of working in the publishing industry. Skilled in Academic Publishing, Publications, Creative Writing, and Text Editing. Strong media and communication professional with substantial experience in Communications, Media, Print Design with a strong scholarly journal publishing background. He has written on a wide range of subjects beyond his area of study, agriculture. He has published articles in different publications as well as book chapters in his long academic and professional career. He has also authored and co-authored several research and development books. The subjects he has written on range from management and administration of research to information technology. Nayan is described as a man with conviction and commitment, responsible for the education of countless postgraduate students from all over the world. He is a brilliant and intelligent communicator who has devoted himself for the promotion of academic publications not only for Malaysia, but also for the developing world and for the entire humanity. There must be some method to his madness that single-handed he has created this mammoth publishing impact. He is full of surprises and his level of energy is very high and contagious". Professor Nayan Kanwal has authored and co-authored numerous academic books and journals, served as a reviewer to many SCOPUS-indexed journals. He has also served as an external examiner/ evaluator for PHD thesis with several universities around the globe. He has delivered countless lecturers, invited by universities in Malaysia, Thailand and Indonesia; attended copious Seminars/Workshops/Courses and has been invited as a Special Guest at more than a hundred Plenary/ Keynote/ Invited Talks. In addition, he has also been involved in research consultancies in Indonesia, Thailand, Vietnam and Malaysia. He is a Fellow of the Royal Society of Arts (FRSA), United Kingdom, a Life Member of the British Institute of Management (BIM), United Kingdom, an Associate Member of the Marketing Institute of Singapore (AMIS) and an Associate Member of the Australian Institute of Agricultural Science and Technology (AIAST).

Swapnamayee Sahoo (PhD) is presently working as an Assistant Professor at the School of Management Studies GIET University Gunupur Odisha. She has more than 13 years of teaching, research and industry experience. She has more than 9 articles published in The International Journal of analytical and experimental model analysis and Journal of Interdisciplinary Cycle Research, Indian council of social science and research few book chapters and few National and International Patents. She has attended many FDPs, national and international seminars, paper presented in conferences, attended in international webinars and some workshops he teaches marketing specialization subjects, Human Resources Management, Entrepreneurship development. Her research area is employees perception towards performance appraisal.

Priyank Kumar Singh is working as an Assistant Professor in School of Management, Doon University. He completed his high school from Sherwood College, Nainital. He graduated in Bachelor of Engineering in Electronics and Communication Engineering from Thapar University, Patiala with Master of Business Administration in Marketing and Entrepreneurship, he has a PhD Degree in Management from Doon University, Dehradun. He has written several research papers in various journals. He has participated in various conferences at National and International level as a paper presenter. Also, a voracious reader and a sports lover.

Mohammad Badruddoza Talukder is an Associate Professor and head of the Department of Tourism and Hospitality Management, Daffodil Institute of Information Technology (at the National University), Dhaka, Bangladesh. He completed his Ph.D. in Hotel Management at the School of Hotel Management and Tourism, Lovely Professional University, India. He holds a bachelor's and a master's degree in Hotel Management from India. He has been teaching various courses in the Department of Tourism and Hospitality at various universities in Bangladesh since 2009. His research areas include tourism management, hotel management, hospitality management, food and beverage management, and accommodation management, where he has published research papers in well-known journals in Bangladesh and abroad. Dr. Talukder is one of the executive members of the Tourism Educators Association of Bangladesh. He has led training and counseling for various hospitality organizations in Bangladesh. As an administrator, Dr. Talukder served as a debate advisor at the University coordinator for courses and exams in the Department of Tourism and Hotel Management. He has experience as a manager in various business-class hotels in Bangladesh. He is one of the certified trainers for the food and beverage service department of the SIEP project from Bangladesh. He became an honorary facilitator at Bangladesh Tourism Board's Bangabandhu International Tourism and Hospitality Training Institute.

Index

G

H

I

M

N

P

R

S

U

Premier Reference Source
The Use of Artificial Intelligence in Digital Marketing
IGI Global

Premier Reference Source
Innovations in Materials Chemistry, Physics, and Engineering Research
IGI Global

Premier Reference Source
Experimental and Clinical Evidence of the Neuropathology of Parkinson's Disease
IGI Global

Premier Reference Source
Balance and Boundaries in Creating Meaningful Relationships in Online Higher Education
IGI Global

www.ingramcontent.com/pod-product-compliance
Lightning Source LLC
LaVergne TN
LVHW081328300926
849161LV00008B/1908
* 9 7 9 8 3 6 9 3 0 7 2 4 3 *